Crime, Justice, and Social Order

CLARENDON STUDIES IN CRIMINOLOGY

Published under the auspices of the Institute of Criminology, University of Cambridge; the Mannheim Centre, London School of Economics; and the Centre for Criminology, University of Oxford.

RECENT TITLES IN THIS SERIES:

Policing Human Rights: Law, Narratives, and Practice
Martin

Normalizing Extreme Imprisonment:
The Case of Life Without Parole in California
Vannier

Respect and Criminal Justice
Watson

Neighbourhood Policing: The Rise and
Fall of a Policing Model
Innes, Roberts, Lowe, and Innes

Respectable Citizens – Shady Practices:
The Economic Morality of the Middle Classes
Farrall and Karstedt

Advocates of Humanity: Human Rights NGOs in
International Criminal Justice
Lohne

Intimate Crimes: Kidnapping, Gangs, and
Trust in Mexico City
Ochoa

Police Community Support Officers: Cultures and
Identities within Pluralised Policing
O'Neill

Last Chance for Life: Clemency in
Southeast Asian Death Penalty Cases
Pascoe

Crime, Justice, and Social Order

Essays in Honour of A. E. Bottoms

Edited by

ALISON LIEBLING

JOANNA SHAPLAND

RICHARD SPARKS

and

JUSTICE TANKEBE

OXFORD

UNIVERSITY PRESS

OXFORD
UNIVERSITY PRESS

Great Clarendon Street, Oxford, OX2 6DP,
United Kingdom

Oxford University Press is a department of the University of Oxford.
It furthers the University's objective of excellence in research, scholarship,
and education by publishing worldwide. Oxford is a registered trade mark of
Oxford University Press in the UK and in certain other countries

First Edition published in 2022

Impression: 2

Published in the United States of America by Oxford University Press
198 Madison Avenue, New York, NY 10016, United States of America

British Library Cataloguing in Publication Data

Data available

Library of Congress Control Number: 2021951954

ISBN 978–0–19–285960–0

DOI: 10.1093/oso/9780192859600.001.0001

Printed and bound by
CPI Group (UK) Ltd, Croydon, CR0 4YY

Sir Anthony Bottoms

General Editors' Introduction

The *Clarendon Studies in Criminology series* aims to provide a forum for outstanding theoretical and empirical work in all aspects of criminology and criminal justice, broadly understood. The Editors welcome submissions from established scholars, as well as manuscripts based on excellent PhD dissertations. The Series was inaugurated in 1994, with Roger Hood as its first General Editor, following discussions between Oxford University Press and Oxford's then Centre for Criminological Research. It is edited under the auspices of three centres: The Centre for Criminology at the University of Oxford, the Institute of Criminology at the University of Cambridge, and the Mannheim Centre for Criminology at the London School of Economics. Each supplies members of the Editorial Board and, in turn, the Series General Editor or Editors.

In this intimate collection of essays, we learn about the life and times of Tony Bottoms as well as his lasting intellectual impact on the discipline of criminology. From the introduction, through the first two chapters which include a contribution from Tony himself, this is not a usual Festschrift. Instead, many of the essays in this book brim with life and passion, reflecting the evident affection with which the contributors hold the man this book celebrates.

The essays are not marked out simply by their emotional cast, but also by the variety of approaches they take and the disciplines on which they draw. From moral philosophy to the hard science of quantitative method, the papers demonstrate not just the impact of this one scholar on a variety of fields, but also the vigour of much contemporary criminology and its creative impulses.

For those interested in thorny questions of punishment, morality, and justice, as well as crime and the environment, the work of Tony Bottoms has always been a rich source of inspiration. As these essays demonstrate, his work has touched many in areas far beyond his own. Written by a selection of his former colleagues and students, these chapters demonstrate his wide and lasting intellectual and personal impact. They also point to the enduring nature of his work, since many of the key issues which drew him into the discipline in the first place remain relevant and just as urgent today.

In building this collection of papers the editors both honour their friend and colleague, and set out a methodological and intellectual framework that will further consolidate Tony's reach and impact. We are pleased to include it in the Clarendon Studies in Criminology series.

Mary Bosworth and Carolyn Hoyle
General Editors
Centre for Criminology, University of Oxford
July 2021

Acknowledgements

The editors would like to thank Charlotte Dove, Louise Foster, Sarah Rosella, and Giulia Contò for administrative assistance in the preparation of this manuscript. We thank Stephen Bottoms for helpful conversations along the way, as well as for his growing interest in all things penological. We are grateful for warm and enthusiastic remarks from three anonymous reviewers and to Mary Bosworth and Carolyn Hoyle, as General Editors, and the OUP team for supportive handling throughout.

Contents

List of Figures

List of Tables

List of Abbreviations

ACE	Assessment, Case Management and Evaluation
CJA 2003	Criminal Justice Act 2003
CRC	Control Review Committee
CRCs	Community Rehabilitation Companies
DEA model	Developmental Ecological Action model
IEP	incentives and earned privileges
IT	intermediate treatment
JRC	Justice Research Consortium
NIJ	National Institute of Justice
OASys	Offender Assessment System
OLS	ordinary least squares
PADS+	Peterborough Adolescent and Young Adult Development Study
RAG	Research and Advisory Group on the Penal System
RCT	randomised controlled trial
SAT	Situational Action Theory
SCCJR	Scottish Centre for Crime and Justice Research
SFC	Scottish Funding Council
SPOA	Scottish Prison Officers Association
WORP	Women's Offending Reduction Programme

List of Contributors

Professor Antje du Bois-Pedain

Antje du Bois-Pedain is Professor of Criminal Law and Philosophy in the Faculty of Law and Director of the Centre for Penal Theory and Penal Ethics at the Institute of Criminology, University of Cambridge. Following earlier work on transitional justice, published inter alia in the monograph *Transitional Amnesty in South Africa* (CUP 2007) and the edited collection *Justice and Reconciliation in Post-Apartheid South Africa* (CUP 2008), her research has concentrated on the justification of criminal justice practices, where recent publications include co-edited volumes on *Criminal Law and the Authority of the State* (Hart/Bloomsbury 2017) and on *Penal Censure: Engagements Within and Beyond Desert Theory* (Hart/Bloomsbury 2019).

Professor Sir Anthony Bottoms

Anthony Bottoms is Emeritus Wolfson Professor of Criminology at the University of Cambridge, and Honorary Professor of Criminology at the University of Sheffield. He is also a Fellow of the British Academy; a Life Fellow of Fitzwilliam College, Cambridge; and an Honorary Fellow of Corpus Christi College, Oxford.

Professor David Garland

David Garland is the Arthur T. Vanderbilt Professor of Law and Professor of Sociology at New York University. Born and raised in Scotland, he is a graduate of the University of Edinburgh and taught there from 1979 to 1997 before moving to the USA. Garland is a Fellow of the British Academy and the American Academy of Arts and Sciences, and the author of a series of award-winning books on punishment and criminal justice, including *Punishment and Welfare* (1985; reprint edition 2018); *Punishment and Modern Society* (1990); *The Culture of Control* (2001); and *Peculiar Institution: America's Death Penalty in an Age of Abolition* (2010). He is also the editor of *Mass Imprisonment: Social Causes and Consequences* (2001). His most recent book, *The Welfare State: A Very Short Introduction*, was published by Oxford University Press in 2016.

Professor Loraine Gelsthorpe

Loraine Gelsthorpe is Director and Professor of Criminology and Criminal Justice at the Institute of Criminology, University of Cambridge. She is also a Fellow at Pembroke College. In addition to the above roles, Loraine chairs the University's Post-Graduate Research Committee, and sits on various other University

Committees including the General Board Education Committee. Loraine has wide interests in the links between criminal justice and social justice, looking at race, gender, and social exclusion; women and sentencing; and women in the criminal justice system more generally. Her research includes a focus on the effectiveness of youth and community penalties, on pre-sentence reports, and on deaths under community supervision. She also has a strong interest in research methodologies and research ethics, human trafficking, and the criminalisation of migrants. Loraine is a Fellow of the Royal Society of Arts (2009), a Fellow of the Academy of Social Sciences (2014), and a UKCP-registered and accredited psychoanalytical psychotherapist.

Professor Jonathan Jacobs

Jonathan Jacobs is Professor and Chair of the Department of Philosophy, and Director of the Institute of Criminal Justice at John Jay College of Criminal Justice/CUNY. He is also a member of the Doctoral Faculties of Philosophy and Criminal Justice at the City University of New York Graduate Center. He received his PhD in Philosophy from the University of Pennsylvania in 1983. He has published widely in moral philosophy, criminal justice, moral psychology, and the history of philosophy. Much of his work in moral philosophy concerns the understanding of moral agency and the role of character in moral judgment and motivation. He recently completed *The Liberal Polity and Criminal Sanction: Can We Achieve Both Justice and Civility?* to be published by Oxford University Press, and he has written ten other books and more than one hundred articles. Professor Jacobs has been a Visiting Professor or Visiting Scholar at Oxford, Cambridge, the University of Edinburgh, the Chinese University of Hong Kong, the Hebrew University of Jerusalem, the University of St. Andrews and other universities.

Dr Caroline Lanskey

Caroline Lanskey is Assistant Professor of Criminology and Criminal Justice at the Institute of Criminology and a deputy director of the Institute's research Centre for Community, Gender and Social Justice. Her research interests stem from her cross-disciplinary professional experience of education and criminology and include youth justice, education and the arts in criminal justice, citizenship and migration, youth voice and participation, the experiences of prisoners' families, and research methodologies. She is currently Principal Investigator on the ESRC Families and Imprisonment Research (FAIR) Study and co-Principal Investigator on the ESRC Inspiring Futures Footprint research on the arts in criminal justice. She recently worked with Tony Bottoms on an analysis of the qualitative data from the Sheffield Desistance Study which resulted in a co-authored conference paper entitled 'Ethical Dimensions of Journeys towards Desistance'.

Professor Alison Liebling

Alison Liebling is Professor of Criminology and Criminal Justice at the University of Cambridge and the Director of the Institute of Criminology's Prisons Research Centre. She has carried out research on prison suicide, conceptualising and measuring the moral quality of prison life, the management of difficult prisoners, incentives and earned privileges, staff–prisoner relationships, values, practices and outcomes in public and private sector corrections, the changing nature of staff–prisoner and prisoner–prisoner relationships in high-security prisons, and the changing role of trust and forms of order in prison. She was awarded an ESRC-funded 'Transforming Social Science' grant for 2012–2014 and was made a Fellow of the British Academy in 2018. Her books include *Prisons and their Moral Performance: A Study of Values, Quality and Prison Life* (2004, with Helen Arnold), *The Effects of Imprisonment* (2005, with Shadd Maruna), *The Prison Officer* (2nd edition 2011, with David Price and Guy Shefer), and *Legitimacy and Criminal Justice: International Explorations* (2013, with Justice Tankebe). She was awarded a Leverhulme Major Research Fellowship for 2020–2023 to carry out the project '*Moral rules, social science and forms of order in prison*'.

Professor Ian Loader

Ian Loader is Professor of Criminology at the University of Oxford and Professorial Fellow of All Souls College. Ian has written extensively on policing, private security, public sensibilities towards crime, penal policy and culture, the politics of crime control, and the public roles of criminology. He has written and edited a number of books including (with Richard Sparks) *Public Criminology*? (Routledge 2010). He is Editor-in-Chief of the *Howard Journal of Crime and Justice*.

Professor Mike Nellis

Mike Nellis is Emeritus Professor of Criminal and Community Justice in the Centre for Law, Crime & Justice, Law School at the University of Strathclyde. He was formerly a social worker with young offenders in London and was involved in the training of probation officers at the University of Birmingham. He has a PhD from the Institute of Criminology in Cambridge (supervised by Professor Bottoms). He has written widely on the fortunes of the probation service, alternatives to imprisonment, and particularly the electronic monitoring of offenders, on which he is an acknowledged expert. He was actively involved between 2005 and 2014 in the planning of a series of European probation conferences on EM, and gave the jubilee lecture at the 2014 event. Between 2011 and 2013 he acted as one of two advisers to a Council of Europe Committee on Penal Affairs which drew up an ethical recommendation on EM, for circulation in the Council's member countries, and subsequently led two workshops in Strasbourg with representatives of countries developing their EM programmes. He was a member of the Scottish Government's

EM Working Party 2014–2016, and is currently a member of England and Wales Ministry of Justice's EM Advisory Group and the Pew Centre's EM Advisory Group in Washington, USA. He teachers a Master's degree course on surveillance, technology and criminal justice studies in the Strathclyde Law School. He co-edited *Electronically Monitored Punishment: International and Critical Perspectives* (2013) with Belgian colleagues Kristel Beyens and Dan Kaminski, and has been the international editor of the *Journal of Offender Monitoring*.

Dr Peter Neyroud CBE QPM PhD

Peter Neyroud is Deputy Director of the Police Executive Programme and Associate Professor of Evidence-based policing in the Jerry Lee Centre for Experimental Criminology at the Institute of Criminology, University of Cambridge. His PhD focused on field experiments in policing. He was a police officer for more than 30 years, serving in Hampshire, West Mercia, Thames Valley (as Chief Constable), and the National Policing Improvement Agency (as CEO). In 2010 he carried out the 'Review of Police Leadership and Training', which led to the establishment of the new National College of Policing in 2012. He is the Co-Chair of the Campbell Collaboration Crime and Justice Coordinating Group.

Professor Joanna Shapland

Professor Joanna Shapland is Edward Bramley Professor of Criminal Justice and Director of the Centre for Criminological Research at the University of Sheffield, UK. She has researched on desistance from offending (with Professor Sir Anthony Bottoms), victimology, restorative justice, and the informal economy. She is Chair of the Restorative Justice Forum (Scotland) and Executive Editor of the *International Review of Victimology*. She has advised the Ministry of Justice and the Home Office in England and Wales, the Scottish Government, and the Council of Europe and the United Nations.

Professor Richard Sparks

Richard Sparks is Professor of Criminology at the University of Edinburgh. Among many long-standing connections, Richard's first research post was on a project directed by Tony Bottoms on 'Control Problems and the Long-Term Prisoner', which among other things resulted in their book with Will Hay: *Prisons and the Problem of Order* by Richard Sparks, Anthony Bottoms and Will Hay (Clarendon Press, 1996). He has written and edited several other books, including (with Ian Loader) *Public Criminology?* (Routledge 2010). Richard is Convenor of Howard League Scotland.

Dr Justice Tankebe

Justice Tankebe is Associate Professor of Criminology and a Fellow at St. Edmund's College, University of Cambridge. Justice has held postdoctoral research fellowships from the ESRC, the British Academy, and Fitzwilliam College. Prior to his current appointment, he was a teaching associate on the Police Executive Programme at the

Institute of Criminology, Cambridge. Justice's interests include policing, legitimation and legitimacy, organisational justice, violence, and corruption. His recent research projects include legitimacy and counter-terrorism policing, and corruption among prospective elites in Ghana. He co-edited *Legitimacy and Criminal Justice* (2013, with Alison Liebling) and *Trust and Legitimacy in Criminal Justice* (2015, with Gorazd Meško). He is Associate Editor of *Criminology and Public Policy*.

Professor Per-Olof H. Wikström

Per-Olof H. Wikström (PhD, Docent, Stockholm University), FBA, is Professor of Ecological and Developmental Criminology at the Institute of Criminology, Director of the Centre for Analytic Criminology (https://www.cac.crim.cam.ac.uk/), University of Cambridge, and Professorial Fellow of Girton College. He is the Principal Investigator of the world-renowned *Peterborough Adolescent and Young Adult Development Study* (*PADS+*), a major ESRC-funded research project which aims to advance knowledge about crime causation and prevention. Professor Wikström's main research interests are developing unified theory of the causes of crime (Situational Action Theory), its empirical testing and its application to devising knowledge-based prevention policies. In 1994, he received the Sellin-Glueck Award for outstanding contributions to international criminology from the American Society of Criminology, in 2002 he was made a Fellow of the Center for Advanced Study in the Behavioral Sciences, Stanford and in 2010 he was made a Fellow of the American Society of Criminology, in 2011 he was elected a Fellow of the British Academy, in 2016 he was a winner of the 2016 Stockholm Prize in Criminology and in 2017 he received an Honorary Doctorate from UNED, Madrid.

PART I
INTRODUCTION

1

Professor Sir Anthony Bottoms, Citizen Scholar

An Appreciation

Alison Liebling, Joanna Shapland, Richard Sparks, and Justice Tankebe

> [This story] speaks to us, in our situation, by emphasising the need to treat offenders, victims and witnesses as people; by calling attention to the sinfulness of all those involved in the criminal justice system, and hence the need to create proper structures of accountability; by reminding us that the full enforcement of the law is not always the most constructive solution; by reasserting the importance of moral standards; and by calling us to create conditions in our society which will reduce the likelihood of offending, including an Old Testament concern for social justice. (Anthony E. Bottoms, sermon preached in Manchester Cathedral on 5 October 1986, on the occasion of the annual service of Her Majesty's Judges)[1]
>
> Criminology inevitably involves analyses of social values and normative choices.
>
> Part of the task of analysing values is a task in social and moral philosophy; that is, centrally confronting in an intellectually serious fashion, the grounds for making certain value choices in the definition of crime, in the enforcement of criminal justice, and in punishment. (Anthony E. Bottoms, 'Reflections on the Criminological Enterprise', Inaugural Lecture as Wolfson Professor of Criminology, 24 October 1986, published in *The Cambridge Law Journal* 46(2) July 1987: 261)

[1] The story Tony refers to here is of the woman taken in adultery, found in John ch. 7 v 53–ch. 8 v 11.

Alison Liebling, Joanna Shapland, Richard Sparks, and Justice Tankebe, *Professor Sir Anthony Bottoms, Citizen Scholar*. In: *Crime, Justice, and Social Order*. Edited by: Alison Liebling, Joanna Shapland, Richard Sparks, and Justice Tankebe, Oxford University Press. © Alison Liebling, Joanna Shapland, Richard Sparks, and Justice Tankebe 2022. DOI: 10.1093/oso/9780192859600.003.0001

> University researchers can only honestly conduct 'policy-relevant' research if they are allowed at the same time to operate with what they would regard as the true criteria for social science. (Ibid: 245)

Professor Sir Anthony Bottoms is unique in British criminology. He has achieved mastery of all the disciplines which rightly require attention if criminological questions are to be adequately addressed, including law, social science, social theory, moral philosophy, and matters of 'administrative criminology': from uses of the fine, to the origins and functions of the probation service. He was, of course, once a probation officer, based in Essex. This is one of the keys to his outstanding contribution to our field. He combines an unusually broad range of intellectual interests with a steadfast dedication to 'the person' living a troubled life (in a specific place). He has conducted outstanding empirical research in each of these areas, addressing each subject in a way that generates clear and original theoretical and normative analysis: the long and elegant essay is his trademark. He can organise his thoughts (and those of others) in exceptionally precise and orderly ways. He has dedicated his professional life to 'doing the sociologist's work of studying real crime and punishment in real society' (Bottoms 1978: 504), attracting the label of 'democratic under-labourer' from Loader and Sparks in their book *Public Criminology*. They explain:

> Anthony Bottoms has ... combined patient, multi-method empirical enquiry into criminal behaviour and crime patterns in urban contexts and the operation of criminal justice institutions and prevention programmes, with an explanatory ambition that links criminological and social theory (Baldwin and Bottoms 1976; Bottoms 2003, 2007). He has also developed in various ways the idea that criminology is a moral enterprise (Bottoms and Preston 1980; Bottoms 1987a, 2002b) as well as being able to think in policy terms about the import of his work. (Loader and Sparks 2011: 127–8)

Tony's intellectual and 'real life' interests in crime and the environment, the changing nature of modern societies, fairness, power and order, and the role of moral values in crime, punishment, and offending and in desistance from crime, have made him a model and leading scholar in our field. His academic record is without parallel in British criminology. Partly for this reason, we have done several things that are unusual in a festschrift. We wanted him present in the book. This has been arranged in two ways. First, we invited one of those long and elegant essays, on a theme that matters to him, and he chose to offer us his 2019 Cambridge Valedictory Lecture on 'Criminology and Positive Morality'. We made this decision in part because he continues to have so much to say that is wise and original, and also because he is continuing to develop his thoughts on the role of agent-centred morality, and 'the virtues' in the development of character. We were committed to representing this intellectual trajectory first-hand in the book. This chapter opens the first substantive section of the book (see chapter 3). We also invited him to reflect out loud at two separate events at Cambridge (a Prisons Research Centre conference and an MPhil Guest seminar) about his professional life, and then supplemented these events with several formal interviews. This exchange has been edited and annotated by two of his close colleagues (Richard Sparks and Caroline Lanskey) and provides a personal form of elaboration on some of the themes we introduce here. We hope that this 'presence' in the book adds to its value and spirit. Overall, we wish for this collection to represent as well as celebrate his work, and communicate the affection and gratitude felt by so many.

Biographical note

Anthony Bottoms was born on 29 August 1939 in Shillong, India, to medical missionary parents. His father was one of only two doctors, who together ran both a small hospital and a leper colony in the Chittagong Hill Tracts (now part of Bangladesh). His mother he describes as 'one of the most loving people in the world'. Both parents had strong religious convictions and his father in particular encouraged intellectual debate but also believed passionately in the 'practice' of ideas in the real world. He was the middle child, with an older brother and younger sister.

The family returned to England at the end of the Second World War, but it was not practicable for Tony to be educated in the Chittagong area, so he remained in England when his parents went back to the hospital in 1946. Missionaries' 'furloughs' in England lasted a year, but they happened only at lengthy intervals, so between 1946 and his parents' retirement from the mission in 1960 he saw both parents together for only two years (when he was aged 11–12 and 17–18), plus a precious extra few months with his mother when he was 14. In this respect he would be regarded by those who know him well, and perhaps by those he studies, as a deprived child. Yet one of his most striking professional characteristics is his willingness and capacity to help others, especially more junior scholars, to flourish. He learned his key values—of service, humility, and devotion—from his parents, but perhaps the combined effects of their absence and their love generated a commitment to others in him that has made him entirely, and more than intellectually, present to others.

As Loraine Gelsthorpe observed, in her contribution on Tony in the volume 'Fifty Key Thinkers in Criminology':

> In many ways this unusual childhood—which combined strong Christian roots, some social marginality and an excellent formal education—has shaped his life's work both in terms of public service, and in terms of an interest in 'other lives', social welfare and social justice. (Gelsthorpe 2010: 227)

From the age of eight, Tony was educated at Eltham College, which had been founded as a school for the sons of Free Church missionaries and which, when he was there, still housed about 50 boys (out of 500) in that category. He was a boarder, and in the holidays he and his siblings lived with an aunt and uncle. From Eltham, Tony won a scholarship in Modern Subjects (intended as a prelude to PPE) to Corpus Christi College, Oxford. However, his history master was convinced that he would be better suited to law, to which he therefore changed. The history master was, Tony now thinks, probably wrong, but he is nevertheless grateful for the advice, because if he had not read law, he would not have gravitated to criminology; also, the exposure in his law degree to 'lots of logic chopping' served him well in later years as he returned to his more natural intellectual instincts in social and moral theory. At university he 'knew nothing of the world', and he has always been too modest to be 'a networker', but he found himself in the 'uncomfortable position of talking to people in power', often in order to defend hard-earned research results (including those of his younger colleagues).

He met Janet, a scholar of English literature, at Oxford; their three children, Cathy, Erica, and Stephen, describe a childhood spent 'navigating their way around Britain by prison location' and 'going to the beach to listen to readings of classic children's literature'. Their childhood was characterised by 'faith, hope and love'. His family have always been prominent in his life, and Janet is a familiar figure at many criminological, Institute, and related events and celebrations. Tony and Janet happily celebrated their 50th wedding anniversary in Westminster College, Cambridge, among family, friends, and colleagues in 2012.

Tony took the first Postgraduate Diploma in Criminology at the University of Cambridge, in 1961/1962 ('from which he emerged with the highest distinction', according to Sir Leon Radzinowicz). Among his teachers on the first Diploma, besides Sir Leon Radzinowicz, were Joan King, Derick McClintock, Donald West, and John Martin. He turned down a research post to work as a probation officer for two years (1962–1964) before being persuaded back into academic life as a research officer at the Institute of Criminology, University of Cambridge (1964–1968), working on the Dover Borstal project directed by Derick McClintock, from whom he received much good tuition and wise guidance. This led to *Criminals Coming of Age* (Bottoms and McClintock 1973: 'a volume of unusual perception, posing many first time questions').[2] If his move from law to criminology was motivated by a preference for the human rather than the rule, he nevertheless retained his capacity to think in highly organised ways, to take rules and their effects on social life seriously, and to study and teach legal topics to an exacting standard, as anyone who has taught *Criminology, Sentencing and the Penal System* to undergraduates alongside him knows only too well.

He became the first Lecturer in Criminology at the University of Sheffield in 1968(–1972) in their School of Law, a position which allowed him to help to build a discipline 'still barely recognised in Britain'.[3] He was promoted to Senior Lecturer there (1972–1976), and then to Professor in 1976, at the age of 37 (see his inaugural lecture, *Reflections on the Renaissance of Dangerousness*: Bottoms 1977). He worked alongside Ian Taylor and Paul Wiles, the latter becoming an especially close friend and colleague. Professor John Wood was his head of department, and a conversation between them stimulated a realisation that Sheffield was an interesting city because of its distinctive urban development. The work arising from that

[2] Sir Leon Radzinowicz, in a statement read at a dinner to mark Tony's retirement from the Directorship of the Institute of Criminology, January 1999.

[3] See the article, 'Professor Sir Anthony Bottoms: The Making of a Criminologist' by Sara Harrop in the Newsletter of the Cambridge Institute of Criminology, 2002: 4. Both Tony's lectureship, and a university-funded Research Assistantship (held by John Baldwin, then by Rob Mawby) arose from a decision by Sheffield University to select criminology as one of its 'growth point subjects' in the 1960s era of university expansion. There was, however, at first insufficient criminology teaching to fill a standard lectureship load, so Tony also taught criminal law for several years.

realisation became *The Urban Criminal* (1976). This marked the making of an environmental criminologist.

He stayed in Sheffield until 1984, when he succeeded Nigel Walker as the third Wolfson Chair in Criminology in Cambridge—a position he held until his 'formal retirement' in 2006 (we celebrated his 'real retirement' in September 2019). He was Cambridge Institute of Criminology's Director from 1984 to 1998, during which time he established the Institute's Master of Studies Programme in Applied Criminology and Management for senior practitioners, increased its staffing from six permanent positions to eight, and persuaded the University that the Institute needed a properly designed building in which to house its expanding activities and staff numbers.

Tony was made an emeritus professor in 2006, and he continues to occupy an office on the third floor of the building he helped so significantly to bring into being in 2005, among the Institute's PhD students and serving staff. He continues to be consulted regularly, and to be almost full-time in his dedication to ongoing research and writing. He still taught regularly on the Master of Studies and other programmes until 2019 and remains wholeheartedly committed to the enrichment of the professional lives and thinking of practitioners in criminal justice as well as the research lives of his younger colleagues. He has been a devoted and appropriately demanding PhD supervisor and examiner to more than two generations of criminological scholars. Since his entry into criminology in 1961, it has evolved from a marginal and 'delinquent' subject (with 'a precarious childhood': Rock 1988) conducted within a largely psychiatric and medico-legal framework, to a recognised, intellectually flourishing, and empirically 'cutting edge' social-scientific field of inquiry. Tony's contributions have done much to take it there.

Towards the end of his formal career, Tony returned part-time to the University of Sheffield as a Professorial Fellow (2002–2007), in order to co-direct the Sheffield Desistance Study (see below) while retaining his Cambridge Chair. He was then made Honorary Professor at Sheffield (2008–present). His 'dual' geographical and institutional commitments do not reduce his affection or loyalty for each place but have given him two rich intellectual homes. These places have shaped him and his life's work too.

He served as editor of the *Howard Journal of Penology and Crime Prevention* from 1975 to 1981. He held a visiting professor position at Queen's University, Belfast from 1999 to 2000 (also acting as a member of their advisory committee). He served as chairman of trustees at

Westminster Theological College Cambridge (from 2008 to 2014) and helped to secure the funding needed to set the college on a new trajectory.

He was made a Fellow of the British Academy in 1997. He was made Knight Bachelor in 2001 for services to the criminal justice system. He is a life fellow at Fitzwilliam College, Cambridge, where he served as President (or Vice-Master) from 1994 to 1998.

Tony was nominated for the Sellin-Glueck Award by the American Society of Criminology in 1996, and the European Criminology Award (by the European Society of Criminology) in 2007. He was awarded an Honorary LLD from Queen's University Belfast in 2003, from the University of Sheffield in 2009, and from the University of Edinburgh in 2015. He also received honorary PhDs from Malmo University, Sweden, in 2014 and the Autonomous University of Barcelona in 2021. He was made an honorary Fellow of Corpus Christi College Oxford in 2012. He enthusiastically took up the co-Directorship of the Institute of Criminology's Centre for Penal Theory and Penal Ethics in 2012, following its magnificent stewardship by Andreas von Hirsch since 2001. He handed over the reins of the Centre to others from 2019, but we hope that it will still serve as his intellectual home in retirement!

Tony's criminology

Tony has been deeply influential in the development of British criminology from its intellectual infancy. He stayed committed to it throughout its adolescent turmoil and has helped to steer it into 'emergent adulthood' (see Liebling et al. 2017; Bottoms 1987b). His areas of expertise are many: cities and crime, youth justice, sentencing, prisons, community penalties, crime and desistance, punishment and deterrence, legitimacy, social theory, and the law. The key master themes that characterise his work are social justice and community, hope, personhood and morality, and compliance and order. During his early period in Sheffield he developed his major interest in environmental, or socio-spatial, criminology. Among the key fruits of this work were (with John Baldwin) *The Urban Criminal* (1976), which developed the idea of 'tipping points' in the trajectories of urban areas. His work in Sheffield also disclosed the unintended effects of housing policies in reproducing the idea of certain estates as persistently problematic across time. The 'Sheffield study' has become well known alongside the original Chicago studies as the study that established environmental criminology, although it was its *difference* from Chicago as a city (it did not have concentric rings) that precipitated Tony's interest. Several generations of criminological scholars were involved in this work, including Monica Walker, John Baldwin, Rob Mawby, Polii Xanthos, Paul Wiles, Andrew Wilson, and Andrew Costello. Key insights from that study included the distinction between an area's offence rate (where offences were committed) and its offender rate (where offenders lived). Areas, as well as offenders, had criminal careers, and even well-meaning decisions by local governments about housing allocation could significantly affect crime rates and residents' perceptions. In recent years, when environmental criminology has swung towards a heavy concentration on the study of local offence rates, Tony has insisted that focusing on high-offender neighbourhoods remains vital to the adequate explanation of urban crime rates; moreover, and contrary to the findings of the Chicago School, the social character of such neighbourhoods can vary significantly (Bottoms 2018a).

Tony's pioneering work in environmental criminology made him the key figure invited to review the state of development of that field in the *Oxford Handbook of Criminology* when that important publishing venture was first launched in 1994. He continued to provide that chapter in successive editions until the fifth (see Bottoms 2012), with comprehensive revision and updating for each edition. The chapters in the second and third editions were written jointly with Paul Wiles, with whom he developed a very creative partnership on environmental criminology, including analyses of the changing nature of urban space in late modernity.[4]

Following his return to Cambridge as Wolfson Professor and Director of the Institute of Criminology, Tony's work focused for some years primarily on research in prisons (see Bottoms and Light 1987; Bottoms 1990; Sparks et al. 1996; Bottoms 1999a), youth justice (e.g. Bottoms et al. 1990; Bottoms 1995a), and community penalties/alternatives to prison (e.g. Bottoms 1987a; Bottoms and Spelman 1988; Bottoms et al. 2001; 2004a). His work with Richard Sparks and Will Hay on problems of order in maximum security imprisonment in England and Wales was an early contribution to the revival of prison studies in Britain since the 1980s. Their book *Prisons and*

[4] This collaboration began with a paper for *Crime and Justice* on the concept of a 'community crime career' and the importance of housing markets in shaping such careers (Bottoms and Wiles 1986). Later work focused especially on the relevance of the changes of late modernity for environmental criminology and for crime prevention (Bottoms and Wiles 1995, 1996). Their joint work was not able to continue after Paul Wiles's appointment as Chief Scientific Adviser to the Home Office.

the Problem of Order emphasised the significance of legitimacy in the exercise of authority as a critical dimension of social relations in prisons and other penal contexts. As well as having a significant bearing on subsequent studies of prisons and in some degree on penal practice and training (the work was referred to, for example, in Lord Woolf's inquiry into the prison disturbances in the English prison system in 1990), this was a starting point for his later work (the body of work that has occupied much of his attention ever since) on questions of compliance in legal settings. His focus on the role of legitimacy in relation to order in general, and especially on the question of the normative basis for compliance with legal authorities, has continued to be of central interest in theoretical criminology, as well as being widely influential in policy discussions of prisons and non-custodial sanctions, and, more recently, in the field of desistance from crime. He expanded these themes in his thorough account of an evaluation of a policy of incentives and earned privileges in 2003, showing how incentives and sanctions have very different effects on different types of offenders, according to the fairness or otherwise of their administration (see Bottoms 2003). This study—conducted with Alison Liebling, Grant Muir, and Gerry Rose, and following soon after *Prisons and the Problem of Order*—stimulated his longstanding interest in ethical experience and reasoning, and their relationship to law and behaviour, in earnest.

It is clear that Tony's work has long been characterised by an interest in normative problems of legal theory, and more broadly in ethics and moral philosophy. These have become deeper and more explicit in his later work on compliance (Bottoms 2002b, 2019b), desistance (see below), and, latterly, repentance (Bottoms 2019b).

However, his work in and since *Prisons and the Problem of Order*—on many topics, not just prisons—has also demonstrated a deep interest in systematic social theory, especially on questions of agency and structure; the timing and spacing of everyday life; and the broad effects of social transitions associated with the concept of late modernity. Many of these themes arose from an encounter with the work of Anthony Giddens (especially Giddens 1984 and 1990), but they have since extended much more broadly.

All the empirical questions addressed in his later work (legitimacy, compliance, desistance) share a concern with the ordering of social relations as a matter of more fundamental theoretical import than the 'causes' or motivations of law-breaking as such.

His more recent theoretical development of this work on how legitimate power relations work, with his former PhD student (now Lecturer at the Cambridge Institute of Criminology) Justice Tankebe (on the dialogic nature of legitimacy, and on power holder self-legitimacy), takes the field 'beyond procedural justice' in several extremely important ways (see Bottoms and Tankebe 2012, 2013, 2017). The authors show how the dual and interactive character of legitimacy, which necessarily involves both power-holders and audiences, has been largely neglected in criminological analysis to date. This situation has arisen because criminologists have not fully explored the political science literature on legitimacy. Developing the field in the light of moral and political philosophical insights, the authors both clarify and transform the future research agenda in this area.

Tony has also worked on deterrence (e.g. von Hirsch et al. 1999) and desistance (see below), as well as continuing his interest in youth justice (e.g. Bottoms 2002a) and area dimensions of crime (e.g. Bottoms 2012, 2018a). Alongside Andrew von Hirsch, who was its founding Director, he has developed a thriving intellectual culture in the Centre for Penal Theory and Penal Ethics since becoming its co-Director in 2012 and its Director in 2016. With founding editor Andrew von Hirsch and colleague Antje du Bois-Pedain, he has co-edited their outstanding series *Studies in Penal Theory and Penal Ethics* with Hart since 2000 (e.g. Simester and von Hirsch 2006; du Bois-Pedain and Bottoms 2019), publishing collections of thoughtful chapters on punishment and sentencing theory arising from its many symposia.

Throughout his career Tony's work has been marked by a concern to combine detailed and often highly local or specific empirical investigations (for example, on the use and decline of the suspended sentence: see e.g. Bottoms and Stevenson 1992) with theoretical curiosity and, especially, to make connections between criminology and normative political and moral theory (see his exemplary essay on the relationship between theory and empirical observation in criminology: Bottoms 2008b). One of many early fruits of this concern was the publication in 1980 of *The Coming Penal Crisis: A Criminological and Theological Exploration*, co-edited with R. H. Preston, then Professor of Social and Pastoral Theology at the University of Manchester. Across the great range of his interests in probation, prisons, sentencing, socio-spatial criminology, compliance theory, and criminal careers and desistance, Tony has displayed an uncanny gift for intuiting the central problem and focusing his attention directly there. His work on managerialism, human rights, and the changing nature of modern social communities in criminal justice, for example, in the 'philosophy and politics of punishment and sentencing', provides a shrewd and conceptually groundbreaking account of the changing shape of criminal justice and sentencing policy in England and Wales since the 1980s, with relevance to many other Western countries (Bottoms 1995a). This is, as it happens, his most cited paper.

Tony's most recent work, an empirical and theoretical project with Joanna Shapland on desistance ('the Sheffield Desistance Study'), and his theoretical project with Justice Tankebe on legitimacy (see above) have both developed into outstanding contributions to the field and together represent a distinctive intellectual 'coming of age', in which Tony unites theory, moral philosophy, and empirical data in a powerful analysis of human potential in societies.

The Sheffield Desistance Study, a follow-up study over 3–4 years of a cohort of persistent young adult offenders, has moved the field forward in subtle and significant ways (for a summary account, see Bottoms and Shapland 2016; see also Bottoms and Shapland 2011; Shapland and Bottoms 2011). With his co-author Joanna Shapland, Tony has shown that the social and moral values of young recidivist offenders are in some ways surprisingly conformist, as are their future aspirations. They want to change, but they face significant obstacles in doing so—and these include some obstacles that have been previously neglected in the academic literature, such as the emotional excitement of continued offending, and how to cope with a loss of income when fewer property crimes are committed. The study also identifies the concept of 'diachronic self-control' as a way in which would-be desisters become able to navigate a pathway out of crime (Shapland and Bottoms 2011; Bottoms 2013). As a theoretical prelude to the study, Tony wrote an exploratory essay on the concept of agency and its relevance for criminology (Bottoms 2006)—a theme to which he returns in his chapter in this volume. These are fitting projects to occupy a much loved, well-respected, and honourable criminologist, who has been happy in his non-retirement. He has continued to be active as Emeritus Professor at the Cambridge Institute of Criminology and as Honorary Professor at the University of Sheffield and to be a critical intellectual presence in both worlds.

It matters to Tony that 'empirical studies have been returned to with full vigour' (Bottoms 1987b: 242) after the sustained (and in many ways deserved) critiques of mainstream criminology during the 1970s and since. He has pursued, and been part of, its complex intellectual development as a discipline and practice, and was pleased when it 'rediscovered its links with mainstream sociology, and ... therefore recaptured its European heritage'

(Bottoms 1978: 503). As David Garland says in his contribution to this volume, Tony is a powerful exemplar of engaged and expert scholarship. He finds his way to 'moral clarification' (Bottoms 1987b), and to broad social theory, via careful and relevant empirical studies.

Tony's Christianity and public service

Tony's Christian faith is relevant to his own life and work in many respects—it lies in the background, shaping his analysis of the proper role of the human being, and his efforts to encourage the flourishing of others. His strong belief that human beings must live in communities has made him a dutiful caretaker of several relevant institutions. Tony has observed that 'there is a serious purpose to the State', and that, at its best, 'it represents the community' in a neutral way. His support of its institutions, and his patience in the process, is testament to the seriousness with which he has taken the concept of 'good social order' over his lifetime. Tony has always believed strongly in the importance of greater engagement between policy-makers and academics in the field of criminology, and he has over the years taken on a number of public service roles. The several institutions to which he has dedicated his life, apart from his family, include the Institute of Criminology (and the Faculty of Law to which it belongs), the University of Sheffield (where he began his formal academic and research career, and to which he returned to continue both teaching and research in his later professional life), Fitzwilliam College, and Westminster Theological College, to which he devoted considerable time and energy as Chair of Trustees between 2008 and 2014, helping to raise £7 million for a refurbishment programme and negotiating a lease on its land to allow the construction of a new building to house the Woolf Institute, an independent research centre dedicated to researching and understanding relations between Jews, Christians, and Muslims. He is an active member of a local United Reformed church in Cambridge. Each of these institutions feels his devotion as if it is the key figure, a trick he manages to accomplish by the attentive presence he practices, as well as by occasionally depriving himself of leisure.

There have been other significant institutions which have benefited from his support. He was a member of the Parole Board for England and Wales between 1974 and 1976. At that time the Board did not give reasons to prisoners for refusals of parole, and Tony was one of a small number of members of the Board who argued unsuccessfully for this practice to be changed. While that particular situation has improved, the recent controversy surrounding the John Worboys case shows how transparency in parole decisions remains a public concern.

After his move to Cambridge, Tony was for six years (1984–1990) a member of the Home Office Research and Advisory Group on the Long-term Prison System, which was set up following a number of incidents of loss of control in high-security prisons. It was because of his membership of this Group that he was invited to lead the research that was eventually published as *Prisons and the Problem of Order* (with Richard Sparks and Will Hay).

Tony has also worked on criminal justice issues in both Northern Ireland and Scotland. He was on three occasions (1998, 2003–2004, and 2007) a special adviser to the House of Commons Select Committee for Northern Ireland Affairs for their inquiries into prisons in Northern Ireland in the decade following the Good Friday Agreement. Then in 2003 the Scottish Government commissioned him to write a report on Scottish criminological research and the possible creation of a university-based Scottish Criminal Justice Research Centre. Tony's report to the Scottish Funding Council in 2004 on questions of research capacity in criminology and criminal justice in Scotland led directly to the formation on the Scottish Centre for Crime and Justice Research (SCCJR), a consortium led by Edinburgh, Stirling, Glasgow, and Glasgow Caledonian Universities, with funding from the Scottish Funding Council (SFC) and Scottish Government Justice Analytical Services. As confirmed in an independent evaluation conducted by Professor Paul Wiles (formerly Chief Scientific Advisor to the Home Office) in 2012, SCCJR has produced a step-change in research capacity and doctoral supervision in Scottish criminology and has provided a forum for frequent exchange and advice between the academic community and policy-makers. This change in the landscape of Scottish criminology—once described by Hans Jurgen Kerner, former President of the European Society of Criminology, as 'the most exciting development in European criminology'—could not have occurred without Tony's intervention.

Tony's public service roles have continued into the period of his 'retirement'. In 2007 he was asked by the then Deputy Commissioner of the Metropolitan Police to act as Chair of the Academic Reference Group for the London Criminal Justice Partnership's ambitious 'Diamond Project', which aimed to provide re-settlement support for released short-term prisoners in high-crime areas. More recently, he was commissioned in 2017 by the Sentencing Council for England and Wales to conduct a short review of the work of the Council, with special reference to the ways in which it might more effectively fulfil its statutory duties (Bottoms 2018b). These two experiences highlight the importance, but also the challenges, of research-policy engagements; the less-than-positive eventual research results from the Diamond Project proved tricky to handle, and the Sentencing Council, while warmly receiving Tony's report, showed more interest in its organisational than its research-based recommendations.

Conclusion, and introduction to the volume

Professor Sir Anthony Bottoms (we prefer Tony) is a man with moral vision, strong loyalties, and a deep commitment to synthesis. If Britain (including its criminology) is 'handicapped by an educational system that produces illiterate scientists or innumerate artists' (Holmes 1993: 2) then Tony did what he could to challenge this, bringing both quantitative and qualitative expertise to his own studies, and never flinching from the mastery of statistical as well as theoretical and narrative skills (in fact, he continued to learn statistical skills and use them himself throughout his professional life). He has been acutely aware of the seismic social and cultural shifts taking place around him (the onset of late modernity) and their effects on communities and institutions, and his sympathetic analyses of these trends and developments have added to his own deep relationships with the criminal justice professions.

In addition to his many achievements, Professor Bottoms is a person of enormous integrity and quiet conviction, and one whose personal influence has shaped the careers and commitments of generations of scholars. He is deservedly loved and admired by many criminologists of several generations. He is a 'citizen scholar' in the truest sense of these words.

Tony continues to be a prolific writer. His contributions are sometimes long and may be daunting to the faint-hearted. But they always repay close scrutiny. They are written with care and devotion, as chapter 3 illustrates. We are delighted that Tony has contributed a chapter to this festschrift, at our request. For the rest, we have tried to select authors and topics that do justice to Tony's longstanding interests, while acknowledging that other authors and topics might have been included in a volume dedicated to such a prolific and eclectic scholar. Many of these authors are collaborators, or past students, or both, and all have enthusiastically accepted our invitation to contribute to what we hope is a fitting dedication to our friend and colleague. All of these chapters pay tribute to aspects of Tony's work and, as such, this volume is a celebration of an outstanding professional career, a deeply human man, and a well-loved and continuing intellectual companion.

There were many others who expressed interest in writing contributions or who wished to express their admiration and love for Tony the citizen-scholar-criminologist. Many have expressed a wish to be present at the event we shall hold on this book's publication, to honour, thank, and pay tribute to a criminologist who inspired, supported, and nourished them, and who continues to be one of the most outstanding criminological scholars. On the occasion of Tony's retirement from the Directorship of the Cambridge Institute, Sir Leon Radzinowicz paid tribute to Tony as follows:

> There emerged a man—not always at peace with himself—modest, even humble, sensitive, loyal, fair, with a steadfast attachment to the institutions he was called on to serve, preferring quality to pretentiousness, deeply religious but no less tolerant, wedded to social progress but not impatient. He is a man who all of us should be proud to know and be his friends. (Sir Leon Radzinowicz, in a statement read at a dinner to mark Tony's retirement from the Directorship of the Institute of Criminology, January 1999)

We dedicate this book to him as his proud friends.

Alison Liebling
Joanna Shapland
Richard Sparks
Justice Tankebe
Cambridge, Sheffield, and Edinburgh May 2021b

2

Reflections on the Life of a British Criminologist

Tony Bottoms in Conversation

Richard Sparks and Caroline Lanskey

This conversation is a composite of two interviews with Tony Bottoms, conducted by Caroline Lanskey[1] and Richard Sparks,[2] in March and October 2018. The first was a public event, as part of the Institute of Criminology's 'In conversation with . . .' series. The second, intended to pick up issues that were missed or left inadequately discussed first time round, took place at Tony's home.

The end-product has been—in current parlance—curated by the interviewers to emphasise those topics that seemed to us to emerge as most significant. These include: Tony's early career in the context of the development of criminology as an academic field; the changing contours and characteristics of that field; Tony's principal contributions to research, including his views on the relationships between theory, empirical research, and normative argument; and his views on the future of the subject.

While trying to remain faithful to the substance of both interviews, we have felt reasonably free (with our subject's permission) to edit, merge,

[1] Caroline Lanskey is a lecturer in Criminology and Criminal Justice at the Institute of Criminology, University of Cambridge. Her research interests stem from her cross-disciplinary experience of education and criminology and include youth justice, education and the arts in criminal justice, citizenship and migration, youth voice and participation, and experiences of prisoners' families. She has recently worked with Tony Bottoms on an analysis of the qualitative data from the Sheffield Desistance Study which has resulted in a co-authored conference paper entitled 'Ethical Dimensions of Journeys towards Desistance'.

[2] Richard Sparks is Professor of Criminology at the University of Edinburgh. Among many long-standing connections, Richard's first research post was on a project directed by Tony Bottoms on 'Control Problems and the Long-Term Prisoner', which among other things resulted in their book with Will Hay: *Prisons and the Problem of Order* by Richard Sparks, Anthony Bottoms, and Will Hay. Clarendon Press 1996.

Richard Sparks and Caroline Lanskey, *Reflections on the Life of a British Criminologist.* In: *Crime, Justice, and Social Order.* Edited by: Alison Liebling, Joanna Shapland, Richard Sparks, and Justice Tankebe, Oxford University Press.
DOI: 10.1093/oso/9780192859600.003.0002

and reassemble this material into what we hope is a readable and coherent format. Our aim is to offer the reader an overview of Tony's varied career, and the nature of his principal contributions to the field, as far as possible in his own words (if not always, to paraphrase Eric Morecambe, in the original order). Where it is clear that the conversation relates to a specific publication or project we provide a citation; and there are a few footnotes, where this seems necessary to clarify dates or other contextual points.

***

CAROLINE LANSKEY (CL): **I'm really interested in understanding how you started off in this field. So, at the age of 16, when young Tony was thinking about his future and where he was going, what was going through your mind? What were your interests and motivations there?**

TONY BOTTOMS (AEB): I was a sixth-former[3] [laughter]. Like lots of sixth-formers I hadn't a clue what my career was going to be. I was doing well at school, but I didn't have a clue. I was being groomed for Oxbridge. I was planning to read PPE at Oxford, and then one day my history master, who was the first person who really taught me to think—and I owe him a great deal—he said to me, 'I've been thinking about you and I think that probably you shouldn't read PPE, you should read Law.' This was the first time this had ever occurred to me, but he said, 'The problem is because you've had this sheltered childhood you really don't know much about the world.' This was true [laughs]. 'And PPE really requires knowing something about the world, but Law doesn't.' [laughter] Sadly there is some truth in it.

So I read Law. I complied [laughter]. What I discovered however when I was reading Law was that indeed a lot of it didn't have much to do with the real world, but I was still passionately interested in the real world. I had planned to become a barrister, but some of the more technical legal stuff like land law I never could get my head round. And I also met a few rather pompous barristers who rather put me off the notion of being a barrister. I'm sure not all barristers—well, I *know* not all barristers are pompous. But I did meet some pompous ones [laughter], and I thought I don't want to finish up like that. And just at that moment when I was really uncertain what I was going to do at the end of my law

[3] 'Sixth-former' in British English designates an advanced 'high school' student, generally between 16 and 18 years of age, often preparing for university entrance.

course, just then the advert for the criminology course at Cambridge[4] arrived and I thought that's it because that allows me, with my interest in the social world, if you like, to mix my law with the social stuff. And so it has proved.

CL: **So what has been the lasting significance of your Law training in your intellectual life?**

AEB: I've always had a wide focus, and I think the fact that I read Law is part of the reason for this. Actually reading Law is quite useful for a criminologist because when the lawyers start talking you understand what they're talking about. You can actually do the legal side when required. Like when I do sentencing stuff, I know what they're on about and I can read the cases. But, as many people who are criminologists who started as lawyers have said, the transition from being a lawyer to being a criminologist is harder in the first instance than from being a sociologist. Because criminology is primarily a social science, the jump between legal methodology and social science methodology is much larger than the jump from sociology, for example.

I feel I have stayed closer to Law than many other criminologists. So I [am able to] use legal frameworks. But then some legally minded colleagues find it very strange that I, having done an analysis in legal philosophy, I then say okay, so let's have a look at some empirical evidence. [They] think that's very odd [laughs]. They find it strange that I always tend to put, even in legal philosophical papers, some empirical research. But it's all part of the world.

And then of course more recently [this helps explain] how I eventually got into ethics. I've always been interested in ethics, but legal philosophy is a very good route into ethics, as is some of the stuff in prisons research. For example, the Incentives Project[5] and why these incentives, which were supposed to work, didn't and they didn't basically because they were administered in unfair ways and people said 'Stuff you.' That raises whole questions, which we've recently been exploring, about how people reach ethical views and so on.

[4] Cambridge University (Corpus Christi College), 1961/1962; Diploma in Criminology 1962.

[5] 'Incentives and Earned Privileges for Prisoners: An Evaluation', *Research Findings No.87*, London: Home Office Research, Development and Statistics Directorate (1999): 1–4 (with Alison Liebling, Grant Muir and Gerry Rose).

But that required starting to read ethics rather more than I previously had. [Initially] I had only assimilated utilitarianism—or consequentialism more generally—and versions of Kantianism. And then there was this whole virtue ethics tradition that I didn't know anything about but which when I started doing the desistance research[6] I suddenly came across something to do with virtue ethics. Hey! This is what [laughs] is going on here [in relation to desistance journeys].

But that's the way I tend to work. That's a good example probably, and it happened in a bookshop originally. I was doing the desistance research. I'd been brought up on utilitarianism and Kantianism. Then I saw this book called *Agent-Centred Morality*,[7] and I thought wow, that's interesting [laughs], what is this agent-centred morality? Because I was doing agent-centred research, and that introduced me to this whole virtue ethics stuff. I've tried to take it from there.

Richard Sparks (RS): Does this help explain why the connection between academic life and professional practice has been important for you?

YES. I came on the first postgraduate criminology course. Life really was different then. I graduated with a Distinction in the Diploma and they promptly offered me a research assistantship. This doesn't happen anymore! With no interview, no nothing, 'Would you like a research position?' [laughter] And I said no. Why did I say no? [laughs] Because I had, prior to that, already negotiated a direct entry into the Probation Service and they wanted me to drop that and become a research assistant. I was well aware that there was this world out there, and I thought if I take this job I'm never going to get out of the universities and I really need to get out of the universities for my own good [laughs].

So I went to the direct entry probation route which I've never regretted and really helped me in all kinds of ways. Whether it helped the probationers I don't know [laughter], but it certainly helped me. I only spent a couple of years in the probation service and the reason I came back was because Derick McClintock—it was a different world—contacted me and said 'Would you like to come back to a research assistantship?' No interview, no nothing. And I said 'Well, I've only been a couple

[6] See *inter alia* 'Towards Desistance: Theoretical Underpinnings for an Empirical Study', *Howard Journal of Criminal Justice* (2004b) vol. 43: 368–389 (with J. Shapland, A. Costello, D. Holmes, and G. Muir).

[7] George W. Harris, *Agent-Centered Morality: An Aristotelian Alternative to Kantian Internalism*. University of California Press 1999.

of years in probation.' 'Yes, but this research involves lots of interviewing of offenders because it's an action-research study, we're trying to change a traditional borstal to a more treatment-oriented borstal and then evaluate it, so there will be lots of hands-on work with offenders', which there was. So I said 'Yes, okay.'

So, for about four years, two years as a probation officer, first two years at the borstal study,[8] I was very hands-on with offenders. And frankly, I've never much seen the point of criminology unless it connects with the real world.

CL: **In what ways do you feel that doing probation work was good for you?**

AEB: Well it was good for my self-confidence because, having had a sheltered childhood—I'd probably better explain a bit more about that. My parents were missionaries, my father was a medical missionary who ran a hospital in what's now Bangladesh, and this was in the days before rapid air travel. So they spent five years at a time over there and I was at boarding school. So in those circumstances it's actually quite difficult, you're in boarding school, and in the holidays you're in a town where you don't know anybody, it's a bit sheltered.

Being thrown into life as a probation officer was certainly different [laughs]. I worked in Basildon and Wickford in Essex. Basildon was a new town, that's where the office was. In those days, males supervised males and females supervised females. I was the only male probation officer in Wickford so I did all of the Wickford cases. But I discovered that actually this wasn't beyond me; I could do it. That gave me a good deal of self-confidence.

So then I worked here as a research assistant to Derick McClintock, who generously made me a co-author of the book that we wrote. And then I went to Sheffield and at Sheffield I was the first lecturer in Criminology. They decided they wanted to develop criminology at Sheffield, and so they called it a 'growth point subject', that was a technical term within Sheffield University. And so they appointed me as a lecturer aged 29 and said 'Okay, you're a lecturer and here's a research assistant and think of something for him to do for the next three years.'

[8] A. E. Bottoms and F. H. McClintock, *Criminals Coming of Age: A Study of Institutional Adaptation in the Treatment of Adolescent Offenders*. Heinemann Educational Books 1973.

That's actually a huge privilege of course for a young lecturer, aged 29, but I had to think of something for him to do [laughs]. In the days of generalism, what I decided was I had up to then focused almost exclusively on penology, punishment of offenders, especially in this borstal study. So I thought that it would be a good idea to do something completely different with the research assistant, particularly because we were trying to start criminology in a new city, that is an interesting city that is an interesting size, it's half a million, it's a good size of city to work with. So I decided that we would do a study of crime in Sheffield and its distribution geographically and so on. And so that led, eventually, to my longstanding interest in environmental criminology.[9]

And when I went to Sheffield, initially about half my teaching load was criminology and the other half was criminal law. I then set up the MA in criminology at Sheffield and so on and there was enough criminology teaching that I didn't have to do any Law teaching anymore. But I did all that.

And because I'd done all that, it was always easy for me to talk to the lawyers in a way that understood their language. And so eventually I became Dean of Law at Sheffield, from 1981 to 1984, which was difficult because it was the time of the first Thatcher cuts. And then I came here [to Cambridge], and institutionally when I came here it was actually very important that I'd read Law and had inhabited a Law faculty for 16 years. There were significant tensions, when I arrived, between the Law Faculty and the Institute. In fact, the previous year, two somewhat conservative members of the Law Faculty had actually taken a motion to the Law Faculty Board saying that the Institute of Criminology should be ejected from the Faculty of Law and transferred to some other bit of the university [laughs].

RS: Why was that?

AEB: Because it's nothing to do with law.

RS: Simply there is no intellectual overlap between the two? That's what they saw?

[9] See, for example, *The Urban Criminal: A Study in Sheffield* by John Baldwin and A. E. Bottoms, in collaboration with Monica A. Walker. Tavistock Publications 1976. 'Housing Policy and Crime in the British Public Sector' in *Environmental Criminology*, ed. Paul Brantingham and Patricia Brantingham. Sage 1981: 203–225 [with Polii Xanthos]. 'Environmental Criminology' in *The Oxford Handbook of Criminology*, ed. Mike Maguire, Rod Morgan, and Robert Reiner. Clarendon Press 1994: 585–656. 'The Importance of High Offender Neighborhoods within Environmental Criminology' in *The Oxford Handbook of Environmental Criminology*, ed. Gerben Bruinsma and Shane Johnson. Oxford University Press 2018a: 119–149.

AEB: That's what they said. So, Nigel Walker[10] and Donald West[11] together managed to do enough politicking in the Law Faculty with good friends like David Williams and Peter Stein and so on and they managed to defeat the resolution. But that was the kind of climate that I walked into, and the fact that I knew how to talk to lawyers [laughs] was a huge help.

CL: [In the course of your career] you've covered youth justice, prisons, probation, sentencing, environmental criminology—a whole range of different areas. Did you set out to become a generalist in this way?

AEB: No [laughter]. And probably it's not possible to be a generalist in quite the way I am any more as a criminologist. But you have to remember that when I started criminology was very, very young in this country. It was better developed both in the United States, where it was particularly sociological at that time, and on the continent of Europe, where it was particularly psychological and psychiatric. But here, as I have said, I was on the very first full-time postgraduate course in criminology anywhere in the UK. It's that recent that criminology first came in. It's almost impossible now to imagine, but until 1974 there was only one professor of criminology in the UK. Now there are about 100 I should think, or more [laughs]. But until 1974, there was only one and that was Leon Radzinowicz and then Nigel Walker, and then after that Derick McClintock became Professor of Criminology at Edinburgh. So you have to remember that very early development of criminology.

That more or less forces you to become a bit of a generalist because you're expected—certainly when I went to Sheffield I was expected to teach a course in criminology covering the whole of the causes of crime and sentencing and the penal system, all by myself. So, there is a degree of generalism almost built into a nascent subject like that.

RS: So, you don't think it would be possible to have this type of career today if you were starting out?

AEB: Not quite as broad as I've done, but I do want to say that I think that it is possible ... [For instance] recently had a study group in the Prisons Research Centre where we've been talking about the new anthropology of ethics and how it relates to prison studies. And I'm very excited about

[10] Professor Nigel Walker, CBE (6 August 1917–13 September 2014) was Wolfson Professor of Criminology at Cambridge, 1973–1984, and Director of the Institute of Criminology, 1973–1981.

[11] Donald West was Professor of Clinical Criminology at the Institute of Criminology and Director of the Institute of Criminology, 1981–1984.

that. So even if you decide 'I'm going to be a prisons specialist'—and that's a very good thing to do!—it doesn't mean you just go on and do prison study after boring prison study. You have new ways of thinking and so on. The development of the anthropology of ethics, potentially in relation to prison studies, is very new, and there's always an opportunity to try and think outside the box. There's no point in thinking outside the box just for the sake of it, and any theory that I've done has always been, I hope, linked to empirical issues.[12] That's the way I prefer to do theory, linking it to empirical issues. But it's certainly possible to select a particular area, like policing or prisons or environmental criminology, and then think it through in its various dimensions.

I do like to work in a detailed way. I do like to have a pretty firm grip on what the empirical evidence is saying. But I think my work is not just detail and I do like to feel there's a big question here, and let's try and get at the big question. So, in the 'Renaissance of Dangerousness' paper,[13] the issue was at that time suddenly people started talking about introducing dangerousness sentences, longer than normal sentences for explicitly dangerous offenders. But this had suddenly bubbled up in the last two or three years and so obviously I wanted to document that but I also wanted to say *why* is this happening? What is going on here? And so on. And then later, there were a couple of projects. One was the project led by Alison [Liebling] on incentives and privileges, where she was asked by the Home Office—and I helped—to investigate the introduction of incentives into English prisons. Basically it was supposed to improve behaviour, in the first year, it clearly didn't. And the Home Office hated the results, they spent a long time trying to show that the research was faulty, they completely failed—the research was fine. So we published it. And then when the Labour government came into power in 1997, we were asked by the Home Office—I was still Director of the Institute, just—to do a literature review on the deterrent effect of longer sentences, for obvious political reasons. And we did that and we found that

12 See, e.g., 'Recent Criminological and Social Theory: The Problem of Integrating Knowledge about Individual Criminal Acts and Careers and Areal Dimensions of Crime', in *Integrating Individual and Ecological Aspects of Crime*, ed. D. P. Farrington, R. J. Sampson and P-O. H. Wikström. National Council for Crime Prevention, Sweden, 1993: 57–108; 'The Relationship between Theory and Research in Criminology', in *Doing Research on Crime and Justice*, ed. Roy D. King and Emma Wincup. Oxford University Press 2000: 15–60.

13 'Reflections on the Renaissance of Dangerousness', *Howard Journal of Penology and Crime Prevention* (1977), vol. 16: 70–96 [Inaugural Lecture, University of Sheffield].

almost always, imposing a longer sentence doesn't improve the deterrent effect on other people.[14]

And these two things had happened in relatively close proximity time-wise, and I was intrigued by this. Because in a rational choice perspective, which Michael Howard introduced in the incentives thing—it's important to say that the privileges in the incentives and privileges project were real privileges. They weren't rubbish, they were real privileges, which prisoners valued. But the introduction of this policy didn't improve behaviour. Longer sentences didn't reduce offending. From a rational choice perspective, these things are both counter-intuitive. So I was intrigued by this, I wrote a paper specifically about that in the context of incentives and privileges and what was going on.[15] But that's what led me then to think much more broadly about *compliance*. Traditional criminology, the kind I was brought up on, is all about law-breaking. How do we explain law-breaking? But actually most people don't break the law most of the time, so it's also an interesting question, why do people comply? And particularly if the so-called incentives and disincentives are not working, what's going on? What's going on here?

So, I then wrote a couple of papers trying to set out a typology of modes of compliance,[16] which highlighted particularly the normative dimension, which of course is legitimacy, which we [Bottoms and Sparks] worked on.[17] It's part of this but has other dimensions as well, like moral values and so on.

RS: So, another feature of your work that I think is quite distinctive, although many people would think of you as being a model of a criminologist, if anybody is, is that it's also continually drawing in ideas from where you find them that don't necessarily originate in or anywhere particularly close to criminology. Is that fair? I think that's a distinctive aspect.

[14] *Criminal Deterrence and Sentence Severity: An Analysis of Recent Research* by Andrew von Hirsch, Anthony E. Bottoms, Elizabeth Burney, and P.-O. H. Wikström. Hart Publishing 1999.

[15] 'Theoretical Reflections on the Evaluation of a Penal Policy Initiative' in *The Criminological Foundations of Penal Policy: Essays in Honour of Roger Hood*, ed. Lucia Zedner and Andrew Ashworth. Oxford University Press 2003: 107–194.

[16] 'Morality, Crime, Compliance and Public Policy', in *Ideology, Crime and Criminal Justice*, ed. Anthony Bottoms and Michael Tonry. Willan 2002b: 20–51.

[17] 'Legitimacy and Order in Prisons', *British Journal of Sociology* (1995) vol. 46: 45–62 (with Richard Sparks). '"A Voice Within": Power-Holders' Perspectives on Authority and Legitimacy' in *Legitimacy and Criminal Justice: An International Exploration*, ed. Justice Tankebe and Alison Liebling, Oxford University Press 2013: 60–82 (with Justice Tankebe).

AEB: I don't know whether it's distinctive, but yes, it's true. As Janet, my wife, will tell you, I spend too long in bookshops, [laughter] probing around.

I've always quite liked David Downes's comment that criminology is a rendezvous subject, although rendezvous doesn't quite get it, does it, because it's quite good as a starting concept but when you think about a rendezvous you don't actually get anywhere in depth at a rendezvous, you just meet each other [laughs].

However, the point is it isn't in itself an academic discipline in the way that sociology or psychology are, it's a rendezvous subject. It's an area of interest on which various different disciplines converge. And in principle there is absolutely no reason why any of them couldn't have something to say. And that includes not only the standard sociology, psychology, law, medicine, but also geography, economics, philosophy, and so on. All of which makes it, I think, at the same time both really exciting and really terrifying, because nobody can be a master of all of those disciplines. But I've always been interested in having a wide focus and trying to see what some of the things in those other disciplines can say to criminology.

So I think it is terribly important to see that criminology has so much to learn from other disciplines, and one of the things that upsets me a bit about American criminology, and this might be an argument against institutionalisation in general, but once you acquire an institutionalised criminology it becomes somewhat self-referential. So you look at most American criminology, it doesn't on the whole bring in stuff from other disciplines.

The exceptions to that are people like Tom Tyler who actually started out as something completely different, as a research psychologist. But those who are in the mainstream of American criminology tend to recite all those really not very helpful theories like differential association and the General Theory of Crime and all that stuff. I don't think that's where the action is, really [laughs]. And I have always found—yes, it's true I look at bookshops—inspiration really in other disciplines, and I think we should always be willing to look at those other disciplines. So I don't really care *where* criminology is located in the university. I do think though that there is a very good case for having a separate institute of criminology rather than being organically within a Law faculty.

CL: Looking back over your career, then, what would you say are the main connecting threads?

AEB: I'm not sure that there's a connecting thread. But the fact that the normative dimension of human life has come out in my late work, you do things and then you look back and say 'what on earth have I been doing?'

I was always interested in ethics, as we have mentioned. I don't know whether anybody here knows anything about the history of ethics as a subject. But if you have read anything about that you will know that by pretty much common consent among moral philosophers, ethics in the 1950s and 1960s was pretty much in the doldrums. It was all about what kind of linguistic game we're playing when we make moral statements and stuff like this. You probably know we have visits from Jonathan Jacobs.[18] He's a moral philosopher and I've learnt a lot from him because he's one of the few moral philosophers who is really interested in criminology. I once mentioned this book to him which I had tried to read years before (I won't name the author) and he said 'Oh, it's still unreadable, Tony' [laughter]. But moral philosophy since then has absolutely flourished. And it has changed in all sorts of ways, and in particular it used to be just a choice between roughly Kantianism and some other deontological ethical theory and utilitarianism, or some wider version of consequentialism. But both of those are about how do we choose the right action. And as a result particularly of the arrival of virtue ethics or the rediscovery of virtue ethics, because of course they go back to Aristotle, we're now asking much more interesting questions about which we were talking earlier this afternoon, about how do people make moral choices and what do those moral choices involve and so on.

In the early period of criminology in this country, those were forbidden questions. Because the dominant discourse was positivist, and positivism has many virtues—in particular, it forces you to look at the evidence, and so on and so forth—but it's very bad on human agency because it basically says everybody is determined. So I've always been interested in ethics, but ethics in the first half of my career was more or less forbidden [laughter] as a criminological topic, and it's only more recently with the arrival of things like legitimacy and desistance and

[18] Jonathan Jacobs is Presidential Scholar in Philosophy at John Jay College of Criminal Justice, New York, a member of the Doctoral Faculty of Philosophy at the CUNY Graduate Center, and a member of the Doctoral Faculty of Criminal Justice at the CUNY Graduate Center. See his chapter in this volume.

agency as a part of desistance, this whole stuff is now absolutely on the table. I've gone on a bit but I hope that's a reasonable answer.

RS: It is, and actually I'm interested to ask you also: how did you feel about presenting writing or thinking that was clearly contradictory to the mainstream of thinking at the time?

AEB: Oh, I've never been fussed about that [laughter]. No, seriously, I have never been fussed about that. The test is truth, and that might be an unfashionable thing to say for the postmodernists and all that, but for me the test is truth and if human beings are moral beings, which they are, then we need to study that. Truth is not a simple concept. But it's the touchstone.

CL: Something that I've observed is you started off particularly in criminal justice. Has the concept of justice been important to you?

AEB: Oh yes, yes. I am a Christian and that probably in part comes from that, and the notion of seeing each individual really as an equal person and trying to create a society that is just and so on. These have always been important underlying values, and in my case they're Christian values but they can also come of course from secular contexts, so I'm not claiming anything particularly religious about them. But in my case, they had a religious dimension.

RS: When you returned to Cambridge in 1984, soon after that you gave an inaugural lecture, 'Reflections on the Criminological Enterprise'. I was there [laughter]! I imagine other people here were also there.

AEB: I think they're all too young [laughter].

RS: Some of us were there [laughter]. And it was partly a descriptive thing of what was going on and it was partly a diagnosis of the health of the subject, I suppose, and it was partly about its future challenges. So just imagine that you were charged with giving a lecture called 'Reflections on the Criminological Enterprise' now [laughter]. We'd probably give you a bit of time to prepare! How would it look? Could one still do that? Is there *a* criminological enterprise? And what would the chief challenges be? How are they different from those ones?

AEB: They would certainly be different, for example because the moral dimension that I've been talking about didn't really exist then. And so one of the challenges certainly, which is what we were talking about earlier today, is if we take this ... I'm not sure how many people know this stuff, but within anthropology, within social anthropology there's a wonderful short article by James Laidlaw from the Anthropology department [at University of Cambridge] in a recent encyclopaedia where he says well, of course anthropology has always been about morals, because it studies customs of people in the Trobriand islands or wherever. But that was a rather solidified version of morals, so there were these customs of these strange people and they were all therefore acting out their customs and so on. So in a strange kind of way, although it was moral, it was also rather positivistic. And some of the early subcultural stuff in criminology was a bit like that too.

And what's different now in the new anthropology of ethics is much more of a flexible notion of ethics and seeing ethics as a series of choices about really quite small things. And certainly one of the challenges of criminology is, I think, to take that anthropology of ethics seriously and to try to incorporate it within criminology, which people within the Prisons Research Centre here are trying to do. I'm quite sure that's a dialogue that we as criminologists need to take seriously.

What other things does criminology need to do? [laughs] Well, it needs to do all the good things, continue doing what it's doing, not worry too much about qualitative/quantitative distinctions, look for the best possible way of getting the evidence, and so on and so forth.

RS: Is criminology still a rendezvous subject? Do you still see it as that?

AEB: Absolutely I see it as a rendezvous subject.

RS: Do we need to invite new people?

AEB: Some new people into the rendezvous, and occasionally we need to shake things up a bit!

PART II

SOCIAL ORDER AND THE CRIMINOLOGICAL ENTERPRISE

3
Criminology and 'Positive Morality'

Anthony Bottoms

This chapter is a revised version of a Valedictory Lecture delivered in Cambridge in September 2019 as a contribution to the celebrations marking the 60th anniversary of the founding of the Institute of Criminology. It was a privilege to be invited to deliver such a lecture.[1]

It probably surprised few people that, on this occasion, I chose to address some aspects of the connection between criminology and morality. The main research topics on which I have worked in recent years have been compliance with law, desistance from crime, and the legitimacy of criminal justice institutions; and each of these topics has some clear connections with moral issues.[2] Also, in an earlier paper on compliance, I made what some have regarded as the bold claim that 'if they are to be true to their calling, all criminologists have to be interested in morality' (Bottoms 2002b: 24). I am gratified that this remark has been quoted with approval on a number of occasions, including once in a Presidential Address to the American Society of Criminology by Steven Messner (2012: 7), and once as an epigraph at the head of a chapter in the *Oxford Handbook of Criminology* by my colleague Per-Olof H. Wikström (2017).[3]

By way of introduction, I shall offer two preliminary comments about the concept of 'morality'. First, when discussing morality in a social scientific context, it is necessary to draw a distinction between two separate aspects of the topic, which were described by the legal theorist H. L. A. Hart

[1] This chapter has the same structure as the Valedictory Lecture. The sections discussing empirical research are largely unchanged, but the section on human agency has been significantly revised. Footnotes and references have also been added.

[2] On compliance see now Bottoms (2019b); on desistance, see the references in the section on desistance later in this chapter; on legitimacy, see Bottoms and Tankebe (2012, 2017).

[3] The citation by Messner is contained in a section of his address which bears the heading 'The Glimmer of a Moral Awakening in Criminology'. It is sad that, at this stage in the development of our discipline, such a heading cannot truthfully be accused of understatement.

Anthony Bottoms, *Criminology and 'Positive Morality'*. In: *Crime, Justice, and Social Order*. Edited by: Alison Liebling, Joanna Shapland, Richard Sparks, and Justice Tankebe, Oxford University Press. © Alison Liebling, Joanna Shapland, Richard Sparks, and Justice Tankebe 2022. DOI: 10.1093/oso/9780192859600.003.0003

(1963: 20) as 'positive morality' and 'critical morality'. 'Positive morality' refers to the morality that we can see around us in the world, whether we agree with it or not: an example would be the fact that, prior to 1967, many people in England morally supported the law which at that time criminalised even fully consensual homosexual acts between adult males. Positive morality can therefore, in principle, be *observed* and *described* by social scientists. By contrast, 'critical morality' is a concept that is intrinsically *evaluative*: it raises questions, for example, about how people ought to behave, or whether particular social structures or institutions are or are not morally commendable. (Thus, examples of critical morality would include saying that a police officer had behaved 'very courageously' in a certain situation (positive evaluation), or describing the pre-1967 English law on consensual homosexual behaviour as 'fundamentally unjust' (negative evaluation).) In my view, careful attention to both positive morality and critical morality is important for criminologists, but in order to keep the discussion within bounds I will in this chapter focus only on positive morality.

Secondly, I am aware from various informal discussions that some people find the word 'morality' itself unsettling; it can conjure up images of strict schoolteachers, or perhaps of being preached at. It is true that, in modern English, the word 'morality' has in some contexts acquired connotations of a 'special moral obligation'; and this led a prominent British moral philosopher (Bernard Williams) to draw a distinction between the general field of ethics and the special features of what he called 'the morality system'.[4] In the present context, however, I am following the more usual practice of treating 'ethics' and 'morality' as synonymous terms, the one derived etymologically from Greek and the other from Latin. Accordingly, readers for whom 'morality' is an unsettling term are invited to substitute 'ethics' in its place.

Approaching 'positive morality'

Although my interest in the intersection of criminology and morality has become more pronounced in recent years, like most criminologists I encountered 'positive morality' from an early stage of my career, when doing

[4] See Williams (1985/2006: ch. 10). According to Williams, 'in the morality system, moral obligation is expressed in one especially important kind of deliberative conclusion—a conclusion that is directed toward what to do, governed by moral reasons, and concerned with a particular situation' (pp. 174–175).

or supervising research fieldwork. So let me begin the substantive discussion of this chapter by describing an event that took place in 1978.

I was attending a conference on Environmental Criminology in Stockholm, at which I presented a co-authored paper reporting some results from an empirical study of crime in public sector housing estates in Sheffield. Two of the areas described had a very similar population composition, and they were situated adjacent to each other, separated only by a main road. Surprisingly, however, their crime and offender rates were very different: one estate had rates that were at least double those of the other area—and maybe more, depending on the measure used. Our suggested explanation for this large difference was complex, but in essence it turned on the operations of the local housing market, which had allowed and then sustained the development of a mild criminal subculture in one of the areas, which we called Gardenia. This subculture, we suggested, had made it more morally permissible for young people in Gardenia to commit offences.[5]

In the coffee break, I was confronted aggressively by a very senior American criminologist. He asked: did the suggested explanation rely, in part, on normative differences between the two areas? Yes, it did. But, he said, that's a very serious mistake. Had I ever actually *seen* a norm? And didn't I realise that proper social science insists that human behaviour is best explained by conditioning, and focuses only on behaviour, without any appeal to people's thoughts and feelings? (Yes, he was a radical behaviourist.)

So, for this American colleague, science, including social science, can't deal with morals. Was he right? Well, a significant number of scholars have thought so. For example, a 2006 book on norms and developmental psychology ['DP'] begins with a statement (which its author, Leslie Smith, goes on to challenge) that 'the question "Can [DP] deal with normativity" has a standard answer "No"' (Smith 2006: 1). Yet a central topic within developmental psychology is, of course, parenting, and all parents know that an important element of parenting is clarifying for their children what are good actions and what are bad actions—in other words, moral education. So how did so many people, in developmental psychology and elsewhere, come to exclude morals (and other normative phenomena) as a topic for social-scientific exploration? The short answer to this question seems to lie

5 The paper given at the Stockholm conference was published in 1981 in a volume arising from that conference (Bottoms and Xanthos 1981). In that paper, 'Gardenia' was labelled 'CHH'. A fuller account of the striking contrast between Gardenia and its neighbouring estate ('Stonewall') was written at a later date (Bottoms et al. 1989).

in a widely held view that science deals in facts, but that moral judgements are not facts. As Leslie Smith (2006: 8) summarises this argument: 'If DP is an empirical science [engaged in a] search for natural laws and their explanation through causal theories, norms would be absent from its domain of investigation. This is because facts and norms are independent of each other.' That view, it will be noted, rests upon two assumptions: first, that 'facts' and 'values' never intersect, and secondly, that DP, as a science, can deal only with facts.[6]

But this intellectual stance—and the similar view expressed by my American critic—is surely very strange. For example, suppose that a woman holding sincere pro-life views unexpectedly becomes pregnant. For various reasons, she is not happy about this but, true to her moral beliefs, she does not even consider having an abortion. Are we really supposed to say that these beliefs are of no social-scientific interest in this situation? Stated differently, is it not a fact that her values have significantly influenced her decision?

Accordingly, I shall henceforth assume that it makes perfect sense for social scientists to study empirically people's 'morality' (or their 'ethics'). But when they do this, what exactly should they be examining? Unfortunately, at this point we immediately run into difficulty, because moral philosophers—the supposed experts in this field—have themselves understood the nature of morality in different ways at different times. Indeed, by an interesting coincidence, the first stirrings of what were eventually to be seen as some very important changes in Anglophone moral philosophy were taking place in Oxford in the late 1950s, at exactly the same time as the Institute of Criminology was being founded here in Cambridge.

The dominant intellectual approach within English moral philosophy in the 1950s was *prescriptivism*, a theory which holds that moral language has the character, directly or indirectly, of universal imperatives. A central claim of prescriptivism is that 'moral terms are used primarily for guiding action, for telling people what to do ... As such they are similar to imperatives, which also have prescriptive meaning' (Norman 2005). Thus, if we declare that 'theft is wrong' we are in effect saying, in the imperative tense, 'don't steal', and we are also saying that this prescription must be universally adhered to (that is, we are attempting to guide people's actions). Given this

[6] The stated view also implicitly assumes that there is no significant methodological difference between the natural sciences and the social sciences—a much debated proposition to which we must return.

emphasis on universal imperatives, prescriptivism naturally focuses its attention almost exclusively on *moral rules*. There is certainly merit in this approach, because there is little doubt that moral rules are important both for ethical conduct and for social order. Indeed, in his final publication the late Meyer Fortes, a distinguished Cambridge social anthropologist, made the strong claim that 'the capacity and the need to have, to make, to follow and to enforce rules are of cardinal importance for human social existence ... For without rules there can be neither society nor culture' (Fortes 1983: 6).[7]

Notwithstanding the importance of moral rules, however, there is now a broad consensus among moral philosophers that, as a *total* approach to their subject, prescriptivism has some important limitations. First, its focus is very predominantly on the question of what it is right to *do* in a particular situation, so that broader ethical questions such as 'what is it good to *be*?' or 'how shall I lead my life?' are largely left aside.[8] Secondly, if indeed we are interested in 'what it is good to *be*', then some appropriate answers might be personal and particular rather than universalist. Thirdly, prescriptivism leaves no conceptual space for people's inner moral lives, as in quiet moments they reflect upon and give their *attention* to various moral issues—a point that was particularly emphasised in the 1960s by the philosopher-novelist Iris Murdoch.[9]

In light of these criticisms, it seems sensible for social scientists interested in positive morality to adopt a wide view of 'morality'. This will of course include the study of moral rules and their effects; but it will also embrace matters such as people's inner ethical lives, and what have been described as their 'ground projects'—that is, the plans and commitments

[7] Similarly, the philosopher Bernard Williams (1972/1976: 20) had earlier stated that 'there can be no society without some moral rules'. Given the anniversary character of this Valedictory Lecture, it is a pleasure to record here that both Fortes and Williams were at different times active and helpful members of the Committee of Management of the Institute of Criminology—Fortes in the 1960s, and Williams in the 1980s.

[8] As Charles Taylor (1989: 84) argued of prescriptivism and some other then-contemporary philosophical approaches: 'The focus is on the principles, or injunctions, or standards which guide *action*, while visions of the good are altogether neglected. Morality is [seen as] narrowly concerned with what we ought to *do*, and not also with what is valuable in itself, or what we should admire or love' (emphasis in original).

[9] Murdoch (1970: 16–23) famously described the hypothetical case of a mother (M) who initially feels hostility to her new daughter-in-law (D). M is however capable both of thinking carefully and of self-criticism, and she quietly gives *attention* to her views, attempting to put hostility aside and to see D 'justly or lovingly' (1970: 22). Gradually, M's vision of D alters. Murdoch explicitly contrasts this kind of inner moral reflection with the worldview of prescriptivism, where 'morality resides at the point of action' (1970: 15).

that they have in their lives, and the values that underpin these.[10] A useful umbrella term for this broad approach, which was coined by the Canadian philosopher Charles Taylor, is the concept of a person's *moral framework*. As a commentator on Taylor's work explains, in his philosophy moral frameworks 'give shape and meaning to individuals' lives and provide answers, no matter how tacitly, to the existential questions that [Taylor] believes face all individuals about the purpose, conduct and direction of their lives' (Abbey 2000: 34).

As well as coining the term 'moral frameworks', Taylor makes two further important points about them. First, within their moral framework most people have a bundle of different values and commitments, of varying strength. These might involve, for example, commitments or values arising from family ties or personal friendships, as well as political or religious beliefs. Each of these might influence some of a person's actions; and, of course, they can also change over time. Secondly, people's moral frameworks are usually a very important element within their sense of self.[11] I shall come back to these matters later.

Once the issues have been, philosophically speaking, set out in this way, it becomes much easier to build a constructive bridge between the contributions of philosophers and of social scientists to the study of morality. That is because social scientists are very aware that people's 'moral frameworks' are often significantly influenced by the people with whom they share homes, schools, workplaces, neighbourhoods, and so on, and also by the specific social situations in which they find themselves. Indeed, that is what my colleagues and I found in Gardenia, the high-crime Sheffield estate that we were describing in Stockholm. At one end of that estate, over

[10] For a pioneering and influential use of the concept of a 'ground project' within empirical social science, see Cheryl Mattingly's (2014) study of Californian mothers caring for seriously sick children. She adopted this concept from the philosophical writing of Bernard Williams (1981). Mattingly (2013: 310) defined ground projects as 'the kinds of commitment that people find so deep to who they are that they might not care to go on with their lives without them, or would not know themselves if they no longer had them'. I shall however propose later in this chapter that the concept of a ground project can also be fruitful when researching less 'deep' commitments.

[11] As Abbey (2000: 34–35) explains, for Taylor moral frameworks 'orient people in moral space … [I]ndividuals feel themselves to exist within a space of moral questions about what is the right thing to do, what goods to pursue and what is the right direction for their lives to take … Just as individuals orient themselves in physical space and find it hard to function if disorientated, so we orient ourselves in moral space.' Of course, this 'does not deny that some individuals can feel themselves as lacking these reference points'. However, such 'feelings of uncertainty [and] of flailing around morally, typify a situation of moral and identity crisis'. This indicates 'how closely intertwined the self and morality are for Taylor'.

time a group of families with extensive criminal records had congregated, with a significant degree of inter-marriage. They didn't hide their non-mainstream moral values, which were also absorbed by their children. They didn't actively try to persuade other residents of their views, but since all the children from the area went to the same secondary school, such views were regularly available as a potential source of influence to all the teenagers of the estate, and they did influence some of them. In short, and surely not surprisingly, aspects of the moral climate of the estate influenced the actions of some people, especially younger people (see Bottoms et al. 1989).

In the remainder of this chapter, I propose to consider three separate strands of research in empirical criminology that have taken the concept of morality seriously. These strands involve, respectively, issues concerning moral rules, shifting values, and social order; and in view of the anniversary character of the original paper, I shall focus especially (but not exclusively) on research contributions authored or co-authored by scholars from the Institute of Criminology. Examination of these various research endeavours will, I hope, provide some constructive lessons on how we can take forward the study of positive morality within criminology. Between the first and the second strands, I will also tackle a related and important conceptual issue: that of human agency.

Empirical studies I: Studies relating to moral rules

First, then, let us consider some empirical studies relating to the concept of moral rules.

Per-Olof H. Wikström (2017, 2019) has developed an important criminological theory called Situational Action Theory (or SAT). SAT is an attempt to provide a general theory of how crimes come to be committed; thus, it ambitiously aims to explain not only the development and cessation of criminal careers, but also the geographical distribution of crimes. The basic structure of the theory is set out in Figure 3.1.

We are trying to explain an action—that of committing an act that has been prohibited by law. Anyone thinking of doing such an act must go through a process of perception of the particular situation; he or she then *chooses* (note that word) whether or not to commit the socially forbidden act. (Of course, all this can happen very quickly, almost instantaneously, in some cases.) According to SAT, the two main matters contributing to this

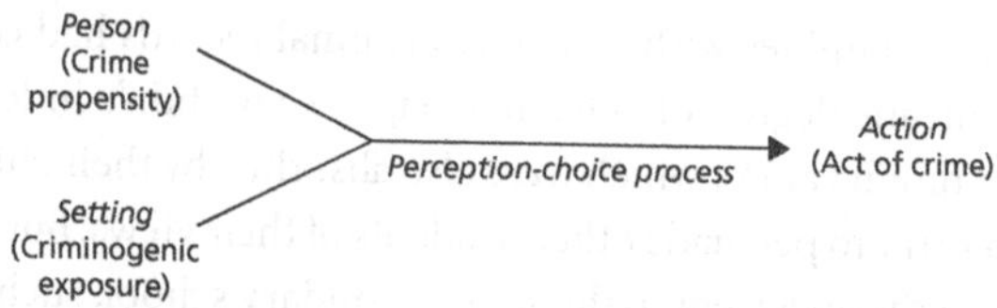

Figure 3.1 Situational Action Theory: the basic theoretical framework
Source: Wikström et al. (2012: 17)

perception–choice process are, first, the individual's general *propensity* to commit crimes, and secondly, the extent to which the particular situation, or geographical *setting*, encourages or discourages crime (in other words, the extent to which it acts as an *environmental inducement*).

Within the theory, both propensity and settings are seen as having some significantly moral dimensions. To take propensity first, SAT explicitly postulates that a person's 'morality is the *basic* personal factor' (Wikström et al. 2012: 16, emphasis added) that shapes crime propensity, although this is supplemented by an individual's ability to exercise self-control. As regards settings, SAT proposes that different kinds of setting 'present different *moral contexts*, that is, different *moral norms* and *levels of enforcement* ... which means they differ in the extent to which they encourage or discourage breaches of rules' (Wikström et al. 2012: 16, emphasis in original). (This is similar to what colleagues and I had suggested was happening in Gardenia: that is, aspects of the moral context of that setting did not discourage rule-breaking.) But although, within SAT, propensity and settings are key concepts, in the last resort the theory sees committing an act of crime as a *choice*, in the standard meaning of that term: that is, the actor chooses to do the criminal act, but he or she could have chosen not to do so. The formal term for a person's capacity to make choices is *human agency*, and I shall discuss this concept more fully shortly.

Given the suspicion of morality in much social science, including criminology, it was very courageous of P.-O. H. Wikström to develop a general explanatory theory that proposes such a large role for moral factors. But his courage has paid off empirically, because the testing of this theory has yielded strongly confirmatory results, notably in the study that he and his colleagues carried out among a large sample of adolescents in Peterborough (Wikström et al. 2012) but also, to a significant extent, in replication studies elsewhere.[12] To give just one example of the strength of the theory, social

[12] For references to some of these replications, see Wikström (2019: 278). As Wikström comments, the findings of these studies are in general 'very supportive' of the hypotheses of

disadvantage is often thought of as generating criminality. In Peterborough, however, a combined index of family and neighbourhood disadvantage explained only 4% of the variance in the frequency of crimes committed by adolescents; by contrast, the combined dimensions of *propensity* and *exposure to criminogenic settings* (as we have seen, two key concepts within SAT) explained 56% of this variance (Wikström and Treiber 2016).

For the purposes of the present discussion, it is important to consider what SAT researchers mean by 'morality'. Within the concept of 'propensity', 'morality' is measured using individuals' responses to two sets of questionnaire items. The first set contains questions relating to respondents' acceptance or otherwise of various *moral rules*, with each question asking, on a four-point scale: 'How wrong is it for someone your age to [do XYZ]?'[13] The second set of questions asks about respondents' experience of the *moral emotions* of shame and guilt. Empirically, these two measures—'moral rules' and 'moral emotions'—are strongly correlated, so usually only the data on moral rules are used in analyses. Turning to the separate issue of measuring the *moral contexts of settings*, here SAT researchers have used individuals' time-budget data to construct an *index of criminogenic exposure*, which measures the time that young people have spent in what are described as 'unstructured peer-oriented activities' in places with a higher-than-average crime rate—that is, time spent in situations where the norms against lawbreaking are likely to be less strong than in other contexts.[14]

In the Peterborough study, both 'propensity' and the 'moral contexts of settings' were found to be strongly related to the commission of crimes. Empirically speaking, this is a powerful demonstration of the importance, as potentially criminogenic factors, of both people's acceptance or otherwise of moral rules, and the moral contexts of settings. Even more

SAT; however, there is a problem in that 'few existing studies have fully appropriate data and methodologies to test the situational model' within the theory.

[13] There are 14 items on the scale, which is reproduced in Wikström et al. (2012: 134). The listed items include, e.g., 'Go skateboarding in a place where skateboarding is not allowed'; 'Skip school without an excuse'; 'Hit another young person who makes a rude comment'; 'Smoke cannabis'; and 'Smash a street light for fun'.

[14] More specifically, the index of criminogenic exposure is a combination of two measures, namely: (i) time spent in unstructured peer-oriented activities in residential areas with poor 'collective efficacy'; and (ii) time spent in unstructured peer-oriented activities in the city centre or in local shopping centres (Wikström et al. 2012: 147). Local areas of both these types have relatively high crime rates. Note also that 'time spent in unstructured peer-oriented activities' is by definition time spent away from the normative frameworks of adult presence and/or socially structured activities.

importantly, however, there is a strong *interactive* effect between propensity and settings. This can be seen in Figure 3.2, which shows that adolescents with a given measure of 'propensity to offend' tend to commit crimes to a very different extent when they are in different kinds of social settings.

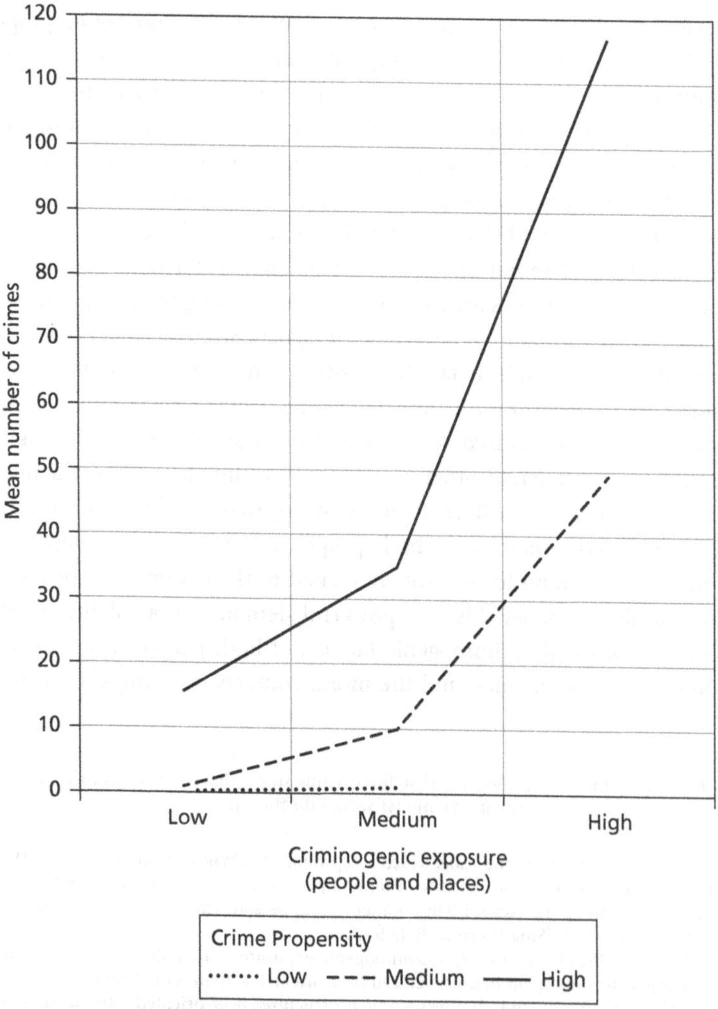

Figure 3.2 Interaction between crime propensity and criminogenic exposure in predicting adolescents' involvement in acts of crime in Peterborough
Source: Wikström et al. (2012: 156)

So, for example, 'high propensity' individuals have a rate of offending that is more than five times as high when they are in 'high exposure' settings rather than in 'low exposure' settings, and 'medium propensity' individuals have a higher rate of offending when they are in 'high exposure' settings than do 'high propensity' individuals in 'medium exposure' settings.

But, having shown—through a discussion of SAT and the Peterborough study—the importance of moral rules and moral settings in influencing behaviour, I now want to consider a slightly different issue about moral rules. That issue is: can people who sincerely accept a moral rule sometimes set this rule aside, and behave in a way that seems contrary to the rule? This issue has been considered, in a very illuminating way, in a recent qualitative research study by Monica Bell (2016) of Harvard.

Bell became interested in the concept of 'legal cynicism', which she defined as a strong 'distrust of the law and legal authorities', especially the police (2016: 318).[15] For present purposes, it is important to note that legal cynicism carries with it a moral rule that 'you don't snitch to the police' except in emergencies. Bell noted the extensive evidence that legal cynicism is pervasive among residents of poor, black neighbourhoods in the US, but was also struck by some less frequently cited data which show that African Americans have, even when one controls for crime rates, at least as high a rate of calls to police as other citizens (2016: 315). To explore this apparent paradox, Bell conducted 50 lengthy qualitative interviews with poor African-American mothers living in Washington DC. She found considerable evidence of legal cynicism in her sample: for example, she reports that respondents were 'deeply wary of police', regarding them as 'corrupt [and] biased on the basis of race and class' (2016: 326–327). Yet two-thirds of Bell's respondents also said that they had called the police at least once (2016: 325). Why? Broadly, there were two main kinds of reason. The first was what Bell calls 'officer exceptionalism'; that is, some women were willing to trust certain individual officers who they had come to know personally, while still not placing any 'legitimacy or trust in the broader system of crime control' (2016: 329).[16] Then, secondly, there were various

[15] Bell notes that the term 'legal cynicism' had been coined by Sampson and Bartusch (1998). She adds that these authors referred to legal cynicism as 'anomie about law', and carefully 'distinguished it from a subcultural tolerance of violence among African Americans' (2016: 318).

[16] In Washington, there had in recent decades been an increase in police presence in the kinds of neighbourhoods where the mothers lived, so it was not uncommon for them to 'encounter police as part of everyday life' (2016: 328). Hence, a main reason for this exception was that respondents tended to 'decouple "the police" as an institution from officers as

circumstances in which the mothers might turn to the police because police seemed likely to offer better solutions than anyone else to specific problems.[17] For example, one woman, while saying that she agreed with the 'street code' against calling the police, also reported that she had several times called police to help friends facing domestic violence, and to help control her teenage children (Bell 2016: 332–333). This example illustrates a further finding of Bell's study, namely that calls to the police were usually made about issues arising within or physically near to the women's homes, or those of their families or close friends, in an effort to regain or retain control of situations that were, literally, 'close to home'. For more distant issues, such as drug trafficking and violent crime in the streets, the community norm against snitching held powerful sway, and the police were not called.

There are of course some limitations to Bell's study, but these need not detain us here. What the study demonstrates is the complexity and specificity of the moral choices made by these mothers. If they had been respondents in a standard survey on police trust and legitimacy, the answers of most of the sample would probably have been simply negative; accordingly, such a survey would have failed to capture the subtle nuances of their moral choices. That is a useful lesson for criminologists interested in studying morality. For some purposes, general measurements of acceptance of a moral rule can be very useful. However, sometimes these measures might hide important qualifications to the general views expressed, and these qualifications might be important for both explanatory and policy purposes.

Human agency within social science

We have seen that a central concept in SAT is the 'perception–choice process', which implies that the people choosing have human agency. But what exactly do we mean by 'agency'? This concept has recently become

individuals' (2016: 327). However, even where officers showed procedural justice (Tyler 1990/2006) and won the respect and trust of mothers, the effects were localised, and 'stop[ped] short of building a sense of legitimacy or trust in the broader system of policing' (2016: 329).

[17] In more detail, Bell distinguished cases where (i) women thought that police would be the most effective agency to handle a particular problem ('domain specificity'); or (ii) they foresaw some beneficial outcome in a given situation ('therapeutic consequences'); or (iii) they turned to the police in a quest for protection or to secure leverage with other power-holders ('institutional navigation').

controversial within criminology, so a brief look at some key questions is essential.

Everyday language assumes that each of us has the capacity to choose between alternatives, and that when we make a choice we could—as philosophers tend to phrase the matter—'have done otherwise'. Our legal system makes the same assumption, and holds us responsible for those choices unless there are special reasons not to do so, for example because we were sleepwalking at the time of the act, or literally coerced to do the act by someone else. Philosophically, this terminology assumes that we have *free will*, and as such it seems to be in some apparent tension with the standard working practices of much social science, which continually searches for the *causes* of actions.

The strongest recent advocate of the importance of human agency within criminology was the late Ray Paternoster of the University of Maryland. His final published paper, which appeared shortly after his sadly early death in 2017, was explicitly focused on articulating the meaning and implications of the concept of human agency for criminologists.

In this paper, Paternoster (2017: 350) rightly observed that a growing—although still limited—number of criminologists 'have incorporated notions of human agency into their theories', although he regretted that few of them had offered any 'detailed conceptualization of precisely what is meant' by this term. He conceded that this criticism does not apply to every scholar, and I am happy to report that I am one of those who was exempted (see Bottoms 2005). But he added (2017: 353, n. 4) that he did not endorse my work either, because the conception of agency that I have worked with is, in his judgement, too social, and not sufficiently 'individualistic'. I will come back to this point shortly.

So how does Paternoster understand agency? In the abstract of his paper, he summarises as follows:

> At its core, human agency is . . . *action*—deliberate and intended or willed conduct. When persons act as agents, they direct their behavior toward some goal . . . preceded by processes of deliberation, decision-making, intention formation, [and] volition or activation of the will . . . *This notion of human agency is incompatible with event causality but is entirely consistent with a teleological explanation*, an explanation of human behavior in terms of the goals that are sought by persons. (2017: 350, emphasis added)

I will consider here two key issues that are raised by Paternoster in this paper: first, his claim that 'human agency is incompatible with event causality', and secondly, his insistence that agency must be conceptualised in an 'individualistic' way.

The issue of 'event causality' was very quickly taken up in print by Francis Cullen, who is—as Paternoster also was—a senior and well-respected American criminologist. Cullen (2017) pays tribute to Ray Paternoster's very considerable contribution to criminology, but he argues strongly against the proposal that human agency should become an important organising concept within our discipline. Cullen declares himself to be an 'unabashed positivist' (2017: 375), and he states robustly that the 'study of causality cannot be avoided if the criminological enterprise is to be scientific' (2017: 373). So we have an apparent stand-off between Paternoster's advocacy of agency and free will, and Cullen's insistence on the importance of causality for criminological explanation.

In my judgement, this is an unhelpfully binary view of the relevant issues. In particular, neither of these scholars takes adequate account of the potential contribution of a type of methodological approach to social science that can be traced back to the work of Max Weber (1922/1978). Crucially, methodologies of this kind explicitly try to hold together 'agentic understanding' (*verstehen*) and causal explanation.[18] Within the *verstehen* dimension, they broadly agree with Paternoster that a person's reasons for action can be treated as a teleological explanation: that is, actions can be (at least partly) explained in terms of the goals that a person has chosen, and his or her reasons for acting.[19] However, such teleology can, it is argued, without impropriety be combined with more traditional social scientific strategies, among other things by asking the question: '*why* did this person choose X rather than Y?'[20]

[18] This issue is, of course, linked to the much debated question of the extent to which the natural sciences and the social sciences share the same methodology. With regard to such debates, Runciman (1983: 2) notes, with regret, the apparently 'persistent compulsion of one side to reject all of the recommendations of the other'. He further suggests that the few scholars who have made a lasting contribution to the debate 'have for the most part done so, as Max Weber did ... by occupying and holding a limited area of the middle ground against attacks directed from either front'.

[19] The agreement is, however, only 'broad' because Paternoster's conception of teleology is more cognitive and individualised than that of most who follow a Weberian approach. See the further discussion of Paternoster's conception below.

[20] Interestingly, although Francis Cullen (2017) declares himself to be an 'unabashed positivist', he does not adopt the fully fledged determinism of most positivists. Instead, he states that he has 'little doubt that "will" or "conscious choice" is involved in offenders' decisions'. However, he goes on to say—and indeed to emphasise—that criminologists can legitimately

All this is made particularly clear in a methodological treatise in the Weberian tradition by the Cambridge sociologist W. G. Runciman (1983: ch. 1).[21] Runciman argues persuasively that a successful piece of social scientific research usually needs to include adequate accounts of three separate matters: first, *what* is being studied ('reportage'); secondly, *how actors* in the studied social context *perceive and understand* that situation ('appreciative description'); and thirdly, *why* matters turned out as they did ('explanation').[22] He further proposes that neither 'reportage' nor 'explanation' differ in principle as between the natural and the social sciences, but that 'appreciative description' is unique to social science. It seems to be an implication of Runciman's account that some social science research can be adequately conducted without including an element of appreciative description, but that such an element is usually beneficial, and sometimes essential.

Issues of this kind can be illustrated by considering some research carried out in the Institute of Criminology in the late 1990s by a team led by Alison Liebling.[23] This was a government-funded study, which was commissioned to evaluate a new prison-based policy called the 'Incentives and Earned Privileges' (or IEP) initiative, introduced with the aim of improving the behaviour of prisoners in England and Wales. The central maxim of this policy was that 'prison privileges must be earned by good behaviour'. It was decided that every prisoner would be placed in one of three new privilege categories ('basic', 'standard' and 'enhanced'), with each of these categories linked to a set of specific privileges that were—by common consent—valued by prisoners. The theoretical framework underpinning the policy was, therefore, that of Rational Choice Theory (RCT): the expectation was that prisoners would act instrumentally, and improve their behaviour in

ask relevant questions about the 'factors that *cause* certain choices to be made' (2017: 375, emphasis in original). Formally, he therefore seems to come close to a Weberian synthesis of 'understanding' (*verstehen*) and 'explanation'. However, in his paper there is little attention to, or development of, the dimension of 'conscious choice'; accordingly, Cullen is perhaps best described as a *de facto* positivist.

[21] As a precursor to this treatise, Runciman (1972) had also published a sympathetic but stringent critique of Weber's methodological writings.

[22] Runciman uses the term 'understanding' as a generic concept to embrace all three of these matters, but I have avoided this terminology because some respected philosophers of social science (e.g., Hollis 2001) have spoken of a tension between 'explanation' and 'understanding'. I have also expanded the name of Runciman's 'description' to 'appreciative description', in order to give a fuller sense of what was intended.

[23] Other members of the team were Grant Muir, Gerry Rose, and myself. I acted as a theoretical and methodological adviser, and took no part in the research fieldwork.

order to secure valued privileges. Given this framework, the governmental sponsors of the research were both surprised and disconcerted when the empirical results of the research—conducted in five prisons chosen by the prison service—found no behavioural improvements in the first year of operation of the IEP policy (Liebling et al. 1999b, Bottoms 2003). The reason for this finding was, however, uncovered by the 'appreciative description' element of the research methods that were utilised in the study. Prisoners were generally supportive of the basic principle that privileges should follow good behaviour, but for various reasons (too complex to explain in detail here), they considered that the way in which the new policy had been introduced had in practice resulted in a significant degree of *unfairness*.[24] In consequence, many prisoners chose not to engage positively with the new incentives structure. In other words, the expected 'rational choice' effects were displaced by a widespread sense among prisoners that the policy, as they actually experienced it, lacked legitimacy. These findings do not comport well with Paternoster's theoretical formulations, in two respects. First, although the agency of prisoners was crucial to the explanation of the lack of behavioural effects, their main agentic response could not be adequately described as a process of 'deliberation, decision-making, intention-formation and volition or activation of the will' (Paternoster 2017: 350); rather, it was simply an evaluative reaction against important aspects of the way in which the new policy was implemented. Secondly, and contrary to Paternoster's further suggestion that 'human agency is incompatible with event causality' (2017: 350), the results of this study suggest that the prisoners' *agentic moral response* to the policy (as it was implemented) was *caused* by aspects of the prison service's implementation of the policy.[25]

However, in his 'agency' paper, Ray Paternoster seems more interested in individual cases than in social-institutional contexts such as prisons. So let us also briefly consider a hypothetical example of the Weberian

[24] The perceived unfairness was found in all the prisons studied, although in detail it differed in different institutions. One important general issue was that the new policy significantly enhanced the discretionary decision-making powers of prison officers, and prisoners considered that these powers were often being used in an arbitrary way.

[25] It follows—as the authors of the IEP research made clear—that with better fairness safeguards in place, the IEP policy could in principle lead to improved prisoner behaviour. In response to the research results, prison service managers in England and Wales amended several aspects of the policy in an attempt to reduce perceived unfairness (see Bottoms 2003 for details); however, the revised scheme was not formally evaluated. Interestingly, a few years later a very similar IEP scheme was introduced in Swedish prisons. Research found essentially the same results as in the English study (Liebling 2008), which led the Swedish prison service to abandon the policy.

methodological approach as applied to an individual case. Gary is an ex-prisoner who has decided that he definitely wants to stop offending; his wish to change has been reinforced by a recently begun relationship with a caring partner. He therefore takes steps to change some of his daily routines. Unfortunately, however, like many ex-prisoners, Gary has had trouble finding a job, and so he is short of money. One day, he happens to meet some old friends who are planning what they believe will be a lucrative crime, and they invite him to join them. It is not hard to agree with Paternoster that Gary has a genuine agentic choice whether to accept their offer; but it is also not hard to see that whichever choice he might make, we will be able to provide a causal explanation of why he chose it.

As one philosopher has put it, the Weberian style of holistic social science research—combining reportage, appreciative description, and causal explanation—is 'tantalising' but very difficult. It is tantalising because it allows us to think about social action as a blend of 'strategically rational choice, intelligent fulfilling of [social] roles ... an openness to moral concerns' (Hollis 2002: 255), and the influences both of our personal and social backgrounds and of our current situation. It is nevertheless difficult, because it requires us to hold together coherently some very different types of issue in our search for explanation. Nevertheless, in my experience it is a deeply enriching way in which to carry out social scientific research.

There is, however, one important consequence of this kind of approach. It offers a creative and inclusive approach to explanation; but free choice still lies at the heart of what we are trying to explain, and that means that we cannot *predict* with any certainty which choice an individual will make in a given situation. This is one of the crucial differences between social science and natural science—which is related, of course, to the very existence of human consciousness, reflexivity, and agency.

To complete this discussion of agency, it is necessary to assess the adequacy of Paternoster's expressed preference for what he describes as a 'very individualistic and cognitive' (2017: 350) view of this concept. Curiously, although Paternoster is well aware that other social scientists have theorised agency in a more social manner than he does, he makes no attempt to argue in detail for the view that he prefers. Instead, he simply records in a footnote (2017: 353 n. 4) that while others have taken a different approach,[26] for him 'agency is very much understood to be more of an individualistic mental

[26] The specified others are Emirbayer and Mische (1998), Hitlin and Elder (2007), and Bottoms (2005).

product, and less a social one . . . it is important to keep in mind that deliberations, intentions and volitions are acts of the mind'. Despite the brevity of this discussion, it seems clear that, for Paternoster, there is a close connection between the individualistic character of agency and a perception of agency as primarily 'cognitive', involving 'acts of the mind'. Given this, it is perhaps not surprising that Paternoster is drawn to link agency explicitly to RCT. However, he is at pains to argue that the source of a person's choices is to be found not only in:

> a common staple of rational choice theory—the reasons for one's actions are sourced in one's own self-interests—[but also in] an important extension of rational choice theory in criminology, [namely that] fully fledged human agency occurs when persons transcend their own interests and defer to a more common good. Rational choice theory, therefore, need not be tied to an image of human beings simply as bargain hunters. (2017: 364)

This is an interesting extension of RCT, and it allows Paternoster to theorise some individuals' decisions to desist from crime in terms of their concerns for others, such as loved ones or victims.[27] 'Human agency', however, is still seen in terms of cognitive deliberation and rational choice. Is this an adequate picture?

To assess this question, consider another example of an individual exercising agency, this time involving a real person. 'Len' was a persistent young adult offender who had served one sentence in a Young Offenders' Institution.[28] His relationship with his mother had broken down, as a result of which he had for a time been homeless, which he found very difficult. He therefore decided to change his lifestyle and try to avoid offending. He had taken some steps along this road, helped by a placement in a city-centre hostel, until one day he met one of his former delinquent friends. They bonded again, then they got drunk, decided to steal a car, and were arrested while driving it erratically.

How can such an episode be theorised? Len had made a rational, agentic decision to desist from crime, and he was trying to re-orient his life on that

[27] Paternoster has, with colleagues, contributed substantially to the research literature on desistance from crime with the so-called identity theory of desistance: see for example Paternoster and Bushway (2009) and Paternoster et al. (2015).

[28] Len's case is briefly discussed in Bottoms and Shapland (2016: 111–113).

basis. However, on the evening in question he had acted in a way that was clearly contrary to that decision—as he himself was very quick to realise after the event.[29] In the language of philosophers, he had therefore acted with 'weakness of will', that is, he had knowingly acted against his own best moral judgement about how he should be living his life.[30] Although the research interview with Len did not explore in detail how this had happened, it is not hard to construct a plausible account. Perhaps, then, meeting and bonding with his old friend created a mood of happiness, and this was then heightened by the consumption of alcohol, which also lowered inhibitions. The decision to take and drive away the car was of course a deliberate decision, very likely influenced by the known excitement that acts of law-breaking often generate among offenders in this age group.[31] Accordingly, there was indeed teleology involved in taking the car, but this teleology was based on short-term considerations (having fun that evening) rather than Len's long-term goal to stop offending. The act was also certainly influenced by the immediate social circumstances of the evening, operating as they did upon someone who was not unused to acts of crime. SAT researchers would have no difficulty in explaining the action, based on issues of propensity and situational context. However, it is very difficult to see how Len's action can be explained by Paternoster's individualistic, cognitive, and (modified) rational-choice conception of human agency. This is because, even in Len's own terms, the act was not rational; moreover, it was primarily influenced by emotional and social factors rather than cognitive and individualistic ones.

It will be recalled that for Paternoster (2017: 350) 'at its core, human agency is understood to be *action*—deliberate and intended or willed conduct' (emphasis in original). The strong focus in his theorisation on the *moral act* is—albeit in a different context—reminiscent of the tendency within prescriptivism to prioritise the importance of adherence to moral rules over other aspects of morality. As Iris Murdoch (1970: 15) shrewdly

[29] Len was, in retrospect, shocked that he had acted in the way he had. In response to this event, and because his relationship with his mother had been improving, he moved back to her home and significantly changed his lifestyle, staying at home to a much greater extent.

[30] 'Weakness of will' is a major topic within moral philosophy, with contributions going back to some of the dialogues of Plato. For essays on historical and contemporary debates, see for example the collections edited by Mortimore (1971) and Stroud and Tappolet (2003).

[31] In the Sheffield Desistance Study (to be discussed later), a sample of young adult recidivist offenders was offered a list of 14 things that 'others have said have made it more difficult to go straight or to stay straight'. At each of four interviews, the item 'need for excitement or to relieve boredom' was ranked third in the proportion of respondents checking the item (Bottoms and Shapland 2011: 61, Table 2.4).

observed, in that kind of moral philosophy 'morality resides at the point of action'; hence, 'until the moment of choice, *the agent is outside the machinery*' (emphasis added). For adequate criminological explanation, we need to bring agents into the 'machinery' in all aspects of their lives, and that requires that our conception of agency will be more social than Ray Paternoster was willing to allow.

Empirical studies II: Shifting values—desistance from crime

Len's case, described above, is taken from a research study of desistance from crime. It therefore forms a natural bridge to the next strand of empirical research that I propose to consider, which concerns that topic.

Studies have shown that most offenders, even persistent offenders, eventually desist from crime, and the age group during which persistent offenders show the fastest deceleration in their rate of offending is the early twenties (Piquero et al. 2007: 136). Naturally, these findings have led to a spate of studies which have tried to understand how and why such processes occur. Within the framework of this chapter, I cannot deal fully with this literature; instead, I shall outline some relevant findings from the Sheffield Desistance Study (SDS), which I co-led with Joanna Shapland of the University of Sheffield.[32]

Because of the known importance of the early twenties as a period of offence reduction, we decided in this study to select a sample of male offenders who were aged about 20 at the start of the research. We then followed them over a period of three to four years, using four lengthy interviews. We recruited 113 men, who were mostly persistent offenders: on average, each man had been officially convicted or cautioned for 19 non-motoring offences at the time of the first interview. Given such records, it was not surprising that 80% of the men were reconvicted during the follow-up period; but, crucially, and in line with previous findings, their average rate of recorded offending declined significantly during that period.[33] In the context

[32] For key results from the SDS, see Bottoms and Shapland (2011, 2016) and Shapland and Bottoms (2011); for a general overview of the research literature on desistance, see Shapland and Bottoms (2017).

[33] The decline was from an average of 8.2 recorded 'standard list' offences in the year before the first interview, to an average of 2.6 such offences in the period (usually more than one year) from the third interview to the end of the study. Both figures are standardised to exclude periods in penal custody.

of the present chapter, three sets of research findings from the SDS are of special significance. These concern, respectively, 'ground projects', values, and dealing with weakness of will.

First, the great majority of the sample, despite their long records, expressed a wish to stop offending, although a minority were not sure that they could achieve this. When asked more generally what kind of person they would like to become in the next few years, the focus was again on normality: the great majority said they hoped they would 'be living a normal, regular life'; 'be a good person'; 'be a family man', and so on. Such aspirations can reasonably be described as forming, for these men, a moral '*ground project*' of the kind brought to prominence by the work of the social anthropologist Cheryl Mattingly (2013, 2014), although using a less 'deep' definition of that concept than the one adopted by Mattingly.[34] However, it was not surprising that, in the SDS as in Mattingly's study, different research subjects pursued their 'ground project' with variable degrees of commitment. Statistically, the Sheffield research found that—consistently with Paternoster's emphasis on 'teleology'—interview-based expressions of a wish to desist did significantly predict less subsequent crime, although this statistical relationship was modest in strength (Shapland and Bottoms 2017b). The main reason why the relationship was modest appeared to be because the lives of many members of the sample were both complex and tangled, and it was very easy for them to revert to old ways in difficult situations—as, indeed, happened in Len's case (see above). Regression analyses on the prediction of desistance reinforced this picture. That is, using measures of self-reported criminality, men were more likely to continue in crime when they had longer criminal records, when they self-reported more current social obstacles to desistance, and when they were not able to secure employment (Bottoms and Shapland 2016: 104). Thus, as other researchers have also found, paths to desistance were normally gradual, with at least one failure on the way. We summarised our findings by saying that '*desistance*

[34] For Mattingly's conceptualisation, see note 10 above. In a criminological context, it seems entirely reasonable to describe as a ground project any serious attempt to change one's lifestyle or habits (whether acquired by nature or nurture). This kind of process has been well described by Jonathan Jacobs (2016: 18): 'One can, for example, strive to control a volatile temper, learn to be more patient and considerate, [or] attempt to acquire a more disciplined approach to one's work and responsibilities ... [T]he possibility of ... realization [about our characters] and the attempt at revision are distinctive capacities of human beings. We do not know whether our efforts will be efficacious because we do not know how fully fixed our dispositions have become. We can still acknowledge reasons for making the effort to change and can be motivated to make the effort.'

is the process of learning to live a non-criminal life when one has been leading a largely criminal life' (Bottoms and Shapland 2016: 109, emphasis in original). This process was often very difficult, just as changing other habitual ways of living, such as smoking or over-eating, can be difficult. Given these difficulties, success in achieving the subject's 'ground project' very often needed support from significant others—especially, in this sample, girlfriends and mothers.[35] Overall, therefore, although the wish to change (and therefore human agency) was crucial to desistance in this sample, our data showed a much more socially embedded picture of agency than is captured by Ray Paternoster's strongly individualistic language of 'decision-making, intention formation, [and] ... activation of the will'.

Secondly, what can be said about *moral values* within the Sheffield men's journeys? Despite their extensive criminal records, it will already be clear from the data on their aspirations for normality that most of the sample were not normatively committed to criminal lifestyles (see more fully Shapland and Bottoms 2011). On the other hand, all of the sample had recently committed offences, and at the beginning of the study 60% said that the excitement of committing crimes was a significant obstacle to going straight. So, to return to Charles Taylor's conceptualisation, the men's *moral frameworks* at the start of the study were complex: they saw offending as something that they could, in some circumstances, contemplate doing; but, looking to their longer-term future, they did not want to go on doing it. In other words, their deepest values were prosocial, but given their recent histories, other values were present in their moral framework. Over the three to four years of the follow-up, however, we were able to identify shifts in the priority of the values of those men who were desisting: more pro-social values came to the fore, usually alongside new relationships or social opportunities, and aided by processes of physiological and psychological maturity.[36] These results are highly congruent with Charles Taylor's

[35] The role of girlfriends and wives in supporting desistance by males is a staple of the desistance literature, albeit subject to detailed empirical debate. The importance of reconnections with families of origin as recidivist offenders attempt desistance in early adulthood (often overcoming previous conflicts with parents) was an original finding in the SDS, although similar findings have now been reported from US research studies (see Giordano 2016: 19–20).

[36] Joanna Shapland and I are most grateful to Professor Joel Robbins of the Social Anthropology Department, Cambridge University, for helping us to see the relevance of a changing priority of values within our data. For a helpful encyclopaedia article on the study of values in social anthropology, see Robbins and Sommerschuh (2016). The leading research study on the importance of developmental processes, including maturity, in understanding desistance from crime in early adulthood is the Pathways to Desistance Study in the United States, led by Edward Mulvey: see for example Mulvey and Schubert (2016).

theorisation about moral frameworks, in which (see above) he emphasised the plurality of values within moral frameworks, and their close connection to people's sense of self.

Thirdly, our research uncovered a particular issue for men in their twenties with offending histories who are trying to desist: namely, how one deals with relationships with former criminal friends. This is not a trivial matter: offending in groups is particularly prevalent at around age 20, and at that age there are often significant bonds of friendship and trust between offenders and their male peers (Warr 2002). In the Sheffield study, therefore, a frequently mentioned issue among those trying to desist was how to avoid the temptations that might arise if one continued to socialise with these friends. Many of our sample did not trust themselves to be strong enough to say 'no' on a face-to-face basis in such situations—in other words, they feared that on these occasions they might act with 'weakness of will' (see previous discussion). In response to these fears, they developed strategies to avoid becoming the subject of such pressures. The main strategies adopted were, first, to avoid certain places, such as specific pubs or clubs, where they thought trouble would be likely to occur; and, secondly, to plan daily routines so as to deliberately avoid possible meetings with old friends. We described such strategies as an exercise of 'diachronic self-control' (that is, self-control in advance of the event), but others have preferred to call them 'self-selection'. Whatever the description, as many as three-quarters of the men in a qualitative subsample had used such tactics (Bottoms 2013). The widespread use of such tactics is surely a very interesting criminological example of everyday morality in action.

Empirical studies III: Prison social order

The final strand of empirical criminology to be considered takes us into the world of prisons, and here I shall focus on a series of studies of prison social order by Alison Liebling, also of the Cambridge Institute. In 2004 she published a book tellingly entitled *Prisons and Their Moral Performance* (Liebling with Arnold 2004), and she has refined and developed her work since then, especially as regards high-security prisons (see for example Liebling, Arnold, and Straub 2011).

Alison Liebling's extensive corpus of research builds on foundations developed through a qualitative methodological approach called Appreciative Inquiry, used particularly with prisoner groups but also with staff. In prisoner-based Appreciative Inquiry, people are asked to reflect upon occasions when they have experienced the institution most positively (for example, when they have felt 'most human'), and to articulate as clearly as possible what it was that made that occasion, or that set of occasions, a positive experience for them. Using this methodological strategy, it became possible for Liebling and her colleagues to identify a set of features of prison life that, according to these accounts of 'best experiences', will allow prisoners to feel that they can not only cope with their sentence, but also start to better develop their potential. Liebling (2015b: 21) has summarised these results as follows:

> [P]risoners need to feel that they are safe; that they are treated with humanity; that they understand the way that the prison system, including [its] release procedures, works; and that they are in a well-organised and professional prison where staff have enough experience and expertise to deal with the issues that matter to them, and where staff use both . . . formal and informal means of authority (including relationships with prisoners) . . . to maintain order. This is not a 'heavy' version of authority. Staff in better prisons . . . are fair, competent, clear and responsive. Not many prisons reach these standards.[37]

Once this set of regime and relational characteristics had been identified through Appreciative Inquiry, it became possible to embody them in a questionnaire format, in order to provide a quantitative measure of how well a given prison is delivering specific moral and regime features. (Alison Liebling describes the use of this questionnaire as 'ethnography-led measurement'.) The resulting instrument, known as Measuring the Quality of Prison Life (or MQPL), is now routinely used by the English prison service to assess what Liebling calls the moral quality of its establishments; it has also attracted significant attention internationally.

But Alison Liebling has not rested content with developing understandings and measurements of the moral quality of regimes. Her first research studies in prisons concerned suicides and attempted suicides, and in this research she showed, among other things—and echoing the classic sociological work of Emile Durkheim (1897/2006)—that suicide rates are not purely a matter of individual decision. Rather, they have a social dimension,

[37] For an account of a prison that did meet these standards, and some comparisons of its MQPL scores with other English prisons, see Liebling et al. (2019).

which in the prisons context means that some kinds of regime are, unfortunately, more likely than others to lead to higher levels of distress, suicide, and attempted suicide (Liebling 1992). Pursuing concerns of this kind in conjunction with her MQPL work, Liebling has shown that regimes that have what might be described as 'good' MQPL profiles (better moral climates) produce better outcomes on a range of matters. These include:

> lower levels of distress and fewer suicides, fewer threats to order, better prospects on release, and better orientations towards faith (that is, there are fewer attractions presented by faith identities linked to 'political charge' or violent extremism). (Liebling 2015b: 21)

This body of work is therefore a further powerful demonstration of the point, also found in the Peterborough study and indeed in Gardenia, that social contexts can influence human action, including moral action. But the studies of prison order are, in my view, also of potentially wider significance for theoretical criminology. Given that most prisoners have broken the law, very often by acts that have put self-interest ahead of the common good, it is not obvious that they would prioritise regime values such as managerial vision and clarity, or staff competence. But most of them do. To explore the implications of this point a little more fully, let us return to the two values articulated at the beginning of the quotation in which Alison Liebling summarises her Appreciative Inquiry studies: 'prisoners need to feel that *they are safe*, [and] that they *are treated with humanity* ...' (emphasis added). Reflecting on these results, I am reminded of Bernard Williams's (2005: 3) argument, in a posthumously published essay, that the 'first political question' in any society is always the 'securing of order, protection, safety, trust and the conditions of co-operation', because without a solution to issues of safety and order, living with others in community can be a nightmare. That, Liebling's results show, is as true in prisons as elsewhere. Nevertheless, safety and order are not the only values of importance in community living. As Geoffrey Hawthorn pointed out in his introduction to Williams's posthumous essays, if a ruler with no moral scruples has access to effective power, then putting a stop to disorder is not difficult. In those circumstances, however, a solution to the 'first question' might well generate a further problem—that of living under despotism. That is why, in Williams's analysis, it is always reasonable for those subject to state power to 'ask what the nature of the state's protection and its price are to be and why, and they will want a reasonable reply' (Hawthorn in Williams (2005: xii)).

This is why prisoners desire not only safety, but also regimes that treat them with humanity and fairness. In short, empirical studies of social order in prisons seem to connect in a very interesting way with an important recent contribution to political philosophy.

One final aspect of Alison Liebling's work must be noted: she has shown that on some occasions *it can be appropriate to inject concepts drawn from critical morality into descriptive social scientific studies*. The best illustration of this point is found in her work on staff–prisoner relationships. When they are speaking about a particular prison, commentators frequently ask whether that institution has 'good staff–prisoner relationships', but Liebling (2011b) has insisted that this is not, ultimately, the correct question. She points out that 'good' relations can simply mean that people are getting on with each other; however, a relationship between an officer and a prisoner can be 'good' but not 'right'. This can happen where, for example, the officer turns a blind eye to drug importation, or is afraid to exert his authority over some powerful prisoners: in such situations the relationship might be socially 'good', but it is not morally 'right'. (There are, of course, parallels to this within policing: for a striking recent study, see Tankebe et al. 2019.) This analysis also has an important wider implication, because it shows that, although in this chapter I have deliberately focused on positive morality, in real social situations positive and critical morality are sometimes intertwined. That is a topic that cannot be further pursued here, but it will need careful attention as criminologists continue to develop their study of the intersection of crime, criminal justice and morality.

Conclusion

In this chapter I have tried to offer a summary account of some recent developments in empirical criminological work that relate, in one way or another, to positive morality. A fair amount of ground has been covered: this includes the importance of moral rules for social life and for the explanation of criminal propensity; the possibility of modifying moral rules within lived everyday morality; the importance of social situations in shaping moral action; the possibility of achieving an altered priority of moral values when people undertake 'ground projects' such as desistance from crime; 'weakness of will' and strategies to avoid it; the perhaps surprising findings arising from asking prisoners to explain, from their experience, when the social order of prisons works best; and the difference between 'good' and 'right' relationships between citizens and criminal justice personnel. In addition, I have attempted to tackle some difficult theoretical issues about the meaning of human agency, and how, methodologically speaking, issues of agency and morality can be coherently related to appropriate social scientific questions about causation and explanation.

It will have become apparent that this field of research is still underdeveloped—necessarily so, because the criminological research community has only recently begun to grasp the full significance of moral issues. Criminology is not unique among the social sciences in this respect: indeed, there have been some recent well-flagged 'moral turns' in other disciplines such as sociology and social anthropology. Criminologists can certainly learn much from these parallel developments, and I have myself particularly benefited from exposure to some of the work of social anthropologists.[38] But we need to focus also on our own subject, which explains the choice of examples in this chapter.[39] As a concluding comment, however, I cannot do better than to quote a contemporary Cambridge social anthropologist, James Laidlaw. His comment is very far removed from the views of the American criminologist who upbraided me in Stockholm, but it is much closer to the realities of everyday life—including crimes and punishments—that we, as criminologists, are committed to studying:

> The ethical dimension of social life—the fact that everyday conduct is constitutively pervaded by reflective evaluation—is irreducible, and ... social theory needs to be reformulated to make our analyses of diverse phenomena and states of affairs cognizant of this. (Laidlaw 2014: 44–45)

[38] Among key recent works on ethics within social anthropology, see Laidlaw (2014), Mattingly (2014), and Lambek at al. (2015).

[39] A text not considered here, but written by a major contributor to criminological studies, is *The Moral Sense* by the late James Q. Wilson (1993). Wilson offered this book as a continuation, in a modern context, of the kind of work 'begun by certain eighteenth-century ... thinkers [such as] ... David Hume and Adam Smith'; that is, he saw it as 'an effort to clarify what ordinary people mean when they speak of their moral feelings and to explain, so far as one can, the origins of those feelings' (p. xiii). His analysis is both complex and controversial, and it deserves a level of serious engagement that could not be provided within the scope of this paper. It is curious that *The Moral Sense* has, to date, been almost completely ignored by criminologists, including those who have contributed to what Messner (2012: 7) described as the beginnings of 'a moral awakening in criminology'.

4

In Dialogue with Philosophy

Recovering the Moral Sciences through Criminology

Jonathan Jacobs

Introduction

One of the most striking features of Tony Bottoms's contributions in recent years is how effectively he has brought philosophical thought about epistemology, methodology, and ethics to bear on empirical criminology. He has addressed several centrally important issues, including the relationship between observations and theory in criminology, the respective roles of agency and causality in explanations of behaviour, the question of the relation between facts and values, and issues concerning the ways moral values can figure in criminological investigations and explanations. Of course, numerous social scientists have explored such matters but Tony recognises that, whatever the state of criminological investigations and theorising, they are accompanied by genuine philosophical issues, and attention to those issues can make important contributions to criminology. There have been numerous philosophical developments concerning epistemology and other key issues in philosophy of science and of social science in recent decades. Tony's work reflects alertness to them and a carefully considered appreciation of their significance for criminology.

One of the ways in which this is especially important is that he sees how empirical inquiry on the one hand, and philosophical analysis and theorising on the other, can be mutually informing in ways that deepen and clarify understanding of problems, issues, methods, and theorising. This is a significant intellectual project both theoretically and practically. In addition to clarifying fundamental aspects of criminological inquiry, it is an essential step in the direction of developing criminal justice ethics as a specific

Jonathan Jacobs, *In Dialogue with Philosophy*. In: *Crime, Justice, and Social Order*. Edited by: Alison Liebling, Joanna Shapland, Richard Sparks, and Justice Tankebe, Oxford University Press. © Alison Liebling, Joanna Shapland, Richard Sparks, and Justice Tankebe 2022. DOI: 10.1093/oso/9780192859600.003.0004

field of study. Also, it can indicate significant respects in which criminological investigation can be a support when policy makers encounter, with apprehension, challenges that clearly have moral aspects.

On a personal note, Tony has very generously included me in various discussions and conferences at the Institute of Criminology at Cambridge and in maintaining an ongoing exchange of ideas that has been an important part of my education, not only regarding criminology, but also my own discipline (philosophy). Tony's wide range of intellectual interests is bolstered by a demanding sense of intellectual integrity. He seeks resources and methods for understanding wherever they may be found and thinks very carefully about how they can contribute. His work demonstrates the exemplary importance of employing conceptual resources and insights from multiple disciplines with an expert hand, attaining depth and clarity.

My discussion of his work will comment on some of the most philosophically important claims and arguments Tony has articulated about theory and observations, agency and causality, the relation between facts and values, and the way that those issues are interrelated. His overall view of that conceptual architecture and its importance to empirical study is especially instructive and impressive.

Some basic issues concerning theory, observation, and explanation

To situate the point I made above regarding the overall character of much of Tony's work, I should say a bit about philosophy and about key issues in the philosophy of social science and social explanation during roughly the past half-century. Regarding the latter, the following are among the most prominent issues: (1) Are explanations in the social sciences methodologically similar to those in the natural sciences? Is the form of explanation and the relevant methodology basically the same in the two areas of inquiry? (2) Is human behaviour to be explained causally in much the same manner as natural phenomena are explained, or does (at least some) human action involve an exercise of agency distinct from what is expressed by causal explanation as generally understood? And finally: (3) How is the relation between facts and values understood, and what are the implications for the relation between social science and morality? Overall, Tony's work builds a very strong case for a non-scientistic conception of criminology as empirical science without sacrificing any of its scientific credentials, while also illuminating important issues concerning values.

Each of those is a complex context involving a number of debates. In the scope of this chapter I can discuss them only briefly. But we can see how each is an important element of Tony's work and we can characterise the significance of his concern to address them in a manner that also examines their interrelations.

In 'The Relationship Between Theory and Empirical Observations in Criminology', Tony identifies two 'key propositions to explicate and defend'. The first is that 'whether one likes it or not (and some do not like it much) some engagement with theory is inevitable if one is to practice social science (including criminology) at all' (Bottoms 2008b: 76). The second is 'that there is a indeed a real world, and that criminologists cannot avoid engagement with that world, whether they like it or not (and some do not like it much)' (Bottoms 2008b: 77). One might suppose that there is some tension between the two propositions, thinking that if we are 'condemned' to theorise, how can we know whether we are, in our investigations and explanations, getting at the world as it is, 'objectively', if one wishes to put it that way? If we cannot avoid theorising, does that imply that whatever we take the world to be like, that view is always a matter of construction on our part, always mediating our view of things by conceptual choices or conceptual lenses that are perhaps not freely chosen, but in any case not a matter of responsiveness to how things are *anyway*, so to speak?

Tony recognises that any attempt to ascertain the facts and to explain them inevitably requires the employment of concepts and theories; facts do not somehow simply disclose themselves in precisely the terms that capture and express their properties so that there is nothing for an investigator to do but record the facts. (They do not come with natural language titles, in the way that paintings are displayed in museums.) Moreover, in attempting to provide *explanations* we need not only concepts but systematic, coherent constellations of concepts, general claims, and hypotheses which can be tested with a view to confirming or disconfirming them and building up an increasingly detailed, accurate, coherent, and illuminating account. We should recognise that concepts and theories are not impediments that come between inquirer and the world, obscuring our grasp of the latter. They need not be 'constructions' that are, so to speak, confined in their reference to the inside of the circle of the inquirer's ideas. Rather, concepts and theories are modes of access to the world, resources for attaining cognition and articulating what there is, what its properties are, and how things happen. The fact that cognition involves *thought* does not put the world out of reach. Rather, though an explanatory cognition of things is not simply evident, disclosed to us without work on our part, concepts and theories can do a better or worse job of attaining that cognition, and we can ascertain whether we are doing a better or worse job. Otherwise, we could think just anything and there would be no reason to either accept or reject that view of things.

Granted, concepts can be confused, distorting, inaccurate, and the like; and theories can be seriously mistaken, held on dogmatic and irrational grounds, and can otherwise fail to describe and explain. But the options are not (i) that unconceptualised, untheorised reality simply presents itself, or (ii) epistemological relativism all the way down, with no friction with reality. In fact, both of those views are very unscientific as well as implausible. The former is a mistake because whatever the issue or the object of interest, experience, or investigation, we can only have any thought of it *under concepts*. One cannot simply count all the *things* in the room. 'Thing' does not specify or identify anything determinate to be counted. One has to count under concepts, under specific descriptions. We can count the wooden chairs, the metal chairs, the white pieces of chalk, the blue pieces of chalk, the sleeping human beings, the note-taking human beings, the linoleum tiles, and so on in the room. There are many different ways of going about counting, some of them scientific, and some very unscientific (e.g., 'how many kinds of things in the room begin with the letter "r" when one is describing things in English?' is typically not a scientific way of counting things). But there is no thinking without concepts. Any explanation, any account depends on a constellation of concepts and the employment, refinement, and revision of them, and the ways they are related to other concepts.

An important part of the scientific project is the formulation and articulation of concepts that can figure in explanations, and explanations typically depend on the theories through which their generality and explanatory relations are expressed. It might be that any theory is imperfect in the sense that, at any given time, it could be more complete, more coherent, more fully confirmed, more fully integrated with other theories we have good reason (thus far) to accept, and so forth. The unavoidability of theory does not imply that we can be certain we are getting things right with regard to some phenomena to be explained. But neither does it mean we encounter insurmountable impediments to 'getting at' the world. In addition, relations between theories become increasingly important as theories are refined, are tested, and find support. We need to consider carefully how our various theories stand with regard to each other and with regard to the observations we make in testing and refining them.

Tony regards himself as 'an unrepentant advocate of serious attempts at synthesis' (Bottoms 2008b: 82). 'A good synthesis seeks to weld theory and data together in an ongoing cumulative search for the truth' (Bottoms 2008b: 83). He recognises the need to be 'open to the insights offered by many theories' (Bottoms, 2008b: 82) and not to turn rival theories into instruments of 'turf wars' rather than explanation. Commitment to a theory need not involve such jealous attachment that other theories are automatically disqualified or assumed to be unworthy rivals. Theories are resources for our projects of seeking intelligibility. We should not become intellectual hostages to favoured theories or elevate them to become objects of theological conviction.

Tony has developed a patient, careful approach to seeing how elements of different theories might be fruitfully integrated. But rather than just borrowing what appear to be attractive pieces of different theories and trying to fit them together, he undertakes a critical exploration of the elements of several different views—their conceptual commitments and the rationales for those commitments. In proceeding that way, we see how the integration achieved is a result of having worked through a complex set of intellectual difficulties, with their points of contact and points of opposition carefully considered. His discussion of behaviour and agency in 'Desistance, Social Bonds, and Human Agency: A Theoretical Exploration' is a model of analytical examination of concepts and theories on the one hand, and a synthesis of explanatory conceptions on the other. In that article he integrates considerations under the heading 'self–other differentiation' and 'self–other coordination' in working towards a more complete notion of agency for the sake of elaborating a theory of desistance. In doing so he is fully alert to the different assumptions, implications, and types of confirming evidence appropriate to diverse approaches. His efforts at synthesis involve judicious acknowledgment of potential challenges and difficulties and are never a matter of enthusiasm for a certain vocabulary substituting for the real work that needs to be done.

He is also alert to the diverse considerations relevant to evaluating theories, and committed to remaining firmly grounded empirically as a way of keeping track of how successfully—or not—a theoretical approach actually produces explanations. Theories need to yield meaningfully testable hypotheses, and the interpretation of data should not be permissive just for the sake of trying to save a theoretical approach one happens to prefer. The relations between theories and observations, and the explication and articulation of concepts involved in theorising, need to meet standards of clarity and rigour. Relativist notions concerning theory evaluation, or maintaining that it is an inquirer's social context that motivates endorsements of theories—treating science as political theatre: those are ways of rendering the notions of *valid*, *explanatory*, *illuminating* empty of meaning. In that case, what does the success or explanatoriness of a theory consist in? Actually, *nothing* that is relevant in epistemic terms.

With regard to the relativism issue, it is important to see—as Tony sees—that conceptual relativism, theoretical relativism, and any of the epistemic versions of relativism do not contribute explanatory illumination. There are genuine and difficult questions about the roles of different descriptions of phenomena in regard to explanation, and difficult questions regarding the relations between different theories—for example, biological, sociological, psychological theories—and the various conceptions of causal processes that they involve. Also, there are justificatory issues concerning the levels of confirmation appropriate to theory-acceptance, and how to adjudicate conflicts between theories. There are also genuine issues concerning the influence of social, institutional, and historical factors on the matter of what theories are accepted, and by whom. But to embrace relativism is to render all of those difficulties nugatory because then there just is no question of addressing or resolving them in better rather than worse ways; of a closer approximation to the truth or of appropriate rather than inappropriate cognitive aspiration. Recognising that there are those sorts of difficulties is not a reason to embrace relativism. The genuineness of the difficulties is a reason *not* to.

The various epistemological and methodological questions concerning criminology and the social sciences generally are connected with the question of whether social sciences should emulate the methods of the natural sciences, whether they should be seen as part of the same overall scientific project, distinguished by focusing on certain classes of phenomena. This is a debate with a multigenerational history by now, and it was made very prominent by the logical positivism that was in ascendance in philosophy (both in Anglo-American philosophy and in a good deal of German-language philosophy on the European continent) during the first half of the twentieth century. The unity of the sciences (through unity of method) was part of the Positivist conception and for a few decades, at least, it seemed as though the epistemology of positivism and the scientific methodology it endorsed might be bringing many of the longstanding disputes about knowledge to an end. But, they did not bring them to an end, and at least in philosophy, logical positivism is now widely regarded as a significant episode in the history of philosophy rather than the once-and-for-all resolution of some of the main problems of philosophy.

Logical positivism underwent a destructive critique of extraordinary thoroughness. Between unanswerable objections to its verifiability criterion of meaning, to the doubts raised concerning positivism's conception of scientific explanation and theory-structure, to the demolition of the notion of a privileged level of description of experience as a basis for confirming hypotheses, to the complexity that was recognised in the process of theory-change, to robust challenges to the conception of reduction that was part of the unity of science view—given all that and more, logical positivism came to be seen as unable to 'deliver' on its extravagant claims. That does not mean that *empiricism* was endangered. Logical positivism is one highly specific version of empiricism and there are robust versions of non-Positivist empiricism. Tony is contributing to the articulation of such empiricism. But it is no longer fraught with the overweening claims distinctive of the triumphalist period of logical positivism.

There is a connection between positivist epistemology on the one hand, and whether there is agency as well as event-causality on the other. In the attempt to emulate the natural sciences many social scientists embraced the notion that the kind of causality that is appropriate to natural scientific explanation is the only kind, and thus, the explanation of human action is to be elaborated in methodologically similar terms. There are difficult questions about what constitute necessary and sufficient conditions for a causal explanation even if agent-causation is rejected. But one way in which positivism was influential was persuading many investigators that there is, so to speak, one kind of causation; there is only event-causation, and not also agent-causation. Thus, 'cause' is to be understood as univocal. Once that one meaning is specified, there would be no further need of reflection on causation, just the business of formulating causal explanations.

Causes and agents

Tony has argued that there is a role for agency, in large part because the understanding of human action is not always a matter of tracing a sequence (even if quite complex) of events.[1] Often, it involves the understanding ('interpretation' in Weberian terms) of action in a way that includes grasping

[1] There is a vast philosophical literature on causation and on agency and the issue of free will. There are influential formulations of the free will issue that do not focus on the question of

the meaning that action has for the agent. That does not mean that the agent always has a correct or honest appreciation of his or her own conduct, but it is important to have a sense of what the agent takes the conduct to be. Most of human behaviour is not just mechanical and explicable in mechanistic terms; people *do* things, and much of what they do, they do for reasons. That is not to say that all or even most action is undertaken for *good* reasons or thoughtfully; it means that human beings often act on the basis of what they take to be desirable, worthwhile, important, opportune, and so forth. Often they deliberate, and when I deliberate it is not just a matter of finding out what I am going to do, but making a determination of what to do. Also, in many cases of acting habitually, a person is acting for reasons but the habit reflects the way in which acting for those reasons has become dispositional.

To be sure, people often act on the basis of strong emotions or intense desires or are caused to act in certain ways by fear, provocation, threat, thoughtless impulse, and a host of other non-deliberative factors. But the facts that there are such actions, and that there are numerous reliable generalisations about how people act, are not evidence of causal determinism in their own right. Many of the latter could be evidence of patterns that reflect rationality, while the former patterns of conduct reflect the pronounced role of other factors. That human conduct reflects certain norms and regularities is hardly surprising. Human beings acquire habits and often settle into certain perspectives and ways of valuing things. For that reason it is rational to expect their behaviour to reflect those pattern-yielding features. Pattern need not imply causal determinism. It *can* reflect that, but it can also reflect what people take to be good reasons for acting in certain ways. If I have internalised certain norms because I believe they are supported by good reasons, and if acting in a particular norm-governed way becomes habitual for me, it is not as though I am no longer acting for reasons. Instead, my behaviour is now indicative of a rational habit. What is habitual need not be thoughtless, even if acting for certain reasons does not require any explicit, self-conscious deliberation in some cases.

determinism or causation but rather on the respective roles of values and desires in our actions or on the question of whether the person identifies with what moves him or her to act. The latter approach takes the issue of free will to be a matter of the reflective structure of the will rather than a matter of what kinds of causes are operating. Thus, the debate about free will is not, as it were, just one debate. It is a quite complex issue. An excellent collection of recent influential works on free will is *Free Will*, ed. Gary Watson, New York: Oxford University Press, 2003. Another, this one including classic as well as modern sources, is *Free Will*, ed. Derk Peerboom, Hackett Publishing Company, Inc., 1997.

Nor is it a necessary truth that we always act on our strongest desires. People sometimes choose to do something other than what they most strongly desire to do, and instead do that for which they think there is the best reason. It won't do to claim that, after all, we can *only* do what we most strongly desire, because it is analytic that if person P did A, then A is what P most wanted to do; that, whatever it is one does, that is *thereby* what the person most wanted to do. It could be that A is what P thought there is the best reason to do, where 'best reason' is not to be explained in terms of the person's wants or strength of desire. The explanations of actions are not analytic truths. We need to *ascertain* what motivates people and what they take to be relevant action-guiding considerations, and whether they have an accurate understanding of their own behaviour in that regard.

Moreover, *desire* is a complex category and many desires are not analogous to mechanical causes. The desire for a drink of water when very thirsty is a very different sort of want than the desire to master Shakespeare's history plays or the desire to marry a coreligionist or the desire to read stories to young children from single-parent households while they are at childcare. What is gratifying about that is quite different from what is gratifying about quenching one's thirst. Some desires have distinctive qualitative feels while others do not. Some are temporally extended and others are episodic; some are the results of careful consideration and others seem to arise without consideration, and so forth.

In addition, one mistake that is sometimes made regarding agency is to claim that if agency is something other than what can be captured and expressed by causal (event-cause) language then it must involve free will in a manner that leaves action utterly unexplained and thereby unintelligible. Actually, this is a mistake of the sort that one makes if a willing hostage to a theory. For example, one criminologist writes, 'The risk with a focus on human agency is thus that it detaches offenders from their personal traits, social context, and evolving life history' (Cullen 2017: 375). Oh? How did 'thus' make its way into the claim? An explanation in terms of agency can ascribe explanatory significance to the person's character, context, and history; in fact, those are just the sorts of considerations likely to figure prominently in one's exercise of agency. An exercise of agency is not something that just inexplicably happens without any basis in the person's character, past, and circumstances.

Dispositions that are elements of one's character, perspectives explicable in terms of one's social circumstances, and the sorts of experiences the individual has had—all of those shape the way a person exercises agency. If it is conceptualized as 'the performance of an action on the basis of nothing whatsoever' it will be a poor candidate for being explanatory. But why conceptualise it that way? Even free will should not be described *like that.* It would be mysterious why anyone would think free will desirable if that is what it is. A conception of free will or agency needs to be suitable to making intelligible distinctions between coercion and voluntariness, between deliberate and inadvertent conduct, between compulsive and self-determined behaviour, between considered and reflex responses, and so forth. It is not a refusal to give an account, asserting, 'the person did it, that's all; there is no explanation of it'.

The need for a carefully elaborated conception of agency is not based mainly on the fact that the law makes a large number of such distinctions so we had better figure out how to make sense of the law. It is because we unavoidably regard ourselves and others *as* agents, at least in the sense that completely abandoning all such distinctions (that is, the carefully made, appropriately qualified versions of them) is a conceptual and pragmatic impossibility. We would be doing without distinctions integral to identifying what actions people have performed. If somewhere a group is found that makes no such distinctions, that is not evidence that we, too, could certainly do without them. First of all, are all such distinctions really altogether absent in that group's social world? Second, would we find rational merit in the attempt to adopt such a way of seeing things? That is not to say that our current specifications of action-types are uniquely correct, but rather that the sorts of distinctions mentioned above (coerced versus voluntary, compulsive versus self-determined, etc.) are indispensable for any kind of social life that we would regard as suitable for beings with the capacities for reasoning, judgement, and choice that we have.

Also, no one defending agency or free will has to claim that all human actions are exercises of free agency. If human beings have free will it is still possible that they can be provoked, that they can act inadvertently, that hunger, fear, exuberance or any number of moods, emotions, and states make a difference to how they act. What is at stake is what is the best general conception of action and what sorts of explanations reflect that conception.

In 'Freedom and Resentment', P. F. Strawson argued that an attempt to regard all of human conduct as causally explainable in such a way that an 'objective' attitude—one suitable towards entities lacking the range of attitudes and sensibility of a volitional agent—would involve a very considerable 'conceptual shock', and probably would not become deeply anchored and enduring. It is too much at odds with basic (non-discretionary) ways in which we conceptualise ourselves, others, and human action. The shock could only be overcome by 'attending to that complicated web of attitudes and feelings which form an essential part of the moral life as we know it, and which are quite opposed to objectivity of attitude' (Strawson 1997: 139). In explicating what he called the 'participant reactive attitudes', he wrote of 'the non-detached attitudes and reactions of people directly involved in transactions with each other; of the attitudes and reactions of offended parties and beneficiaries: of such things as gratitude, resentment, forgiveness, love, and hurt feelings' (Strawson 1997: 122). We should keep in mind that the debate about what kind of causality operates in the context of human action depends in an important way on this larger question of how we conceptualise the context of human action and what sorts of conceptual choices there are—and are not.

Tony's work on desistance is a good example of how agency, along with various other factors, generalisations of diverse types, and especially the sorts of relations persons have with others, figure in the explanations of whether, how, and why offenders desist. Tony recognises that it is crucial to have a conceptually articulate grasp of agency, and he maintains that explanations that are almost exclusively at the level of social factors and institutions are not satisfactory in the respect that they do not register the role of agency:

> First, taking agency seriously *requires* that our research methodology takes full account of the actor's own self-understanding of actions—a dimension that has been singularly absent in much of the positivist-founded research on criminal careers, and even in much recent sociology with its stress on 'social action' rather than 'action'. (Bottoms 2004: 374–375)

The more fully a person can come to understand himself or herself as an agent, the more capable of successfully desisting he or she might become. It is not just stopping; it is coming to see oneself differently. Where there aren't the necessary supports to agency, the effort is much more vulnerable to failure. 'In short, agency may be real, but it is constrained, in explanatory terms, by lack of self-awareness and lack of full contextual awareness' (Bottoms 2004: 375).

If one can only imagine event-causation then an exercise of agency might seem like a gap in the causal chain, and for that reason, an inexplicable occurrence. However, if we think of agency as a capacity exercised by an individual with cognitive abilities, sensibility, desires, emotions, capacity for deliberation and judgement, and relations with other persons, then an exercise of agency can be intelligible in terms of the involvement of those (to varying degrees) in performing an action. Moreover, the universal determinist thesis (i.e., all events are caused by antecedent events, on a univocal sense of 'cause') is neither a truth of reason nor an inductive truth; nor is it demonstrably necessary as a methodological postulate. Inquiring into causes is indeed almost always a rationally appropriate approach to inquiry, but there is no assurance that what will be found will be—or *must* be—a deterministic cause. And the notion of agency does not imply (i) that everything people do, they do freely; or (ii) that there are no degrees of acting freely, and one's behaviour is either free or unfree, full stop; or (iii) that accounts of behaviour in terms of agency have no intelligible relation to accounts of other kinds of phenomena, most of which are explained causally.

Agency needs to be understood in its social context because the concerns, interests, and attitudes that people have are shaped in part by, and are responses to, their social environment. The way one's agency is exercised both impacts and reflects one's setting and context. Tony wrote:

> Extensive literatures exist on issues such as power and social relationships in high security prisons, but much less attention has been paid to how prisoners in such institutions make sense (including moral sense) of the sentence that the court has imposed upon them, in the context of their having to live in confinement for an extended period of time, and eventually return to society. (Bottoms 2019a: 19).

The importance of a point such as this is that it recognises that among the moral features of a situation is the way that the agents involved see it, what kind of valuative significance it has for them, whether it is a textured and reflective appreciation or a simple, thoughtless one. We will take up the issue of facts and values and the understanding of moral features of actions shortly. Here, the chief point is that the putative dilemma 'causal explanation of action or unintelligible free will' is a false dilemma. No one should think those are the only possibilities. When a person gives a rationale for a decision or an action, that is generally a matter of showing the decision or the action to be choiceworthy, desirable, or appropriate, or in some way that it is thought to be the thing to do.

Suppose the person acted quite spontaneously and there was not time to deliberate. The act could still be an exercise of agency insofar as it is an expression of the person's character and dispositions to make judgements in certain ways. Some of our habits are rational habits in the sense that much of what we do habitually we do for reasons, and we could explain what makes the habits rational ones.[2] Given one's states of character, there are certain kinds of consideration that a person typically regards as reasons, as action-guiding. Being truthful or willing to help, or, for that matter, being self-centred and quite mercenary, can be characteristic ways in which persons exercise agency. Character is disclosed in action but that does not mean it is a straightforward cause of action. One's situation and perceptions of it can influence how agency is exercised but they are not straightforward causes of action. A large number of factors can operate as influences on how persons exercise agency. Those are not inconsistent with free will. Again, what would be the point of it if it had no intelligible relation to history, circumstances, abilities, and dispositions?

Granted, there are challenging issues involved in providing a satisfactory account of agency, and among the challenges are ascertaining the degree to which persons' capacities for agency are *effective*; the degree to which, in acting, persons are self-determining. Provocation matters; one's physiology and neurological condition matter; hunger and fatigue can matter; having recently received very bad news can matter, and so on and on. But nothing is gained by dismissing agency because it is contra-causal, as though if we just call it that, we can call it a day. We should instead work at trying to understand the ways in which a large diversity of factors and considerations are involved in the ways persons act, and often as voluntary, accountable agents.

Recall, also, what we said about levels of description and the theory-dependence of how phenomena are described. Are we to simply accept that there is one and only one correct level of description for the causation of human action? What is that level? This is not a point in favour of some sort of theoretical relativism but recognition of something on which we commented above, namely, facts do not come pre-labelled, indicating the unique way for them to be described; instead, conceptualisation and theorising are modes of making facts accessible. As Tony remarks:

[2] I discuss the notion of habits, the voluntariness of habits, and their role in constituting character and explaining voluntary action in my *Choosing Character: Responsibility for Virtue and Vice*, Cornell University Press, 2001, esp. chs 1 and 2.

> [W]e need also to recognize that any serious treatment of the theory/research relationship has to take account of the fact that *there is normally a range of competing theories* . . . available to the researcher in developing and explanation. Part of the researcher's choice of theory must depend on the fit between data and theory, *but part of it must also depend upon the analytical coherence of the different theoretical concepts deployed in the overall explanation*. (Bottoms 2008b: 104)

Though it might be understandable, the tendency on the part of some inquirers to believe that if they have produced what appears to be a satisfactory explanation of some phenomenon, there are no additional illuminating ways of conceptualising relevant causal factors or no illuminating rival theories, is usually just a mistake. A great deal can depend on the relevant level of description and the way that explanation is to fit into some larger theoretical framework. One of the unhelpful biases that seems to have been encouraged by positivism is the notion that there is a single, primary level of description and explanation.

Tony's work on desistance provides helpful illustrations of some of the points made thus far. Tony conceptualises desistance as involving a kind of 'turning around' rather than a deeper kind of repentance of the sort that Antony Duff includes in his view of punishment and secular penance: 'I will explore the application to punishment theory of an understanding of repentance as primarily 'turning around' . . . or "change of mind or purpose" (that is, as *metanoia*, as standardly translated in English bibles)' (Bottoms 2019a: 127). Repentance as traditionally understood has a significant backward-looking element inasmuch as it involves a deep reconsideration of one's values and motives with a view to reorienting oneself.

> By contrast, the primary focus of 'repentance as turning around' is the future state, or future relationship, to which the persons repenting aspires. It is recognised that one needs to move in from—and deal with—the past, but it is the future that is of central significance. (Bottoms, 2019a: 128)

Thus,

> on the 'turning around' concept of repentance, the illocutionary and perlocutionary point of the censure is to prompt not remorse, but a 'change

> of mind or purpose' towards the behavior required by the 'objective values' enshrined in a justifiable criminal code. (Bottoms, 2019a: 129)

Understanding the relevant sort of 'turning around' involved in desistance involves having a conception of agency and how one's self-conception is involved in the process of turning. We might find that an offender in his mid-twenties is more likely to desist if he has a stable relationship with a partner, but it would also help to know if having such a relationship makes a difference to the person's self-conception and what he regards as appropriate motivations, and whether he has a changed view of various other norms. That can lead to a new perspective, perhaps, on law enforcement and on the norms governing various institutions. Perhaps they can begin to seem more reasonable, and the institutions can come to seem less like obstacles and threats. A revision in one's agentic perspective can be centrally important to the account of that person's behaviour. These are not all things that 'happen to' a person as though he or she is a passive subject; these changes often involve efforts, changes of perspective and aspiration best understood in terms of agency. What we need to grasp is not only what factors operate on the person's behaviour but also what sort of agent one takes oneself to be. Much can be understood through comprehension of the subject's conception of his own agency and the enlargement of his view of accountability.

The debate about agency is related in important ways to debates about the appropriate form of explanation and what conditions a satisfactory empirical explanation needs to meet. It is also related to debates concerning relations between facts and values and whether social scientists should recognise a fact/value distinction. Tony has written that 'we see agency as, *inter alia*, intimately linked to intersubjective assumptions of responsible action' (Bottoms 2004: 375). Moreover, 'we consider that the whole concept of agency in criminology is currently under-theorised: the word tends to be used without detailed exploration, and rather differently by different authors' (Bottoms 2004: 376). As Tony has said: 'desistance will very likely include both individual and "community" elements, which may interact' (Bottoms 2004: 379) and 'in the desistance literature there are two important strands: (A) meaningful social attachments (notably marriage and employment; (B) agency and cognitive reorientation' (Bottoms 2004: 381). The alleged fact/value distinction, one of the most disputed aspects of social scientific explanation, is related to the issue we have discussed so far. In part that is because aspects of persons' characters are important elements in many explanations, as are considerations concerning effort, self-conceptions, and responses to one's circumstances and to relations with others. Those are all matters in which moral values can be involved in important ways. We now turn to the issue of facts and values.

Facts and values

Tony recognises that in addition to morally relevant features of human action being more facts about actions, they are constitutive of its normative significance in ways that should not be set aside by criminological inquiry and explanation. That is one reason why agency is so important. It is through exercises of agency that we exhibit commitment to certain norms and rules and make judgements concerning what is to have priority and what we take to be discretionary, and so forth. Moral value is present throughout human beings' lives both in terms of the different contexts in which we each participate and in terms of there being certain values, norms, and ideals most of us believe we should respect in any case, regardless of context. This is so even if some people choose to ignore them or have perverse and deeply wrong conceptions of value.

Normativity in the broad sense is pervasive in human activity. Much of what we do is norm-governed and much of our learning is a matter of internalising norms. What counts as a complete performance of an act of type A can be a norm-governed matter even if values are not part of our interest in the action. Not all normativity is moral normativity but that kind merits a distinctive form of attention, and Tony's work has made significant contributions to the elaboration of that form in ways appropriate to empirical investigation. His discriminating appreciation of the critiques of positivism and the developments regarding the social scientific study of morality in recent decades is reflected in the philosophical fluency of his work. He has argued that the role of moral beliefs and judgements in many of the contexts studied by criminologists is crucial to understanding the issues. Moral considerations should not simply be set aside as unscientific. There can be a substantive explanatory role for them. Tony recognises that this raises the question of the *relation between normative theory and explanatory conception* for criminology, and that must be addressed with great care. Commenting on the powerful influence of the is/ought, and accordingly, fact/value distinction as understood by many positivists, Tony writes: 'That difficulty can be simply stated: it concerns the question of how, if at all, from a positivist perspective one can give any serious weight to moral judgements' (Bottoms 2002b: 22).

Tony is addressing questions about whether criminology can make contributions to what we might call 'moral science', an empirical investigation of how moral values pervade human beings' lives (in the context of criminological issues in particular) and how moral judgement is involved in attaining that understanding. His work has interesting points of contact with James Laidlaw's thinking on the anthropological study of morality. Laidlaw wrote:

> Can people's sense of responsibility and freedom in relation to their own character and conduct really be written off, with a causal story about how, generally speaking, they come to do what society (or their culture or their class) requires of them? Could not anthropologists' knowledge of the diversity of forms of moral life contribute something to debates among philosophers and others about how to understand ethics? (Laidlaw 2017: 4)

Human beings' actions reflect values in the broad sense of disclosing what they regard as worthwhile, important, meriting concern and attention. Something might be valuable on account of being opportune (it has a certain kind of instrumental value), and something might be valuable in its own right and not as a means to something else. Something can have value that is qualified or conditional without that being merely instrumental value. Kant thought of happiness in such terms; it is desirable for its own sake but it is not an unqualified good. (He held that happiness is not distributed in proportion to virtue—as in the case of a happy but morally vicious person—and thus, happiness' value is not unconditional. The undeserved happiness of the morally vicious person is not happiness we can regard as a good without qualification.)

One's view about the relations between facts and values can depend a great deal on how one regards the issues we have discussed so far, and it seems that many social scientists continue to endorse a fact/value distinction. That almost surely reflects the considerable influence of logical positivism in philosophy during the first half of the twentieth century, and then for several decades more in disciplines other than philosophy. Logical positivism seemed to offer a clear, rigorously formulated conception of what makes a mode of inquiry a science, and also a clear account of the distinction between facts and values and the corollary claim that moral claims are to be understood as having expressive meaning while having no cognitive meaning.

A significant implication of such a view is that there is then no basis for a rational critique of moral values or moral judgements. If value commitments and value judgements are not fact-based or rationally grounded then, whatever the facts are, they do not provide grounds for rational argument about values or rational justification of them. There can be a role for instrumental rationality in such a view. For example, if a society values something very highly but is also committed to certain norms and practices that make it impossible to realise what they value, then there is a basis for thinking them irrational in their overall commitments. But what they (or anyone) value—whatever it is that is regarded as intrinsically valuable as an end and not just instrumentally valuable—that is immune to rational criticism. The facts, the way the world is, do not provide reasons for having specific, substantive value commitments, or moral values. Their rational significance is confined to their instrumental role. (With regard to action, the view would be that rationality is always only instrumental rationality. It cannot also judge ends in their own right.)

Hume is widely regarded as the key figure in making the case for a fact/value distinction. His famous observation (in the *Treatise of Human Nature*) that he had never seen an inference from (i) *what is the case* to (ii) what *ought to be* done spelled out in a manner that legitimates the conclusion is generally held to be the *locus classicus* of the fact/value distinction.[3] What is often overlooked is that he went on, in the *Treatise* and the *Enquiry Concerning the Principles of Morals*, to develop a moral theory that, while sharply critical of rationalism, was meant to explain the genuineness and authority of moral considerations on an empirical, naturalistic basis. He was a sceptic regarding moral rationalism; he was not a sceptic regarding morality, and he is a thinker of the first importance with respect to the conception of an empirical 'moral science'. While Hume argued that claims about value cannot be demonstrated on strictly factual grounds, he was not arguing that the facts (what he called 'matters of fact or existence') are irrelevant to prescriptive judgements or to what value commitments it is reasonable to have. Showing that prescriptions are not logically derivable from factual statements is not the same thing as showing that facts lack any ethical significance.

[3] See David Hume, *A Treatise of Human Nature*, 2nd edition, Notes by P. H. Nidditch, Oxford University Press, 1978.

Logical positivists made the argument that moral judgements have no cognitive meaning, and this suggested that, whatever the facts are, *any* moral evaluation could be associated with them because the facts are not a rational basis for moral values.[4] That does not actually describe Hume's view. Moreover, as David Wiggins has remarked:

> Hume's interest in morality was that of a moral scientist or as one would now say moral psychologist. His first question is not the question of the vindication of duty (that question can arise later), but the question of how natural beings such as ourselves can have arrived at the point where we can even think the refined and complex thoughts we do think about morality and its requirements. (Wiggins 1995: 300)

Hume held that the fact that we find something agreeable and useful was crucial to our finding it morally commendable, but by 'agreeable' he did not simply mean blind preference. His discussion of property and the way that property figures in our conception of—and commitment to—principles of justice is evidence of that. And as Wiggins points out, Hume undertook the project of explaining how creatures such as human beings, given what they are like, lead lives in which moral values and moral judgements figure centrally. This was not an attempt to 'explain away' moral values; it was more like an attempt to show how and why they are crucial to our lives despite the fact that moral values are not entities with which we come into contact via reason.

The critique of emotivism and prescriptivism between the 1950s and 1980s resulted in the retrieval of some forms of moral rationalism and several forms of moral cognitivism and moral naturalism.[5] In addition, the forms of emotivism that still have adherents are not based mainly on the sorts of arguments and commitments associated with the fact/value

[4] A classic presentation of the positivist view is Chapter VI of A. J. Ayer, *Language, Truth and Logic*, 2nd edition, Dover Publications, 1952. The chapter is entitled, 'Critique of Ethics and Theology.' A very good collection of influential works on metaethics in the twentieth century is *Essays on Moral Realism*, ed. Geoffrey Sayre-McCord, Cornell University Press, 1988. Another excellent collection on metaethics, focusing on work during the second half of the twentieth century is *Moral Discourse and Practice: Some Philosophical Approaches*, eds S. Darwall, Allan Gibbard, and Peter Railton, Oxford University Press, 1997. It includes works defending various post-positivist antirealist positions as well as non-intuitionist, anti-noncognitivist views.

[5] The papers in Philippa Foot's collection *Virtues and Vices*, University of California Press, 1978 include some of the most important critiques of emotivism and prescriptivism as well as some influential arguments leading to the recovery of virtue-centred ethical thought in the twentieth century. Iris Murdoch's *The Sovereignty of Good*, 2nd edition, Routledge, 2001

distinction of the first half of the century. They have moved on well beyond 'first generation' emotivism. Hume is no longer seen mainly through the lens of 1930s positivism. The fact/value distinction as it is often attributed to positivism no longer has the centrally important role it formerly took in philosophy. To be sure, the fact/value relation remains disputed and there are numerous empiricism-rooted grounds for doubt regarding the objectivity of moral considerations. However, with the positivists' principle of verification and criterion of cognitive meaningfulness near extinction as a result of inability to respond to a steady barrage of critique, current moral sceptics are likely to develop their arguments on grounds other than those bases. (There are important forms of moral scepticism, but they are not based on a theory of meaning in the way that early emotivism centrally involved such a theory.)

That is not to say that Tony regards his task as involving moral evaluation of the behaviour and agents he studies. Rather, the project of understanding people's moral values and motivations is a way to more fully understand their behaviour and understand them as agents, and the understanding of those values and motivations requires the sort of understanding that is crucial to moral thought. In order to study behaviour and social relations scientifically it is not necessary to assume a fact/value distinction and demoralise the social world, but instead to make its moral aspects more fully intelligible.

That can also position the work of criminologists to have a more significant and constructive role in regard to reform of institutions, practices, and changes in policy. The point is not that seeing our way past the putative fact/value distinction implies a burden of moral expertise and responsibility that social scientists must face. Instead, it suggests that the facts and explanations articulated by social scientists can have considerable moral significance, and that is not something to minimise or ignore. The issues that criminologists study unavoidably have multiple morally significant aspects. How society addresses them (or fails to address them) has multiple morally significant aspects. Criminological investigations could make very valuable contributions to moral understanding, to formulation of reforms, and to wider appreciation of the character of the issues.

influenced the development of late twentieth-century moral realism though it was not a direct defence or even presentation of realism. But her critique of emotivism, non-cognitivism, and voluntarism pointed to important directions for the development of realism.

Conclusion

With his grasp of the developments in philosophy, Tony is developing a project of inquiry that upholds standards of scientific rigour and employs quantitative methods, while also responding to issues concerning agency and moral values. A critic might insist that this involves dilution of social science with humanistic interpretation, but the objection reflects a confusion of science with scientism. The latter is a dogmatic insistence that all knowledge is scientific knowledge and it often also insists that scientific knowledge has the form and character attributed to it by logical positivism. The first part of the claim is untenable for several reasons, but one of them is that it is *itself not a scientific claim*. Starting out with a pragmatic contradiction or self-refutation is not an auspicious beginning. The second part—the embrace of logical positivism—ignores several decades of quite conclusive critique of ways that the understanding of the epistemology of science and several other key issues moved on from the wreckage.

Tony's work on desistance is a challenge to the contours of positivism without sacrificing intelligibility based on evidence, conceptual clarity, quantitative measurement, and explanatory precision. The approach can, I think, be characterised as a form of moral science, an approach that includes a philosophically textured appreciation of the presence and role of values in people's reasoning, judgements, and motivations while striving to make that appreciation part of an empirically rigorous account of the topics studied. For scientific purposes it is important to count things, but it is important also to know what is to be counted and why—and what things count for, so to speak. Considerations of value and agency are vitally important to that. For one thing, the concept of *explanation* itself has normative features, and the concept of *agency* can be elaborated and employed in ways that involve empirical methods.

In closing, I want to again express appreciation of Tony's work, the standards it sets for criminology, and the ways in which it is helpful to philosophy through its fruitful interaction with social science. Tony's work brings to criminology an exemplary combination of theoretical sophistication, rigorous methodology, and a philosophically and morally serious determination to clarify and explain the issues in ways fully responsive to their complexity. Those issues include difficult questions concerning agency and values in ways that enlarge and focus the agenda of criminology and also contribute to the important project of connecting philosophical reflection and analysis with empirical social science.

5
Learning to Experiment
The Police, Science, and Evidence-Based Practice

Peter Neyroud

Introduction: From Diamond to evidence-based practice

Building a knowledge base about policing, and ensuring it is applied effectively to improve policing, has become an urgent challenge in the early twenty-first century. Public policing agencies across the developed world are faced with a 'perfect storm': the impact of financial austerity on an institutional structure with embedded inefficiencies and the challenge of demonstrating the effectiveness of the police as traditional crime falls and pressure to tackle cybercrime, terrorism and protect vulnerable victims increases have impacted on the legitimacy of the police (Neyroud and Weisburd 2014; PERF 2014; HMIC 2014; Neyroud 2019). Far from enjoying a 'Cold War' dividend from the crime drop, police have faced renewed scrutiny about their mission, purpose, and contribution (Vitale 2017).

In the past the police might have fallen back on experience and traditional law-and-order rhetoric. However, in the international debate about the reasons for the crime drop, few analyses of these causes have accorded police a central role. Yet, even those commentators who have primarily focused on the impact of the wider safety and security web in encouraging changes in behaviour (by victims and offenders) have found room for better policing as a driver of past and continued reductions (Waller 2014). In doing so, Waller (2014) and other key authors have argued that reliance on experience and traditional tactics is not sufficient. Instead, Laycock and Tilley (2013) have proposed renewing attention to 'professional' problem-solving, Waller (2014) has advocated 'smarter crime control' focusing on 'problem places and problem people' (2014: 52), and Sherman (2013) has

Peter Neyroud, *Learning to Experiment.* In: *Crime, Justice, and Social Order.* Edited by: Alison Liebling, Joanna Shapland, Richard Sparks, and Justice Tankebe, Oxford University Press. © Alison Liebling, Joanna Shapland, Richard Sparks, and Justice Tankebe 2022. DOI: 10.1093/oso/9780192859600.003.0005

set out a 'Triple T' strategy—targeting, testing, and tracking—that uses the best evidence available to inform police decisions. The common strand to each of these is a conception of the future of policing as a new profession, using knowledge to support delivery and innovation and research to test, learn, and develop effective practices (Neyroud and Sherman 2013).

This chapter will draw on research on randomised controlled experiments in policing to explore the lessons from nearly 50 years of police experiments for science in policing and the development of police education. Within this, the chapter also reflects on more than 20 years of the Cambridge Police Executive Programme, a Master's-level programme in Applied Criminology and Police Management that was pioneered by Sir Anthony Bottoms. In 1995, as Director of the Cambridge Institute of Criminology, Tony responded to a commission from the then Director of National Police Training to provide a programme in applied science as part of the Strategic Command Course for UK police officers selected for Chief Officer posts.[1] The ethos of the programme, which has continued to develop under Tony's successor, Lawrence Sherman, has been that the best leaders in policing need to understand the best science—in particular, social science—and evidence about their profession.

The chapter seeks to explore these issues by starting with an example of failed testing—the Diamond Initiative in London. This leads to discussion of the literature on experimentation in policing, before the central section of the chapter draws on the research of Neyroud (2017) on police experiments to set out the evidence for key factors that may be critical in developing a new discipline of learning from testing in policing.

The Diamond Initiative: A failure of field testing

The debate about a new police profession and the relationship of the police to the science of policing is not without controversy. Several authors have expressed doubts about the research on police effectiveness, the ability of the police to utilise that research, and the likely outcomes (Sampson 2010; Manning 2011; Greene 2014).

There is good cause to approach the subject with care and an open mind. There have been many false dawns. One such was the 'Diamond Initiative'

[1] The author was a student on the second cohort of the Police Executive Programme in 1997 and is currently a Lecturer in Evidence-Based Policing within the programme.

in London. In his foreword to the final report of the 'Diamond Initiative', Tony Bottoms, as Chair of the Advisory Board, provided a careful, forensic dissection of the dangers of overstating the potential of any given innovation (Bottoms 2011). Yet, while urging caution, he also praised the London Criminal Justice Board for their 'courage' in setting up the Diamond Initiative, the Board's determination to evaluate it thoroughly, and the way that, even though the promised outcomes had not been achieved, Diamond had produced significant lessons for practice.

Diamond was a major programme designed to support desistance by offenders released from prison after short sentences through partnership between police and probation offender managers. It was launched with great fanfare by the Mayor of London and criminal justice leaders. One focus was on using the capacity of local neighbourhood police officers working alongside probation officers to support desistance. It had promised so much and its interim report hinted at real progress. The final report was 'less encouraging'. Tony remained upbeat: 'the Diamond initiative put into practice a set of principles for which there is considerable empirical support' (Bottoms 2011: 3). In so doing, it was following the path which Tony had encouraged all his police and probation students to take: use the best available evidence and theory to design innovatory practices and then test them rigorously. Furthermore, he encouraged all of us to think in much broader terms than the narrow crime-based output measures, such as prevalence and frequency of re-offending.

Diamond illustrated many of the challenges of learning by testing. It was over-hyped by both its promoters and the media, which contributed to a huge sense of disappointment when the outcomes were not as promised. On the other hand, a careful reading of the report shows that some important lessons emerged. Diamond involved the police in a relatively new role of managing offenders, post-sentence, in the community in partnership with the probation service. This appeared to be the type of cross-agency thinking that the creation of two parallel Master of Studies programmes in policing and penology was designed to foster. One key finding was that the trial had 'certainly demonstrated the feasibility of involving police officers in rehabilitative work with offenders' (Bottoms 2011: 5). However, the evaluation also showed the importance of paying greater attention to the process of implementation and the advantages of a tighter experimental design in order to reduce the problems of selection bias in the samples.

Diamond, in conception, was exactly the sort of 'strongly targeted, offender-focused crime prevention' strategy for which Tony and his co-author Paul Wiles had argued in the 1990s (Bottoms and Wiles 1996: 35), and which Waller has advocated more recently (Waller 2014). It appeared to illustrate the potential for police, probation, and other partners to share information and collaborate in innovative practice to support desistance. At the same time, the evaluation highlighted some of the difficulties in the path of success, the challenges of implementation, and the need to develop better approaches to the conduct and management of such initiatives in order to build and sustain their impact.

The final report of the Diamond Initiative was published in 2011, at a time when the impact of a 'perfect storm' in the area was becoming apparent in England and Wales. Alongside a programme of cuts to budgets and police salaries and pensions, a new model of local accountability, and a realignment of national bodies, the Coalition government responded to the recommendations of this author's Review of Police Leadership and Training (Neyroud 2011) by agreeing to the creation of a new 'College of Policing'. The latter was explicitly designed to develop into a professional body for the police service and all its members. The design included a commitment to 'evidence-based practice' to underpin the new profession.

There are substantial challenges to the evidence-based strategy, which were illustrated by the Diamond Initiative. Choosing the right issues to prioritise (targeting), testing the strategy effectively (testing), and managing the wider implementation of tested tactics and strategies (tracking) are at the heart of what Sherman has labelled the 'triple T' approach (Sherman 2013). Yet, in the course of more than half a century of police research since the Second World War, the police service itself had been at best a junior and, frequently, an unwilling partner. The police had neither embraced research as a key driver of professional practice nor sought to exercise ownership over its focus and direction (Weisburd and Neyroud 2011). This was consistent with an occupational culture in policing in which educational attainment—particularly at graduate and post-graduate level—was neither a qualification for entry nor a mark of credibility.

In other sectors, such as medicine, one yardstick by which to measure the advance of evidence-based approaches has been the growth in the use of experimentation to test treatments (Shepherd 2003). In policing and criminal justice, progress in this area has, until very recently, been glacially slow. As recently as 2014, Braga et al. (2014) suggested that there had been insufficient experiments in policing to build a body of knowledge from which it was possible to develop a more generalised theory and build better practice on how targeting, testing, and tracking can most effectively contribute to the improvement of policing. However, that situation has been changing in the past decade. The Global Police Database—a repository of all the controlled design studies in policing—suggests that by the end of 2018 there had been more than 200 randomised controlled trials and more than 1000 quasi-experiments in policing (Mazerolle, Eggins, and Higginson 2019). Given the accelerating pace of experimentation in policing (Neyroud 2017), it is increasingly possible to frame the main factors that will assist or confound effective testing and, thence, learning from testing in policing (Mazerolle et al. 2014). A necessary pre-condition is, however, to have a field that is receptive to testing and capable of using the lessons.

Educating police leaders

It is important therefore, before discussing experimentation in more detail, to reflect on the education of senior police leaders. Testing—experimentation—requires sanction and support from senior leaders, given that it is likely that the process will either be applied to innovations or be used to challenge existing practices. Both of these present risks to the organisation. In the past, as Weatheritt (1986) documented, much research evaluating policing innovations was designed, where it was actually carried out, to be more confirmatory—a means of demonstrating success—than objective and challenging.

Part of the reason for this was a 'dialogue of the deaf' (Bradley and Nixon 2009) between researchers and senior leaders, neither of whom understood or, in many cases, trusted each other's professions, motivations, or needs. As the author found in a Review of Police Leadership and Training for the UK Government (Neyroud 2011), the training of police officers at all levels has been focused, since the foundation of the modern police force in the early nineteenth century, on legal knowledge and procedures and learning from field experience. The Review found very few credible examples of programmes that endeavoured to bring legal and procedural knowledge together with the research and theory.

The Review's findings illustrate why Tony Bottoms's decision to respond to the commission from National Police Training was so potentially ground-breaking. The creation of an applied criminology programme as an assessed part of the mandatory training for all senior leaders was a significant departure from previous models in which a few selected officers were sponsored for degrees or part-funded for Master's-level study of their own choice. The new programme meant that every Chief Officer—including this author—appointed after 1996 had a post-graduate Diploma in Applied Criminology and Police Management.

Furthermore, although the programme, now entitled the 'Police Executive Programme', was uncoupled from the Strategic Command Course after a number of years, it continued to develop and, partly in order to maintain student numbers, internationalised, drawing in students from Europe; North, South, and Central America; Australasia; and Asia. A major part of the attraction of the programme for police force sponsors had become the combination of applied criminology and police management with thesis research, which has increasingly emphasised the research of professional challenges with organisational ownership.

By 2019, alumni of the Police Executive Programme accounted for more than 15% of all Chief Officers in police forces in England and Wales. The programme has been responsible for a series of internationally important research programmes: the development and evaluation of body-worn cameras (Ariel et al. 2014); the creation and application of 'Crime Harm' indices to provide a harm-weighted index of crime as an alternative to crime counts (Sherman, Neyroud, and Neyroud 2016); field testing of hot-spot patrolling and different strategies and tactics across multiple national contexts (e.g., Sherman et al. 2015). With more than 30 randomised controlled trials conducted by students, the programme has also been a major contributor to the growing body of experimental research in policing. It has, indeed, met Tony's challenge in the foreword to the Diamond report, and demonstrated a willingness to test practices, which makes it all the more important that the programme is supported by a credible framework of research on how to test and how to learn most effectively from testing.

Researching police experiments

The research which underpins this chapter was undertaken by adopting two main approaches (Neyroud 2017): first, a systematic search for all the police experiments completed prior to 2017; secondly, a detailed case study of Operation Turning Point, a randomised controlled trial of police-led diversion conducted in Birmingham between 2011 and 2015. Neyroud (2017) found 122 randomised controlled trials. The published reports were analysed by two principal means: first, a descriptive analysis of the year, topic, principal investigators, and police departments; secondly, an analysis of the treatment integrity of the studies. This focused on the levels of attrition from the randomised samples and delivery of the intended treatments in order to arrive at estimates of the extent to which the experiment was effectively implemented.

In the second phase of this analysis, the high, medium, and low-integrity experiments were examined for factors which appeared to correlate with effective or ineffective implementation. One set of factors, which Neyroud (2017) framed as 'novice theory', appeared to provide a credible explanation for low integrity: experiments in which there were novice investigators (with no prior experience of implementing randomised controlled trials), new interventions, and novice police departments with no track record of field research were strongly associated with low-integrity experiments. In order to explore 'novice theory' and a wider set of factors further, a case study, Operation Turning Point, was explored in greater detail. Before we move on to this, it is important to place this research in the context of the debates about experimentation in policing.

Experimenting in policing

There has been growing interest—and, indeed, controversy—regarding the extent to which the police can improve their practice and effectiveness by science and, above all, through experimentation. Sherman's (1998) 'Evidence-based policing' for the Police Foundation and Weisburd and Neyroud's (2011) 'Police Science: towards a new paradigm' for the Harvard Session on Policing and Public Safety have set out the case for the police to adopt a more evidence-based, scientific approach to their professional practice and development. Both of these papers are seen by some as exclusively advancing the cause of experimental methods (Sampson 2010; Sparrow 2011). However, the core argument in both papers is that policing should use and invest in the best evidence available.

It would be unrealistic to rest the case for evidence-based policing solely on experiments. As the Campbell Collaboration on Crime and Justice has acknowledged, in accepting quasi-experiments and non-experimental designs in systematic reviews, there had, until recently, been too few experiments and some obstacles to their use in criminal justice. Several authors have focused on the reasons for the rarity of RCTs in criminal justice compared to health (Shepherd 2003; Farrington and Welsh 2006; Welsh and Farrington 2012). The complexities of the outcomes, the ethics of experimentation in criminal justice, and the cost of carrying out RCTs have all been cited as barriers. Sampson (2010) and Greene (2014) have been critical of the focus on crime control measures at the expense of wider objectives in policing. Greene (2014) raised particular concerns about the way that experiments can be seen to narrow the role of the police and neglect important social functions that are more difficult to measure with experimental methods. Laycock (2013), on the other hand, has argued that a focus on the police—'police science'—distracts from a broader 'crime science' agenda within which the impact of policing is a relatively weak factor in preventing crime. Sparrow (2011) objected to the expense and timeliness of RCTs and, like Tilley and Laycock (2002), argued instead for more 'realistic' methods of evaluation. While these are important arguments, they do not diminish the strength of the case for RCTs as a means of assessing whether a specific strategy or tactic is or is not capable of producing a given outcome (Weisburd and Hinkle 2012). They do, however, as McGloin and Thomas (2013) also argue, make the case for the use of a broad range of methods to evaluate policing and criminal justice.

Given that, it is important to focus on one other major critique of experiments in criminal justice, which Sparrow (2011) touched on but which has generally received less attention. Even the most ardent advocates of experimentation would agree that RCTs are not usually simple or straightforward to conduct and manage. Indeed, Feder et al. (2000) illustrated the risks in experimentation in this field. In a similar vein, Strang (2012), in an article reflecting on the challenges of experimentation, sets out eloquently the frustrations and challenges. Her particular focus was the fragility of the 'coalition' between practitioners and researchers that she suggested was essential to successful experiments. Equally, Sherman (2010), in setting out a working framework for experimentation, has described the essential components for success—research motivation, an experimental station, a tight process of randomisation and the management of cases and data required for evaluation—but stressed the need for rigorous attention to each element. Both Strang and Sherman highlight the number of 'moving parts' in an experiment and the delicate balancing act that has to be performed by those engaged in the process.

At the heart of that process is a partnership or coalition between the researcher(s) and the practitioners. Engel and Henderson (2013) have recently analysed the academic–practitioner partnership in policing and drawn attention to the tensions and limitations. They were sceptical of the achievability of Weisburd and Neyroud's (2011) vision of a police-owned and police-led science in policing, opting instead for a more incremental collaborative relationship. There has been increasing interest in understanding the range of police experiments, the research community involved, and the impact on policing. Mazerolle et al. (2014) document the developing field and the growing importance of tools such as the Matrix hosted by the George Mason University Center for Evidence-based Crime Policy. The Matrix provides a repository for all the police-involved experiments focused on the prevention of crime. The Matrix is organised into themes based on whether the intervention is targeted individually, at a group, or across a whole jurisdiction. The aim is to encourage practitioners to think carefully through the nature of the problem that they are seeking to address while they search for and access the material (Lum and Koper 2018).

Braga and Walsh (2014) carried out an analysis of the researchers responsible for completed police experiments. To some extent, both the Matrix and Braga and Welsh's analysis lend weight to Engel and Henderson's arguments. Up until 2012, when Braga and Walsh's search concluded, the vast majority of completed experiments had been conducted by a relatively small group of scholars, many of whom had been mentored and trained by an even smaller core of senior academics.

However, Neyroud (2017) found that the situation was changing rapidly, with a significant number of experiments in progress or recently completed that had been led by practitioners with academic support (such as Ariel and Farrar 2013). Many of these were being conducted by practitioners—past and present—as part of a higher degree qualification and therefore with professional academic supervision and support (including Operation Turning Point), or were being conducted and managed wholly within the profession by newly emerging bodies such as the National College of Policing, or even within police forces by police officers with higher degrees. This growing range of options serves to highlight further the need to develop a new discipline of leadership and management for policing which supports the process of testing and learning from the process and outcomes (Sherman 2013). Consistent with this, Neyroud (2017) found that the expanded professional role—beyond sponsorship and into personal engagement in and leadership of field research—indicated a need to ensure that 'novice' professional experimenters were sufficiently well trained and supported to enable credible implementation, valid outcomes, and a balanced approach to learning from, as well as publication and dissemination of, results.

The experiments in policing

A critical source for building our understanding of learning from testing is the collected body of completed experiments. It might be thought that this would be a readily accessible set of research papers. However, there was no systematic collation of the reports until the late 1990s. Only with the recent development of the Global Police Database (Mazerolle et al. 2019) has there been credible progress towards a searchable international repository of experiments.

There are some clear limitations to using the published experiments alone. First, their quality varies: some are published in peer-reviewed journals; some reported to funding bodies like the National Institute of Justice (NIJ); and some simply posted on the internet. Until quite recently, with the standards set by journals such as the *Journal of Experimental Criminology*, the layout and content of articles and reports was inconsistent. Importantly, the published experiments represent 'completed' experiments and are often tightly focused on reporting results. This presents a challenge when seeking to understand conduct and management issues. It is relatively rare for scholars to focus on the problems of implementation, beyond perfunctory methodological issues. Feder et al. (2000) are unusual in dissecting the problems that they experienced in implementing two randomised controlled trials. Secondly, there is likely to be a significant 'file-drawer' of experiments that have not been published or have been only partially published and, therefore, probably encountered significant implementation difficulties, providing a potential bias in the sample of experiments (Shadish et al. 2002). The 'file-drawer' problem may well be less significant in the case of experiments because the method has been so unusual and has tended, until quite recently, to be supported by external funding from government bodies or independent foundations who have a commitment to publication.

The 122 experiments in the sample found by Neyroud (2017) do, however, represent nearly 50 years of police experiments. As Braga and Welsh (2014) have shown, there have been distinct phases in which first one topic, then another, has been the focus of effort. The very first reported experiment by Rose and Hamilton (1970) centred on juvenile justice and diversion in the North-West of England, but this issue, which is central to Operation Turning Point, has been relatively rare in a corpus of experiments that has largely focused on domestic violence, hot-spots, drugs education, restorative justice, and the use of new technology. Within this group of experiments there are also several distinctive randomised controlled designs, ranging from large-scale pipeline experiments such as Turning Point to smaller-scale designs testing line-up identifications (Wells et al. 2011). This heterogeneity of topic, design, timescale, and jurisdiction evidences a need for caution in drawing general lessons for all types of police experiment.

Nevertheless, the fact that the use of RCTs in policing remains so rare when compared to health or education (Welsh and Farrington 2012 and Braga et al. 2014) suggests that there may be a set of common barriers to experimentation in policing. Conversely, it also suggests a pressing need to learn from the experiments that have been done to see if there are common factors which predict successful implementation. An analysis of the literature on experiments in policing and the 122 RCTs completed suggested a high-level set of key issues that could be important for successful testing. These are presented in Table 5.1.

Research motivation is mentioned by Sherman (2010) and in the majority of the study reports. It is of course difficult, without a pre-research protocol (which is a more recent development), to be sure that the motivation set out in the reports and articles matched the initial raison d'être. However, most researchers (e.g., Roman et al. 2009; Lum et al. 2011; Ariel et al. 2014), in addition to setting out the theory and criminological

Table 5.1 Key issues for implementation of RCTs in policing (Neyroud 2017)

Research motivation	**Implementation process**
	Pilot testing
Experimental station	Technology support
	Structured decision-making
Researcher role	
Training and guidance	**Police culture**
Control of random assignment	Professional skills
	Frontline engagement
Leadership commitment	Ownership
	Discretion
Inter-agency decision-making	

justification for their study, make clear the arguments that persuaded the police and, often, the funders to support the research. Sherman (2010) and Strang (2013) suggest that sound theory and a strong research motivation are essential in both getting started and sustaining the effort.

However, it is important to point out that, as Braga et al. (2014) document, the research motivation for most of the first 70 experiments came from funders and researchers rather than being developed within the profession or department. The recent development of more police-led experimentation suggests that departmental or professional sponsorship may have become more important. An exception was Ariel and Farrar's important body-worn camera experiment in Rialto, which was led by Farrar both as the Chief of Police and as a Master's student of the Police Executive Programme, supervised by Ariel (Ariel et al. 2014).

The literature and completed RCTs also emphasise the importance of the 'experimental station'. This is either the police department or the precinct or department within the force in which the research is carried out. For Sherman (2010) the location is more than a geographic location but also requires the development of social relationships between the researchers and the practitioners, which in turn require systematic efforts to be sustained. The Police Executive Programme has sought to build longer-term relationships with departments, with a view to supporting a series of experiments using police Master's students as both learners and field researchers. Operation Turning Point was the second in a series of experiments following this model in partnership with the West Midlands Police (see further below).

The role of the researcher is clearly integral to an RCT—the very nature of the 'controlled design' requires key elements, such as the randomisation process, to be managed tightly. Until the development of tools such as the Cambridge Gateway (Ariel et al. 2012), the external researcher was required to be directly in control of the process, and the reports and articles focus on the level of control to support the internal validity of the experiment. However, tools such as the Gateway have enabled a proliferation of smaller experiments under professional leadership but with experienced academic support. The Gateway was originally developed as a web-based screening and randomisation tool. In Turning Point, custody officers in the police stations within the experiment were asked to open the Gateway every time an offender met the initial threshold for prosecution: the twin criteria of meeting the evidential and public interest tests. The Gateway then asked them to respond to 18 Gateway questions which comprised the agreed eligibility criteria for inclusion for the trial. At this point, if the criteria were all met, the Gateway would perform the randomisation, allocating the offender into either control or treatment conditions.

Leadership, implementation, and police culture tend to feature in discussion of the enablers of or barriers to the experiment. Sherman (2010) and Strang (2013) both emphasise the critical role performed by leaders at all levels in communicating and managing the experiment. On the other hand, quite a number of the reports and articles focus on the resistance to change and the non-experimental mindset within policing (Feder et al. 2000). However, the evidence from the studies is difficult to assess. Successful studies with high levels of statistical significance in the outcomes tend to gloss over the difficulties of implementation, while some other studies (e.g., Giblin 2002) appear to offer culture and implementation difficulties as mitigation for smaller effect sizes. This made it challenging to construct a substantive theory on the conduct and management of experiments in policing from the studies alone. 'Novice theory', as we have outlined above, emerges as a potentially useful framework to explain poor integrity, but a more in-depth examination of an individual case study offered an opportunity to provide a more detailed explanation (Neyroud 2017).

Operation Turning Point: A case study in learning from testing

Operation Turning Point was a randomised controlled trial which compared the effectiveness of court prosecution for low-harm offenders with a structured diversion to a deferred prosecution linked to a 'Turning Point Contract'. Turning Point drew on the lessons of studies such as Operation HOPE (Hawken and Kleiman 2009) which suggest that swift and certain action by criminal justice agencies will have enhanced deterrent effects and on the lessons of criminal career and desistance studies on strategies to encourage offenders to stay out of crime (Neyroud and Slothower 2013).

The full method for Operation Turning Point was published in a Crimport protocol (see Appendix 4 of Neyroud (2017)). The sample for the experiment was offenders whom the police custody officer had decided that it was in the public interest to prosecute—informal warnings and cautions having already been discarded.[2] At that point custody officers were instructed to use the Cambridge Gateway. In Turning Point, the Gateway triaged out offenders with multiple convictions, a high likelihood of prison, and a serious offence. The Gateway was then, if they were triaged as eligible for the experiment, set to randomise them into prosecution or a Turning Point treatment. Offenders randomised to Turning Point were asked to attend a meeting, to take place within 48 hours, with an offender manager or Youth Offending Service officer. They were warned that non-compliance with that requirement, reoffending, or failure to meet the terms of the Turning Point contract would result in prosecution.

In the meeting with the police or Youth Service, they were asked to agree a contract as a result of a structured conversation at their meeting. The conversation was designed to encourage the offender to talk about the factors that were contributing to their offending, with a view to agreeing a set of conditions—rehabilitative, restorative, or deterrent—that would help to prevent reoffending and support desistance. While agreement was voluntary, it was backed up by the threat of prosecution. The incentive was that successful completion of the contract over a four-month period would result in no further action.

Operation Turning Point started in November 2011 in two police areas within West Midlands Police and ran through four phases, in which first the Gateway was piloted and then the Turning Point treatments, before moving to full randomisation and expanding the trial to include all four police areas within Birmingham. Data gathering was completed in June 2014. Alongside the data gathering for the RCT, interviews were carried out with staff involved in November 2013 in the middle of the final phase, Phase IV. The sample of 20 interviewees was determined by the need to focus on a purposeful sample of the most informed participants (Morse 2007). The list of interviewees was thus set around the key processes of the experiment—custody, offender management, and project management. The interviews were focused both on the process of experimentation and on the organisational learning which may have accrued through the experimentation (Bedford and Neyroud 2018).

[2] Both within English law under the Police and Criminal Evidence Act 1984 and supported by the Crown Prosecution Service for this experiment, the Police Custody Officer (a uniform Police Sergeant) had the authority to charge or divert the offender to Turning Point without recourse to referral to the prosecutor.

Some caution needs to be exercised in making comparisons to the wider set of completed experiments, because Turning Point has a relatively unusual design and focus—a pipeline experiment concerned with offenders at the pre-court stage. This places it in a smaller sub-group with Rose and Hamilton's (1970) study of cautioning plus the Restorative Justice experiments (Strang et al. 2013) and the experiments on police-led diversion (Wilson et al. 2018). However, it also seems likely that the unusual duration and complexity of Operation Turning Point, compared to almost any other experiment in the list, may provide a robust exemplar from which to draw lessons. Furthermore, Turning Point was an almost unique experiment among police experiments in that it had to be restarted, after initial problems with treatment integrity. Problems with attrition and treatment fidelity in the original evaluation phase meant that the research team and the police force decided to make changes to the design and treatment and re-run the data gathering. Hence Turning Point also provided a comparison between a phase with problematic implementation and treatment integrity and a final phase in which there was a high level of treatment integrity (Neyroud 2017).

The coding and analysis suggested that the research motivation was important in Operation Turning Point, but was very strongly connected with the ability of the staff involved to connect the experiment with the police force's own priorities and strategy. It was a prominent theme across all the interviews that staff were able to articulate how Turning Point fitted into their work. There were some differences. Some saw it as linked to crime reduction through offender management; others saw it as a means of reducing cost through diversion. In turn, they connected the research motivation to their Chief Officers and cited the strong support that they had received from the top of the organisation as a factor both enabling the experiment and licensing them to step outside the norms of practice. However, in contrast to the analysis of the other completed experiments, the research motivation in Turning Point was seen as coming from the force or, where the researchers' involvement was discussed, from a partnership between the force and the research team. Given that the force and the research team had already partnered in a RCT, this gives some support to Engel and Henderson's preference for building medium or long-term collaborations as a base for learning and research.

There was also recognition that the force was consciously letting itself be used as an 'experimental station'. The staff were aware of previous and ongoing experiments in the force within the same police–academic partnership. There was general support for this, especially within the wider context of 'austerity' in which a commitment to trying different approaches was seen as important. Indeed, the 'experimental station' was viewed by the staff as a deliberate response to the challenges of austerity. Alongside this, one key issue that emerged was the perceived importance of the way in which participating in the experiment had developed the individuals involved, their professional skills, and their understanding of 'police science'. The implementation of the experiment had involved some initial and ongoing training for staff. However, there was a deliberate strategy from the force and the research team to engage the staff in the wider project of evidence-based policing. Sixty staff involved in Phase 1 were invited to the University and given a day's intensive immersion in the theory as well as the detail of the experiment. This was in clear contrast to training models adopted in other diversion tests, which appeared to have concentrated on training procedures rather than attempting a wider scientific education about the process of testing and theory behind the experiment (Ames et al. 2018). In Turning Point, an emphasis on theory as well as practice was repeated as each stage of the training and follow-up was implemented. More than 150 staff—custody officers, offender managers, youth service workers, and drug referral workers—attended these sessions. The fact that those interviewed recognised this process and appeared to value it would seem to lend weight to Sherman's (2010) emphasis on building the social relationships, but to go further and suggest that it may be important in sustaining experiments to connect the process of experimentation with the development of professional skills and knowledge. Given the almost complete absence of police science in the curriculum of formal police training (Neyroud 2011), this might be a particularly important enabler in policing experiments.

In contrast to the generally negative view of police culture as a barrier to experimentation, there was a more nuanced view from the respondents in Turning Point. The force had made an early commitment to encourage officers engaged in the experiment to use and develop their professional discretion. This was, for example, manifested in the design of the Gateway, which allowed custody officers the final say over eligibility contingent upon setting out their reasons for exclusion beyond the standard triage questions. Equally, the initial approach to the setting of Turning Point contracts relied heavily on professional discretion rather than the more normal, restrictive operational rules. In both cases, the custody officers and the offender managers were given opportunities to contribute to the initial design and assist with subsequent improvements. As the models developed, a model of 'bounded discretion' evolved and was critical to ensuring relatively high levels of internal validity in the final phase of the experiment (Slothower 2014).

In Neyroud and Weisburd (2014) we suggested that police 'ownership' of police science may be an important contributor to its adoption as a central component of policing and its future development. We argued that 'ownership' comprised a sense of valuing the science, a level of knowledge of the science and how to use it, and a degree of shared leadership and control over its production and dissemination. Operation Turning Point also suggests the importance of efforts to link the art and craft of policing with the discipline of scientific testing. In this case, the energy invested in blending the officers' cherished professional discretion based on experience with the design of the experiment appears to have contributed to a sense of ownership in the process. That in turn suggests that it is not the experience-based police culture that is the barrier to evidence-based approaches; rather, the barrier is attempts to design experiments which neglect experience or are not perceived to engage officers adequately. Sparrow (2011) argued that experience and experimentation were incompatible. Turning Point suggests, in contradiction to this, that experience is capable of supporting the design and experimentation may be able to contribute to developing and deepening professional skills and experience.

Finally, the role of the research team was explored in some detail. A number of the completed studies provide details of the researchers training, observing, and controlling the randomisation process. Sherman (2010) has argued that there is a need for a permanent, field-management-style presence from the research team in order to ensure compliance with research standards and protocols and to maintain the ongoing relationship within the 'coalition'. The Turning Point respondents provided overwhelming support for this stance. They highlighted the role of the field manager as one of the critical factors in keeping the experiment on track, troubleshooting it, and developing it step by step. They also saw the researchers as an expert resource, contributing scientific analysis to support them. The principal researchers in Turning Point probably provided an unusual mixture of field research and professional experience, but they also, according to the respondents, offered a high degree of credibility and reassurance to the force and the staff involved, given that the experiment was pushing the boundaries of randomisation to include the prosecution decision. In summary, for police-led testing and learning from that testing to work effectively, the quality of the partnership between police forces and researchers is critical.

Shepherd proposed a model for such partnerships which would mirror the relationship between medicine and medical schools, and this research suggests that his proposal has much to commend it (Shepherd 2003). The Police Executive Programme that Tony Bottoms initiated has continued to develop in a way that meets many of the requirements of this model. Tony's insistence on an applied model has been harnessed to a commissioning process in which the police leaders who form the student group are required to negotiate research topics that meet identified strategic needs for either their own organisation or national requirements. In return for meeting an organisational need, the students are given access to datasets and support to analyse them, or are given approval to conduct experimental or qualitative field research. The cycle from research motivation to findings and research lessons is completed by a requirement to present an implementation plan to Chief Officers. This process is now supplemented by a Journal—the *Cambridge Journal of Evidence-based Policing*—and an annual international seminar to publish and disseminate the findings across the profession of policing and beyond.

Towards a discipline of learning from testing

This chapter has been concerned with the learning for policing which can draw from experimentation: both the learning from the process of experimentation and the learning from the evaluation of the outcomes and implementation. The analysis of the body of completed experiments in policing and a more detailed exploration of conduct and management of Operation Turning Point have been used to draw out the emerging framework of a new discipline for policing—learning by testing.

To some extent the Diamond Initiative, which we discussed at the beginning of the chapter, appears to match an older approach to police learning. Even its name—the Diamond 'Initiative'—appears to align itself to a model of police innovation, as Weatheritt (1986) reviewed, in which an innovation is launched, evaluated (usually with limited pre and post designs without controls), and then either discarded or approved for general implementation based on whether it was perceived to have succeeded or failed. On the other hand, in her study of police innovations, Weatheritt (1986) also reviewed an experiment—the Havant Policing Scheme—in which the author was involved as a young constable tasked with evaluating a complex community policing scheme without academic support. As Weatheritt identified, neither academically led nor professionally led models of experimentation are likely to be wholly successful in securing learning and the translation of lessons into policy and practice. The first may well achieve robust research but may lack ownership; the latter may fail to achieve high integrity, while yet enjoying, in many cases, rather too much ownership to be allowed to fail.

Apart from an experimental design, we would argue that Diamond lacked the support of a developed discipline of learning from testing in policing. As we have seen from the analysis above, that discipline is not a simple process of project management or a module in police leadership training. As Fixsen et al. (2005) have shown in their synthesis of the literature on implementation, there are many dimensions to this discipline that need to be understood and managed to enable experimentation (which is, after all, the testing of a change process) to succeed and learning to be derived and disseminated. Indeed, as Nutley et al. (2007) have shown, implementation or the successful conduct and management of the experiment is not enough, because there needs to be a larger commitment to the ownership and integration of the lessons of the research into practice.

Professor Sir Anthony Bottoms pioneered a model of police education—the Police Executive Programme—in which future senior leaders are equipped with the best science in applied criminology and are encouraged to research their own organisation as an informed insider, supported by outside expertise. Looking at the first 50 years of police experimentation, we find that this model, and others like it, appears to present a promising route to enhance police ownership of science and a potential means for police to learn faster and more effectively by testing policies, practices, tactics, and new technology.

6
Reasonable Hopes
Social Theory, Critique, and Reconstruction in Contemporary Criminology

Ian Loader and Richard Sparks

> I am not an optimist; I am a prisoner of hope.
>
> Archbishop Desmond Tutu

Introduction

In this chapter we want to address some themes about the aims of criminological theory and research, especially in relation to social change.[1] This includes the kinds of change that happen whether we want them to or not, and which researchers may variously seek to describe, to interpret, to criticise, and perhaps sometimes to affect by alerting others, campaigning, proposing alternatives, and otherwise resisting. We are also, however, interested in the kinds of change that we might actively seek to promote—those that seem, to the people concerned, to represent qualitatively different and preferable ways of doing things compared to what exists now. How do we ground or justify claims of that sort? What kinds of research, and what conceptual resources, can help people to develop those arguments? How do we distinguish between credible aspirations and vague, fanciful notions?

[1] We have discussed some of the ideas in this chapter with a variety of audiences in the course of its gestation. These included a staff–postgraduate seminar at the Institute of Criminology, University of Cambridge in February 2014; the 2nd Tony Peters Lecture, presented by Richard Sparks, at KU Leuven in April 2014; participants at the postgraduate 'scuola intensiva' at the Universidad Nacional del Litoral, Santa Fe, Argentina in March 2015; and successive meetings of the Law and Society Association in Mexico City and Washington DC in 2017 and 2018. We are grateful to all concerned for their thoughtful questions and criticisms.

Ian Loader and Richard Sparks, *Reasonable Hopes*. In: *Crime, Justice, and Social Order*. Edited by: Alison Liebling, Joanna Shapland, Richard Sparks, and Justice Tankebe, Oxford University Press. © Alison Liebling, Joanna Shapland, Richard Sparks, and Justice Tankebe 2022. DOI: 10.1093/oso/9780192859600.003.0006

In our view, we will not derive much help in this regard from looking for theoretical refreshment only within the traditions of criminological theorising, whatever 'within' and 'criminology' may mean here. One reason for this, we suggest, is that criminology has generally tended to be at its most creative when its defences are down; when it is more open to perspectives arising elsewhere and not focused on policing its borders, declaring disciplinary autonomy or stipulating correct ways of doing things. Another reason, we think—one perhaps more specific to our own times—is that a good deal of recent criminology has become quite dismal in mood and declamatory in tone. To state the matter baldly, much criminological work of the past couple of decades, including some of the most admired and influential, has had too little faith in the future to find it worth the effort of delineating what it might become. Where this arises (and no one need feel they are being asked to wear the cap when it does not fit) it can be a serious problem, intellectually limiting as well as morally and politically inhibiting. If we wish to overcome this situation, then, we will need both to locate it, in terms of the experiences and influences that led there, and to begin to identify bodies of work that may be useful in demonstrating ways of doing things differently, or at least suggesting that this might still be a possibility.

It strikes us as highly appropriate to pursue this argument in a volume dedicated to honouring the contributions of Tony Bottoms. In the course of a career devoted to a succession of rigorous and often very lengthy empirical inquiries, Bottoms has brought to bear an exceptionally wide range of theoretical resources, often ones with which most criminologists were not previously very familiar. In this sense, while never overtly criticising, let alone attacking, criminology as such, the Wolfson Professor of Criminology appears to have been rather little constrained by it, and surprisingly insouciant about transgressing its boundaries. In particular, Bottoms has been one of the rather few empirically oriented criminologists who have thoughtfully applied moral theory and concepts drawn from political theory. The most salient example of the latter, we suggest, concerns the notion of legitimacy, which has been a central concern of Bottoms's work for the past 25 years. Since one of us had a hand in combining with Tony Bottoms and Will Hay to specify some of the criminological applications of that idea (Sparks 1994; Sparks, Bottoms, and Hay 1996; Sparks and Bottoms 2007), it is doubtless not surprising to find that we continue to think it important. As is well known, Bottoms has since developed these ideas much further, both in his work on theories of compliance (Bottoms 2002b) and in his joint work with Justice Tankebe on power-holders' perspectives

(Bottoms and Tankebe 2013) and on the 'dialogic' nature of legitimacy (Bottoms and Tankebe 2012).

We have also argued elsewhere that the question of legitimacy is at the core of understanding why politics and crime matter so much for one another (Loader and Sparks 2013a) and is thus a key component in subjecting developments in crime control and penal policies to a political frame of evaluation. For such reasons, we think there are a number of 'resources of hope' (Williams 1989) in Bottoms's work. It matters little in this regard that Bottoms has never self-identified as a member of a radical wing or group. How far and with what effects one can press the implications of the ideas is of much greater interest.

It is because of this abiding theoretical curiosity, allied to a powerful sense of civic responsibility in the choice of his objects of inquiry and practical engagements, that we mentioned Tony Bottoms (alongside John Braithwaite) as exemplifying some of the virtues that we associated with the figure of the 'democratic under-labourer' in our book *Public Criminology?* (Loader and Sparks 2011). Since that term—no doubt in part through our fault, but also we think at times perversely or obtusely—has been poorly understood in some responses to our work, we take the opportunity to return here to the question of the relationship between criminology's civic missions and virtues and its specifically theoretical and conceptual tasks. In our view, these matters are not just things that accidentally co-exist sometimes. Rather, they are integrally, indeed constitutively, related.

In our view, criminology's 'political frame of evaluation' (Loader and Sparks 2016) is underdeveloped by comparison with the sophistication of some of its empirical techniques and its descriptive capacity. This has contributed to the dismalness and lack of focus on the future that we attribute to much of the field. It has given us some potent depictions of current problems and predicaments, but few really persuasive ways of thinking beyond them. We all experience the weightiness of the present, in our everyday lives as workers, viewers, voters, and so forth, as well as through our research and inquiry. We see how resistant to change current practices and institutions are. We understand the interests that sustain them and hold them in place. By contrast, criminologists lack much in the way of good theories about how to 'unfreeze' (Unger 2005: 184) the present. We therefore think it makes sense to do as creative people such as Bottoms, Braithwaite, and others have long been doing and look further afield for inspiration and assistance. We think we may have found some of this in the form of some themes from the pragmatist tradition in political theory, which we briefly introduce with reference to two of its commanding figures: John Dewey and Roberto Unger. It is indicative, we suggest, that these major figures of, respectively, twentieth and twenty-first-century social and political thought are little known or cited in criminology.

To think about the problems with which criminology grapples through the lens of pragmatism provokes a pronounced change of perspective, we suggest. It requires a refocusing on questions of democracy and democratisation on one hand, and on knowledge, expertise, and inquiry on the other, and proposes some particular ways of thinking about what relationships we should seek to promote between them. Seen in this light, the fixity that criminologists attribute to contemporary conditions may be a theoretical failing as well as a political distraction. We might begin to ask some different questions: not 'why is everything terrible, yet nothing can change?' but rather 'what is the best for which we may reasonably hope?'

The poverty and promises of theory

Theory has a curious and ambivalent place in criminology. Or perhaps it is more accurate to say that criminology has an odd and ambivalent relationship with theory. Most textbook accounts of the subject—and textbooks have proliferated enormously in recent years, in tandem with the institutional embedding of criminology as a disciplinary category—are arranged in terms of a familiar succession of theoretical positions. We begin, generally, with classicism and positivism. We encounter Durkheim, who may or may not have been a positivist, but whom we suspect was a functionalist. Marx may be mentioned at this point, or he may be postponed until later, when critical criminology enters the scene. Once Criminology (now with a big C) naturalises in the United States it begins to seem more credible to speak of *criminological* theory as such, and so the line-up gets more solid: social disorganisation; strain theory and its successors; interactionism; control theory and its recent variants. These are all positions that students can name-check, even if our accounts of them are quite reductive and make rather little reference to whatever the original proponents now assigned to these categories actually thought or said. At a certain point (it is not always made clear exactly why these points occur when they do) some fairly serious people, often in fact much more ardently engaged with Theory (with a big T), turn up demanding admission. Thus radical or critical criminologies, feminism, green criminology, cultural criminology, latterly post-colonial and critical race theories, each present their challenges to the dominant narrative. Some of these generate substantial bodies of research and carry significant implications for practical interventions in the world, yet somehow disrupt the solidity of the standard story less than might thereby be expected. Genuine attempts at integrative theoretical work are quite rare.

These are caricatures, of course, at least to some degree. Why then trouble to rehearse them here at all? One reason is the oddity that these traditions appear to continue to matter at some level. In some other disciplines—psychology, perhaps—while the history of the subject may be a recognised special interest for some, for most practitioners once a theory has been falsified or otherwise superseded it ceases to matter very much. That raises questions about what would constitute progress in criminological theory and about when or how theories become obsolete (Dooley and Goodison 2019). More positively, the way in which we handle the history of theory in criminology could be seen as suggesting a due recognition that contemporary ideas about crime, including those that are mainly designed for purposes of practical intervention, have antecedents and affinities, and are capable of being described or modelled as belonging in one or another family of ideas.

Theory, we might say, is compulsory; but like many obligatory things, it is not always embraced by everyone with conspicuous enthusiasm. Every degree programme has courses in it. Every conference has streams of sessions about it. Every PhD student is greeted by the injunction to theorise their research or state their theoretical position. Yet, in the mainly fairly applied and often policy-focused sphere of criminology, it is the genuine enthusiasm or special interest of relatively few professional scholars, despite the fact that so many students who encounter criminology are switched on by ideas and their transgressive conceptual potential. Moreover, the tendency for those textbooks and conference sessions and courses to focus on 'criminological theories', rather than on theorising as an activity, risks imposing intellectual limits upon the explanatory, interpretive, and contextual resources that people are able to mobilise in designing or reporting their research. In this regard, the teaching and learning of criminology as a distinct body of theories, with most of the institutional accoutrements of a discipline, even where that status is widely denied by its practitioners themselves, is problematic. It stands to insulate it from the wider currents of sociological, legal, psychological, and other traditions of thought that originally animated it and constituted it as a point of intersection and creativity (Garland 2011).

We would like to lodge a series of further challenges to some of the standard ways of thinking about theory that seem to obtain among some criminologists. In particular, we present some arguments about the kinds of effort involved in getting to grips with contemporary economic, political, and cultural change—which is what the best of social theories have always done for their own times—and hence about the kinds of theoretical work that seem to us most necessary now. We have argued elsewhere that the chronological succession of paradigms or positions is a poor way of thinking about the history of ideas (Loader and Sparks 2004). Our argument was that there was a need for investigation of the generative relationship between political responses to crime and criminological knowledge. This, we suggested, demanded an approach that sought to situate criminology's lines of intellectual development in the context of the institutional settings within which it took place, and the broader social, cultural and political contexts that shaped it (cf. Garland 1992).We also argued, further, for an assessment of the ways in which particular forms of criminology have been taken up and used by political actors, have been inscribed in political discourse and professional practice, have become embroiled in political and cultural struggles. Our subsequent book *Public Criminology?* was in part an attempt to make good on those aspirations, as some of our other efforts have also been (Loader and Sparks 2012a, 2013b). We cannot situate criminology properly without both thinking theoretically about 'it' as an object, and thinking historically about its uses of theory. This suggests a particular way of thinking historically about criminology's uses of ideas and the uses of those ideas in the articulation of practices and interventions. Perhaps the most fully realised attempt to achieve this in practice is Dario Melossi's *Controlling Crime, Controlling Society* (2008), but the concern arises everywhere throughout the history of prisons, probation, social work, and so on.

In this respect, our argument in *Public Criminology?* was not primarily directed towards the current preoccupation that scholars have, and are ever more strongly encouraged and enjoined to have, with publicising their work and with bringing it into public discussion through blogging, tweeting, appearing in the media, and so on (the importance and value of which however we have never denied—it's just a slightly different set of questions). Rather, we were concerned with the necessary publicness of research work whose concepts and assumptions inevitably and continuously fall back into the circulation of discourses and professional practices. We have been roundly criticised by some readers who wanted to see much more of the former (for example Wilson 2010), and we happily acknowledge the importance of those concerns for all contemporary knowledge-workers, ourselves included. However, in our view this also risks missing the point we were making, which is a more basic one about the sociology of knowledge and practice in respect of crime control.

There have been many attempts, of course, to capture the constitutive nature of the relationships between the production, circulation, and application of social scientific knowledge on crime and punishment in modernity (a point we develop at more length in other places: Loader and Sparks 2011: ch. 2; Loader and Sparks 2012a; Loader and Sparks 2013b). Indeed, teasing out just how ideas, 'findings', and inventions enter the world of practical action is exactly one of the points on which social theory has a precise bearing on applied subjects like criminology. So, in earlier work we made reference to Giddens's point that the relations between social scientists and their objects of study are characterised by a 'double hermeneutic' in virtue of which 'lay' and 'technical' concepts have a two-way relationship. On this view, 'the concepts of the social sciences are not produced about an independently constituted subject-matter, which continues regardless of what these concepts are. The "findings" of the social sciences very often enter constitutively into the world they describe' (Giddens 1987: 20).

One scholar whose work frequently and intensively addressed the implications of this condition for criminological knowledge and its relations to the worlds of power and policy was the late Richard Ericson. Ericson accepted that for various reasons to do with the differing priorities, needs, vocabularies, and time and resource pressures of the actors involved, the direct and visible impact of social science research on policy may often be slight, but this is a secondary matter compared with their constitutive role in modern societies. Thus:

> As Giddens (1990: 16) remarks, 'the practical impact of social science and sociological theories is enormous, and sociological concepts and findings are constitutively involved in what modernity is'. Sociology originated, developed and sustained legitimacy as part of the modern, liberal, social imaginary of producing data on populations that contribute to governmental programmes of security, wellbeing, prosperity and self-governance (Taylor 2004). As such it has always been integral to policy, defined simply as principled courses of action. Moreover, as analysts of principled courses of action, sociologists cannot escape making choices

> among preferred principles and thereby contribute to policy. (Ericson 2005: 367–368)

If theory matters as much as we suggest then it also matters which theories we deploy, to which ends, and just how we go about developing and using them. We argue here, drawing some of our inspiration from Bottoms's work in ways that might slightly surprise him, that at least one important task of theory, in criminology as elsewhere in the social sciences today, lies in what we call *reconstruction*. Theoretical work in this mode, we argue—following Roberto Unger (2014)—does not aspire only to explain what goes on in the world but also to illuminate the 'penumbra of possibilities' that surround any current course of action. Good theory may not thereby go quite so far as to 'show us which way to move', as Raymond Geuss (1981: 54) once put it, but it may serve to sharpen our awareness of constraints and possibilities and illuminate some part of what lies within the space of (Unger again) 'the adjacent possible' (2007: 86). If we are right about this then we need to draw upon a different and more plural set of theoretical resources than those that are currently most familiar to criminologists, namely theories that have something to say about agency, decision-making, democratic deliberation, and priority-setting, and thus about politics. Our argument is that, following a period characterised by something of a dearth of political creativity and theoretical imagination amongst mainstream criminologists, and indeed by a sometimes over-generalised and disabling pessimism, conceptual tools of the kind we advocate can provide what Raymond Williams illuminatingly termed 'resources of hope' (1989).

In order to defend, and then build upon, these claims we need first to spend a little time explaining quite why some recent modes of writing and theorising in criminology, including some of those that we regard as among the insightful and interesting, have been quite so dismal and often so lacking in respect of political or normative guidance. Elements of this story are already well known, and we too have commented on it before (see in particular Loader and Sparks 2012a), so we try to be brief here. Nevertheless, outlining the nature of the conditions that have provoked these responses, and the precise ways in which they strike us as inadequate or unhelpful, is an important step. In the remainder of the chapter we then seek to sketch what we see as some preferable alternatives to this state of affairs. One strand of that argument is that criminology, in common with other descriptive and policy-focused social sciences, could benefit from sharpening up its ideas about politics. Another is that if we can do that to effect then we can begin to move beyond a rather repetitious set of restatements of the problem towards, if not answers, then at least more fully engaged and strenuous responses to it. At this point, competitive distinctions between theoretical and practical or applied approaches to problems always let one down, since often enough what is felt to be needed (cf Mills 1959) by people engaged in severely practical activities is some conceptual tools for re-describing and re-thinking their predicaments and some action-guiding principles for re-shaping them.

Paradise postponed: Criminologies of disappointment

At the end of our book *Public Criminology*? (Loader and Sparks 2011) we suggested that one of the aspirations of students of crime and punishment (criminologists, for want of a better term) should be to help create the conditions for a better politics of crime. Their special contribution to that objective, we suggested, takes the form of trying to raise the prevailing quality of political argument about crime and social ordering. The ways in which they do this, we suggested, include but are certainly not limited to those of correcting misinformation, weighing evidence about existing policies and practices, and designing alternative interventions. Those certainly do seem to us to be basic, indeed central, obligations for social scientists; and the rigour, persistence, and respect for evidence with which they are pursued are central to what distinguishes their investigation as topics for social science, in quality if not in kind, from other kinds of opinion. However, these objectives, extremely demanding though they clearly are, don't seem to us to be quite enough to capture either the specific responsibilities upon or the opportunities open to people working on problems of crime and punishment. The alternative conception that we presented there (Loader and Sparks 2011: ch. 5) involved cultivating a set of practices and dispositions that we called 'democratic under-labouring'.

Those who want to insist upon the view that criminology is primarily concerned with empirical and pragmatic questions at the expense of normative or political ones risk placing an unnecessary and inhibiting limit on their conception of criminology's civic role, we believe. Those limits have to do with an inability to *explain* how criminological knowledge in fact fares in settings of contemporary policy formation and what often seems like an undefended desire to somehow *replace* politics with what Bruno

Latour calls 'calculative devices' (Latour 2004). Instead, we think there is much to be gained, not from treating criminology as an expert antidote to democratic politics, but from trying to think afresh about criminology's relation to problems, and promises, of democracy. Democracy in this sense is both an established mode of social organisation that all of us who live in the affluent countries of the global North are familiar with (and often disappointed by) and an unfulfilled set of aspirations and possibilities across a range of sites and institutions, including some that have a strong bearing on criminal justice. Among the questions that we took this to raise are: What in a democracy is the public value of criminology? What is the collective good that criminological enquiry seeks to promote? What modes of intervention—and what institutional arrangements—can best realise that good?

The consequences of thinking along these lines, we argued, included a clearer sense of the need for 'argumentative' (Hoppe 1999) or 'intelligent' (Sanderson 2009) rather than simply 'evidence-based' public policy-making. On this view, criminology is committed both to participating within, and to facilitating and extending, institutional spaces that supplement representative politics with inclusive public deliberation about crime and justice matters, whether in local, state, or federal arenas or across emergent transnational spaces. In giving this disposition a name—that of democratic under-labouring—we certainly did not imagine that we were inventing anything, let alone stipulating how everyone ought to behave. But we did and do believe that it was a fairly apt way of trying to draw out some key features of the practices of many thoughtful and engaged people (who by no means all belong to a single school of thought, or generally agree with one another—or, for that matter, with us). For such people—people like us, and we suspect most readers of this book—it is an important challenge to try to reconcile an earnest commitment to scholarship and knowledge generation with an equally sincere and sustained desire to change the world.

Being the stuff of politics, exactly how the world should be changed—how radically, how comprehensively, how quickly, and by which means?—is inherently and chronically contested, between criminologists just as between other citizens. The stuff in question, moreover, is particularly hot and volatile. As the late Jock Young so concisely stated: 'The study of crime is not a marginal concern to the citizen but plunges us immediately into fundamental questions of order and morality in society and to the examination of the very basis of the civilization we live in' (Young 1981: 307). In a somewhat similar vein, Richard Ericson, writing here with Patricia Baranek and Janet Chan, once observed:

> Deviance and control are not marginal to society, but rather of central significance. They are key elements in everyday life, used by all of us to define who we are and what we might become. This is increasingly so in modern, complex societies because moral boundaries are equivocal and constantly shifting in accordance with ongoing negotiation among different interests. The nature of these negotiations . . . who participates in them, what is at stake, whose definitions prevail, and who is affected by them and how—is an essential topic for social research, as it contributes to an understanding of social stability (our sense of order) and social change. (Ericson et al. 1987: 7)

It is small wonder then that debate about such topics sometimes turns a bit intemperate, given all that is at stake. For much of its history, but perhaps especially since about 1970, criminology has been a 'hot spot' for intellectual and political debates that ranged across the social sciences. This is not the place to rehearse, even in summary form, the multiple points of disagreement and dispute between radicals and liberals, feminists and proponents of 'conventional' theories and methods, positivists and constructivists. There has been much of deep significance at issue. As we have attempted to summarise elsewhere, proponents of different criminologies have disagreed about theory, methods, agency, institutions, topics, curricula, priorities, affiliations, diagnoses, objectives, and so on (see Loader and Sparks 2012a). In these respects, criminological theories may not all *be* political theories (often they are all too ignorant of the claims of political theory properly so called—Loader and Sparks 2011: ch. 5). Yet they all, without exception, find their uses and applications in circumstances that are shaped and conditioned by the realm of politics and they carry implications from and for that world.

For all the side-taking and sometimes bitter mutual name-calling, it may also be possible to argue that the proponents of these various positions frequently had a great deal in common. One thing they often shared was a relatively optimistic orientation towards the future. They might berate one another for undue caution, on one hand, or for unbounded radical zeal, on the other. Yet, seen in a slightly longer and wider historical perspective, they often appear to have been disputatious members of a single tribe rather than outright opposed parties—occupants of 'adjacent rather than antithetical positions', as Garland once suggested in a related context (Garland 1995). This is not in any sense to suggest that the arguments were, or are, fictitious; nor that the points of contention were not highly significant. In many cases they went not merely to conceptual and epistemological disagreements but to questions of liberty, legal protection, life chances, and the social distribution of resources (including resources of safety and danger) that posed policy questions, and indeed questions of larger political strategy, of the first importance, domestically and globally. We should accept as a starting point, therefore, that the relations that subsisted between different intellectual and political commitments of both academic criminologists and their kinfolk in the worlds of professional practice and political activism were both complex and frequently contentious, and fully deserving of serious and respectful historical recovery (Loader and Sparks 2004).

Nevertheless, the world has changed in ways that turned out to be disruptive of the hopes and expectations of both the 'mainstream' and the radical factions. Thus, although challenged in some degree from the Left, though largely within the fields of academic knowledge and professional practice rather than in the wider arena of national electoral politics, crime control was—until the 1970s—characterised by what seemed an entrenched matrix of institutions and ideas. The result was an apparently quite stable complex of institutional sites, dispositions, and practices—what Garland (2001: ch. 2) has termed 'the penal-welfare state' (Garland 2001: 46; see generally Young 1999; Hobsbawm 1994: ch. 9; Hay 1996: chs 2–4).

Since the 1970s, this field of control institutions and mentalities has been profoundly called into question and transformed—undone by a perfect storm of rising crime and shifts in political culture. The massive escalation in recorded crime rates between 1945 and the mid-1990s saw criminal victimisation move from the margins of social life to 'become a routine part of modern consciousness, a standing possibility that is constantly to be "kept in mind"' (Garland 2001: 106). This, according to Jock Young (1999: 35), represents 'the central motor of change' in post-war criminal justice and crime control. This process has exposed the limitations of simple social democratic accounts of crime causation (wherein better social conditions should mean less crime) and seen the 'discovery' of hitherto hidden offences and unknown victims (domestic violence, sexual and physical abuse of children, stalking, environmental pollution …). It has also given the crime question (and crime imagery) a prominent, noisy, and hotly disputed place in everyday life and political discourse (Hope and Sparks 2000; Garland 2001: ch. 6).

For some observers, these transformations represent the extinction of many of the values for which they have hoped, studied, and striven. Thus, for example, the later work of Robert Reiner (as we have discussed at more length elsewhere: Loader and Sparks 2012b) has increasingly assumed the form of a lament for social democracy's lost and defeated principles (Reiner 2006). In part, this is straightforward homage to a better past. Recalling the views of authors such as Eric Hobsbawm (1994) and Tony Judt (2010), Reiner writes: 'I have been persuaded ... that the 1950s and 1960s were a sort of golden age in objective terms, and that in the early 1970s something happened to set in train a general—though not unambiguous—decline in the quality of life' (Reiner 2011: xxviii). But this orientation can also be detected in the absence of 'any real confidence' (Reiner 2010: 261) in the capacity of social democracy to exercise much influence under current conditions, even after the 2008 financial crash, or of concrete ideas for how it might begin to do so.

This is a strong form of the argument, but we suggest by no means entirely unrepresentative. Pat O'Malley has, in this regard, argued that 'critical criminology is deep in one of its more pessimistic phases' (O'Malley 2010: 81) and that its exponents 'rarely suggest any way out of the nightmare they depict' (ibid: 6). There may be cogent reasons why observers might see their contribution as in the first instance a defensive one. For example, Wacquant speaks of his interlocutors in Latin America as seeking to create 'civic firebreakers' (2009: 166–167) in the face of a conflagration. The civic project is, in this light, one of trying to shelter existing institutions from an overwhelming threat. It has been very difficult for progressive observers to discern a more appealing future beyond them. Criminologists have become, as John Braithwaite puts it, 'pessimists and cynics' (Braithwaite 1992: 1). In a similar vein, David Brown draws together a list (each fairly familiar in itself, but quite powerful for being collated in this way) of reasons that liberals and progressives on matters of crime and punishment have had to not be cheerful. They include the long rise of prison populations, the demotic public discourse, the intensification of risk-based reasoning and mangerialism, and so on (Brown 2013: 28).

Criminologists, for a range of reasons—among which is the disappointment of a certain set of political aspirations combined with an increasing sense of exclusion from major centres of decision-making—have become adept at charting the many things that they, frequently rightly and eloquently, identify as alarming and dismaying. They are often less proficient at framing any convincing sense of alternative political possibility (see also Matthews 2010). In this regard the impulse towards critique, though frequently developed on the basis of quite powerful empirical evidence, is not matched by equivalent sophistication with respect to normative argument or novel political strategic thinking. Far from suggesting in which direction to move, critique emphasises how stuck we are. Lucia Zedner (2002) has pointed to the danger that critique severed from a sense of social possibility or moral commitment reduces to commentary: 'self-consciously indifferent.' This may well have something to do with a growing dissociation between academics who affiliate to critical schools of thought in their work (for which they—we might better say here 'we'—may be well rewarded in professional terms) and the campaigns and struggles of actual oppositional movements, as Tony Platt (1991, and personal communication), among others, has argued.

Let us suppose for the moment that there is something in these suggestions. One consequence might be that there were few inhibitions against, and often some handsome rewards in professional terms for, proposing accounts of social change that overwhelmingly focused on the negative, even the dystopian, with no corresponding obligation to imagine how the world could be otherwise. That might well produce a discourse fluent in vigorous, eloquent, and often persuasive critique, but not necessarily one that was particularly creative in respect of policy or possibility. Such tendencies would look fairly intelligible in light of Pierre Rosanvallon's (2008) account of what he terms 'counter-democracy'. For Rosanvallon, counter-democracy is something of great importance, a cultural counterpart to the development of the institutions of representative democracy themselves. It consists of the activities of placing democracy under critical inspection through the three-fold mechanisms of 'vigilance', 'denunciation', and 'evaluation':

> By 'counter-democracy' I mean not the opposite of democracy but rather a form of democracy that reinforces the usual electoral democracy as a kind of buttress, a democracy of indirect powers disseminated throughout society—in other words, a durable democracy of distrust, which complements the episodic democracy of the usual electoral-representative system. Thus counter-democracy is part of a larger system that also includes legal democratic institutions and extends their influence, to shore them up. (Rosanvallon 2008: 8)

Nevertheless, Rosanvallon argues, in the present—which he characterises as an age of 'generalized distrust' marked by a pronounced populist temptation (2008: 265) and a 'utopia of transparency' in lieu of substantive political goals—counter-democratic oversight can degenerate into 'a banal form of opposition': 'today's negative politics marks a painful and energy-sapping shrinkage of that activity' (2008: 190). Critical counter-democratic work has become oppositional without also being 'propositional'.

In our view, then, there is a properly theoretical difficulty underpinning these problems of engagement and vision. This is that, by contrast with the increasingly high development of their analytical and interpretive tools, social theories of crime and punishment have a rather weak sense of politics, and in particular a weak grasp of normative political argument. For these reasons, the project that seems to us most necessary now is one that strives to draw productive linkages between accounts of the problems of contemporary democratic politics—such as the vagaries and extravagancies of punishment in advanced capitalist countries today—and efforts to sketch how these matters might be theorised, approached, and done differently. This implies a change of perspective and vantage point. It demands, among other kinds of change, a much closer collaboration between those working in criminology and those for whom democratic politics as such is the primary object of inquiry, and indeed of practical intervention. So, just how should we go about reacquainting democratic theory with the situated investigation of the institutions and practices of crime control?

Resources of hope: Legitimacy, pragmatism, democracy

To seek a more hopeful, future-oriented criminology is not to take refuge in a naive, unworldly optimism. It does not mean forgetting all the hard-won and sometime battle-scarring lessons about the conflicting interests, institutional inertia, or unintended consequences that litter the histories of criminology and of reform movements in crime control and penal politics. To have documented and understood these stands among the most important intellectual contributions of criminologists. The career of the late Stanley Cohen, for example, provided eloquent counsel against gimmicks and enthusiasms of every kind—notably in the brilliant but nowadays too little referenced *Visions of Social Control* (1985). It is generally just not very good social science to imagine that social arrangements are easy to change, or to suppose that there is a historical tide running in favour of what we happen to prefer. Criminologists of all people should not fail to notice that good intentions frequently produce perverse outcomes. In short, optimism is a poor guide.

But optimism and hope are conceptually and practically quite different. Hope, for example, requires elements of commitment that are alien to the sunny disposition of the optimistic. As Christopher Lasch argues:

> Hope implies a deep-seated trust in life that appears absurd to those who lack it. The worst is always what the hopeful are prepared for. Their trust in life would not be worth much if it had not survived disappointments in the past, while the knowledge that the future holds future disappointments demonstrates the continuing need for hope. Improvidence, a blind faith that things will somehow work out for the best, furnishes a poor substitute for the disposition to see things through even when they don't. (Lasch 1991: 81)

As this makes clear, optimists have no need to be hopeful—they already think things are going to turn out for the best. Hope by contrast is a worldly sensibility, grounded in recurrent experiences of disappointment and a sober analysis of the world as one finds it. To maintain hopefulness in this sense is to refuse to call off the search for future possibilities even in the face of rigorous and disillusioned analysis of the weight of the present.

If hope is thus quite different from optimism, it is equally distinct from the pessimistic conviction that nothing much can change or that the acuity and insight of social science has at best a defensive purpose. We certainly do not wish to argue that criminology is mainly or only about either technical interventions designed to enhance the efficiency of existing systems, or about problem-raising, or about damage limitation, or about nostalgia for lost political worlds (see further Loader and Sparks 2012b). Whatever their differences, those orientations have in common that they disclose no coherent vision of possible futures; nor do they venture any clue as to how to think about getting from here to there. For this reason, even when sharply critical of the existing way of doing things (latterly, this means the ubiquitous 'neo-liberalism'), they cede the initiative to it. As O'Malley (2008) points out, neo-liberalism is highly inventive: it operates in large part by providing incentives to produce new 'moral inventions'. One danger, therefore, that is exacerbated by the absence of hopefulness in our conceptions of crime control or penal politics is that we are invited to accept innovation as a surrogate for aspiration. So how can we begin to fashion a more hopeful orientation to the politics of crime? In the remainder of this chapter we suggest that there are (still) good reasons for thinking that a better politics of crime needs to be both robustly democratic and explicitly egalitarian in its commitments.

Among the most important aspects of legitimacy, according to Bottoms and colleagues (Sparks et al. 1996, Sparks and Bottoms 2007, Bottoms and Tankebe 2012), is the view that a person's acceptance of a decision or provision that affects their interests is likely to be grounded in shared beliefs and in the giving of reasons that they can reasonably be supposed to accept as valid. Bottoms and colleagues argued that this applied to the decisions of penal agents (such as prison or probation officers) and their reception by people undergoing penal sanctions (such as prisoners and probationers) just as much as to everyone else. Beetham (1991) argues that all distributions of power seek to legitimate their actions and decisions. The simple fact that a prison is a prison, for example, does not *ipso facto* take it outside some conception or other of what it means to act or decide, to impose demands or withhold benefits, legitimately. Something of this sort is clearly implicit in the gradual extension of rule of law values into penal institutions in the UK and elsewhere in Europe since the 1970s (whereas at least in Britain up until then the courts had largely declined to interest themselves in questions of prison discipline or the application of prison rules). Latterly and increasingly, this has of course taken the form of actions in respect of international human rights instruments (van Zyl Smit and Snacken 2011; Murphy and Whitty 2013). But beyond the fairly rare and unusual issue of recourse to law, the point is that members of democratic polities tend to develop certain fairly firmly held expectations of their treatment by others—such as to be addressed in a civil way, or not to be subject to arbitrary or prejudicial behaviour. Such expectations are not all suspended just because the other people involved happen to be police or prison officers.

We take it that the relevance of these concerns has now been fairly well established in (we may say 'even in') relation to people's experiences of and responses to encounters with criminal justice, such as in policing (Tyler 2004) and prisons (Sparks et al. 1996; Liebling 2004, 2007). However, it also seems possible to connect these 'special' concerns to much wider considerations regarding our views and requirements of criminal justice and crime control as citizens (and thus also as onlookers, readers, viewers, voters, consumers, tweeters, taxpayers, and so on—cf. Jackson et al. 2012). In their extension of accounts of legitimacy in criminal justice 'beyond' the procedural paradigm, Bottoms and Tankebe argue that legitimacy is best thought of as a matter of ongoing dialogue (2012: 139). It involves, they suggest, a continual dynamic of claim and response, and is thus 'more like a perpetual discussion' (Bottoms and Tankebe 2012: 110) than a single assertion of power or command.

We think this is an important insight, but one whose implications we need to press further if we are to fully gather its implications for the development of a better politics of crime. Thus, Bottoms and Tankebe also suggest that understanding the idea of legitimacy in terms of dialogue means transcending the idea that legitimacy has mainly to do with compliance and obedience (ibid: 139). Indeed, it may have much more to do with change and transformation than with order and stability. We would argue that, more especially, it also has to do with contemporary people's expectations of voice or participation in important public questions that affect their lives (Dzur 2019). It is this view that we intend to develop here with regard to the insights of the pragmatist tradition in political theory as resources of hope.

If legitimacy is, for some purposes at least, an idea that suggests dialogue, then legitimate social arrangements might be ones that make space for debates and discussions that inform actions or policies. Those debates and discussions might be expected to involve as many of those affected by the outcomes of such actions as possible, either directly or by some representative mechanism. This further raises the question of what kinds of knowledge the people concerned bring into such discussion, or how knowledge becomes available to them in the course of it. The latter point is, we suggest, at least incidentally interesting as it raises once more the prospects for some degree of mediation between the more scientistic versions of criminology (such as 'experimental criminology') and other, more overtly 'political', wings. Pragmatism, as we shall see, expressly foregrounds the questions both of the social and political value of conversation and of the benefits of experimentation (albeit in a slightly specialised sense of the term 'experiment').

Dewey, experimentalism, and the epistemic powers of democracy

In his long and exceptionally active life (1859–1952) John Dewey produced an expansive corpus of work grounded in an organising commitment to democracy as a moral ideal. For Dewey democracy was not solely or simply a form of government, but a way of life. It was also more particularly the 'precondition for the full application of intelligence to the solution of social problems' (Putnam 1990: 1671), where intelligence means the use of 'inquiry' in the search for an 'inevitably provisional solution to the practical and intellectual problem that sparked inquiry'. Inquiry in this sense is a collective activity, not just a property or disposition of individuals: it is seen as problem-solving, as historical and progressive, and as communal. 'Inquiry' is something undertaken by actors seeking solutions to problems: 'part of an existential struggle to cope with an objectively precarious but improvable environment', or as Dewey put it: 'Prophecy for the future, but one disciplined by serious thought and knowledge' (Dewey 1918: 3).

The key to finding such better solutions, for Dewey, is a certain conception of scientific method and an openness to experimentation. It involves the commitment to 'testing one's ideas in practice and maintaining an attitude of fallibilism towards them', within a 'critical community of inquiry' (Shapiro and Glicksman 2003: 16) whose membership extends well beyond the preserve of specialists or technicians. Thus for Dewey the application of scientific method to social problems was not something reserved to a separate cadre of technically accomplished experts, however important the contribution of such people might be in providing the resources to inform such deliberation. Rather, it presupposed experimental inquiry combined with 'free and full discussion' in as inclusive a way as possible—which means maximising the capacities of citizens for proposing courses of action, testing them, and evaluating the results. As Anderson (2006: 14) puts it:

> John Dewey offered an experimentalist account of the epistemic powers of democracy. He characterized democracy as the use of social intelligence to solve problems of practical interest ... This requires abandoning dogmatism, affirming fallibilism, and accepting the observed consequences of our practices as the key evidence prompting us to revise them. Dewey took democratic decision-making to be the joint exercise of practical intelligence by citizens at large, in interaction with their representatives and other state officials. It is cooperative social experimentation.

In its regard for fallibilism and the testing of propositions, this view of course bears a more than merely passing resemblance to the aspirations of those who seek to make criminology and crime control policy more 'experimental' (e.g., Sherman 2009). But Dewey's express coupling of scientific method with free and full discussion among citizens has far-reaching implications for how we think about experimentalism and its applications to crime control.

First, it means much more than relying on experts—and therefore more than simply introducing more and better evidence to the process of policy-making, as daunting as that in itself can be. Experts, for Dewey, belong to privileged classes and 'all special privilege narrows the outlook of those who possess it' (Dewey and Tufts 1908: 18). For pragmatists, 'the capacity of the wise to discern the public interest tends to be distorted by their position' (Festenstein 2014: 4). Dewey further argues that 'A class of experts is inevitably so removed from common interests as to become a class with private interests and private knowledge, which in social matters is not knowledge at all' (Dewey 1927: 208). Experts also tend to be accustomed to telling people what to do and, for Dewey, social problems cannot be solved by telling people what to do. So expert knowledge has a vital place in the experimental method, but cannot be the only voice, or be determinative of what is to be done. Rather, the key question is how to infiltrate the results of inquiry into social and political deliberation (Knight and Johnson 2014).

Second, experimental method for Dewey is incompatible with social arrangements that rationalise entrenched privilege and deny the underprivileged the opportunity to develop and use their capacities. The ramifications of this mean that any experimental approach to finding better solutions to crime questions needs to do more than privilege certain methods or forms of knowledge. Rather, it requires exploration and development of the institutional preconditions for the full application of social intelligence to these issues, together with an experimentalist orientation to the creation of institutions that can give effect to it. Some commentators influenced by these views note that the inclusive, deliberative activities recommended by Dewey and other pragmatists are important *because of* rather than despite the fact that consensus may be rare, conflict frequent, and divergent interests endemic in human affairs (Smith 2011; cf. Misak 2000). This is an intriguing point for criminologists, whose work so often relates to the aftermath of hostilities or abuses, or to institutional divisions and controversies. In other words, it may be that a more hopeful politics of crime demands a more robustly deliberative conception of democracy—one which calls for its reform and expansion, rather than simply defending (or seeking a shield from) its existing forms.

Unger and democratic experimentalism

Dewey helps us to build a better bridge between criminological analysis and thinking about (better) democracy and its conditions of possibility. But even Dewey's keenest admirers admit that his work lacks attention to institutions, and suffers from programmatic vagueness (Bernstein 2010: 87; but see Ansell 2011; Sabel 2012). A contemporary thinker whose work may offer further assistance in thinking about democratisation, experimentalism, and desired social change is Roberto Unger.

Unger's work is far too extensive for us to do more here than make reference to a few propositions that appear particularly germane. In earlier work (Loader and Sparks 2011) we noted that criminologists tend to express dismay at the extent to which public discourse and political contests around crime have become 'hot' in recent decades. On the whole, our collective response to such heating up is to associate it with rhetorical display (which we frequently call 'overheated') and gestural politics, and with (all too evident) excess in ways of punishing and responding to crime. Many practising criminologists actively seek ways to 'cool things down'.

Unger is somewhat unusual among contemporary political writers in that he uses the idea of 'heat' in a positive way. Unger (2007) suggests that an 'empowered democracy' would be a hotter, more energetic place than contemporary social democratic or neo-liberal societies. But then, he argues, the value of social theory lies in waking people up rather than calling them to order (Unger 1987). Among Unger's most notable contributions to social theory is the idea of 'false necessity'. In a notable interview, he summarises the position thus:

> The great revolutionary idea in classical European social thought, in the tradition that began with thinkers like Montesquieu, was the conception that the arrangements of society—the regime of society—is not a natural phenomenon; it is made and imagined. And you could radicalise this idea in the following way by saying the structures understanding them as both the institutional structures and the ideological structures are a kind of frozen politics; they arise as the result of the temporary interruption or the relative containment of practical and visionary strife over the terms of our access to one another. And then they appear to us as though they were *things*—as if they were a *fate* rather than what they

> really are which is our own creations naturalised. (Unger 2014; emphasis in original)

In Unger's view, such an understanding of ideas like 'structure' and 'institutions' is imaginatively, and hence politically, limiting. He warns against what he calls structural fetishism—denying that we have the power to change the quality as well as the content of our practices—and institutional fetishism—the assumption that our institutional ideas (democracy, say) correspond to a single set of institutional forms (Unger 1998: 25–26). By these means, Unger argues, we systematically understate our capacity to alter the structures that we ourselves create, and we can only imagine a certain limited range of institutional arrangements in terms of which we might organise our collective activities. Unger argues that the social sciences today have contributed to the sense of stasis and lack of vision that he identifies. He alleges that they are in this respect guilty of 'deficiencies at once of hope and insight'. He continues:

> The fundamental problem with the social sciences today is that they have severed the link between insight into what exists and imagination of what might exist at the next steps—the adjacent possible . . . The vocation of social science is to help us understand how we came to be in this present situation, in such a fashion that our understanding of our circumstance, rather than putting us to sleep and inducing this fatalistic superstition, awakens us to the imagination of the adjacent possible. (Unger 2014)

The term 'the adjacent possible' is used by Unger to subvert the commonplace distinction between putatively 'revolutionary' transformation and 'mere' adjustment or reformist 'tinkering'. In Unger's view, every current circumstance is surrounded by a 'penumbra of transformative opportunity' (ibid). Unger's incitement here is to encourage us to develop a richer programmatic/institutional imagination, not make a sharp distinction between our political ideals and the institutions through which we seek to enact them: 'institutional choices are how we work out our plans.' We are inclined to respond to this as an invitation to open up criminological theorising to thinking in our field about the conditions of possibility for democratic experimentalism. What are we to do with such an invitation? How shall we even begin to respond to it?

Crime control and democratic hope: An experimentalist agenda

We do not have a list. Rather, we have identified certain problems. In criminology today, there is a tendency to think about politics primarily as something negative that introduces difficulties and disturbances into the crime control field from outside, rather than to think of crime and politics as constitutively related. One consequence of this, we have argued, is that much criminological thinking is either rather glum and fatalistic, or else excitedly apocalyptic, in content and tone. Neither of those registers, we suggest, are the most helpful or incisive ones with which to think about the future. 'Innovation', on the other hand, tends to have been ceded to colleagues of a more commercially opportunist or more technocratic turn of mind; and there is little from those quarters by way of searching reflection upon ethical or political questions.

We think, by contrast, that one purpose of criminological argument is to help define a better politics of crime. We argue that in the wake of certain major and very disconcerting forms of social and cultural change, criminologists have produced some influential accounts that are simultaneously quite persuasive as narratives of decline and fall, and distressingly weak as political analysis, especially from the point of view of guiding intervention. We have also suggested that social analyses of crime and punishment in particular, but theories of democratic politics too, are enriched by greater mutual contact and impoverished by disciplinary separation.

Some people, of whom Tony Bottoms is very much one, have pursued more challenging and illuminating lines of inquiry. We have begun to try to press certain of their ideas—specifically here the relationship between legitimacy (of criminal justice institutions) and questions of their democratic qualities. To cut a long story short, we suspect that for twenty-first-century people, in and beyond the criminal justice system, outright refusals to explain, consult, engage, or involve (or simple failures to do so) inhibit legitimacy.

In this chapter we therefore took a step back and away to recover some themes within the political thought of John Dewey and the pragmatist tradition of democratic theory that he inspired. These seemed to us to offer some refreshment, especially around the view that democratic legitimacy might be enhanced by, on one hand, a certain conception of experimental inquiry, and on the other by a quite demanding and expansive stipulation about public participation and deliberation. Roberto Unger's account of 'empowered democracy' is in key respects a contemporary development of this idea. We think these authors offer some resources for developing—in our view, much needed—reconstruction in theories of crime and its control. It will not, however, have escaped the attention of readers that the resources we have so far found are far from brand new. Indeed, in respect of Dewey's work in particular, they are not only quite old ideas but ones which in some other contexts (most obviously in education in this case) have already been massively influential. Yet their impact in criminology, and perhaps especially in recent criminology—especially in the Anglo-American worlds—has been rather slight. The particular interest, from our perspective, in encouraging renewed attention to the pragmatist tradition in political thought lies in part in its abiding interest in democratisation (and its insistence on the connection between democracy and the quality of decisions) and in its resolute sense of social possibility.

Despite the dismal tone that we attribute to much recent criminology, we also observe a rekindling of interest in scholarship that seeks to investigate and theorise alternatives (for example Dzur 2019). The predominant focus of such work has, understandably enough and for some time now, been in the domain of restorative justice; and at least for some working on those questions, that work has maintained an open connection to projects of social transformation (Walgrave 2008), deliberation (Aertsen et al. 2006) and republican politics (Braithwaite and Pettit 2000). Indeed, it sometimes appears that restorative justice has provided the primary, if not the sole, repository of hope in what is otherwise regarded as a forbidding and barren landscape. However, other sightings of the adjacent possible can also be discerned, whether in some of the work on justice reinvestment (Schwartz et al. 2012), participatory accounts of criminal justice institutions (Fung 2006; Dzur 2013), the long and deep interest of feminists in women's self-organisation and empowerment (Nelund 2014), or theories of transitional justice, to name but a few. Our own emphasis in thinking about how best to develop these lines of inquiry further—as we hope to have made clear in this chapter—is to encourage deeper and more frequent interaction between those who self-define as criminologists and colleagues working on questions of deliberative or participatory democratic theory. This is one of the points of interest in Bottoms and Tankebe's work, as we note above. It is also a connection that is the focus of our own collaboration with Albert Dzur and others (Dzur et al. 2016). It offers, in our judgement, the firmest ground upon which to develop an agenda of reconstructive theorising, research, and engagement in crime control; an agenda which seeks—in the words of another great twentieth-century pragmatist, Albert Hirschman (2013: 22)—to 'widen the limits of what is or is perceived to be possible'.

A 2020 postscript

This chapter was rather a long time in the making and then, for a host of reasons, a long time in production. These are not necessarily bad things. We *intended* to reflect upon what is now a long collaboration of ours, and quite an expansive set of debates; and it is self-admittedly a mainly conceptual chapter, albeit one that we hoped some readers would find of some use in developing their own more substantive and practical projects.

In the time it took for us to bring out our little chapter, however, the world has turned upside down. In some ways, the chapter's strengths, such as they are—the traditional device of standing somewhat apart from everyday, concrete things in order to review and organise one's thoughts about them—now look a bit remote, and of diminished relevance. The worry is that efforts such as this become 'out of time' in a negative sense—overtaken by time and chance, failing to have much purchase on a world already transformed.

We cannot begin to summarise, let alone engage with, these changes here. The United Kingdom has left the European Union, without ever resolving its own divisions on the matter. Whether or not this in turn will cause one or more of its constituent nations to secede, who knows? It seems more likely than before. In the United States the office of the President was captured by an arch exponent of populist phrase-making and political street-fighting whose divisive tactics enabled the resurgence of white supremacism, among other pathologies. Those tactics found echoes and emulators among demagogic authoritarians from Hungary to the Philippines. There, here, and seemingly almost everywhere, hostility has been incited and channelled—against liberals and 'elites', certainly, but also and more importantly against the excluded and displaced who have been incarcerated, expelled, rejected, or drowned. We never anticipated that a global pandemic would see the imposition of restrictions on movement and association, unprecedented in democracies in modern times outside of war, and so precipitate the greatest ever natural experiment in compliance (and defiance). In 2020 in particular we saw policing and criminal justice take centre stage in the drama of social division, especially in the United States, but not just there. The names of those who have died at the hands of the police

(George Floyd, Breonna Taylor, and many others) or self-justifying vigilantes (Ahmaud Arbery, and all his predecessors) became rallying points not just for resistance to racism, brutality, and the misapplication of lethal force but for the articulation of a radical set of democratic demands.

None of this is to say that our argument here is mistaken in its essentials—indeed in some respects quite the contrary, as we will indicate briefly below. Nor can we somehow turn our somewhat reserved overview into another kind of chapter just by a few rapid references to current events. We didn't quite see 2020 coming, and we don't have 20:20 hindsight about that now.

When Unger developed his arguments for 'empowered' and energised democracy—arguments that have excited and attracted us for quite some time—he may not have anticipated either just how hot or how far-reaching some of these debates would soon become. In that respect, all of us should be careful what we wish for. It does seem apparent, however, that current arguments about reform or abolition of criminal justice institutions (whatever 'defund the police' turns out in practice to involve, and whatever it produces in time) also require democratic experimentation if they are to produce creative, non-violent, sustained change. In these respects, Unger's calls to explore the 'adjacent possible' are only more compelling for the urgency of the moment. This suggests that people currently working in the fields of crime, justice, and policing, if they are to have meaningful contributions to make at all, need to think carefully and in detail, but boldly, about the methods, and forms, and processes of situated (including, of course, online) democratic participation. There will be no renewal, no legitimacy, and no settled peace unless we do so.

PART III
CRIME, JUSTICE, AND COMMUNITIES

7

Keeping a Human Perspective

Some Lessons from Women and Community Justice

Loraine Gelsthorpe

Introduction

As will be clear from the Introduction to this book, Professor Sir Anthony Bottoms (Tony, to all of us) is a man of many parts and interests. Tony's father was a medical missionary who worked in a hospital in what is now Bangladesh. In the absence of adequate schooling there, at the age of eight Tony was sent to Eltham College in London as a boarder, remaining there until 1958. In an era before regular jet travel, the costs of travel precluded summer trips to Bangladesh, so holidays were spent with an aunt and uncle in Yorkshire. Tony's parents returned to Britain for just one year in every six. In some ways, this unusual childhood—which combined strong Christian roots, some social marginality, and an excellent formal education—has shaped his life's work both in terms of public service and in terms of his interest in 'other lives', social welfare, and social justice. Unusually for a modern-day criminologist, Anthony Bottoms spent a two-year period at the beginning of his career as an Assistant Probation Officer. It was clearly an important experience and served to shape later interests in the 'real lives' of offenders and in desistance.

Tony's work characteristically links theory, policy, and practice. This is best reflected in a guided criminological and theological exploration of the 'collapse' of the rehabilitative ideal which had informed so much policy and practice in the 1960s. With a penal crisis on the horizon, a group of criminologists and penal practitioners met to discuss the relevance of Christian theology to issues of crime and punishment (Bottoms and Preston 1990). In other words, there was a search for values and principles: a quest for penal ethics. By all accounts Tony took the lead in this collaborative project,

Loraine Gelsthorpe, *Keeping a Human Perspective*. In: *Crime, Justice, and Social Order*. Edited by: Alison Liebling, Joanna Shapland, Richard Sparks, and Justice Tankebe, Oxford University Press. © Alison Liebling, Joanna Shapland, Richard Sparks, and Justice Tankebe 2022. DOI: 10.1093/oso/9780192859600.003.0007

revealing his capacity to cross not just disciplinary boundaries, but also the boundaries between intellectual and practical pursuits.

It is not my purpose to list all of Tony's many achievements and interests here; the editors and other contributors have covered a good deal of ground. I will mention just two other intellectual highlights before moving to the substantive parts of this chapter. First is Tony's interest in order, compliance, and community penalties (Bottoms 2001), where he outlines the principal basic mechanisms underpinning legally compliant behaviour. There are two dimensions to this: 'community' and 'relational'. With regard to community, Tony was one of the first criminologists to observe that changes in the structure of probation over time have made it less community-based (Bottoms 2008a), notwithstanding moves to ensure the increasing visibility of unpaid work (as a punishment) in the community. Indeed, he argues that this change in practice matters very much from the point of view of both offender rehabilitation and community confidence. Drawing on research completed with colleagues at Sheffield University on young men and desistance (Bottoms et al. 2004b), he points out their telling comments in relation to the challenges of 'going straight' because of where they live. There are other factors at play, including drug taking, a search for excitement, and financial and employment issues, but living in deprived areas featured large. The thrust of Tony's argument is to say that offenders need to be confident that probation supervisors can assist them in dealing with such issues if they are to have influence. They need to be confident that probation officers understand the social world that they inhabit. As Tony puts it: probation officers who rarely emerge from their offices 'to visit the deprived areas in which offenders disproportionately live are unlikely to inspire much confidence' (Bottoms 2008a: 162).

What of the 'relational' dimension? There is a telling clue to his strong interests in this direction in his further work with Sheffield colleagues, this time on the quality of probation supervision (Shapland et al. 2012). Here, Joanna Shapland, Tony Bottoms, and others distil the essence of quality supervision from a myriad of perspectives and research studies. What emerges is a sense that the quality of supervision cannot be attributed to the practitioner, with the service user having only a passive role. Rather, there is strong recognition that the interaction between staff and service users produces a quality product. Thus positive engagement with service users often involves 'going the extra mile'. As the researchers indicated, 'Users will engage with staff who make some effort to find out and match with what users see as their own priorities' (Shapland et al. 2012: 42). We could describe this as 'meeting offenders halfway'. In other words, it is important to find out where offenders are in their desistance journeys, and to understand the practical challenges which may not be apparent at the outset, but which may emerge as the probation supervision progresses.

Secondly, Tony elaborated upon his theoretical understandings of compliance in work on 'Criminology and the Normative', arguing, for example, that criminologists have neglected the moral (normative) dimensions of their subject (Bottoms 2002b). What he means by this is moral judgement and moral responsibility. He goes on to suggest that 'if they are to be true to their calling, all criminologists have to be interested in morality' (Bottoms 2002b: 24).

It is almost the case that Tony has never written specifically about girls or women caught up in the criminal justice system: the exception is a joint article (with John Pratt), 'Intermediate Treatment for Girls in England and Wales', in Maureen Cain (ed.), *Growing Up Good* (1989). The chapter draws on empirical data from a national survey of the provision of intermediate treatment (IT) carried out in 1984–1985 (Bottoms and Pratt 1990).[1] Interestingly, the chapter draws attention to the fact that although girls eventually came to be reasonably well provided for in IT practice, they rarely featured in the accompanying critical discourse. This was largely because in the first phase of the development of IT, activities for young people were physical and adventure-based, and none of the projects were specifically for girls. Gradually, over time, the emphasis shifted from male-oriented activities (as they were perceived at the time) towards non-gender-specific relationships, and discussion. Both the gaining of insight and group work were opened up for mixed groups of boys and girls.

Tony tells a wonderful anecdote about his interest in gender differences in crime. When he was a Research Officer in the Institute in the 1960s (working with Derick McClintock) before he moved to Sheffield, Derick encouraged him to gain teaching experience in order to improve his future employment prospects. So Derick got him a number of criminal law supervisions from some of his Directors of Studies friends in colleges, and also mentioned his name to the then Department of Extra-Mural Studies (now the Institute for Continuing Education at the University of Cambridge). So it came about

[1] Intermediate Treatment was a generic term for a range of provisions in England and Wales for young offenders (from the age of 10 to under-17) judged to be delinquent or in need of official care or considered to be at risk of delinquency or appropriate subjects for official care proceedings. IT was introduced in 1983 but was phased out in various pieces of legislation in 1988, 1989, and 1991.

that the first lectures (as opposed to supervisions) that Tony ever gave were general lectures on 'criminology' to an extra-mural class on Saturday afternoons in Swavesey[2] in 1966. Data on lifetime probabilities of conviction for an indictable offence had recently been published for the first time (everyone has forgotten how primitive criminology was until rather recently)—showing, inter alia, a marked gender gap (from his memory, 29% M, 8% F). Janet and Tony had recently (about a month beforehand) become parents for the first time, so to liven up the lecture he told them this, indicating that he had told his wife that their daughter would have only an 8% probability of becoming delinquent. During the tea break, a lady came up to him and said, 'Mr Bottoms, I do hope that wasn't the ONLY thing you said to your wife when your daughter was born'. He had the frightening thought that she might be seeing him as a completely desiccated human being, interested only in statistics. Nothing could be further from the truth, of course! Importantly, Tony has carried out survey research covering both genders (for example in his Sheffield 'housing and crime' studies). Altogether, one can discern a sympathetic understanding of some of the complexities facing women in conflict with the law.

In this chapter I describe some of the developments in relation to women, crime, and criminal justice, which in some ways can be set against the gloominess of criminal justice in terms of the increased use of imprisonment. I hasten to add that women have not been untouched by the apparent punitive turn, and there are some real concerns in the continuing use of short sentences of imprisonment for women. But there have been positive developments in regard to the development of provision for women lawbreakers based in the community during the past two decades in particular, and there are lessons to be drawn from research in this area. Many of these lessons reflect a relational turn in criminology, assist us in understanding compliance, and help us to keep a human perspective.

Amartya Sen (2009) challenges us by asking what kind of reasoning should count in the assessment of ethical and political concepts such as justice and injustice. 'What is the role of rationality and of reasonableness in understanding the demands of justice?', he asks (2009: viii). I want to suggest that reasonableness is intrinsic to conceptions of justice and compliance, and that 'reasonableness' is very much a human and relational dimension.

[2] Swavesey is a village in Cambridgeshire.

Turning to women, crime, and justice

In the first part of the chapter I provide a brief overview of policy developments in regard to women, crime, and justice, observing a punitive turn in relation to women but also noting complexities which mean that the story is not one of a straightforward 'juggernaut of control' over women (Gelsthorpe 2004), but a rather more subtle penal-welfare panoply of regulation. There are some very positive developments in policy and practice. In the second part of the chapter I discuss some of the significant debates and developments which have marked an increasingly distinct way of dealing with women which includes efforts at normative compliance. In the final section I draw out what we can learn from work with women in the past two decades in particular, and how this fuels thinking about the role of 'community', relational dimensions of criminal justice, values in criminal justice, compliance, and legitimacy. These aspects of service delivery contribute to 'reasonableness' and reflect many of Tony's interests.

A brief overview of policy developments regarding women, crime, and criminal justice

Criminal justice has been characterised by a certain gloominess in the past 40 years, with a disproportionate rise in the women's prison population in England and Wales in the 1990s (Gelsthorpe and Morris 2002). In 1994 men were 21 times more likely to go to prison than women; in 2002 they were only 12 times more likely to do so (Ministry of Justice 2010). The increase in women's imprisonment during this time must be the most oft-quoted statistic. Various explanations were pursued to explain this increase: changes in the nature and seriousness of women's crime; increases in the number of women being convicted; the possibility of women and men being treated more equally in sentencing (women being treated more severely, like men); changes in sentencing patterns; increases in the length of women's sentences of imprisonment; and changes in the 'type' of women sentenced to imprisonment (Gelsthorpe and Morris 2002; Hedderman 2004). None of these matters alone provided an adequate answer to the evident punitive turn towards women. Indeed, most of the women in prison in 2002 remained criminally unsophisticated, serving their first custodial sentence and received into prison for property-related offending. They were really the same as those who were in prison in 1990.

A key explanation for the 'punitive turn' towards women comes from David Garland's (2001) work on the 'culture of control', where he describes a shift from rehabilitative interventions to more negative and retributive punishments. This shift has had twists and turns in regard to women, not least because of the themes of pathology, domesticity, and respectability which have dominated criminal justice discourses relating to women. This has meant that a penal-welfare approach has endured. These themes (all of which have been subject to strong critique) lend themselves to notions of women being 'mad, bad, or sad', or either caring or neglectful mothers, and to familial justice. In turn, these things mean that the punitive turn towards women has never been as 'complete' as it has towards men (Gelsthorpe, 2004) but this is a side issue in the context of the narrative here.

A related explanation for the increase in the use of custodial sentences for women relates to Pat Carlen's (2002) notion of 'carceral clawback'. Despite increasing acceptance that the needs of women offenders were different from those of men and required different provision, it was evident that there was a pervasive and enduring belief that only relatively minor and superficial modifications to existing provision within existing structures were required. Yet, as Carlen (2002) argued, it is important to resist the myth that, as a result of feminist-informed reforms, women's prisons were becoming benign places of treatment and rehabilitation. She warned against being distracted from the reality that prisons (including women's prisons) are places of control where matters of security will always prevail over more constructive considerations such as education, drug treatment, or rehabilitative programmes.

Putting these complexities aside, what is more interesting is why there was a gradual falling off in the use of imprisonment for women. Indeed, data show that the annual number of women received into custody on remand (pre-trial and pre-sentence) decreased by 18% between 2002 and 2009; the decrease for males was 12% (Ministry of Justice 2009). What is relevant here is that the cumulative and compelling body of research seeking to remove barriers to the provision of more appropriate methods of dealing with women offenders began to emerge in the 1980s and early 1990s; these research findings identified that women offenders needed specifically women-centred provision.

Awareness of criminal justice discrimination on grounds of race and gender came from different quarters. By 1989 an interest in race and gender had become embedded in probation service culture, and probation officer training in particular. The *Probation Journal* reflected this heightened professional and political sensitivity by publishing articles on the criminalisation and imprisonment of black women (Chigwada 1989), mothers in custody and the punishment of children (White 1989), empowering women (Buckley and Wilson 1989) and women-wise penology (Carlen 1989). In a sense, these articles provided a comprehensive and sophisticated analysis of the *practical problems* of working with female offenders, increasing numbers of whom were being sent to prison. But they also suggest a willingness to locate those problems within a broad critique of social and criminal justice policy.

Around this time, there was increasing recognition that women who offend often have different needs from men, as well as growing awareness that female offenders frequently have histories of abuse. Such awakenings (often feminist-inspired) prompted a bottom-up development of group work programmes for women in some probation services (Mistry 1989; Jones et al. 1991). The development of these programmes was regarded as a means of ensuring that the particular needs of women were addressed in a safe and non-threatening environment that was conducive to the development of the 'reciprocal relationships' which practitioners had frequently identified as central to women's growth and change. The establishment of a major women's groupwork programme in 1993 in the Hereford and Worcester Probation Service similarly reflected the need to provide women with the kind of support that was appropriate, as well as to provide the courts with constructive alternatives to imprisonment (Roberts 2002). In much of this work there was a conscious aim to contextualise rather than pathologise women offenders' problems by facilitating links with outside agencies: a holistic approach was needed, partnerships were important, and linking women into normal mainstream services was paramount (Worrall and Gelsthorpe 2009). There was even the emergence of the notion of a 'gender-conscious service' (Wright and Kemshall 1994: 73) and encouragement to recognise the reality of women offenders' daily lives and the obstacles they faced in reporting and engaging with supervision (Wright and Kemshall 1994: 73). This went beyond the 'bottom up' groupwork initiatives to call for changes at practice, organisational, and structural levels to achieve 'feminist probation practice'. 'Gender is on the agenda', it was conceded, 'but a co-ordinated approach is required if consistent *best practice* is to be achieved' (1994: 79; emphasis added).

In a Special Issue of the Probation Journal on the Criminal Justice Act 1991, Orme (1992) took issue with the rather nebulous statement regarding the introduction of section 95 requiring the Secretary of State to publish annual information so as to facilitate the avoidance of discrimination on grounds of race or sex or any other improper ground in the administration of criminal justice. She doubted that sufficient information could be gathered, and even more that it would make a difference to the treatment of women. Her Majesty's Inspectorate of Probation slowly caught on to all these concerns, reviewed progress, and began to look more carefully at the provisions for women who had offended. Early contentions that women offenders were not dealt with by the probation service in the same way as men, with the result that they were sometimes precluded, inadvertently, from the full range of community sentences, were rehearsed and addressed. 'Providing appropriate supervision provision for the relatively small numbers of women on community sentences was often seen to be economically unviable' and community service (now known as unpaid work) was perceived to be a particularly 'macho environment' (HMIP 1996: 13–14). The same report expressed concern that the provision of accommodation, both pre and post-trial, for women who needed a safe and secure environment was patchy. The unsatisfactory nature of hostel accommodation provision for women had been recognised from the early years of the 1990s. The small numbers requiring such accommodation meant that women had either to travel many miles from their homes to reside in women-only hostels, or to be accommodated in mixed hostels that reserved a small number of beds for women. In 1996, Emma Wincup reported on research that demonstrated the difficulties in guaranteeing privacy, safety, and equality of service for female residents in mixed hostels (Wincup 1996).

By 1998, offending behaviour programmes based on cognitive behavioural psychology were central to the delivery of probation supervision but there were concerns about the absence of such programmes for 'serious or persistent women offenders in an all-female environment in the community' (Hay and Stirling 1998: 36). I should add that the case for 'all-female' groups (with all-female staff) had been made almost a decade earlier by Pat Carlen (1990) and was well recognised by many female probation officers, but it had to be restated.

With cumulative evidence and gathering concerns, slowly it was recognised that formal equality before the law regarding men and women could result in inequality of impact. Underpinning a number of critical contributions on sentencing, community sentences, and probation practice regarding women was a strong assumption that women should be kept out of prison. The role of commentators, whether academic or practice-based, was to highlight the discriminatory impact of sentencing decisions. However, the policy climate only began to thaw when campaigning organisations (especially the Prison Reform Trust and the Fawcett Society) raised the public profile of women offenders.

The increasing recognition that women have different 'criminogenic'/crime-related needs gradually led to policy and practice changes. While research evidence indicates that *some* factors may be *similar* (unemployment and substance misuse, for instance), there is now convincing evidence that how difficulties have come about and how they contribute to offending may be different for women and men, and that there are other difficulties which appear to be more specific to women too (physical and sexual abuse, for example: Hollin and Palmer 2006). There is now a substantial body of methodologically sound work which supports interventions informed by women's needs. Blanchette and Brown's (2006) analysis of the assessment and treatment of women offenders highlights the need for gender-sensitive risk assessment and for treatment services to be delivered in a style and a mode that match the learning style and needs of offenders.

Accountability towards people who have offended

Serving offenders in this way, being accountable towards them by recognising differences between them, is important. A common approach to accountability revolves around managerial and cost issues (good stewardship of taxpayers' money) and around obligations towards 'the community' (Clarke and Newman 1997). Equally, debates about accountability often include an important focus on responsibilities towards victims (Crawford and Goodey 2000). What about accountability towards the offender as well? Arguably, it is incumbent upon the criminal justice system to sentence offenders to disposals that actually work or are useful (notwithstanding the different aims of sentencing). By its very intervention into offenders' lives, the criminal justice system is seeking to inculcate values which we would associate with good citizenship. A respect for individuality and social diversity is arguably a key corollary both of an adequate concept of citizenship and of the principle of social inclusion. Thus accountability towards the offender can be conceptualised *socially and culturally*; that is, we need to recognise social differences (*gender differences* chief among these) in order to maximise the potential for effectiveness. As Tom Tyler (1990) has suggested, normative compliance may arise from an individual's general moral sense, or from a changed perspective on the world due to some life event (such as marriage). It may also come from a morally based perception that the demand for compliance (law-abiding behaviour) derives from legal authorities that are *legitimate*. This means procedural justice, but it means other things too. Paternoster et al. (1997) spell out the essential ingredients of justice which appear to facilitate legitimacy: representation, consistency, impartiality, accuracy, correctability, and *ethicality*. It is this last point which interests me here, for if legitimacy demands that legal authorities treat offenders with respect and dignity, we might argue that recognition of gender differences in the delivery of penalties is an essential part of the required respect for offenders in order to facilitate active citizenship on their part (Gelsthorpe 2001). This is an essential part of the 'reasonableness' to which Sen (2009) draws our attention. All of this has obvious implications for the focus and content of interventions for women and there is evidence of attempts to implement practical, positive, and gender-specific interventions for women in the community in particular.

Community-based developments

Some practice-led developments deserve more attention than I can give here, but to give a handful, Hereford and Worcestershire—under Chief Officer Jenny Roberts—moved from a group work programme for women to recognition that they needed women-centred provision. Following research on women's needs—including careful analysis of Hereford and Worcestershire caseloads—poverty, abusive relationships, child abuse survival, alcohol, and drugs were identified as key areas. Acknowledging women's distinctive and multiple needs, a multi-session programme—a 'model of change'—for women offenders was created (Roberts 2002: 113). The programme sessions were firmly placed in the context of crime reduction and delivered through a single centre (the Asha Centre) by specialist women supervising officers. The work there was supported by the use of Assessment, Case Management and Evaluation (ACE), subsequently superseded by an Offender Assessment System (OASys) in England and Wales, but still used in other jurisdictions. This was a radical and innovative step. Following submissions from the Chief Officers of Probation, the Government's Strategy for Women Offenders in 2000 could identify only 19 group work programmes specifically for women and only one pilot offending behaviour programme, with another 'being developed' (Home Office 2000: 18). Despite the increase in Community Service Orders (as they were then) being given to women, none of the six community service pathfinders[3] (funded by the Home Office) was aimed exclusively at women offenders.

However, these practice-based developments fuelled energy. While there was no avowed interest in decarceration, the Labour years between 1997 and 2010 produced a range of progressive ideas and practical developments: a Women's Offending Reduction Programme (WORP) in 2002, an Action Plan in 2004, a cross-departmental liaison group in 2006, guidance concerning services for women on probation, and support to existing initiatives to improve community-based responses to women's mental health needs. The Women's Policy Team negotiated £9.15 million to build on best practice developed by small-scale initiatives such as the 218 Residential Centre for women in Scotland and the Asha Community Centre in England and Wales, and supported a demonstration programme, *Together Women* (TW) (five projects across two regions of the country), which sought to provide holistic support for women who were formerly or currently convicted or whose social exclusion needs were thought to put them at risk of offending. The Ministry of Justice's own analysis of the creation of these centres[4] for convicted women and those at risk of offending—which were introduced between late 2006 and early 2007—suggested that TW was seen by local stakeholders as filling an important gap in provision (though there were still concerns about the supply of suitable accommodation for women, access to counselling, and mental health outreach services). One distinctive feature of these community-based centres was the acknowledgement that women could continue to turn to the TW projects whenever they felt they were struggling, long after court orders had ended and long after other agencies, and perhaps even families and friends, had given up on them. In other words, they served as community drop-in *centres*.

Where were these *community* services based? Not in the middle of housing estates where women lived, but certainly in the centre of towns and cities, accessible on bus routes, child-friendly, where women might drop in

[3] Community Service Pathfinders were part of the programme of research funded under the Crime Reduction Programme. These innovative and evaluative projects were developed as part of the 'What Works' initiative which had been pursued by the Probation Service since the mid-1990s.

[4] The centres (known as services in some areas) typically provide holistic support for women who are vulnerable in other ways, offering debt counselling, personal counselling, employment skills development, help with formal educational qualifications, clothing exchanges, a place to meet their probation officers, and offending-based programmes (e.g. acquisitive crime programmes), for example.

for a cuppa as well as to see their probation officer. While Tony has offered insightful criticism of the lack of community-based provision for offenders, the development of women-specific provision has made a return to the community in a most meaningful way.

Baroness Jean Corston's Report (2007) and the further development of holistic services in the community

A further drive to create community centres for women came when the Labour government was still in power. Partly triggered by the high number of suicides in a single year by women prisoners in Styal prison, Baroness Corston, an experienced Labour Party politician, was commissioned to 'conduct an independent review of "vulnerable" women offenders and other vulnerable women who come into contact with the police or courts, identifying gaps in provision for their needs within the criminal justice system and related health services'.

The requirement was that:

> The review should be focused on the group of women offenders who have multiple needs, particularly those women whose risk factors could lead them to harm themselves in prison, and take fully into account existing and planned work. (Corston 2007, Review Terms of Reference, 2007, Appendix B)

Baroness Jean Corston's expressions of dismay when she introduced her report on women with particular vulnerabilities in the criminal justice system in 2007 were profound and far-reaching:

> I have been dismayed at the high prevalence of institutional misunderstanding within the criminal justice system of the things that matter to women and at the shocking level of unmet need. Yet the compelling body of research which has accumulated over many years consistently points to remedies . . . There can be few topics that have been so exhaustively researched to such little practical effect as the plight of women in the criminal justice system. The volume of material might lead one to suppose that this is a highly controversial area, which might account in some way for the lack of progress and insight in the way women

continue to be treated. This is not the case. There is a great deal of evidence of fundamental differences between male and female offenders. (Corston 2007: 16)

Jean Corston's input not only made a major contribution to the cumulative arguments that gender-sensitive and gender-specific approaches are important, but also prompted the government to give further funding for community centres. The report contained 43 recommendations which revolved around the need for holistic care for women in conflict with the law in the community. This main recommendation for community centres to continue to offer holistic care for women was reinforced by the almost simultaneous publication of the Fawcett Society's commissioned survey of existing community centres and services which could potentially be adapted for women offenders (Gelsthorpe et al. 2007). The survey report fuelled debate by identifying nine lessons to be taken into account when providing services for women in the community. Drawing on an extensive range of literature on women's needs, 'what works' with women, and 'women and desistance', the researchers argued that services should:

1. Be women-only (or women-centred) to foster safety and a sense of community, and to enable staff to develop expertise in work with women.
2. Integrate offenders with non-offenders so as to normalise women's experiences and facilitate a supportive environment for learning.
3. Foster women's empowerment so they gain sufficient self-esteem to engage directly in problem-solving themselves, and feel motivated to seek appropriate employment.
4. Utilise ways of working with women which draw on what is known about their effective learning styles.
5. Take a holistic and practical stance to helping women address social problems which may be linked to their offending.
6. Facilitate links with mainstream agencies—especially health, debt advice, and counselling.
7. Have the capacity and flexibility to allow women to return to the centre or programme for 'top ups' of continued support and development where required.
8. Ensure that women have a supportive milieu or mentor to whom they can turn when they have completed any offending-related

programmes, since personal support is likely to be as important as any direct input addressing offending behaviour.

9. Provide women with practical help with transport and childcare so that they can maintain their involvement in the centre. (Gelsthorpe et al. 2007)

Thus there was huge momentum for change. Drawing on the favourable impact of the TW project and existing expertise from practitioners (probation and voluntary sector organisations), and prompted by Baroness Corston's report,[5] the Ministry of Justice found funding (some £15m) to promote the extension of work in women's community centres around the country to provide service interventions for women in contact with the criminal justice system. The creation and promotion of an 'Equality Duty', embodied in the Equality Act 2010, also served an important purpose in emphasising that discrimination needed to be addressed, including discrimination against women, and that women's needs ought to be properly recognised.

There has been continued evidence of the need for gender-responsiveness over the years, with rapid evidence assessments of what works with women (Lart et al. 2008; Stewart and Gobeil 2015). The second of these, in particular, provides some interesting insights. The authors suggest that substance abuse treatment interventions in prisons, in particular, or structured therapeutic community-based programmes which apply cognitive behavioural practices focusing on skills development, are helpful. There is also suggestion that a gender-responsive cognitive behavioural programme with emphasis on existing strengths and competencies, as well as skills acquisition, is useful to facilitate pathways out of crime. Further, community-based opioid maintenance can result in reduced offending patterns while women are in treatment. Booster programmes and treatment reflecting gender-responsive approaches show promise relative to gender-neutral programmes.

We have also seen the production of a National Framework for Women Offenders (NOMS 2008) which sets out the kinds of services which were to be provided (subsequently replaced by a NOMS Women and Equalities-authored report, *A Distinct Approach: A Guide to Working with Women Offenders* (NOMS 2012)). The government's most recent 'framework' for

[5] With support from the Equalities Office and a collaboration of grant-making trusts and foundations who wanted to see action following the report.

addressing the needs of women was published as the Government's *Female Offender Strategy* (Ministry of Justice 2018).

Beyond this, and building on early work on the importance of addressing women's needs directly, the New Economics Foundation (2008) strongly suggested that we *all* benefit from investing in alternatives to prison for women offenders. The authors went so far as to indicate that using women's centre provision as an alternative to custody can deliver £14 of social value for every £1 invested. Later research from the New Economics Foundation (Nicholles and Whitehead 2012) investigated the impact of the 'Women's Centres' on women offenders across five sites, and suggested improvement in relation to women's optimism, autonomy, and self-efficacy, and establishing supportive relationships.

We have also witnessed growth in the number of women's centres. Indeed, there were nearly 50 community centres for women at one point. Needless to say, this is not a story of success after success; every positive step has been hard fought for, and there have been particular challenges and reverses along the way. The funding from government has often been uncertain, leaving coalitions of funders to plug gaps; some centres have closed because of a lack of funding (Gelsthorpe and Russell 2018). The Offender Rehabilitation Act 2014 introduced an extension of post-custody statutory monitoring and supervision to people who have offended, for a mandatory period of 12 months. It also amended licence conditions for those serving sentences of 12 to 24 months in order to ensure that they do not receive shorter periods of supervision than those serving sentences of less than one year. The Act also created a divided service provision for those under supervision in the community, with the less serious offenders to be supervised by staff within the 21 Community Rehabilitation Companies (CRCs) commissioned by government to work across 21 contract package areas, and the National Probation Service to manage and supervise the more serious offenders. Combined, these two structural changes raised concerns about how far women law-breakers' needs would be met. Would the newly created CRCs be able to address women's needs, for example, or would the incentive of 'payment by results' lead the CRCs to focus on larger cohorts of men? Would women benefit from the new supervision arrangements, given that they generally fall within the 'less serious' offending groups? There is a telling clue to the success *or otherwise* of the government's move to privatise elements of supervision in the fact that further structural change, from 26 June 2021, made the National Probation Service responsible for the supervision of everyone subject to supervision within the community; in other words, the probation service is to be reunified and returned to the public sector. While some agencies involved in the CRCS will continue to provide specialist rehabilitation services, payment by results will be no more (Ministry of Justice 2021). As for the impact of introducing supervision for women (and men) receiving short sentences of custody, this has not been a success. On the contrary, the number of women recalled to prison has risen dramatically since the end of 2014. Many women have been recalled for breaching the conditions of their licence rather than for new offending (Ministry of Justice 2017). We might add that the high use of short custody sentences for women has continued and the use of community orders has continued to decline (ibid). Moreover, the government's announcement in December 2020 that that it intends to create 500 more prison places for women (Grierson 2021), flies in the face of evidence of what is needed, and that of the Female Offender Strategy (Ministry of Justice 2018), with its emphasis on 'taking an evidence-based approach to rehabilitating offenders', which argues that 'short custodial sentences are less effective in reducing reoffending than community penalties' and 'good community management works'.

There is more to say about reverses, missed opportunities, and contradictions in the development of policy regarding women, but it is important not to lose sight of some of the positive action witnessed over time, and here there is resonance with Tony's vision and values for criminal justice.

The relational dimension: Being human and going the extra mile

In describing the government-sponsored prototype for community centres, Hedderman et al. (2011), who evaluated *Together Women*, make a plea to learn from women themselves. Outcome evaluations which rely exclusively or mainly on information in project databases and criminal records may not capture key elements which make an intervention 'work'. Neglecting service users' insights may lead to underestimates of resource needs, unrealistic target setting, and the eventual abandonment of promising ideas.

What have we learned from women as service users? Women involved with the community projects developed a sense of 'respect and community' which made them feel optimistic about the future (Hedderman et al. 2011: 30). The feeling that *Together Women* workers were genuinely interested in the women's welfare led to positive responses to visits and to the telephone calls they received to remind them of appointments. As Hedderman et al. (2011: 11) indicate, one client returned to the project after not attending for some time and found:

> It's nice to know that somebody thinks about you and that, you know, there is somebody there to turn to … I thought it'd be like another authority … like, erm, police, probation, social services kind of, you know, making these rules, setting down, I must do this, and I must do that, and it's not been anything like that … obviously, they're not gonna put up with my bloomin' nonsense, and all that sort of thing—but they just tell me what I should be doing, really, and then basically they leave it to me whether I take it on board, or phone me and try to encourage me, 'Have you done that?' you know.

Another woman explained:

> I went to anger management but then I wasn't so good at coming so I stopped. I got two letters from them writing and saying I haven't been for a few days asking if I'm alright, they said if there's any problems get in touch with them, that they're looking forward to hearing from you. They wrote twice in four days. I live on my own so that was good of them wasn't it? Someone does care. I was thrilled to bits when I opened the letter. (Cited in Hedderman et al. 2011: 11).

The key themes which emerge are that what matters to women as service users is experience of key workers who 'see service users as people, not cases', 'being accepted and respected', 'being in a women only environment', and being in a 'quality' environment—by which is meant a good physical environment where colour schemes were bright and furniture modern and comfortable. As one woman put it:

> Yeah, I've been in trouble with the law again, actually, but that was through me alcohol and through me partner, but I would've possibly been in *more* trouble had I not had this place … You know, if I didn't have this place to come to, I would've just totally gave up, I think, a couple of time, you know. But instead, I've got myself up and come here instead and it's helped me. (Cited in Hedderman et al. 2011: 14)

Other service users have described matters in similar ways. ISIS is a community service for women offenders in Gloucestershire. In an evaluation report, one service user explained why she attended in this way: 'It's somewhere I can come and be safe. There's a day centre just down the road, where my doctors is … where I have to go, but all they talk about is drugs, drink, jail, down there, and here they talk about recovery. (ISIS 2012: 3).

Such claims are repeated in a number of evaluations of women's community centres and services. At the Turnaround Project in Wales, the clients were unanimously positive about their experiences (Holloway and Brookman 2010). Issues that were highlighted as being particularly positive included the range of support that was offered, the flexible pace of working, the confidential nature of discussions, the non-judgemental nature of the staff, and the ability of staff to uplift them and instil confidence and self-esteem in them. The women were also aware that the project was helping to empower them in various ways. As one woman put it:

> I can do that now. I'll go to this place and that person and it's just giving me all the knowledge or helping me to gain the knowledge because I was making phone calls this morning to the repairs and [she] said 'I'm not making them, you pick up the phone and you do it'. Y'know putting the power … responsibility back onto me so I can be responsible for my own life instead of looking to other people to solve everything for me. (Cited in Holloway and Brookman 2010: 19).

In Scotland, the 218 Service, based in Glasgow, opened in 2003 as a specialist facility (day and residential provision) for women offenders and as a direct response to reviews of experiences (especially the experiences of highly vulnerable women repeatedly sent to prison for short sentences). The 218 Service also emerged out of recognition that that there had to be a better way of working with women to offer a safe place and space, help them reintegrate into society, and enable them to reconnect with their communities (Beglan 2013). As Beglan (2013) describes, regular reviews demonstrate an increase in positive outcomes for the women over time in relation to substance misuse, living situation, social functioning, physical health, psychological well-being, and, importantly, criminal activity. As one service user put it:

> ... was just amazing and I'm so glad I had the opportunity and took on board everything that we had done. I didn't think I could have done half of it and I finished and completed it. It's made me look at myself differently as well, and that I can do things and it's given me confidence in myself. I didn't like myself for a long, long time and it's just wee bits, but it's coming together... (Cited in Beglan 2013: 164).

Another woman indicated that 'if it wasn't for 218 I don't know where I'd be. I'd be in jail or up the road doing something stupid but I'm here and I'm straight and I've never had that in all those years. I don't know where I'd be without this place' (cited in Beglan 2013: 166).

The Inspire Women's Project in Northern Ireland has also produced positive findings. The community-based project aimed to 'develop and deliver in the community a new, enhanced range of women-specific services which directly contribute to reducing women's offending through targeted community-based interventions' (DOJ 2010). The evaluation involved analysis of a group of women who were referred to Inspire between October 2008 and July 2010, with the majority of women (89%) being on community sentences. Most of the women (72%) were compliant with their community sentences and the women were very positive about the quality and variety of support made available to them, including the women-only space (for reasons relating to feeling safe), peer support, and practical help in dealing with debts and housing (Easton and Matthews 2011). Interviews with 29 out of the 37 women involved indicated that they had not committed any further offences since engaging with Inspire in Belfast (a rate of 78%). The holistic approach to women's problems and experiences rather than an exclusive focus on offending behaviour, combined with a supportive non-judgmental approach, contributed to its success.

When Helen Grant (then Justice Minister) chatted to 'Hilary', sent to the Anawim Centre in Birmingham in 2013 under the specified activity requirement of her court order, Hilary said:

> Anawim has been my godsend ... I was scared stiff of coming here, but the minute you walk through the door, everyone is so positive. They know why you're here, but it doesn't seem to matter. (Staffordshire and West Midlands Probation Trust, 2013)

From a qualitative analysis of interviews with service users in a range of community centres for women in England and Wales, Radcliffe, Hunter, and Vass (2015) concluded that relationships with key workers and peers, alongside the facilitation of education and employment opportunities, were crucial in supporting women to get their lives in order and to set a clear track for desistance from crime. While measurement of reoffending following contact with the community centres was initially very complex (Jolliffe et al. 2011), the Inspire Project at Brighton Women's Centre produced a similar story of success, with 90% of women referred to the Centre within a particular cohort completing their Community Orders through the support of the Centre, and with notable reductions in reoffending (Inspire 2017).

Compliance and legitimacy

As previously indicated, Tony is chief among the researchers who have looked at compliance (Bottoms 2001). Tony has identified four types of compliance relevant to community sentence completion: instrumental; constraint-based; routinised; and normative. In instrumental compliance, the offender weighs the pros and cons attached to programme completion, concluding that it is in his or her best interests to complete it. For example, s/he may deem it preferable to complete a programme and remain in the community rather than refusing and being sent to prison because of being in breach of conditions attached to a community order. Constraint-based compliance is a product of specific restrictions, either physical or social (such as residency requirements, target hardening, or curfews—with electronic monitoring to enforce this), which limit an offender's ability to avoid compliance. Routinised compliance, on the other hand, is automated and a function of habit. Here, programme attendance becomes such a regular part of the offender's schedule that s/he no longer needs to actively decide to comply. Finally, normative compliance stems from an offender's belief in the legitimacy of the sentencing authority. For example, an offender recognises that s/he has a problem (e.g., substance misuse or anger management) that programme compliance might help to solve. It represents an internalisation of the values of the supervisory authority and indicates compliance with the spirit (substantive) as well as the letter (formal) dimensions of the sentence or requirements (McBarnet 2004; Carlen 2002).

Robinson and McNeill (2010) have taken this work further by giving attention to the idea that 'formal' and 'substantive' dimensions of compliance need to be recognised. 'Formal compliance' is characterised by an offender who 'technically' complies with the requirements or conditions set, but who does not actively engage beyond that point. Substantive compliance is characterised by the active engagement of an offender who not only meets the requirements or conditions, but who also seeks to engage and address issues. It is this '[un] auditable' compliance which Robinson and McNeill (2010: 370) see as problematic, yet essential to 'normative compliance', where the offender desists from offending behaviour because they have understood the good sense in not doing so—for themselves and others.

Thus compliance can arise from self-interest, social norms, force, or simple habit as well as any combination of these. Ideally, the different dimensions might work together to promote both short (programme completion) and long-term (desistance) compliance. However, the precise mechanisms involved might vary between people who have offended. Certainly, recognition of gendered 'needs' would need to be considered here alongside the age/crime curve, the seriousness of offences committed, the length of orders, and the number of requirements or conditions attached.

From the evidence of the operation of community centres for women, there is strong indication of moves towards compliance in terms of women living less chaotic and more regulated lives. The evaluation of the women-only demonstration projects alone—*Together Women*—have been seen by local stakeholders as not only 'filling an important gap in provision by linking up what was already available more effectively and by adding to the range of services available' (Hedderman et al. 2008: 26), but also having an impact on reconvictions. The 'women-only' nature of the projects has proved to be important, as have service users' feelings that the staff in the centres (projects) seem 'genuinely interested in them as individuals' and are 'prepared to go the extra mile' (2008: 26). Judith Rumgay's (2004) use of the concept of 'normalsmiths' is relevant here: that is, women in conflict with the law belong alongside other women, emphasising that they are women first, and 'offenders' second.

The small-scale nature of the evaluation studies mentioned supports the idea that a more focused and systematic analysis of women's compliance is required, but we can also draw from other research evidence which suggests that women's engagement in existing interventions is determined by the fact that they learn in different ways to men (Belenky et al. 1986; see also Covington 1998). Women-only environments are also thought to facilitate growth and development (Zaplin 1998) and thus the evidence adds up to a need to work with women in non-authoritarian co-operative settings, where women are empowered to engage in social and personal change (Gelsthorpe 2020).

The range of women's community centres and services which have been built up over time embody these principles or variants on them (Gelsthorpe and Russell 2018), including strong relational dimensions. The message is clear: situational, practical, and gender-specific factors are relevant to compliance. We have learned a good deal from the women's centres and from women users. There has been movement away from generic programmes which aim to address women's *presumed* needs to gender-sensitive and gender-specific interventions. This may be the product of women recognising or believing that the interventions to which they are assigned can help address the problems which led to the offending behaviour. Certainly, there is strong indication that the interventions via community centres are legitimate. Compliance will only work when interventions themselves make sense. Returning to Shapland and Bottoms et al. (2012: 43): 'Building genuine relationships that demonstrate "care" about the person being supervised, their desistance, and their future, and not just control/monitoring/surveillance' is one of the keys to effective supervision and a route to compliance.

Towards a conclusion: Values and vision

Thus far I have provided an overview of developments in regard to provision for women in the criminal justice system, focusing particularly on accountability towards people who have offended, the creation of community centres, the experience of service users who use such centres and services and who convey the importance of non-judgmental relationships, and the impact of this kind of holistic and problem-solving approach on compliance. I want to return to the question of values here, touching on Tony's quest for a value-laden criminal justice system and on his interest in theology.

As Tony and Ronald Preston argue in *The Coming Penal Crisis*, theology is about so much more than the exigesis of the best texts or sacred books, or doctrinal issues or ecclesiastical institutions: it is concerned with understanding the nature and significance of human life and human well-being in society, 'including the State, and the legal and penal systems which go with it' (Bottoms and Preston, 1980: Preface x). *The Coming Penal Crisis* was the result of a consultation between academic criminologists and a group of theologians, including representatives from the probation and prison services, prison chaplains, and the then director of the Howard League for Penal Reform. It was written in 1980 in the midst of a penal crisis regarding overcrowded prisons, prison riots, and the collapse of the rehabilitative ideal, following strong theoretical objections (American Friends Service Committee (1971) and damning indictment of costs and ineffectiveness (Martinson 1974). Thus the interdisciplinary consultation involved searching for values to fill the serious vacuum in penal thought. Notwithstanding the fact that we live in a context of pluralistic religious, philosophical, and value commitments in society, exploration of Christian values to fill the vacuum makes as much sense now as it did then. At its simplest, theology is about what it is, or might be, to be human in the world. Christian doctrine involves a set of principles by which to live (if aspirationally); this involves considerations of 'sin', 'free will' and evil, moral repugnance, just deserts and how we work them out, the State's duty to care, and how to create communities which protect and enable human living together, as well as notions of responsibility (am I my brother's keeper?), how to maximise 'good', what to value and what not to value, and other complex strands of thinking.

In the closing pages of that book, Tony and Michael Taylor acknowledge the complexities of the task of identifying future penal policy options. There was no absolute consensus in the consultations which led to the book, but there was agreement on one thing: acceptance of the structural changes in the penal system that the critique of treatment requires, 'coupled with insistence that hope for the future and respect for persons must not be abandoned in penal systems'. This strikes me as being a good place to reassert this value, and to suggest that it shines through all the work on women in conflict with the law. Rowan Williams, in *Being Human*, discusses this question in some detail via 'consciousness' and 'what makes us persons', concluding that a person 'is the point at which relationships intersect, where a difference may be made and new relations created' (Williams 2018: 32). Being in relationship is a way in which 'each of us has a presence or a meaning in someone else's existence' (Williams 2018: 33). Christian philosophy is relevant in that biblical teachings emphasise that the human condition is one of created beings who are in relationship with another; relationships through which we are called to love.

Work with women who have offended in communities, alongside other women, where (largely third sector) staff, in conjunction with visiting probation staff, have demonstrated that a non-judgmental attitude can bring hope to individual women via an emphasis on the relational, is telling. Many have written about the 'theology of hope' (see, e.g., Pannenberg and Grenz 1990). Equally important is the work of Bonhoeffer (Green 1999), with his theology of sociality, incorporating the basic Christian concepts of 'person', 'primal state', 'sin', and 'revelation'. In Matthew 25, Christ identifies himself with the poor, the prisoner, and the foreigner. Christian salvation is not a private reality occurring in the solitude of the inner self, but something which requires charity. Charity requires justice, and arguably justice would decay without charity. In other words, there is a responsibility to participate in the public square. While one cannot legislate for criminal justice to be based on such precepts, one can seek out opportunities to infuse criminal justice practice with these values. In discussions, Tony frequently reminds people that we are social beings, with all the complexity that this brings, and with all the opportunities for relational moments and positive possibilities.

8

Desistance from Crime and the Potential Role of Restorative Justice

Joanna Shapland[1]

Criminology: Making links or creating fissures?

As an academic area evolves and becomes more populated, there seems to be an immutable progression from the early, tentative and exploratory, forays into the new subject to deeper and more content-limited work. Subject areas become more specialised; they develop their own technical language ('jargon') and specialised terms; and the literature to which each sub-area refers may become more self-referential and more self-contained. Occasional interdisciplinary pioneers or refugees from other academic disciplines may enter, bringing with them fresh breaths of outside air, but there is often little overlap between what may become parallel evolutions of ideas in different sub-areas or sub-disciplines.

Criminology is no different from other disciplines in this evolution. It may itself have been created originally from law, sociology, and medicine, but initial disputes about whether it was merely an offshoot of what were often seen as more solidly founded parent disciplines (Rock 2007) have given way to specialism within criminology. Scholars are often now defined as specialists in crime prevention, or policing, or youth justice, or victims (Sebba and Berenblum 2014), or critical criminology, or media, or many other areas. This is not surprising: it is very difficult to be expert in all the methodologies used or keep up with the ever-increasing literature.

[1] An earlier version of this chapter was presented in a paper given at the conference to celebrate the work of Professor Sir Anthony Bottoms in Cambridge on 30 November 2007.

Joanna Shapland, *Desistance from Crime and the Potential Role of Restorative Justice*. In: *Crime, Justice, and Social Order*. Edited by: Alison Liebling, Joanna Shapland, Richard Sparks, and Justice Tankebe,
Oxford University Press. © Alison Liebling, Joanna Shapland, Richard Sparks, and Justice Tankebe 2022.
DOI: 10.1093/oso/9780192859600.003.0008

The danger in this increasing specialism arises, though, if it is merely an academic preoccupation, not shared by those involved in the professional development of systems of justice or in the lives of those studied by researchers. In other words, the academic study of policing may come to perceive itself as completely other than the academic study of penology, or judging, or media depictions of crime, but are the concepts used in policing fundamentally different from the work of probation or judging or journalists? Is the way in which people start offending and increase their participation different from the way in which they move out of it? Is there anyone there to make the theoretical and practical links?

Tony Bottoms (2008b), in his essay on 'the relationship between theory and empirical observations in criminology', comments: 'A "theory" can be a theory of anything' (2008b: 76). How that subject matter is bounded and informed—its theoretical 'spectacles'—is therefore really important, because that will both guide our empirical observations and also influence our realist judgements of how accurate our observations are.[2] He warns specifically against theoretical preoccupations becoming divorced from empirical study.

He also refers to the perceived need for younger researchers to 'get their name known' by presenting themselves as specialists. This can lead—but in his view and my view should not lead—to 'theoretical pigeonholing' (p. 82), whereby the researcher labels particular other researchers as adhering to a different theoretical standpoint and so having nothing of interest to say on that particular area. This forms another danger of specialists becoming 'islands' of theoretical development and knowledge.

In the early 1980s, I had the privilege to assist in the translation and editing of Hurwitz and Christiansen's (1983) *Criminology*, originally published in Danish. It is an omnivorous tome covering the 'science of criminology', but looking at sociological, economic, psychiatric, psychological, and legal elements which affect criminality and the occurrence of crime. It ranges from the early strain of economic work of Bonger (1905) and von Mayr (1914), who related crime levels to the price of grain, to family relationships. Its very omnivorousness has proved its strength over time: it is still one of my sources on surprisingly little-researched questions

[2] Those holding a strongly constructivist view will of course not wish to make any judgements about the accuracy of observations, because all observations will, for them, be constructed by the researcher and the observer. However, such a strongly relativist position does not make it easy to progress the discipline's understanding of its subject matter.

about crime such as 'What happens if there suddenly aren't any police?', or the rather up-to-date problem, in our insecure age, about what happens to crime rates in time of war. Hurwitz and Christiansen's strength is in their attempts to hold all these different approaches to crime together and to compare and contrast them.

It would be impossible to produce such an omnibus volume today that could cover all the current topics of research on crime and criminal justice. Even such key reference tomes as the *Oxford Handbook of Criminology* (Liebling et al. 2017) have made a selection of major topics. Criminology has matured and specialised. My question in this chapter is whether middle-aged criminology is acquiring the deep, rich patina of age, similar to that of really good furniture or Italian Renaissance painting.[3] Has criminology managed to build on its foundations, recognising dead ends, celebrating insights, integrating empirical knowledge? Or has it fissured into a thousand theoretical positions so that there are many different schools, each talking to itself, each pursuing its own little patch, which becomes ever more specialised? Celebrating difference and endlessly creating greater apparent variance between various theoretical positions and their corresponding methods can be good for academic careers, but it can also create artificial barriers to theoretical advance. Are criminologists still capable of seeing the links and the applicability of one strand of work, from, say, penology, to another on, say, crime careers?

This ability to see the links, to build theoretical castles from very different kinds of stone, is one which has characterised Tony Bottoms's work throughout his career. He has worked on many fields—on social theory, on social policy, on penology, on crime, on neighbourhoods and environmental criminology, on moral philosophy—and the list continues. He would see them as all potentially contributing to the problem at hand. Having the great privilege of working with him on the Sheffield Desistance Study (Bottoms and Shapland 2016), I know how he can meld philosophy with empirical findings, empirical work

[3] The interface between leisure and work, or, alternatively, the dominance of crime thinking and security over everything else, was illustrated on a holiday in Italy. I bought a not very expensive small painting, a still life, in which the painter was experimenting with Renaissance techniques in preparing paint. She insisted that it be tightly wrapped with a letter explaining that this was modern work, so that I was not immediately accused of heritage theft by the Italian police and customs. The letter gave her name, address, telephone number, and e-mail address so that the police could contact her if they were suspicious of me.

on prison with work on adolescents, and so forth, all to the benefit of the theoretical work being developed. In other words, he is a master of 'synthesis'—a principled and justified combination of parts or elements to form a whole.

Maybe this link-making is catching. Over the past 15 years or so, I was working simultaneously on an evaluation of restorative justice and on the Sheffield Desistance Study, which has been exploring processes of early desistance among men in their early twenties. The offenders involved in both studies have tended to be mostly of a similar age group, mirroring that of the largest age group of prosecuted, convicted, and imprisoned men in England and Wales, who tend to be aged 18 to 29. It has become clearer that there are potential links between the kinds of situations which facilitate processes which those who are thinking about desisting may need to go through, and the situations which restorative justice conferencing aims to create. These similarities can still only currently be seen as tentative—neither study was designed to explore these possibilities, though they have given rise to some limited empirical work by Bart Claes in Belgium and England (Claes and Shapland 2016), which has tended to confirm the links. However, prevalent theoretical perspectives underlying restorative justice do not necessarily—as we shall see below—link the use of restorative justice to reducing reoffending. The theoretical vocabularies and developmental pathways of restorative justice and desistance have often been very different.

The impetus for the link between desistance and restorative justice came inductively from the participants in each study. There was a sense of déjà vu when hearing offenders from one study in the context of the other. What the persistent offenders in the desistance study were saying in their interviews with the research team seemed to be echoing some of what the offenders in the restorative justice evaluation were saying in our observations of their conferences and direct mediations and interviews with them. The aim of this chapter is to develop this initial idea, expressed by Gwen Robinson and myself briefly in Robinson and Shapland (2008), to explore whether the link could be real or is instead artefactual, and to see what kinds of theoretical mechanisms, derived from both bodies of theory, might explain it. Hopefully, this will be synthesis rather than eclecticism (Bottoms 2008b: 82). First, however, it is necessary to describe each study, its methods, and its limitations.

The research studies

The evaluation of restorative justice

The evaluation of restorative justice was funded by the Home Office (it is now the purview of the Ministry of Justice) under its Crime Reduction Programme, and aimed to evaluate three restorative justice schemes. The three schemes, CONNECT, Justice Research Consortium (JRC), and REMEDI, differed from most restorative justice in England and Wales at that time in that they involved primarily adult offenders and often were concerned with serious offences, such as burglary, robbery, and violence (Shapland et al. 2011). The schemes took cases from 2001 to 2003/2004, with the evaluation continuing until 2007 to look at reoffending over two years. The restorative justice processes, which were voluntary for both offenders and victims, ran alongside the normal criminal justice process. Hence restorative justice was experienced:

- As diversion for young offenders as part of a final warning (JRC Northumbria, REMEDI in South Yorkshire)
- As part of a referral order for young offenders, decided upon by a referral panel (REMEDI in South Yorkshire)
- Pre-sentence for adult offenders (at the magistrates' court—CONNECT in London and JRC Northumbria; and at the Crown Court—JRC in London)
- During community sentences for adult offenders (JRC Thames Valley, REMEDI in South Yorkshire)
- Prior to release from prison for adult offenders (JRC Thames Valley, REMEDI in South Yorkshire).

CONNECT and REMEDI primarily used mediation, where the restorative justice was either a direct meeting between victim and offender, with a mediator; or indirect ('shuttle') mediation involving the exchange of information between victim and offender. JRC only used conferencing, involving a direct meeting between victim and offender, with a facilitator, where both victim and offender were encouraged to bring supporters. JRC used random assignment of cases to restorative justice or a control group, after both parties had consented to participate. CONNECT and REMEDI did not use random assignment and so control groups had to be constructed by the evaluators by individually matching offenders (Shapland et al. 2008).

The initiative had two key aims: to meet the needs of victims and to reduce reoffending by offenders. It was therefore important not only to undertake a detailed process evaluation and to observe the restorative justice events, but also to interview both victims and offenders to understand how these outcomes might have arisen. Our emphasis was hence as much on offenders' views of the processes and of criminal and restorative justice as on victims' views. This has been rare in evaluations of restorative justice, which have tended either to explore victims' views in detail (e.g., Strang 2002; Umbreit et al. 1995) or to focus on reoffending but without exploring why the reoffending or reduction in reoffending might have occurred. It is this focus on both observation of direct meetings and interviewing offenders which has allowed the links to be made between potential desistance and restorative justice.

The later research by Bart Claes was in one prison in Belgium and one in England. At the time, the dominant model for restorative justice in Belgium was victim–offender mediation, which involved a meeting between victim and offender but in which, like in the two mediation schemes in England evaluated by Shapland et al. (2011), outcome agreements were rare and there was not necessarily discussion of future paths for offenders. In the English prison, the dominant model was conferencing with a future orientation. In both countries a primarily ethnographic approach was taken, involving observation in the prisons and interviews with prisoners, as well as staff.

The Sheffield Desistance Study

The Sheffield Desistance Study is a longitudinal study of 113 young adult men who were persistent offenders, followed and interviewed up to four times from the age of 19 to 22 (at first interview) for a period of around three years (Bottoms and Shapland 2011). The idea was to look in depth, through long interviews with the men about all aspects of their lives, at a period of time when they may, according to the age–crime curve, be starting to desist. Offending was studied both using official records of convictions (through the PNC), as in the restorative justice evaluation, and through self-report. Both studies involved quite sizeable teams of dedicated researchers[4] and employed somewhat different methods.

[4] Those working on the Ministry of Justice-funded evaluation of restorative justice schemes have been Anne Atkinson, Helen Atkinson, Becca Chapman, Emily Colledge, Jim Dignan,

Initial awareness of potential links—was it an artefact?

I had no expectation, therefore, of any links between the studies. However, when observing restorative justice meetings and reading the synopses of such events prepared by other team members who had observed them, the kinds of statements that offenders made during the events seemed to be very similar to the kinds of statements being made by the offenders in the Sheffield Desistance Study.

My initial reaction was that this was an artefact—I was involved in both studies as director or co-director and my brain was just merging one with another. Or, alternatively, I was twisting one set of data (or both sets, partially) to fit the same theoretical 'spectacles' or worldview. However, on reflection, this was not likely. Those observing the restorative justice events and carrying out the interviews with offenders in the evaluation of restorative justice were not the same people who were undertaking the interviews in the Sheffield Desistance Study—and I only played a very minor part in either. Moreover, the process of analysing the data for the restorative justice evaluation was a group process where small teams analysed each kind of material (interviews, observations, process observations, reoffending rates) and compared notes. The elements and discourses that offenders were producing were contributed by others, as well as myself. The links did not seem to be a product of there being one or two workers in common to both studies. Nor, given the different initial theoretical foci of both studies,[5] did they come from a common theoretical school of thought, though both studies respected participants' perspectives and agency rather than taking an entirely deductive approach.

Jeremy Hibbert, Marie Howes, Jennifer Johnstone, Rachel Pennant, Gwen Robinson, Angela Sorsby, and the present author. Those working on the Sheffield Desistance Study have been Helen Atkinson, Tony Bottoms, Andrew Costello, Deidre Healy, Deborah Holmes, Grant Muir, and the present author. The Sheffield Desistance Study was funded by the Economic and Social Research Council of the UK and by a Leverhulme Trust fellowship to Tony Bottoms, and was part of the SCOPIC network on pathways into and out of crime, coordinated by P.-O. H. Wikström. Bart Claes's work on prisoners in Belgium and Sheffield was funded by a Marie Curie postdoctoral fellowship, held at the University of Sheffield, for which the present author was the mentor.

[5] See Bottoms et al. (2004b) and Bottoms and Shapland (2016) for a statement of the theoretical ideas of the Sheffield Desistance Study and Shapland et al. (2011) for an analysis of the aims of the restorative justice schemes. Different schemes had rather different priorities in terms of restorative justice theory.

The reader may be puzzled as to why I was worrying about making links between desistance and restorative justice. The key reason is that the two studies came from different criminological and theoretical traditions—and that the scholars who had developed each tradition and undertaken the major empirical studies had been working to develop these theories rather separately. This of course, as described above, is within the dominant paradigm of social science and, within that, criminology—that one should keep one's criminological theory and resulting methods pure in the traditions of that theoretical approach. Theorists such as Maruna (e.g., Burnett and Maruna 2006) and Bazemore (Bazemore and Erbe 2004), who have worked on desistance and on community sentences, have also put forward potential links between restorative justice and desistance, though they have primarily developed these theoretically.

The surprise for myself, however, back in the mid-2000s, was that it was the offenders who were saying the same things—for me, this was an inductive link. Yet, should I have been surprised? After all, an offender who has committed many offences and is now trying to desist is the same person whether they are talking about their current lifestyle and its difficulties to an interviewer, or saying the same things to the victim, their own supporters, and the victim's supporters in a restorative justice conference. It is only the criminological literature which has followed different paths and may have created apparent divergence. Let us consider, then, how each literature has developed.

Desistance research and restorative justice research

Interest in desistance has developed from a number of strands. One has, not surprisingly, arisen from interest in resettlement from prison and corrections, including, more recently, the ways in which community sanctions may aid desistance. This strand has tended to arise from evaluations of correctional initiatives, including the prominent Risk-Need-Responsivity work exemplified by the 'what works' paradigm and cognitive behavioural programmes (Andrews et al. 1990; Bonta et al. 2008). The timescales of studies in this paradigm have tended to be bounded by the timescales of initiatives and of measuring reoffending—a few years. Longitudinal research has been rare, with the honourable exception of Farrall (2002; Farrall et al. 2014). Desistance research from this perspective has therefore been somewhat hobbled by its timeframe, though it has started to emphasise social capital and relationships, as well as the practical obstacles to ex-offenders ceasing offending (McNeill 2006).

Another strand is exemplified by developmental and life-course criminology, which has been dominated by much longer longitudinal studies, and which has been primarily an empirically based and quantitative branch of criminology. Most effort in developmental criminology has been put into trying to explain and understand the sequencing and causal elements involved with risk factors and protective factors in the rising part of the age–crime curve in adolescence. Those studies, including the work of P.-O. H. Wikström and his team on the Peterborough study (see Wikström et al. 2012) and also the outstanding work of David Farrington, Donald West, and the Cambridge Study of Delinquent Development (e.g., Farrington et al. 2006; Farrington 2019), have led to the current UK crime reduction policy emphasis on early intervention in childhood to encourage good parenting and opportunities in more deprived areas (such as the 'Sure Start' programme). Relatively less effort has been put into work on late adolescence and adulthood, though this is beginning to change, and so it is only in the past ten years or so that it has become clearer that the kinds of factors which predict pathways into crime are not necessarily the same factors that predict desistance from crime (Stouthamer-Loeber et al. 2004). Moreover, early childhood and even adolescence are not noted as life stages in which people tend to spend their time introspecting about who they are and where they are going in life and explaining it in great detail to interviewers. Hence the kinds of studies which have, until recently, characterised developmental criminology and which have focused upon the pathways into crime have tended to concentrate upon researchers asking 'what happens?' rather than 'why does it happen?', or asking subjects 'why do you think your life is happening like this?' This may explain the relative absence of agentic emphasis in theories about the childhood and adolescence areas of developmental criminology.

In the past ten years there has been much more interest, within lifecourse studies, in desistance—stopping offending. This has concentrated upon young adults and older people, and has started to shift methods towards those, allowing more attention to attitudes, identities, and plans. Work by Laub and Sampson (2003), Burnett (1992), Farrall et al. (2014), Maruna (2000), Giordano (2016), and ourselves (Bottoms and Shapland 2016) all stresses offenders' agency as being important to desistance, alongside structural features of modern society and contextual changes in offenders' lives.

In the Sheffield Desistance Study (Bottoms and Shapland 2011), it was found that decisions to desist among persistent young adult offenders are both surprisingly common and an important element in their own views of who they are and where they are going. A majority of the male offenders in the study, from the first interview at age 19–22, said that they had taken a definite decision to desist. That decision seemed to be linked with becoming fed up with their current lifestyle or realising that they did not wish to continue with this lifestyle much longer. This might be related to the realisation that continuing offending was likely to lead to a life led with the continuing likelihood of a police knock on the door, or longer spells in prison, or feeling that 'now I am an adult'—or all of these. Of course, decisions to desist, as all probation officers will know, do not necessarily result in being able to do it immediately—or at all. We have adopted the philosophical term 'weakness of will' to indicate the situation—common, I suspect, to all of us in our struggles with our bad habits—where we may want not to do something and we could potentially control ourselves not to do it, but we still find ourselves doing it (Shapland and Bottoms 2007). Decisions to desist, once taken, could—and did—also waver or change for some over the following months. Desistance, for those who reduced their frequency of committing crime or even stopped entirely, tended to be a process—only very rarely an all-or-nothing Damascean moment. Desistance itself was linked to the concurrence of personal and social contexts with structures which facilitated that decision being realised. We found, however, that decisions to desist seemed to predict greater desistance at subsequent interviews, while the initial amount of self-reported offending, for example, did not (Bottoms and Shapland 2011). People's own views of where they want to go and whether they think they will get there were clearly important.

Restorative justice has come from a different set of theoretical imperatives. In this chapter I am concentrating largely on offender-related theoretical perspectives, because I am comparing restorative justice with desistance, which has been almost entirely offender-focused. However, it is important to remember that restorative justice sees victim perspectives and needs as equally important—and our evaluation considered both victim and offender views.

Restorative justice is now clearly an umbrella concept: it embraces victim–offender mediation, conferencing, circle sentencing, and peacemaking for transitional societies. Moreover, restorative practices and restorative values have been adopted to deal with a wide range of disputes across the civil and criminal spectrum.[6] Not surprisingly, therefore,

[6] I am using the term 'restorative justice' to denote an exchange of information in both directions between an offender and the direct victim of the offence committed by that offender, as

restorative justice has several theoretical aims and values. Braithwaite (1989; Braithwaite and Pettit 1990), for example, has emphasised democratic or republican participation (all those affected by the crime should be involved), communication between the parties, and reintegrative shaming (deplore the offence; see the potential in and keep caring for the offender). Zehr (1990) and others have tended to focus on the potential for repairing the (emotional) harm done, restoring the victim, and healing. Tyler (1990; Tyler and Huo 2002) has concentrated upon the processual values involved in creating proper communication in a safe manner: allowing everyone to speak; being respectful. Tyler et al. (2007b) have linked restorative justice with Tyler's theory of procedural justice concerning civil and criminal justice: that allowing people to communicate in this manner will increase respect for and the perceived legitimacy of the law.

Not all of these perspectives would see restorative justice as leading directly to or being causal in reducing reoffending. This has been discussed in greater depth in Robinson and Shapland (2008), but essentially those theories which lay stress upon the potential for healing or repairing harm or problem-solving between the individual offender and victim in the instant offence would not expect a general reduction in reoffending by that offender (desistance), though they would hope that there would be a reduction in reoccurrence of the identical offence. Many of these theoretical perspectives do not take a criminal justice perspective or see links with criminal justice as important—indeed, some, such as that of Christie (1977), would find it far preferable for restorative justice to take place outside of and preferably without criminal justice. Other theories, such as those of Braithwaite and Tyler, do see the processes fostered by restorative justice as tying the offender more closely into mainstream society and societal values, so reducing the potential for reoffending generally.

One element that all these restorative justice perspectives have in common is active communication between the parties involved and the need for participation in restorative justice to be voluntary. Hence the research methods associated with restorative justice need to incorporate these values. They are necessarily interpretative: looking at what is happening, what people

exemplified, for example, in Marshall's (1999) well-known definition: 'Restorative justice is a process whereby all parties with a stake in a particular offence come together to resolve collectively how to deal with the aftermath of the offence and its implications for the future' (Marshall 1999: 5). Restorative practices, a wider concept, also encompass work with indirect victims and the community, as well as contacts between offenders and victims who do not share a particular offence or dispute in common.

feel. In restorative justice, participants' agency is not only assumed but required and is seen as a major contrast with so-called traditional criminal justice. Though researchers have undertaken outcome-focused studies of, for example, the effect on reoffending (Latimer et al. 2005; Sherman and Strang 2007), they have tended to investigate participant-focused reasons why reoffending might reduce. So, for example, Morris and Maxwell (1998; Maxwell and Morris 2001) have found that offenders feeling remorseful and apologising to the victim characterised those New Zealand young offenders who subsequently reoffended less. In the evaluation of the three schemes in England and Wales, we found that standard demographic factors played no part in distinguishing offenders who were more likely to reoffend between the randomly assigned restorative justice and control groups—but what did characterise those less likely to reoffend was how they reacted to the conference, specifically the extent to which offenders felt that the conference had made them realise the harm done by the offence, whether the offender said they wanted to meet the victim, the extent to which the offender was actively engaged in the conference, and how useful the process was found to be for the offender (Shapland et al. 2011).

Resonances between offender accounts of desistance and restorative justice

Given the different theoretical roots of desistance research and restorative justice research, what resonances began to stand out in the empirical work on desistance and on restorative justice? The similarities were not just that both concerned ceasing offending or reducing the frequency of offending. These were not just official aims, but offenders' accounts of what was happening in their lives when they started to try to desist and when they were reflecting on their experiences of restorative justice meetings.

Both pieces of research were dealing with a similar age profile of the offenders taking part. The Sheffield Desistance Study concerned male young adult offenders between the ages of approximately 19 and 25. The restorative justice evaluation did not select its offenders by age, but for serious offences the main age group for conviction is 20s–30s. The mean age of offenders in our evaluation was 31 years for CONNECT (with 88% male), 31 years for JRC London burglary offenders and 29 years for JRC robbery offenders (but with 42% between 18 and 24), 25 years for Northumbria court offenders (but with 66% between 18 and 24 and then an older group), and 27 years for Thames Valley prison and community group offenders (Shapland et al. 2006). The relatively similar age groups are, I think, important, because it means that the two studies were at similar life points, but that did not cause the sense of déjà vu.

What was striking was the similarities between, on the one hand, what offenders were saying in restorative justice conferences (and, to a lesser extent, direct mediations) and, on the other hand, how the offenders in the Sheffield Desistance Study were describing their struggles to desist. I shall argue in this chapter that restorative justice and desistance are theoretically more intimately connected than any simple statistical correlation in terms of age. Nor is this just a link in terms of preventing reoffending: that, in some circumstances for some people, restorative justice may reduce reoffending. I argue that restorative justice events can provide a boost to desistance for those who have already decided to desist: that they embody a stage on which desistance hopes, means, and social capital can be displayed. There are a number of elements to this proposition, which are set out below. First, to what extent are participants in restorative justice likely to be potential desisters? Secondly, what elements of the restorative justice meeting may link to desistance? Thirdly, what elements of the restorative justice outcome agreements may relate to desistance?

1. Restorative justice offender participants are likely to have decided to desist

Let us first consider which offenders are likely to agree to participate in a restorative justice conference, where both the victim and the offender's own supporters are likely to be present. Participation needs to be entirely voluntary, as the UN ECOSOC Resolution (2002) states: 'Restorative processes should be used only where there is sufficient evidence to charge the offender and with the free and voluntary consent of the victim and the offender. The victim and the offender should be able to withdraw such consent at any time during the process. Agreements should be arrived at voluntarily' (s. 7). This was the case in all the schemes we evaluated. Restorative justice was also only offered after it was clear who had responsibility for the offence, and after the offender had acknowledged that responsibility by pleading guilty or admitting the offence. The restorative justice encounter did not take the place of a trial—and indeed it was the (very rare) conferences in which offender and victim did not agree on what happened during the offence/on who did what that were much less successful and could end without an agreement (Shapland et al. 2011). Hence offenders who had agreed to come to a conference had agreed that they had done the offence and that they were prepared to meet the victim.

What did that involve? It meant that the offender was prepared to admit to themselves and to the victim that they had done the offence and that they were responsible for it and for the harm that had been caused. Moreover, these were conferences attended by supporters of the offender and victim. Supporters were generally those close to the main participants, whom they trusted—normally relatives, key workers, or close friends. Agreeing to participate hence meant that offenders were prepared to own up to all this before others, knowing that they would be asked questions not only about the offence but also about themselves—why did they do it? What part does offending play in their lives? The offenders we interviewed prior to a conference were very aware that victims would have questions—and were highly nervous about what would happen, though they had decided that they should do it. Very often, they had decided that they would apologise to the victim and wished to do so (79% of offenders attending conferences said it was very or quite important to them to try to repair the harm done, and 84% of offenders envisaged they would apologise to the victim—though victims did not have such high expectations: Shapland et al. 2011).

Let us think a little further about what an apology is in these circumstances, particularly in relation to a serious offence. Apologising is admitting wrong, but it is also normally accompanied by wishing to make things right (Shapland 1981; Tavuchis 1991). We need to add to that the knowledge of both victims and offenders that a simple apology, though hard in itself, is not likely to be sufficient for a serious offence (Shapland et al. 2011; Tavuchis 1991; Choi and Severson 2009). Offenders would often say sorry many times during the conference—but that also may not convey sufficiently the appreciation of the effects of a serious offence (and it can be taken as 'maybe he protests too much'). Instead, we have argued that offenders showing that they are taking steps to change their lives, to stop offending, is itself a form of symbolic reparation to victims.

An offender who has admitted responsibility for the offence, who is prepared to say this to the victim, who realises the victim will ask questions about why that offending has occurred, and who is prepared to engage in a discussion about symbolic reparation and the way he or she is leading his/her life is, in my view, an offender who has already travelled quite a way down the mental path to desistance. As discussed above, the path to desistance is normally a process—one which Anthony Bottoms and I have postulated tends to start with the realisation that the offender is fed up with his current lifestyle and wishes to contemplate a different kind of life: one with less offending. We would argue that a key prerequisite for desistance is being prepared to envisage a different lifestyle, one with less offending—a change which may well occur because the offender has become tired of the downsides of and meagre rewards from a persistently offending lifestyle (see also Shover 1996; Maguire and Bennett 1982; Paternoster and Bushway 2009).

Being prepared to envisage a life without (or with less) crime does not of course mean that the person will succeed in this, as Shover (1998) and we (Bottoms and Shapland) have shown. In other words, our model suggests that the path to desistance tends to start with a provisional decision to try to desist (Bottoms and Shapland 2011). Because of the mental processes involved in preparing for restorative justice, outlined above, I would argue that those offenders who agree to participate in restorative justice, as long as they are not doing it for purely instrumental reasons (to obtain a lower sentence), seem likely to be offenders who are contemplating a different life and who are prepared to think about desistance.

2. Are there elements of the restorative justice process which link to desistance?

Offenders approaching those forms of restorative justice which involve a direct meeting between victim and offender are likely, therefore, to be those who are contemplating changing their lifestyle (in the direction towards desistance). May the restorative justice process itself then encourage these aspects? The key value of restorative justice processes is facilitating communication between offender and victim. It was also the aspect most appreciated by both victims and offenders in the evaluation of the three schemes (Shapland et al. 2011). We need to remember that all the schemes were operating restorative justice in addition to, and therefore in parallel with, the normal traditional criminal justice processes which victims and offenders therefore also experienced. In fact, 71% of JRC offenders were very or quite satisfied with what the criminal justice system had done about the offence and 70% of JRC offenders thought the criminal justice process was very fair or somewhat fair (Shapland et al. 2011). However, offenders were even more positive about the restorative justice experience.

Offenders were very positive about the JRC conference itself, both in the follow-up interview a few weeks afterwards and in final interviews some 8 to 9 months afterwards, at which point 80 per cent of offenders were very or quite satisfied with their JRC conference. Communication (direct, face-to-face communication) with the other party was the most valued element of the conference and was rated highly by all those interviewed (Shapland et al. 2011). As an illustration of this, we can see that conferencing provided a far greater opportunity than the normal criminal justice process to make and receive an apology: in findings very similar to those of Heather Strang (2002) on the experiences of Australian restorative justice victims, in JRC 90% of conference group victims said their offenders had apologised, while in the control group, which did not experience a conference, only 19% of victims interviewed had had their offender apologise to them. Restorative justice provided the opportunity for direct, two-way, question-and-answer communication, as opposed to the formal speeches and directed answers of criminal justice.

Moreover, restorative justice also provided the opportunity to learn about these possibilities for communication in preparation sessions. These sessions were not rehearsals for the meeting itself—that would have led to speeches, rather than communication in the conference itself. However, the preparation sessions did enable participants to think about the kinds of points they wanted to make to the other party and to their own supporters: for offenders to prepare what they might want to say about how they wished to lead their lives.

Another element was the opportunity, in conferences, to have supporters there and for those supporters to contribute—restorative justice is inclusive in communication and participation. It also aims to separate the person of the offender from the offence that person has committed—shaming the offence, but not the offender, as Braithwaite (1989) puts it in his theory of reintegrative shaming. How might this be relevant to desistance? Desistance can be characterised as a process of learning to lead a new life and, eventually, creating a new identity as a non-offender. A justice process which elides the past offence with the identity of the offender, as traditional criminal justice and sentencing based solely on retribution or deterrence may, is likely to impair that cognitive process of desistance, or make the offender feel that he or she will never attain the status of a full member of society. A justice process such as restorative justice—which separates the intrinsic person from the offence, pouring shame on the offence but affirming that the offender could change—is likely to underline any pro-desisting ideas the offender may have.

Moreover, during the conference, other participants may support and affirm pro-desistance statements by the offender. It is highly likely that the victim and offender supporters (as well as victim supporters) will react positively to statements by the offender that he or she takes responsibility for the offence, is sorry, intends to change, and is prepared to share ideas about what may contribute to the offending. In studies, supporters were also positive about any practical, concrete ideas from the offender about how to change. All this will provide reinforcement for pro-change views of the offender. Essentially, not only is the victim looking positively on the offender—and expecting such change to start to happen—but supporters close to the offender are saying the same things. This contribution by supporters is one of the reasons why we think that conferencing holds more promise in relation to desistance than mediation does.

Further positive contributory factors to ideas of desistance are the procedural legitimacy (Tyler and Huo 2002) and deliberative accountability (Roche 2003) which the procedural justice of restorative processes can provide. Tyler's theory of procedural justice suggests that if participants in a justice process feel that decision makers are acting fairly and if they themselves have been treated fairly and given the opportunity to put their case, then this will increase the extent to which they think that the justice process is legitimate. The justice process is itself a proclamation of conventional, societal moral values and the importance of obeying the law. If, then, participants in a justice process feel they have been treated fairly, this will, argues Tyler, promote pro-social views and bind participants more closely to conventional society. Tyler has himself amassed empirical evidence to support his theory from criminal justice, restorative justice, and civil justice processes (Tyler et al. 2007b; Tyler and Huo 2002).

Roche's (2003) theory of deliberative accountability concerns rather different mechanisms, but again relates legitimacy to justice processes. Roche argues that processes are just and seen as legitimate if participants are accountable to each other during the process, that is, if participants can question and take up points raised by other participants.

Both theoretical views would regard justice processes which promote communication in a fair way as promoting legitimacy. This would need to include that all participants are able to say what they need to say, without any participant dominating, in a safe environment. This could be within the remit of traditional criminal justice or restorative justice (Tyler et al.

2007b). However, it is likely that the opportunities afforded by well-run restorative justice mechanisms will be greater than traditional criminal justice in England and Wales, in which offenders are either legally represented and do not speak themselves or find it difficult to say much during the opportunity provided in mitigation (Shapland 1981). In the traditional criminal justice process between conviction and sentence, obtaining relevant information is key, but the process is designed to promote the obtaining of information for the sentencer rather than offenders feeling they have had a reasonable opportunity to say what they wish to say themselves. In contrast, the need to promote communication to all is embedded in the core values of restorative justice (Braithwaite and Mugford 1994). Few evaluations have directly compared participants' own views on criminal justice and restorative justice in the context of processes which involve participation in both in full, but the evaluation of the three schemes did just that. It found that offenders were remarkably positive about criminal justice, as shown above. However, more offenders were positive about restorative justice than criminal justice. Indeed, offenders who had attended a conference run by Justice Research Consortium were significantly more satisfied with what the criminal justice system had done generally in their case than offenders from the control group, who had been randomised out and had not attended a conference (Shapland et al. 2011).

A final key aspect of some restorative justice processes which may link to desistance is the opportunity in restorative justice for participants to communicate about the future: to think themselves about what might mitigate the effects of the offence and to problem solve. They are invited to try to address the problems lying behind the offending and so reduce reoffending. This is an element which traditional criminal justice, at sentencing, reserves for the judiciary and other professionals, such as the probation service. The Practice Direction governing sentencing in England and Wales firmly states that victims are not supposed to express their opinion about sentencing at all in any victim personal statement—they should confine themselves to writing about the effects of the offence (Practice Direction [2001] 4 All ER 640). However, talking about the future, what might reduce reoffending, and how to influence the factors leading to offending were the tasks which both victims and offenders (and their supporters) set themselves in the third stage of the conferencing model used by Justice Research Consortium (see Shapland et al. 2011).

In the subsequent research in Belgium done by Bart Claes (Claes and Shapland 2016), the model of restorative justice used was mediation, involving just the prisoner and the victim with the mediator (no supporters). The advantage of the mediation was that the dominance of discourse about the offence within criminal justice could continue to trap offenders in an offending identity, one which is accentuated by normal prison practice. As one offender said:

> The system focuses on all your negative characteristics, or defaults ... I also have some good things about me. I am a whole person, with bad but also good parts, I don't like it being reduced to just the crimes I have committed. You know who the first person was who addressed me as [...], my mediator.

Mediation offered motivation to continue with programmes they had started in prison and aided in maintaining desires to desist. It sometimes increased social capital by reconnecting with family members.

However, the mediation rarely had a forward-facing focus involving concrete plans for the offender, and so was not able to address structural and practical problems likely to be encountered on release. Only a fifth of the mediations resulted in outcome agreements. This is in contrast to the future-oriented communication about possibilities to reduce offending in the conferencing evaluated in England and Wales by Shapland et al. (2011). We think that having a forward-facing emphasis as part of restorative justice is important for both victims and offenders. Where restorative processes are more backwards-looking, thinking only about the offence and its effects—as in some forms of mediation—then they may help to answer questions and provide some closure, but they do not allow participants to move on to problem-solve about the future. Moreover, the presence of supporters can also be important in suggesting possibilities for preventing re-offending and in helping them to be realised. Some supporters are relatives, who may be able to provide support to offenders to accomplish elements of the outcome agreement (Shapland et al. 2011). Some supporters or participants may be professionals, who may have information about relevant opportunities or programmes to deal with offending-related problems, such as drug dependence. Conferences, with their cast of supporters and professionals, may be more helpful in creating and accomplishing these forward-looking initiatives than some forms of mediation.

There are then aspects of the restorative justice conferencing process itself which may encourage an offender who is beginning to think about desistance and maintain that impetus. They include the potential for putting those thoughts about leading life in a different, less offending way into words—words which will be heard and supported by both supporters and the victim. In a sense, a restorative justice meeting provides a stage for conversation about desistance in a safe environment. If the restorative justice has a final, future-oriented stage, then more practical elements of a less offending life can be discussed and promises made by the offender to try those elements.

So far, we have been seeing restorative justice processes as encouraging and amplifying preliminary decisions to desist—where those decisions began to be formulated before the meeting with the victim (and supporters). Other restorative justice theorists would go much further, to hypothesise that it is the encounter itself that can provide the push towards changing offenders' views—that it is the words of the victim in the meeting which create the remorse or empathy which change offenders (Zehr 1990; Harris et al. 2004). We do not deny that this could occur: that offenders who have remained resistant to desistance or gone into restorative justice meetings for instrumental reasons might then be affected by what victims say. We suspect, however, that preparation and the power of anticipation play a large role in offenders thinking through what they might say, which then is cemented in the meeting itself. Either possibility, of course, requires the meeting to occur.

3. Are there elements related to restorative justice outcome agreements which link to desistance?

From a wish to desist to the accomplishment of a non-offending lifestyle is a considerable journey. Are there elements of restorative justice outcome agreements which may aid in that journey? We need to bear in mind, as discussed above, that not all restorative justice processes end in outcome agreements. In our evaluation of the three restorative justice schemes, REMEDI, for example, would only envisage outcome agreements where the victim and offender themselves wished to do this and raised it during the mediation meeting: a written agreement only occurred in 31% of direct mediations (Shapland et al. 2006). Indirect mediation undertaken by REMEDI and CONNECT did not feature outcome agreements. JRC, in contrast, had a third, future-oriented stage to the conference which emphasised all participants trying to come to an outcome agreement. There was an outcome agreement made in 98% of JRC conferences. There is clearly a difference in participants' behaviour between mediation and conferencing. We think part of this was due to expectations, from facilitators' descriptions, of what was expected to occur, and part due to the very much smaller cast list in mediation compared to conferencing (where supporters are also present).

If outcome agreements were due to facilitator-inspired expectations, were they then created by facilitators and the items suggested by them? Were outcome agreements really the individualised, offender- and victim-inspired collective agreements envisaged by restorative justice theorists (Christie 1977)? Or were they rather an outpost of rehabilitation, directed by criminal justice-focused facilitators? Our observations suggest that, though lay participants at conferences sometimes hesitated before plunging into a discussion of the future—almost waiting for permission to talk about matters normally reserved for criminal justice professionals—they then took the major part in that future-oriented discussion which led to the outcome agreement. In only 3% of JRC conferences observed did the facilitator seem to direct this phase of the conference, though the facilitator did often play a part (Shapland et al. 2006a).

These future-oriented discussions at the ends of conferences tended to revolve around the offender and what the offender should do. Of the JRC conferences, 83% specifically discussed how to stop the offender committing similar types of offence again, with 60% discussing offenders' previous offending patterns. Problems which were linked to offending commonly featured, especially in conferences which concerned more serious offences (Shapland et al. 2006). In accordance with victims' expectations and wishes, reparation was only rarely discussed (though this seems to have a cultural element, because it more commonly occurs in Belgium (Claes and Shapland 2016; Van Camp 2014). What victims did want to see was that the offender was not just saying sorry, but taking steps to change their lives so that others would not suffer from future reoffending.

Key characteristics of the outcome agreements made were that they were practical and related to that situation and that offender. So, conferences which stemmed from long-running disputes among people who knew each other—in the neighbourhood, through membership of leisure facilities, by being extended families—tended to focus on how to intervene in potential future flare-ups by informing a neutral agreed person, and how to avoid exacerbating the dispute by agreeing not to gossip to others in the area (Shapland 2009). Conferences which were discussing persistent patterns of offending tended to concentrate upon factors which led to such offending: 28% of JRC outcome agreements featured offenders applying to or attending a drug programme, 7% an alcohol programme, 5% an anger management programme, 8% counselling, 15% engaging in education, and 14% seeking employment (Shapland et al. 2006). What was important, though, was that those elements were agreed by offenders themselves, in the context of the discussion, as being relevant to where they were then in terms of trying to reduce offending. These were individualised desistance plans. Moreover, on occasions, they were desistance plans which were to be supported by other participants, such as offender supporters.

Could, then, the outcome agreement be characterised as purely a rehabilitational form of lay sentencing? Is restorative justice just a way of imposing change on offenders? We would argue that it is qualitatively different from rehabilitational sentencing, in terms of achieving agentic-focused progress towards desistance. First, this is voluntary participation by all those who meet—rather different from attending a sentencing hearing, or even having supervision imposed upon oneself. Secondly, in restorative justice, this is the offender suggesting, or at least agreeing to, each item in the outcome agreement, rather than professionally prescribed elements in presentence reports. Thirdly, outcome agreements in restorative justice are intended to be the marshalling of resources to fit that offender's needs and the holding of the state to account as to whether such resources are available (Morris and Maxwell 2000), rather than the marshalling of offenders to fit the state's prescription of what penological resources it wishes to provide.

Hence, we would argue that when the participants were concentrating on the future and solving problems in devising outcome agreements, including preventing reoffending, this did not mean that restorative justice is rehabilitational, in its traditional sense, in value and purposes. We have argued that restorative justice is intrinsically what the participants bring to it—it is democratic and participative, and its essence is communication (Shapland et al. 2011). If it is not left to the participants, then it is not restorative justice. It was the expectation of the lay participants that offenders would engage in a discourse about the symbolic reparation of reducing offending—desistance—and their future lives.

Empirical work on desistance has pointed out that, in the journey towards desistance, offenders are often hampered by practical obstacles—difficulties in obtaining work, in dealing with debt, in acquiring qualifications, in housing—which they have few resources to surmount. It has been argued that, in Western countries, political trends have made it more difficult for offenders to desist and have put more structural obstacles in their way in recent years (Farrall et al. 2010). The lack of resources essentially reflects offenders' limited social and human capital. Persistent offenders are likely not to have participated particularly effectively in education, and indeed young offenders are often excluded from school (Farrington et al. 2006; Bottoms and Shapland 2011). They have a very limited work portfolio and few contacts through which to obtain work (Bottoms and Shapland 2011).

Restorative justice involving problem solving for the future has the potential to add possibilities for attaining social capital for offenders during the discussion of the outcome agreement. If, for example, offenders have lost touch with relatives or friends who are important to them, perhaps through imprisonment, then the process initiated by the facilitator to bring together the 'community of care' or 'micro-community' (Braithwaite 1989; McCold 2004) for conferencing of people important to the offender may bring these relatives back into contact, as was found in the research by Shapland et al. (2011) and Claes and Shapland (2016). Personal contacts may provide initial employment opportunities for offenders (Calverley 2009). Moreover, facilitators or schemes themselves may involve professionals who know of relevant programmes for offenders (Campbell et al. 2005).

Restorative justice and desistance languages—different terminologies, same sense?

To summarise, I have been arguing that restorative justice events, particularly conferencing, may provide opportunities for offenders to work through their ideas for desistance. They are participant-focused events which, through their design, bring together those harmed and those important to the offender. Key aspects of the restorative justice which maintain a desire for desistance seem to be, as argued above, the opportunity for the offender to state their desire to desist; the support for that desire shown by victims and by offender supporters; the acknowledgement of the potential for the offender to change and not retain an offending identity; a future-oriented phase to discuss practical and structural possibilities for desistance; the offering of social capital by professionals and supporters to aid these possibilities; and the cementing of these possibilities into a doable, realistic package for which the offender will be held accountable.

The two theoretical traditions, each with their own multiple strands, of restorative justice and of desistance, have their own languages to express all this, as shown in Table 8.1.

These are different words from quite different theoretical and empirical traditions. My forcible association of them and translation between them could be seriously problematic or even eclectic. There are major dangers in

Table 8.1 Theoretical traditions of restorative justice and desistance

In **restorative justice language**, conferences, with the direct victim and offender and victim supporters, may provide:	We can translate these into **desistance language**, when they become:
• Communication between relevant parties, answering questions: some closure for victims and the opportunity for the offender to show altruism towards that particular victim.	• Communication about how their offending happens and potentially greater clarity for offenders about which aspects of their lifestyles they need to change to reduce weakness of will.
• The opportunity to take responsibility for the offence, apologise, and move on: closure for offenders.	• The opportunity to state to others their intention to desist, together with emotional closure for that offence and the opportunity to show altruism for that individual victim.
• Affirmation for offenders' apologies through acceptance that they have made them by victims and affirmation for any expressed desire by offenders to change their lives towards less reoffending: elements of reintegrative shaming.	• Reinforcement that there is a different potential future and a different potential identity as a non-offender (or not so persistent or serious offender).
• Concrete elements in an outcome agreement which are clear and possible for the offender to undertake, directed at offending-related problems.	• Practical steps to address offending-related problems and solve practical difficulties.
• Opportunities for support in undertaking those items from supporters and practical steps to access relevant programmes from professionals.	• Increasing social capital if supporters present at the conference decide to help the offender address offending-related problems, plus potentially thicker positive relationships with those same supporters. Increasing social capital through bringing in professionals to link offenders to sources of future help.

making such transitions between theoretical traditions and their associated empirical streams of work, as Bottoms (2008b) has shown. They are similar to the dangers of comparative criminology and criminal justice between countries (Nelken 2010). For a synthesis, rather than eclecticism, one needs to display '*appropriate sensitivity to the overall theoretical contexts* within which the concept(s) were first generated' (Bottoms 2008b: 104, italics in original). Yet I think there is power in comparing and contrasting different criminological traditions which have grown apart into separate streams of work. It is after all the same offenders, victims, and offences who are researched in both.

I do not want to suggest that all the elements listed above happen, perfectly, for and in every restorative justice conference. They do not. But these elements of restorative justice conferences include many of the key elements in the emerging desistance literature which are beginning to be seen as important in both desistance and resettlement: close family bonds; practical opportunities; people who will care. They also indicate that it is those who have already moved some way on the (mental) path to desistance who may benefit most from restorative justice: those who have already made a decision to desist, even if it is only a provisional decision. Certainly, where conferences (and other forms of restorative justice) broke down in our evaluation was where offenders were not prepared to take responsibility; where they wished to go on offending; where offender and victim differed substantially on who was responsible for all the elements of the offence. Is volunteering for restorative justice conferences (as long as it is not being done entirely instrumentally) predictive of being on the path to a decision to desist?

Dignan et al. (2007) have likened restorative justice events to staged theatre plays. In desistance terms, we might see them as relatively public staged desistance events. Restorative justice events are not open to the public, but those important to that offender and affected by that offence are present. The outcome, in restorative justice linked to criminal justice, is made known to criminal justice personnel and the offender will be held accountable for it (Campbell et al. 2005; Shapland et al. 2011). In theoretical terms, making these kinds of desistance declarations during restorative justice may operate as a boost for the wavering self-belief of the intending desister. They state and make conceivable a different identity as a conforming normal member of the public. However, it remains vital that restorative justice does not become merely a tool to benefit desistance in offenders—its victim-oriented roots and the needs and requirements of victims are equally important.

Restorative justice events may now be one of the rare opportunities which can operate in this desistance-promoting way for offenders in the criminal justice system in England and Wales. Court appearances have been so streamlined in an understandable attempt to reduce delay that they have lost any meaningful input from (or to) offenders. Though probation appointments can also fulfil some of these functions, they only rarely bring in important offender supporters such as partners and parents. We may need to start thinking in both desistance and restorative terms in order to provide means through which offenders, victims, their supporters, and professionals can pick up possibilities for desistance and restoration.

9

Towards a True Social Ecology of Crime

On the Limitations of a Criminology Without People

Per-Olof H. Wikström

My first contact with Tony Bottoms and his scholarly work was through his seminal book with John Baldwin, *The Urban Criminal* (Baldwin and Bottoms 1976). I was working on a large-scale project on urban crime and violence in Sweden (Wikström 1985, 1991) and was looking for other major contemporary European studies on the topic. They were hard to come by and, as Tony noted in his introductory essay to the book, 'the specifically urban and areal dimensions of the social processes that are connected with crime have been seriously understated in much recent criminological work' (Baldwin and Bottoms 1976: 1). This is a claim that probably cannot be made today, with the strong expansion of research into the area and place dimensions of urban crime that has taken place.

The publication of *The Urban Criminal* contributed to the revitalisation of the social ecology of crime and brought some new and fresh ideas and insights to its study (such as the role of local housing markets and the importance of better analysing and understanding the problem of crime and distance).[1] In his subsequent works, a prime focus for Tony has been arguing for the need to bridge the gap between the classic Chicago School approach into the study of urban crime (e.g., Shaw and McKay 1969) and the later emerging environmental criminology (e.g., Brantingham and Brantingham 1981), as exemplified by his recent paper 'Crime specifics,

[1] Although Tony has an impressively wide variety of criminological and criminal justice interests (the hallmark of his outstanding contribution to criminology), his active engagement with the study of the social ecology of crime has persisted over the years (e.g., Bottoms and Wiles 1986; Bottoms, Claytor, and Wiles 1992; Bottoms 1993, 2007, 2012, 2017a, 2018a).

Per-Olof H. Wikström, *Towards a True Social Ecology of Crime*. In: *Crime, Justice, and Social Order*. Edited by: Alison Liebling, Joanna Shapland, Richard Sparks, and Justice Tankebe, Oxford University Press.
DOI: 10.1093/oso/9780192859600.003.0009

offender residences, and social change: Developing the criminology of place' (Bottoms 2017a).

Urban crime is not the only interest I share with Tony: we both have a profound interest and belief in the importance of analysing and understanding the moral dimensions of the crime problem, albeit with a somewhat different focus (e.g., Bottoms 2003; Wikström 2010). What I have really come to appreciate about Tony's scholarship is that his contributions are always open-minded (non-tribal) and thoughtful, and commonly draw upon not only the criminological but also the wider philosophical and social and behavioural science literature. He is a master of addressing criminological topics by synthesising relevant theoretical and empirical knowledge. On a more personal level, I cherish Tony's friendship and support (he talked me into a move to Cambridge in 1997 and provided a very helpful introduction to the peculiar environment that is Cambridge University) and I value our scholarly interactions and exchange of ideas over the years.

Towards a true social ecology of crime

In my view, one fundamental problem that has always impeded, and which still hampers, the advancement of a true social ecology of crime is its common neglect of proper consideration of the role of people (actors), and particularly the person–environment interaction in crime causation. The social ecology of crime is essentially a criminology without people (actors).

In this chapter I shall discuss the social ecology of crime from a Situational Action Theory perspective (e.g., Wikström 2006, 2017, 2019a, 2019b) and how it may help create a much-needed truly ecological perspective in the study of crime and its causes.

My central argument is:

> *If we want to understand how the environment affects crime, we first must understand what factors and processes move people to engage in acts of crime.*

Without knowing what factors and processes are involved in moving people to commit acts of crime, it is difficult to identify and assess what environmental factors and processes (directly as causes, or indirectly as 'causes of the causes') are involved in crime causation. Moreover, such improved knowledge (if utilised) will certainly assist policy-makers and practitioners in making better designs in, and more effective and targeted implementations of, crime prevention policy and interventions.

The social ecology of crime

Arguably, a truly social ecological approach (together with an adequate action theory) is the foundation for a proper understanding of human actions such as acts of crime. One can, of course, disagree about what genuine social ecology entails, but I take it that lexically *ecology* generally refers to the science of the study of the relationship between organisms and their environment and *social ecology* (or human ecology) concerns the study of the social and behavioural outcomes and consequences of the interaction between man and his environment (including the man-made physical environment). Acts of crime are one kind of behavioural outcome and, therefore, the *social ecology of crime* may be regarded as the study of the role of the person–environment interaction in crime causation. However, the various approaches normally thought of and referred to as ecological approaches in the study of crime are essentially environment-oriented perspectives on crime, its causes, and its prevention. They typically leave out the role of individual differences and their role in the person–environment interaction (and its changes).

Two major strands of research into the social ecology of crime

This is not the place for a comprehensive review of studies on the social ecology of crime: there are many works that undertake or include such reviews (e.g., Kornhauser 1978; Brantingham and Brantingham 1984; Bursik and Grasmick 1993; Wikström 1998, 2007; Pratt and Cullen 2005; Bottoms 2007, 2012; Sampson 2012). Here I will only briefly summarise some key pointers as a background to my discussion of the limitations of a social ecology without people (actors).

The social ecology of crime may broadly be divided into 'classic crime ecology' and 'environmental criminology', although there have been convincing arguments for the value of integrating the two or parts thereof, and some initial attempts to do so, of which much of Tony Bottoms's recent work is a good example. *Classic crime ecology* originated in the early twentieth century as part of the Chicago School's research into urban growth and residential segregation and its social consequences,[2] including neighbourhood variations in the rates of offenders[3] and other types of social problems (e.g., Shaw and Mckay 1969). That research and subsequent studies in this tradition became the foundation for the development of social disorganization (e.g., Kornhauser 1978, Sampson 1988; Bursik and Grasmick 1993) and collective efficacy theory (e.g., Sampson, Raudenbush, and Earls 1997; Sampson 2012). Policy and prevention approaches emerging from this line of research are typically referred to as 'social prevention' and tend generally to focus on programmes directed towards influencing neighbourhood social conditions and institutions (e.g., family and school conditions; the provision and organisation of young people's leisure activities). The 'communities that care' programme is probably a prime example of this line of community-oriented prevention (e.g., Hawkins and Catalano 1992).

Environmental criminology (or 'opportunity theory', as it is sometimes called) appeared as a major criminological perspective around the late 1970s and early 1980s, with a focus on the role of criminogenic micro-environments (settings) and their emergence in the explanation of crime events and spatio-temporal crime patterns. Key initial theoretical contributions in this movement included the work of Cohen and Felson (1979) on routine activity theory and that of Brantingham and Brantingham (1981, 1993) on crime pattern theory. This strand also includes as major subsequent contributions research aiming to identify crime hot spots (e.g., Sherman, Gartin, and Buerger 1989) and to elucidate the criminology of place (e.g., Weisburd, Groff, and Yang 2012). Environmental criminology is closely linked in its policy applications to the 'situational crime prevention' approach initially developed by Ron Clarke and Derek Cornish (1985).

Table 9.1 illustrates schematically some major differences in focus of the two perspectives and points of their potential integration. What these different approaches have in common is a strong focus (theoretically[4] and methodologically) on the role of the environment in crime causation (and prevention) at the same time as they typically, and sometimes explicitly,

[2] Partly against the backdrop of and inspiration from European social theory (e.g., Emile Durkheim) and research into the crime distribution in the population (e.g., Adolphe Quetelet) and specifically Charles Darwin's ecological theory (see, e.g., Burgess 1925; Park 1961).

[3] Subsequent research in this tradition has increasingly also considered the neighbourhood rates of crime events.

[4] Some research in the ecological tradition is rather untheoretical, mostly concerned with mapping out crime patterns and their environmental correlates (and therefore reminiscent of the risk-factor approach common in developmental and life-course criminology).

Table 9.1 Two major strands in the social ecology of crime. A schematic overview of some key differences in focus, points of integration (↔) and policy application

Classic crime ecology		Environmental criminology
Residential segregation	↔	Land use
Community social organisation	↔	Routine Activities /places (social and physical layout)
Neighbourhood offender rates (crime rates)	↔	Place variation in crime rates/crime events
Neighbourhood crime careers	↔	Places crime careers
Social prevention	↔	Situational prevention

ignore (or downplay) the role of personal characteristics and experiences, and, particularly, the role of the person–environment interaction. Why is this problematic?

The poverty of a criminology without people (actors)

There are at least three major reasons why a criminology without people (actors) is problematic and limits our understanding of the role of the environment in crime causation:

1. People are the source of their actions (and intentional inactions).
2. People are different; they react differently to the same (immediate) environment.
3. The causes of action are situational; people's actions are an outcome of the person–environment interaction.

I will develop these arguments in some detail, but first I provide some basic definitions of certain key concepts I will use in the subsequent discussion.

Human *actions* ('doings') are intentional bodily movements[5] (e.g., talking or hitting) or purposely withheld movements. A particular 'action' may include a series of different bodily movements (such as in the act of beating up another person). *Crimes* are actions (or intentional inactions) that break rules of conduct stated in law. As such they are essentially no different from rule-breaking more generally (i.e., they are governed and explained by the same basic processes). What any theory of crime causation should essentially explain is why people follow and break rules of conduct.

The 'environment' is not an easily defined concept and its definition often depends on the research topic at hand. Typically, it refers to a geographic/spatial unit (e.g., a country, neighbourhood, school, prison, or street corner) and its social and physical characteristics. From the point of view of the person, the environment is all that is outside and accessible to the person. When explaining action, the *causally relevant environment* is the immediate environment that a person can access with her or his senses at a specific moment in time (this includes any accessible information from any media present). This may be referred to as the *setting* (i.e., the action-relevant environment). The configuration of settings in which a person takes part during a specific period (e.g., a day, a month, or a year) may be referred to as her or his *activity field* (for that period). Its stability and changes are an important source of continuity and change in people's crime propensity and exposure to criminogenic settings.

People are the source of their actions (and intentional inactions)

Environments do not act; only people do. People do as they do because of the choices they make among the action alternatives they perceive in relation to the motivators they experience (Wikström 2019b). Because people are the source of their actions, any environmental influence on their actions must arise through its influence on the content and efficacy of the mental processes impacting on how they come to see and choose certain action alternatives.

[5] Excluding reflexes but not habits (on the role of deliberate and habitual choices in crime causation, see Wikström 2019b: 273–274).

Crucially, the environment does not cause acts of crime, but it may cause some people (depending on their propensities) to commit acts of crime. Only environmental features that affect how a person sees her or his action alternatives and makes choices in relation to motivators are causally relevant in the explanation of environmental influences on action, such as acts of crime. Ignoring the role of the mental process (the perception–choice process) by which people react and respond to environmental influences limits our understanding of the role of the environment in crime causation. A proper understanding of the workings of the action-relevant mental processes helps us identify what aspects of the environment are causally relevant in the explanation of acts of crime. This requires an adequate action theory.

People are different; they react differently to the same (immediate) environment

People react and respond to the settings in which they take part, and depending on who is in what setting, certain actions may be likely. Different people pay attention to different aspects of, and react and respond differently to, the same environmental conditions and circumstances, with the important implication that the relevance and strength of influence of specific environmental conditions and circumstances differ among people.

People vary in their *preferences and sensitivities* and, therefore, differ in what opportunities and frictions in a setting may motivate them (create specific goal-directed attention). People also, and crucially, vary in their *personal morals* (what actions are considered acceptable or unacceptable responses to a motivator in the circumstance) and *ability to exercise self-control* (the ability to act in accordance with their own morality when externally pressurised to do otherwise), and, therefore, differ in what action alternatives they may see as viable and acceptable and what action-choices they may make in response to a specific motivator (temptation or provocation) in the particular circumstance (moral context). While some people may see and choose an act of crime as a viable and acceptable action alternative in a specific setting, others in the same setting may not. Ignoring the role of individual differences in environmental influences limits our understanding of the role of the environment in crime causation. These are fundamental arguments of Situational Action Theory (SAT) as regards the importance of the study of the person–environment interaction in crime causation (e.g., Wikström 2019a, 2019b). It is all about interactions!

The causes of crime are situational

If people are the source of their action, and people are different (pay attention to and react and respond differently to particular characteristics of the environments), and settings are different (provide different kinds of action-inducements), combinations of particular kinds of people and particular kinds of settings are likely to encourage particular kinds of actions (and in some cases stimulate the perception and choice of crime as an action alternative in relation to a motivator). If we are interested in the role of the environment in crime causation, the central question thus becomes: *What kind of settings encourage what kinds of people to do what kinds of crime?*

It is important not to conflate the concept of 'situation' with that of 'the immediate environment', as is commonly done in criminological (and other) studies (see further, Wikström and Treiber 2015). SAT proposes that, as the product of the person–environment interaction, the *situation* is 'the action alternatives a person perceives in relation to any motivator she or he experiences'. The situation is thus neither the person nor the setting, but the outcome of the combination of the two (i.e., motivations and action alternatives).

The importance of action theory

Action theory tells us what moves people to action. A well-developed action theory connects person (propensities), environment (incitements), and action (outcomes). It helps us specify how the human–environment interaction affects what action alternative we see and what action choices we make in relation to the motivations we experience. The better we can understand how this works, the better we can explain why people act as they do, including why they commit acts of crime. This is also the foundation for assessing which (and how) macro-level (e.g., inequality and segregation) and developmental (e.g., socialisation) factors and processes are implicated (as causes of the causes) in crime causation.

Situational Action Theory (SAT): The core model

The core argument of SAT is that people do as they do because of who they are (their action-propensities) and the setting in which they take part (its action-inducements). When it comes to the explanation of *crime events*, it is the interaction between people's crime propensities and the setting's criminogenic inducements that is crucial. People vary in their *crime propensity* (their tendency to see crime as an action alternative in relation to particular motivators in specific circumstances) depending on their personal morals and ability to exercise self-control (see further, Wikström 2019b). A person who sees crime as an action alternative in many different circumstances can be regarded as a person with a high crime propensity, while a person who rarely sees crime as an action alternative can be considered as a person with a low crime propensity.

Settings vary in their *criminogenic inducements* (their tendency to encourage criminal acts as a response to the opportunities provided and frictions created) depending on the setting's moral context (its moral norms and their enforcement relevant to its opportunities and frictions) (see, further, Wikström 2019b). A highly criminogenic setting is one that creates strong encouragements to conduct acts of crime as a response to its opportunities and/or frictions. However, the proposed relationship between propensity and exposure is not simply additive: *people with a very low crime propensity are largely immune to settings' criminogenic inducements, while people with higher levels of crime propensity are vulnerable to criminogenic inducements, and increasingly so the higher their crime propensity is* (for an empirical test and corroboration of this assumption, see Wikström, Mann, and Hardie 2018).

The basic action-process according to SAT is illustrated in Figure 9.1. A person's crime propensity and the setting's criminogenic inducements are the *inputs* to, and their specific combination the *trigger* of, the perception-choice *process*, whose *outcome* will determine what actions, if any, are taken (and, crucially, whether or not an act of crime is performed).

A person's particular crime propensities are *activated* by a setting's specific criminogenic inducements, and a setting's particular criminogenic inducements are *made relevant* by a person's specific crime propensities. This interaction will influence what kind of action alternatives the person will see and what choices she or he will make in relation to the motivators experienced, and, in turn, what kind of actions may follow. The relative

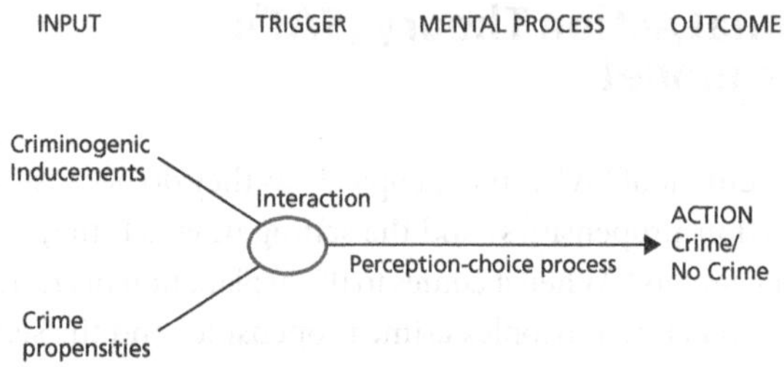

Figure 9.1 The basic action-process according to SAT

strength of a person's specific crime propensities and the setting's specific criminogenic inducements may vary by circumstance and, hence, their relative importance for the outcome. But there will always be an interaction between the two.

The model in Figure 9.1 illustrates the basic proposed action process according to SAT (for details and suggested key elements of the perception-choice process, that is, motivation—moral filter—controls—action, see, e.g., Wikström 2006: 76–84; Wikström 2017: 511–513; Wikström 2019b: 270–274). It highlights the shortcomings of considering only one of the major inputs (environmental inducements *or* person propensities) in the explanation of crime events. Again, my central argument is that a proper explanation of crime events needs both: the causes of crime are situational, a result of the choices a person makes based on the motivations and perception of action alternatives that are triggered by the interaction between the person's propensities and the setting's inducements. The role of the environment in crime causation cannot be seen in isolation (as little as the role of the person (actor) cannot be isolated from that of the setting).

SAT: The Developmental Ecological Action (DEA) model

The environment is not only important situationally, as part of what creates crime events, but also developmentally, as part of the processes that affect the emergence of and changes in people's crime propensities and their levels of exposure to criminogenic settings. It is important not to confuse the immediate (situational) role of the environment in explaining crime events with its longer-term (developmental) role in explaining stability and changes in people's crime propensity and criminogenic exposure (although this seems commonly to be the case: for an illustrative example, see Wikström 2019b: 267–268).

The *Developmental Ecological Action model* of SAT (the DEA model) proposes that a criminal career (an individual's age-trajectory of crime involvement) is best analysed as a series of crime events, where each event is explained as an outcome of the crime propensity–criminogenic inducement interaction in the circumstance. Stability and changes in people's crime involvement are outcomes of stability and changes in the input to the perception-choice process, that is, a result of continuity and changes in people's crime propensities and/or criminogenic exposures (Figure 9.2). The model further suggests that stability and changes in people's crime propensities are largely a result of psychosocial processes of moral education and cognitive nurturing, and that permanence and changes in exposure to criminogenic settings are largely a consequence of socio-ecological processes of social and self-selection. These are lifelong processes in which *current* states (propensities, exposures) are a result of *past* developments (influences) at the same time as they set the stage for *future* developments (influences). For a more in-depth overview of the DEA model of SAT and its proposed core processes, see Wikström (2019a); for its empirical testing, see Wikström, Treiber, and Roman (2022).

In the next two sections I will argue for and illustrate the value of a true social ecology of crime by briefly examining and discussing *how* two major topics in the social ecology of crime tradition (the study of 'neighbourhoods and crime' and 'crime opportunities') are limited by fundamentally

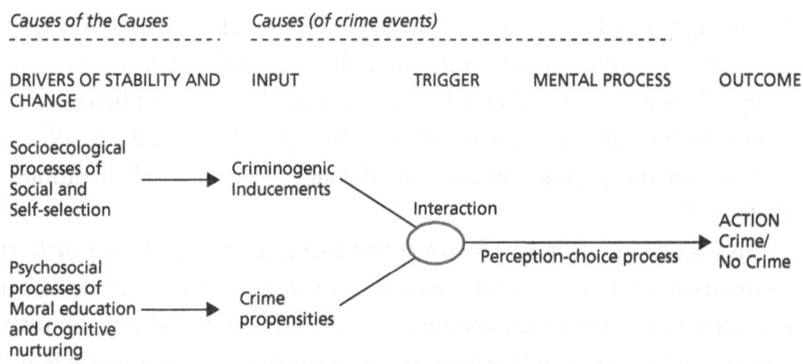

Figure 9.2 The drivers of stability and change in crime involvement according to SAT

ignoring the role in crime causation that is played by people (actors) and their interaction with the environment.

Neighbourhoods and crime

> *[A]dvancement in the understanding of the role of community context in crime causation requires better theorizing of social mechanisms that link community context to individual development and acts, improved 'ecometrics', and a focus of study on cross-level interactions.*
>
> Per-Olof Wikström and Robert Sampson (2003: 118)

Does it matter where we grow up and live? Does it influence the likelihood that we will develop a higher crime propensity and get involved in crime? That it does seems to be the fundamental assumption of the classic ecology of crime tradition, with its strong focus on the role of neighbourhoods ('communities') in crime causation. Early Chicagoans saw the city (and its various environments) as 'a laboratory or clinic in which human nature and social processes may be conveniently and profitably studied' (Park [1925] 1967: 45–46), and Clifford Shaw and Henry McKay (the Chicago School's prime criminologists of the time) mapped out area-level (aggregate) associations between (primarily) the rate of young offenders and various other social problems and area structural characteristics, such as population low SES, heterogeneity, and turnover (findings that largely still stand in contemporaneous neighbourhood and crime analyses—e.g., Wikström 1991; Sampson 1997; Sampson and Wikström 2008; Wikström et al. 2012: 171–185; Sampson 2012). Shaw and McKay interpreted the neighbourhood variations in young offender rates as reflecting different levels of social disorganisation, arguing that 'a high incidence of delinquent behavior indicates the breakdown of the machinery through which needs of different segments of the population are met through conventional institutions' (1969: 384).

This argument was taken forward and theoretically developed by Ruth Kornhauser (1978: 70–82). She defined *social disorganisation* as the lack of 'a structure through which common values can be realised and common problems solved' (ibid: 63). A typical neighbourhood 'common problem' is high levels of crime and disorder among the young, primarily emerging in poor, residentially unstable, and heterogeneous communities because (i) it is difficult to realise common values and solve common problems, due to such factors as poor communication resulting from residents' diverse and changing cultural backgrounds and experiences (creating a lack of cohesion and poor trust), but also the fact that (ii) key social institutions (e.g., the family and schools), due to factors such as lack of money, skills, and personal investments by residents, tend to be inadequate, isolated from each other, and unstable. Poorly functioning social institutions and a lack of common values among community residents result in poor informal social controls and defective socialisation, which in turn cause high rates of offending by community residents (particularly among young people).

Robert Sampson further refined social disorganisation theory by suggesting the concept of *collective efficacy*, a concept that subsumes the concepts of social cohesion (a community's ability to generate moral and social integration among its residents: Sampson 1993) and informal social control (monitoring and intervention) and describes *residents' willingness to intervene for the common good* (i.e., their potential to exercise informal social control if needed) *as the result of shared expectations and mutual trust* in the community (Sampson, Raudenbush, and Earls 1997; Sampson, Morenoff, and Earls 1999). Unlike social disorganisation theory, which assumes that effective social control is based on strong ties between neighbours (friendship, kinship), this is not a necessary prerequisite in collective efficacy theory, maintaining that it is the trust-based *anticipation* that one's neighbours would intervene for the common good *if needed* that is the basis for strong neighbourhood informal social control (Sampson 2012: 152).

Why some and not others?

While classic crime ecology has contributed significantly by identifying certain general environmental conditions (residential community contexts) linked to area variation in offender and crime *rates*, it has not succeeded equally well in empirically exploring and theoretically explaining the *cross-level* (neighbourhood to individual) processes involved. The focus on explaining and exploring crime and offender rates rather than individuals' crime propensities and acts of crime prevents a fuller understanding of the role of neighbourhoods (and the environment more generally) in crime causation. For example, using the offender rate as outcome masks the fact that there is a substantial (typically theoretically unexplained) *within*-neighbourhood variation in residents' crime involvement: questions such as *why some but not others* in a neighbourhood are, or become, persistent and serious offenders are rarely effectively addressed.

This problem is well illustrated by some basic findings from the Peterborough Adolescent and Young Adult Development Study (PADS+) which show that self-reported crime involvement in adolescence (ages 13–17) varies considerably *within* all quintiles of neighbourhood disadvantage (measured at age 12),[6] notwithstanding that there are more young people with no or few crimes in the more advantaged areas and more young people with high crime involvement in the more disadvantaged areas.[7] For instance, 39% in the most advantaged compared to 23% in the most disadvantaged areas had committed no crime, and 1% in the most advantaged compared to 7% in the most disadvantaged areas had committed 100 or more crimes (Figure 9.3).

If we only consider serious crimes of theft (burglaries, theft of and from cars, and personal robberies), the proportion of young people who reported having engaged in such crimes in adolescence (ages 13–17) varies from 15% in the most advantaged to 28% in the most disadvantaged areas.[8] *The overwhelming majority of young people in all areas are not involved in serious theft crimes, while there are some in all areas that are* (Table 9.2).
This is not a problem confined to studies of neighbourhood effects but applies to all studies using rates (aggregated actions) as *outcome* when explaining human behaviour, for instance, explicating historical (e.g., annual), national, regional, institutional (e.g., school), or demographic (e.g., gender) differences in the rates of offenders or crime events. Typically, there is always a substantial within-group variation that requires explanation (e.g., even if men, on average, are found to commit more crimes than women, there is considerable variation among males in their crime involvement, as there is among females—see, e.g., Wikström and Wikström 2019).

[6] For information about the PADS + study and its design see chapter 3 in Wikström et al. (2022). The neighbourhood unit of analysis here is the *output area*. Two thirds (75%) of the subjects lived in the same address during ages 13–17 as at age 12, and of the 25% who moved, 60% moved to an address in an output area within the same or worse disadvantage quintile. The measure of neighbourhood disadvantage is based on output area census data on residents' socioeconomic characteristics (for details see Wikström et al. 2012: 174).

[7] In this context it can be mentioned that the neighbourhood level of disadvantage is strongly correlated with the neighbourhood level of poor collective efficacy (r. = 0.67): see Wikström 2012: 181.

[8] Although the *frequency* (crimes per offender) of serious thefts is generally higher among serious theft offenders living in more disadvantaged areas.

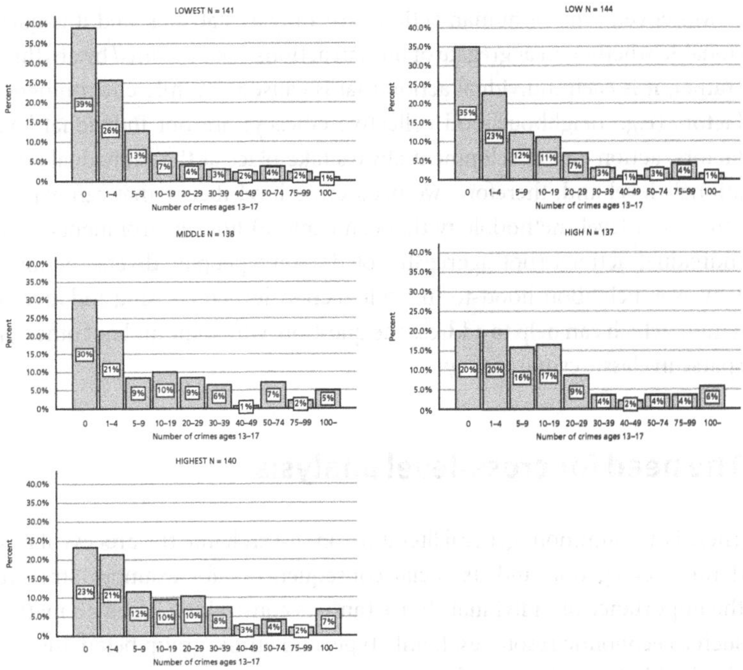

Figure 9.3 Crime distribution, total number of crimes ages 13–17, by childhood (age 12) neighbourhood disadvantage (quintiles). Data from the PADS+ study.

Table 9.2 Percent young people that have been involved in serious theft crimes* (ages 13–17) by childhood (age 12) neighbourhood disadvantage group (quintiles)

Disadvantage Groups (quintiles)	Serious theft (%)			
	YES	NO	TOTAL	N
Lowest	15	85	100	141
Low	14	86	100	144
Middle	28	72	100	138
High	23	77	100	137
Highest	28	72	100	140

*Residential and non-residential burglaries, thefts of and from cars, personal robberies.

Moreover, *rates* of human action exist only as statistics, and it is questionable whether an aggregate of human actions can be *caused* by anything (rather, it is each individual action that is caused).[9] While environmental factors (e.g., neighbourhood collective efficacy) are not individual-level factors, action and development always take place at the individual (situational) level and, therefore, we need cross-level theory that can explain (and cross-level methodology that can explore) how environments affect individual actions (not aggregates of different people's diverse actions). However, neighbourhood-to-individual cross-level theorising and investigation, which can help to address the question 'why some and not others', is sparse in classic crime ecology.

The need for cross-level analysis

There is a voluminous general literature on research into the process of residential segregation and its social consequences—for example, stressing the importance of individual choice (and its constraints) based on matters such as economic resources, family type, and ethnic group belonging, but also highlighting the role of the content and workings of housing markets and related processes of neighbourhood gentrification and decline (the role of local housing markets, with special reference to the crime problem, is a topic to which Tony Bottoms and colleagues have made seminal contributions—see, e.g., Bottoms and Wiles 1986 and Bottoms et al. 1992). This is not the place to review this literature: it will suffice to say that research into the causes and consequences of residential segregation (i.e., residential differentiation and its social consequences) constitutes an important background to and framework for analysis of the neighbourhood crime problem.

In a paper on neighbourhood effects generally (i.e., not confined to the problem of crime), Patrick Sharkey and Jacob Faber elegantly summarise the neighbourhood crime problem by arguing that the central question is 'when, where, why, and for whom [does] residential context matter'

[9] It is of course possible to argue that we can have causation at the aggregate level explaining human actions (although I have found no convincing arguments for such position), or that this doesn't matter (is not important); that one is satisfied with demonstrating prediction at the aggregate level and just takes for granted that this association represent some underlying process of individual-level action causation (in spite of the risk of an ecological fallacy—see, e.g., Hammond 1973).

(2014: 562)—and to that I would add, crucially, *how*. To explicate these processes requires cross-level analyses that connect the neighbourhood context (and its changes) to individual action and developments (e.g., linking neighbourhood contextual features to people's individual acts of crime and criminal careers). Such studies are still in their infancy and are comparatively rare in criminology, and typically not part of the classic crime ecology tradition (e.g., Simcha-Fagan and Schwartz 1986; Loeber and Wikström 1993; Wikström and Loeber 2000; Lynham et al. 2000; Lanctot and Smith 2001; Henry et al. 2014), and notwithstanding that these studies are a vast improvement over studies using aggregates of action as outcome, there is yet something central missing—the important role of settings for human action and development.

The missing link: Settings

Neighbourhood cultural (rule-based) and structural (resource-based) features are *manifested* in, and exert influence through, micro-environments (settings). A neighbourhood[10] is typically a specific mosaic of diverse private (e.g., homes), semi-private (e.g., schools), and public (e.g., street segments) micro-environments, varying in the moral content and efficacy of the opportunities they provide and frictions they create (and in their role and importance for processes of moral education and cognitive nurturing), to which residents (and visitors) may be differently exposed (concurrently and over time) through processes of social and self-selection. Their relevance for residents—and residents' reactions to them—may vary (and change) depending on the residents' existing personal characteristics, life stages, and circumstances, resulting in specific developmental influences and behavioural consequences.

Any impact of neighbourhood contextual characteristics, such as concentrated disadvantage and poor collective efficacy, only happens through its influence on the content and efficacy of the settings in which people act and develop. In other words, *settings are the intermediating link between neighbourhood context and individual action and development.* It is the

[10] There is no universally accepted definition of the concept of neighbourhood. The early Chicagoans thought of neighbourhoods as 'natural areas' created in the process of residential segregation but most research into neighbourhood effects uses pre-defined administrative areas (such as census tracts) as measures (proxies) of neighbourhoods.

specific qualities of the various micro-environments in which people actually take part in their daily life (the kind of people with whom they meet and interact, the kinds of activities to which they are exposed and in which they participate,[11] and, importantly nowadays, their social media encounters and endeavours) that affect the formation of and changes to people's preferences and sensitivities (of relevance for what motivates them) and their personal morals and ability to exercise self-control (of relevance for their crime propensity), and in which they may face circumstances (moral contexts of opportunities and frictions) that are criminogenic and that may entice some to get involved in acts of crime. The criminological relevance of all this is that some neighbourhood contexts will produce more criminogenic settings, and more settings promoting the development of a higher crime propensity, than others, impacting their crime and offender rates. However, this will not help to explain why some but not others living in a specific neighbourhood are more frequently involved in acts of crime, or why some but not others develop persistent and serious criminal careers.

People matters

A question that has always haunted classic crime ecology is whether high neighbourhood offender and crime rates are a result of more crime-prone people being segregated into some residential areas, rather than the environment of these areas being responsible for the higher rates. Robert Sampson and colleagues argue that 'the issue of selection bias is probably the biggest challenge facing neighbourhood-level research' (Sampson, Morenoff, and Gannon-Rowley 2002: 466). However, this is probably a misspecified problem because if one accepts that acts of crime (and people's crime propensities) are always an outcome of person-environment interactions, both the kinds of people segregated into neighbourhoods and the kinds of micro-environment a neighbourhood provides (not unrelated to the outcomes of population residential segregation)—and, crucially, their specific interactions—will matter for offender and crime rates.

[11] This point is well argued and expounded in Bronfenbrenner's (1979) ecology of human development, maintaining that it is the individuals' day-to-day routines and activities, 'the objects to which she or he responds and the people with whom she or he interacts on a face-to-face basis', that have a direct influence on her or his development.

People are different, and which micro-environments will be accessible and relevant to and influence them, and in which ways, will vary depending on their current personal characteristics (what social categories they belong to and their psychological make-up[12]) and their past experiences. For instance, certain settings may generally be more open, relevant, and attractive to some social categories than to others: for example, to males rather than females; to younger rather than older people; to wealthy rather than poor people; and to some ethnic groups rather than others.[13]

People's agency (based on their human, economic, and social capital) and personal preferences will also influence what settings they can take part in and find relevant and attractive. Social category-induced influences may be thought of as processes of social selection, and personal agency and preference-based influences may be thought of as processes of self-selection. *Social selection* refers to 'the process by which cultural and structural forces enable (encourage or compel) or restrict (discourage or bar) particular kinds of people from taking part in particular kinds of time- and place-based activities' and *self-selection* refers to 'the agency and preference-based choices people make to attend particular time and place-based activities within the constraints of the forces of social selection' (Wikström 2019b: 275).[14] *The kind of settings a person will take part in depends on the process of self-selection constrained by processes of social selection.*[15] The criminological relevance of all this is that some people, both generally and in specific neighbourhoods (due to processes of social and self-selection), will be more exposed, and more exposed at certain stages of their life-course, to criminogenic settings and settings that promote the development and sustainability of a higher crime propensity. This will help explain both within-neighbourhood individual and between-neighbourhood rate variations in people's crime involvement and criminal careers. However, and crucially, *people do not only live their lives and exclusively commit their crimes in their own neighbourhood.*

[12] Of which some may have a grounding in their genetic make-up.

[13] Importantly, specific kinds of settings' accessibility and attractiveness for different social categories may vary between countries and change over time in the same country.

[14] For an interesting application of the role of self-selection to the problem of desistence (although he discusses it in terms of self-control), see Bottoms (2013).

[15] At birth and early life social selection will obviously have the dominant influence, but with rising age self-selection will increasingly—but unequally so for different people—become an important part of processes of selection relevant to people's differential exposure to specific configurations of settings, with implications for the formation of their crime propensity and involvement in acts of crime.

Beyond neighbourhoods: The importance of people's activity fields

People who live in the same neighbourhood (even in the same household) may, depending on processes of social and self-selection, have very different exposures to different settings within and outside their neighbourhood. People's *activity field* may stretch far outside the area of their place of residence (e.g., due to the out-of-neighbourhood locations of relevant and attractive leisure, shopping, and work settings and friends and relatives' home locations), and hence environmental influences on their development and actions are not restricted to their specific exposures to the micro-environments in their neighbourhood (see Wikström et al. 2010 for an example as regards adolescents' activity fields). Using the neighbourhood as a sole measure of people's environment, which is common in criminological studies into the role of person–environment interactions (e.g., Simcha-Fagan and Schwartz 1986; Gottfredson, McNeill III and Gottfredson 1991; Wikström and Loeber 2000; Lynham et al. 2000; Henry et al. 2014), restricts our understanding of the role of the person–environment interaction in crime causation. This has obvious implications for the understanding and explanation of the sources of neighbourhood offender and crime rates.

The problem of *crime and distance* (i.e., the distance between the place of crime commission and the location of the offender's residence) is central to the analysis of the relationship between neighbourhood characteristics and its crime and offender rates. The neighbourhood crime and offender rates do not only reflect crimes committed by residents in their own neighbourhood (Baldwin and Bottoms 1976; Bottoms 2007; Brantingham and Brantingham 1993 2008; Wikström 1991; Wikström et al. 2012). A neighbourhood's *offender rate* is a result of the combination of crimes that its offenders have committed inside and outside their neighbourhood, and the neighbourhood *crime rate* is a result of the combination of crimes committed in the neighbourhood by residents and visitors (Figure 9.4). If all crimes in a neighbourhood were only committed by its residents and all offenders in a neighbourhood only committed their crimes in their own neighbourhood (which rarely, if ever, is the case), the neighbourhood context would be the only relevant environment when studying the causes of crime events.[16]

[16] Although this does not exclude the possibility of influences from people's participation in external settings on the formation of their crime propensity.

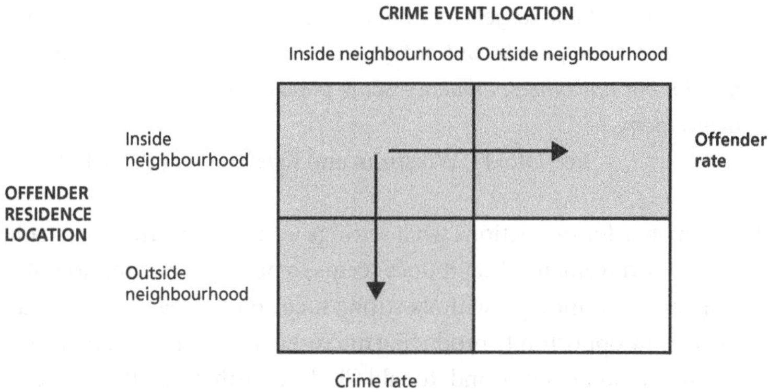

Figure 9.4 Neighbourhood crime and offender rates deconstructed[a]

[a] The lower right-hand white box represents all crimes in which neither the crime occurs in nor the offender resides in the neighbourhood in question.

To get a proper understanding of the role of environment in crime causation rather than using people's neighbourhoods as their environment, we need to focus on explicating and investigating their activity field, which often spreads well outside their neighbourhood. This may also further help to explain why some and not others living in a neighbourhood are more heavily involved in crime and develop persistent and serious criminal careers. The main methodological implication of this is that we need research techniques that allow the study of activity fields (the configuration of the different kinds of the settings in which people actually take part), of which *space–time budgets combined with small area community surveys* are a prime example (Wikström et al. 2011). While classic crime ecology has not paid much attention to the role of settings in crime causation, it is a prime focus for so-called opportunity theories.

Opportunities and crime

Arguing that if someone is motivated to commit a crime and faces a suitable target lacking adequate guardianship, he or she will commit an act of crime does not take us very far towards understanding what causes that crime, or the role of the environment. For example, it does not explain why some people, but not others, commit an act of crime in response to

> *(particular) suitable targets lacking guardianship; why some targets are suitable to some people, but not others; or why some forms of guardianship, but not others, influence some people's, but not others', crime involvement.*
>
> Per-Olof H. Wikström and Kyle Treiber (2015: 420)

Does it matter for our actions what settings we take part in? Does it affect our crime involvement? That it does seems to be a core assumption of environmental criminology, with its strong focus on the role in crime causation of crime opportunity producing micro-environments and their social emergence. Marcus Felson and Ronald Clarke state that 'the theory of crime settings rests on a single principle: that *easy or tempting opportunities entice people into criminal action.* This principle is found in each of the new opportunity theories of crime, including the routine activity approach, crime pattern theory and the rational choice perspective' (1998: 3, my emphasis). The idea that the manipulation of opportunities (e.g., making crime harder to commit and less profitable) is crucial for successful crime prevention is central among advocates of situational crime prevention and is expressed in slogans such as 'opportunity makes the thief' and 'to prevent crime, ignore the offender'.

In many respects, the emergence of environmental criminology was a reaction to people-based explanations of the causes of crime:

> Individual behaviour is a product of an interaction between the person and the setting. Most criminological theory pays attention only to the first, asking why certain people might be more criminally inclined or less so. This neglects the second, the important features of each setting that help to translate criminal inclinations into action. (Felson and Clarke 1998: 1)

While Felson and Clarke's critique of the common disregard in criminology for the importance of the setting in crime causation was largely valid at the time, in practice the approach they and other opportunity theorists took instead led, ironically, to the equally problematic neglect of the role of people and their individual differences. Hence there was a *missed opportunity* to advance a proper ecological perspective on crime and its causes by not taking seriously the role of people (actors) and their interactions with the environment (see further, Wikström and Treiber 2015).

A missed opportunity

Lawrence Cohen and Marcus Felson's *Routine Activity Theory* (RAT) is probably the most well-known and influential theory in the environmental criminology tradition.[17] RAT proposes that 'the probability that a violation will occur at any specific time and place might be taken as a function of the convergence of likely offenders and suitable targets in the absence of capable guardians' (Cohen and Felson 1979: 590).[18] The theory has at its core an interactional model stressing the person–environment interaction and as such it provides an embryo for the development of a proper situational explanation of crime and its causes.

However, in its initial formulation and subsequent applications RAT downplays and largely ignores the role of individual differences in crime causation and fails to provide an action theory (other than occasionally alluding to rational choice theory) that details how the proposed person–environment convergence moves people to commit acts of crime. Cohen and Felson maintain that 'unlike many criminological inquiries, we do not examine why individuals or groups are inclined criminally, but rather we take criminal inclination as given' (1979: 589). Felson acknowledges that 'the routine activity approach implied a decisional offender, but did not make the decision process explicit' (2008: 73). While RAT does recognise that there are individual differences in crime propensity, at best it pays lip service to its role in crime causation. Felson and Eckart sum up the position well, arguing that 'offenders are but one element in a crime, and probably not even the most important' and going on to claim that 'opportunity is a root cause of crime' (2019: 42). What does this mean?

The concept of opportunity

The argument that to do something you need the *opportunity*—the possibility—to do so is pretty self-evident, and in itself does not provide much of an explanation for why certain actions take place (e.g., to shoplift you

[17] Alongside with Clarke and Cornish's application of Rational Choice Theory to the problem of crime (1985), and Brantingham and Brantingham's Crime Pattern Theory (1993).

[18] Writing in the RAT tradition sometimes talks about 'likely offenders' and other times about 'motivated offenders', two concepts that appear to be used exchangeably, as I will do here.

need a store with merchandise you can steal).[19] If opportunity only refers to the possibility to commit crime (e.g., the possibility to hit someone or to steal or vandalise an object), there are endless opportunities to do so for (almost) everybody in their daily living, and this hardly constitutes a good explanation of why crime happens (most opportunities (possibilities) will not result in acts of crime[20]).

However, there are two other aspects of the concept of opportunity that make its role more interesting to consider: the question of what makes a *good opportunity* to commit acts of crime (e.g., shoplifting may, for various reasons, be more attractive and easier in some shops as opposed to others), and the question whether, and to what extent, good opportunities are what *motivate* people to commit acts of crime (e.g., the extent to which shoplifting is a result of people being enticed to steal by coming across good theft opportunities in-store).

The value of a pure 'opportunity' explanation of people's crime involvement depends on the extent to which people's crimes are a result of motivational forces inherent to the setting, and the extent to which suggested motivational features of the setting (e.g., presence of a suitable target in absence of guardianship) are those that generally move people to engage in an act of crime. If the suggested motivational forces of the setting are the sole explanation for why people commit acts of crime, people's differential exposure to good crime opportunities would be the lone explanation for their differential crime involvement, without any need to involve any reference to their crime propensity (or differences therein). However, this would be a tough case to convincingly argue.

Not everyone is enticed to steal attractive unguarded cars

According to RAT, what (almost always) creates a good crime opportunity is *a suitable target in the absence of a capable guardian* that may be acted

[19] Although it may go some way to explain where and when certain types of crime may happen (e.g., shoplifting can only happen at places where there are shops, and at times when they are open).

[20] When considering some specific crime categories, such as insider trading, opportunities may be restricted to certain people, but even among those with the possibility of committing insider trading only a limited number of people would engage in the crime.

upon by a motivated (likely) offender. A suitable target has been defined as 'any person or thing that draws the offender toward a crime' (Felson and Boba 2010: 28), and guardianship as 'the presence of a human element which acts—whether intentionally or not—to deter the would-be offender from committing a crime against an available target' (Hollis, Felson, and Welsh 2013: 76). Cohen and Felson state 'that the analytic distinction between target and guardian is not important in those cases where a personal target engages in self-protection' (Cohen and Felson 1979: 590, footnote 2). In RAT terms, a good crime opportunity is thus when people take part in a setting, in which a person or a thing draws them to do a crime (e.g., 'a car that invites him to steal' or 'somebody who provokes him into a fight'[21]), and there is no human element that would prevent it or deter them.

However, it is hard to define a *good* crime opportunity (or to define a *suitable* target or a *capable* guardian, for that matter) without reference to the actor and her or his relevant preferences and sensitivities. People are different and react and respond differently to the same setting and circumstances. A suitable target for some is not one for others. A capable guardian for some is not one for others. For example, most people would not see an unguarded, attractive car that they come across in their daily life as a potential theft opportunity, but some would. To find objective site characteristics that would entice everyone (or even a majority) to engage in acts of crime would be difficult.

The insight that people do crime (even the same kind of crime) for various reasons, and that some things are more tempting for some people than others, and that some people and their actions (for some persons) are more provocative than others, and that some guardians are more deterring for some than for others, does not take us very far in understanding the causes of crime events. It does not help us explain *why some but not others* engage in acts of crime when they are confronted with what they see as an attractive target in the absence of a capable guardian (e.g., when they come across an unguarded car of the kind they like). A good opportunity is not enough. There is something crucial missing.

[21] Within-bracket quotes taken from Felson and Eckart 2019: 31.

Thieves take opportunities

People are the source of their actions, and they react and respond differently to the circumstances of the setting. Some people are more crime-prone than others; they are more likely than others to see and chose crime as an action alternative in response to certain setting characteristics. *However, what makes some people more crime-prone than others is not a question that preoccupies opportunity theorists.* The definition of 'motivated offender' in RAT, just as the definitions of suitable target and capable guardian, is vague (and tends to blur the difference between motivation and propensity in crime causation). What makes a person criminally inclined, and what makes some more crime-prone than others, is rather unclear.[22]

Cohen and Felson (1979: 590) recognise that a crime requires 'an offender with both criminal inclinations and an ability to carry out those inclinations'. Clarke and Felson (1993: 2) contend that a motivated offender may be 'anybody who for any reason might commit a crime'. The basic proposition of RAT seems to be that what motivates people (anyone) to commit acts of crime is the exposure to crime opportunities, and that the motivational forces of the setting are more important than any influence by people's (differential) crime propensity, illustrated by Felson and Eckart's presumption that 'within-in person variation far exceeds between-person variation' (2019: 50).[23]

This supposition is well illustrated by their discussion of self-control—the only personal characteristic, to my knowledge, that Marcus Felson occasionally alludes to as relevant for people's crime involvement, although stressing that its role should not be overstated: 'the correlation between self-control and delinquency should be duly noted, but not exaggerated' (Felson and Eckart 2019: 52), arguing that 'self-control is not just an individual trait' (ibid: 51) and that 'the power of self-control itself rises and declines in different situations' (ibid: 50). The role of self-control in RAT is undeveloped and far from crystal clear, possibly as a result of a failure to clearly distinguish between a person's *ability* to exercise self-control (as a

[22] For an overview of opportunity theory advocates' reasons for scepticism concerning the value and importance of considering people's differential crime propensities in the explanation and prevention of crime, see Weisburd et al. (2016: 149–150). In my opinion, these are mostly not very convincing arguments, and arguments that generally do not tally very well with our PADS + research findings.

[23] An assumption that appears problematic considering that many people rarely or never engage in acts of crime.

somewhat stable personal trait) and her or his *application* of this ability to the conditions and circumstances of the specific settings in which she or he takes part (for which its relevance and efficacy may vary). For example, peer pressure does not affect a person's ability to exercise self-control, but her or his ability to exercise self-control determines how well she or he can withstand peer pressure.

It is perhaps symptomatic that the reasoning in opportunity theory (and situational crime prevention, for that matter) mostly focuses on how motivated (likely) *offenders* respond to crime opportunities (and how they can be influenced). It is probably fair to say that RAT predominantly is a theory focused on how people who (for whatever reason) are motivated offenders are affected by crime opportunities. Probably, the slogan 'thieves take opportunities' is more fitting to the thrust of opportunity theories than 'opportunity makes the thief'.

Why the few and not the many?

One of the central problems that troubles opportunity theory is why more people do not more often commit acts of crimes if crime essentially is a matter of exposure to crime opportunities (which are all over the place), and whether this is not a consequence of the fact that people vary in their crime propensity and, crucially, that most people tend to have a low crime propensity (being largely resistant to most crime opportunities). It is true that opportunity theorists and researchers at times allude to the role of crime propensity, but mostly as a 'get out of jail free card', without seriously considering its implications for their theorising, research designs, and crime prevention suggestions.

A well-known statistic, largely ignored in RAT theorising, is the fact that the distribution of crime in the population is heavily skewed: a few commit a lot of the crimes, particularly of the more serious kind (e.g., Piquero, Farrington, and Blumstein 2007: 17–19; Wikström 1990). This consistent finding tallies badly with the idea that opportunity is the main (most important) cause of people's crime involvement, unless one makes the less realistic assumption that the skewed distribution of crime in the population mainly reflects people's differential exposure to suitable targets without guardianship.

Our PADS + research show that young people's crime hotspots are a result of the coming together of crime-prone young people and criminogenic settings[24] (Wikström et al. 2012: 315) and that young people with a low crime propensity are largely unaffected by the influence of taking part in criminogenic settings (Wikström, Mann, and Hardie 2019), demonstrating the shortcomings of ignoring people (actors) and their interaction with the environment in the study of crime causation. We have also established that stability and changes in people's crime involvement in adolescence and young adulthood (their different crime trajectories) largely reflect stability and changes in their levels of crime propensity and criminogenic exposure (Wikström, Treiber, and Roman 2022).

I would not go so far as to argue that crime opportunities (in the RAT sense) are unimportant (the deterrent qualities of a setting clearly play a role for crime-prone people), but I would insist that other aspects of the setting are far more important in the explanation of why crime happens—why some and not others are enticed to commit acts of crime in certain settings.

The moral filter

In a Situational Action Theory (SAT) framework, instead of talking about opportunities we talk about motivators and we argue that there are two main kinds: temptations and provocations. A *temptation* occurs when a person's preference-based desires connect with an opportunity (possibility) to satisfy the desire, and a *provocation* arises when a person's specific sensitivities are activated by encountering a friction (e.g., someone blocking your way or making insulting comments). In both cases *the motivation is an outcome of (triggered by) the person–environment interaction* (i.e., it depends on who is in what setting). Motivators provide goal-directed orientation.

However, in SAT, motivation is not enough for a crime to happen: there are typically both legal and illegal action alternatives to respond to a specific motivator (or one can refrain from responding at all)—it also requires that the person sees and choses crime as an action alternative. The crucial ingredient here is the *moral filter* (determining the perception of what are viable and acceptable action alternatives in relation to an experienced motivator). This is an outcome of *the actor's application of her or his personal morals to*

[24] *Crime propensity* was measured as an index of scales of law-relevant morality and ability to exercise self-control, and a *criminogenic setting* was measured as a residential area with poor collective efficacy or a city or local centre area in which the young person spent time with peers, unsupervised and engaged in unstructured activities.

the moral context of the setting in which she or he takes part (its perceived relevant moral norms and their significance). If a person does not perceive crime as an action alternative, her or his ability to exercise self-control and the setting's deterrent qualities (capable guardians, in opportunity theory terminology) does not come into play (does not affect the action-choice). Importantly, the matter of what action alternatives a person sees and chooses is not a straightforward (one-to-one) function of the actor's personal morals, but a result of the *application* of her or his personal morals to the moral context in which she or he takes part. It is always about the interaction.

Examples of criminological concepts that tap into the importance of *the moral contexts of action* are Robert Sampson's concept of 'collective efficacy' as applied to settings (see Wikström et al. 2012) and 'the moral code of the streets' as applied to the settings of street segments (Andersson 1999). It is interesting to note that in some later developments in opportunity theory-based situational crime prevention techniques (Clarke 1997: 23–24), certain suggested new practices seem to directly target the moral context of the setting: in addition to the original three main techniques, 'increasing efforts', 'increasing risk', and 'reducing rewards', a fourth main technique labelled 'removal of excuses' was added, including the subcategories 'rule-setting' and 'stimulating conscience'.

Coda

In this chapter I have argued, from a Situational Action Theory perspective, for the value of a true social ecology of crime that incorporates and integrates key knowledge and insights from person-oriented and place-oriented criminology. I have highlighted and explored key problems of neglecting the role of people (actors) and their individual characteristics when assessing the role of the environment in crime causation. I have specifically exemplified these problems in relation to two prominent study areas in the social ecology of crime tradition: the study of neighbourhoods and crime and the role of opportunities in crime causation.

Unnecessary conflicts between person-oriented and place-oriented perspectives in the study and explanation of crime are unhelpful and hinder the advancement of our knowledge of crime, its causes and prevention. It is easy to agree with Albert J. Reiss Jr, who some time ago, with reference to the individual and ecological traditions of research into crime, convincingly argued that 'more is to be gained by linking those traditions than by their continued separate development and testing' (1986: 29). The question is not whether a person-oriented or a place-oriented approach to the understanding and explanation of crime is the better one, but how we can combine the key insights from the two to get a more comprehensive and in-depth understanding of the crime problem. Situational Action Theory is an attempt to do just that.

10

Constructive Sentencing through Custody-Avoiding Sanctions

Theoretical Foundations and Practical Challenges

Antje du Bois-Pedain

Introduction

In recent years, sentencing innovations that permit courts to impose what one may think of as 'bespoke' sentences, which are aimed at helping the offender stay away from crime, have received renewed attention from scholars and policy-makers alike.[1] In the United States, a backlash against sentencing guidelines that produced oppressive patterns of mass incarceration is in full swing.[2] It includes, at the policy level, a renewal of diversion strategies for certain offender groups,[3] and at court level, an increasing willingness to revert to individualised sentencing practices.[4] At first blush, the embedding of sentencing guidelines in England and Wales over the past decade or so, and the introduction of guideline options in the Scottish criminal justice system, may point in a different direction. However, in aspiration at least, these guideline regimes aim to preserve possibilities for constructive, individualised sentencing, which are often of greatest interest

[1] See, e.g., Cullen et al. (2017), and (for early prescient criticism of the turn away from correctional rehabilitation) Cullen and Gilbert (1982).

[2] On the phenomenon and causes of mass incarceration, see, e.g., National Research Council (2014); Gottschalk (2015). On changes to sentencing, see Lamb (2015), Adelman (2016), and the contributions to Tonry (2019).

[3] Influential documents include a 2013 report by the American Probation and Parole Association (APPA 2013) and the National Center for State Courts on effective responses to offender behaviour, and numerous manuals on risk and needs assessments in sentencing prepared by the latter organisation.

[4] For the latter, see, e.g., Commonwealth of Massachusetts Superior Court (2016).

Antje du Bois-Pedain, *Constructive Sentencing through Custody-Avoiding Sanctions*. In: *Crime, Justice, and Social Order*. Edited by: Alison Liebling, Joanna Shapland, Richard Sparks, and Justice Tankebe, Oxford University Press.
DOI: 10.1093/oso/9780192859600.003.0010

when they can reduce reliance on imprisonment. Indeed, developments towards meaningful alternatives to imprisonment have been a central concern for Tony Bottoms throughout his long career, with some of his most influential publications concerning the present and future of probation, suspended sentences, and other community-based disposals (see esp. Bottoms 1980, 1981, 1987a, 1989, 1998, 2008a, 2017b; Bottoms et al. 2002, 2004a). Before embarking on an academic career, Tony Bottoms worked for some time as a probation officer, and from many conversations with him about law and justice I feel sure that experiences from and concerns formed during this time have always been key to his academic outlook (and perhaps no less to his ineradicable belief in the possibility of personal improvement, which infuses his work on community-based rehabilitation and desistance alike).

This chapter therefore focuses, in Tony's honour, on the types of sanctions that have been of such longstanding concern for him, namely custody-avoiding sanctions—the collective term I use for community sanctions and measures and for suspended sentences of imprisonment. Of course, as we shall see, the technical legal construction standardly placed on the latter is that of a sentence of imprisonment, the mere enforcement of which is modified or suspended. This, however, does not change the fact that the sentencer's intention when imposing this type of sentence is to avoid sending the offender to prison (and this will also be the practical outcome if the offender successfully completes the operational period of the sentence). I also, for the most part, restrict my discussion of suspended sentences to those which are suspended entirely. Partially suspended sentences, given their similarity to early release on parole under conditions, raise partly overlapping but also significantly different issues.

My use of the term 'bespoke sentences' differs from some earlier understandings in the literature. I use this expression to refer to individualised sentences, where sentencers choose from a selection of generally available, standardised sentence elements in order to meet the stated sentencing objectives. In some of the earlier discussions (e.g., von Hirsch 1993: ch. 8), by contrast, the notion of 'bespoke' sentencing was associated with sanction packages that, in an effort to tailor a punishment precisely to the circumstances and criminal behaviour of a particular offender, could include burdens and requirements not standardly available as sentence options; for instance, sentencing a slum landlord to a short term of residence in his slum building (a real-life example considered by Duff 1991: 245 and von Hirsch 1993: 76). Such non-standard disposal options raise additional concerns, particularly regarding a lack of legal certainty and the risk that conditions are imposed which violate offenders' basic rights (for discussion, see O'Malley 2018: 42–43). My analysis is concerned with the model for bespoke sentences that has been adopted in England and Wales: a model that restricts sentencers to the making of certain types of orders, where the 'bespoke' dimension resides in the range of orders available, and in the possibility of their flexible combination.

My discussion takes up the twin challenges of providing a coherent penal–theoretical conceptualisation of custody-avoiding sentencing options and of integrating these options into a comprehensive theory of criminal punishment capable of underpinning constructive sentencing practices.

I first address the conceptual question whether criminal case disposals such as suspended sentences of imprisonment, unpaid work requirements, drug rehabilitation treatment, and other lifestyle-modifying obligations are best understood as falling within the general category of punishments, and (if so) whether they are best theorised as intermediate sanctions. After presenting relevant legal arrangements and empirical findings pertaining to the English and German contexts, I ask to what extent an analysis of these punishments as 'intermediate sanctions' is helpful in understanding their place in the system of criminal disposals, and in what respects this categorisation appears to miss important dimensions of these sanctions. This leads me to focus on three destabilising features associated with these sanctions: wide interpersonal variation of perceptions of severity, instability of content, and malleability of penal function. The latter two are shown to be key to an appropriate theoretical understanding and practical deployment of these types of sanctions. The array of penal aims pursued through the imposition of a concrete sanction package requires a degree of conditionality and resolves the apparent contradiction in the fact that these sanctions are always imposed by sentencers as precisely the right sanction for the case at hand, and yet are also sometimes seen and justified as constituting a deliberate underpunishment. These features also, in large part, explain why views about the absolute and relative severity of these sanctions differ so profoundly, and help us understand why the theorisation of these sanctions as intermediate penal disposals is insufficiently complex.

I then consider what penal theory can underpin these sanctions and provide guidance for their imposition. I argue that, when punishment is viewed as an ongoing process of setting reasonable terms for continued coexistence between the polity and an offender, the theoretical justification for the imposition of custody-avoiding intermediate sanctions becomes continuous with the justification for imposing other types of sanctions. This approach stands in marked contrast to most current sentencing regimes, which make community-based disposals, but not imprisonment, subject to additional suitability requirements. It is capable of integrating custody-avoiding sanctions seamlessly into a sanctions regime, putting an end to community sanction 'exceptionalism' by insisting that all punishments, not merely community-based ones, must be suitable as well as proportionate. This assists the integration of non-custodial sanctions into the penal–theoretical landscape in another way, too. The exceptionalist perspective is often taken by those who see custody-avoiding intermediate sanctions (more so than other sanctions) as giving effect to the value of parsimony (e.g. Tonry 1994) or penal restraint (Irwin-Rogers and Roberts 2019: 155). While parsimony is indeed a value that ought to shape and constrain penal impositions, arguments of this kind can easily lead to a bifurcated division of penal disposals into parsimonious and non-parsimonious options, to be chosen for different offenders placed on, so to speak, different tracks—with all the questions this raises about equality between offenders. In response to such views, it is suggested that a uniform approach to punishment's justification, combined with a more capacious conceptualisation of proportionality judgements as 'bifocal' (as developed in du Bois-Pedain 2017), provides a superior theoretical framework in which to develop criteria for choices between different kinds of sanctions, fully integrating the value of parsimony into every sentencing decision.

The nature of the beast: Conceptualising the penal content of suspended sentences of imprisonment and community sanctions and measures

Theorisation of the wide and varied array of community-based, custody-avoiding penal disposals now available in many jurisdictions is made difficult by what Gazal-Ayal and Roberts (2019: v) call the 'protean nature of suspended and conditional sentences', explaining that '[i]f they are construed to allow a court great flexibility in terms of the number and intrusiveness of conditions, as well as the duration of the order, it becomes hard to locate them on a scale of severity'. Indeed, the specifically 'punitive' content of some non-custodial orders may be not only difficult to quantify but elusive to identify in view of the penal objectives this particular order may be designed and understood to serve. Consequently, it may become difficult to conceive of some of these disposals as punishments at all, and it certainly is difficult to fit them into a desert-based sentencing scheme (cf. Bottoms 2017b; see also Bottoms 1998 in respect of probation orders).

One factor that contributes to the difficulty of conceptualising various custody-avoiding disposals as punishments is that their design and use differs considerably between criminal justice systems, and even within the same jurisdiction over time. Take suspended sentences of imprisonment. One possible understanding of a suspended sentence is that of a suspension of the imposition of punishment as such. Actual punishment for the offence is reserved rather than imposed. While this is not the construction standardly adopted by legislators, especially on the Continent (see Ancel 1971), it may exceptionally be the case that legislation treats the imposition and not merely the execution of the sentence as having been suspended. This was how suspended sentences functioned when they were first introduced in South Australia in 1887 (Smith 2016: 242), and some Nordic countries also permit a suspension of the sentencing decision as such (Lappi-Seppälä 2019: 20–22). The suspended sentence then does not even register as a punishment until the suspension is revoked and the sentencing process activated. In such a system, further conditions of suspension (even if they are onerous to comply with for the individual concerned, and run the full gamut of what other systems provide for as non-custodial punishments) may then quite possibly not register as penal hardships, and the question whether they are convincing punishments from a sociological perspective or appropriate punishments from a normative one may not even be asked. In South Australia, for instance, sentencers conceive of the suspended sentence as a 'form of bond "with teeth in it"' (Smith 2016: 247, quoting Dengate 1978: 41). Indeed, there are even examples of suspended sentences emerging entirely informally through local court practice. In Ireland, the Law Reform Commission (2017) explains, the introduction of suspended sentences 'has [been] attributed . . . to Sir Thomas O'Shaughnessey, Recorder of Dublin between 1905 and 1924 who formulated 'a probation system of his own" whereby "the prisoner is not asked to serve [his or her sentence] unless and until he [or she] breaks the law again"' (Law Reform Commission 2017: 10, quoting Osborough 1982). Similarly, when probation first emerged in England in the second half of the nineteenth century, it did so as a sentence-avoiding diversionary option where courts entrusted private individuals with charitable ambitions with the task of helping first-time offenders avoid brushes with law enforcement in the future (Vanstone 2004; on the conceptual differences between probation and Continental-style suspended sentences, see especially van Zyl Smit et al. 2015: 6–7). While the creation of the probation service and the professionalisation of probation work led to the state involving itself in probation provision, this was initially located within the state's welfare delivery. It was only in the 1990s that probation formally became a type of sentence to be imposed post-conviction; a change that was accompanied by a reduction in welfare orientation and a gearing up of offender monitoring and control (see, e.g., Farrant 2006, Raynor 2018). Before that change, probation in England was more similar to a conditional discharge than it was to suspended sentences of imprisonment, in that an offender who was given probation would avoid the imposition of a criminal sentence if successful during the probationary period (see also Bottoms 2017b: 566–571).

This section of the chapter is intended to lay some groundwork for the ensuing discussion by introducing readers to the legislative framing of sentencing options in two jurisdictions, one Anglo-American (England and Wales; hereafter: England), the other Continental (Germany). The subsequent discussion will build its conclusions on the sometimes similar, sometimes different patterns and problems observable in these jurisdictions.

Available penal disposals and their interrelation in German law

German law recognises only two types of primary sanctions: fines and imprisonment. Following tentative beginnings from the 1950s onwards, in 1969 the legislator—in connection with a thoroughgoing reform and revision of the penal system in the late 1960s—created the regime for the suspension of sentences of imprisonment which is still in force today. The 1969 revisions of the German Penal Code (StGB) not only provide sentencers with the option to suspend sentences of up to two years' imprisonment (section 56(1) and (2) StGB), but also require that sentencers suspend sentences of less than six months unless, owing to special features of the offence or the character and personality of the offender, actual imprisonment is necessary in order to influence the offender or to maintain respect for the legal order (section 47(1) StGB). The operative period of a suspended sentence must be between two and five years (section 56a StGB). The main condition imposed by a suspended sentence of imprisonment is the condition not to reoffend during the operative period of the sentence.

Community orders do not exist as autonomous sanctions in the German system, but the kinds of conditions familiar from the English sentencers' menu of community-based disposals can in Germany be imposed as adjuncts to a suspended sentence of imprisonment, in the form of additional requirements (*Auflagen*, section 56b StGB) or instructions (*Weisungen*, section 56c StGB) to the offender. In this context, the offender can also be placed under the supervision of a probation officer (section 56d StGB). The breach of a suspended sentence can result in the revocation of the suspension by the court (section 56f StGB). There is only one kind of non-custodial sanction that can be imposed as an adjunct to a fine in order to increase the sanction's overall punitive content: this is a driving ban, when it is imposed unconnected to the commission of any driving offences (section 44(1), second sentence StGB). Before this possibility was introduced in 2017, it was not open to the sentencing court to impose any further non-custodial sanction alongside a fine.

For the range of cases where a sentence of imprisonment is short enough to be capable of suspension, the legislative scheme treats suspended and unsuspended sentences of imprisonment as interchangeable sanctions in terms of their penal value (one day of unsuspended imprisonment equals one day of suspended imprisonment).[5] Sentencers are instructed to make the choice between these sanction types on special-preventive and general-deterrent—and hence on utilitarian rather than on retributive—grounds (see section 56a StGB). On a technical-doctrinal level, the suspended sentence is construed as a modification of the enforcement of a prison sentence (see, e.g., Heinz 2005). At the end of the operational period, provided the suspension has not been revoked in response to breaches, the court is instructed to remit the sentence (section 56g StGB). This construction applies both to simple suspended sentences and to suspended sentences to which further conditions are attached.

This legislative scheme notwithstanding, empirical research into sentencers' understandings and attitudes, and actual court practice, has established conclusively that the suspended sentence of imprisonment is

[5] For suspended sentences, this is not explicitly spelled out but treated as self-evident. For fines, which are expressed in a multiple of units that equate to an offender's actual or potential daily income (day-fine system), the conversion rate for unpaid fines, that one day-fine unit equals one day of imprisonment, is laid down in section 43 StGB.

treated by practitioners as a sentence option in its own right, located—in terms of severity—between fines and imprisonment (see, e.g., Harrendorf 2017). Practitioners will, for instance, discuss whether a particular case of medium seriousness can still be dealt with 'by a suspended sentence', not whether 'the deserved period of imprisonment can be suspended'. It is often only after agreement has been reached, in the more serious cases, that a suspended sentence is still an option that its length is fixed (at the legal maximum for periods of imprisonment that can be suspended, which is two years of imprisonment), and further conditions (e.g., making a significant payment to a designated charity) are attached to the suspended sentence to increase its total onerousness to a level considered appropriate for the crime. Harrendorf (2017: 523) describes these arrangements as 'strategies of mitigation' employed to achieve 'suspendability' and suggests that these strategies may be particularly prevalent in the context of German-style sentence negotiations. In practice, the suspended sentence registers with sentencers as a custody-avoiding option, selected when the offending behaviour does not require immediate imprisonment.

The simple suspended sentence (without further conditions attached) is considered less severe than a suspended sentence to which further conditions have been attached (irrespective of whether these are explicitly punitive conditions or designed to assist the offender in managing personal issues that place him at risk of reoffending). Gauging the severity of such 'suspension-plus' sentences brings with it the difficulty of placing, on a scale concerned with punitiveness or penal hardship, some impositions whose primary purpose and function is not to create hardship (an issue to which I will return below).

Available penal disposals and their interrelation in English law

The present English sentencing regime provides for fines, community sanctions and measures, suspended sentences of imprisonment, and non-suspended sentences of imprisonment as types of penal sanctions. Absolute and conditional discharges may be imposed in cases where there is no mandatory sentence and the court considers it 'inexpedient to inflict punishment' (section 12(1) of the Powers of the Criminal Courts (Sentencing Act 2000). Probation, which (as mentioned above) was initially conceived in England as a *punishment*-avoiding disposal, became a sentence in its own right in 1991. Subsequently, however, probation was subsumed within the broader notion of a community order to which a supervision requirement was attached (see generally Bottoms 2017: 578ff; Mair 2011).[6] It therefore does not feature as a separate sentencing option in the analysis that follows.

English sentencing law has seen a huge expansion of freestanding community-based disposal options since the 1960s. In their latest incarnation, courts can choose from a wide list of requirements to form part of the community order.[7] These requirements must not only be 'the most suitable for the offender' but also, to the extent that they restrict the offender's liberty, 'such as in the opinion of the court are commensurate with the seriousness of the offence' (section 148(2)(a) and (b) of the Criminal Justice Act (CJA 2003). Prior to 2013, the courts were otherwise simply instructed to have regard to the five statutory purposes of sentencing (punishment, crime reduction, rehabilitation, public protection and reparation) when imposing a community order. Following a legislative amendment by the Crime and Courts Act 2013, however, at least one condition or requirement must be imposed on the offender 'for the purposes of punishment', or he must in addition to the community order also be given a fine. The newly inserted provision (section 177(2A) CJA 2003) does not specify which requirements fulfil 'the purposes of punishment' but leaves this for the court

[6] The tortuous history of changes to probation service delivery in England and Wales in the last few decades, connected to ongoing reinventions of probation's place within the criminal justice system, is also reflected in changing terminology. Initially rebranded as a 'community rehabilitation order' in 2001, probation was removed as an autonomous disposal by the Criminal Justice Act (CJA) 2003, which instead allowed sentencers to attach a supervision requirement to custody-avoiding disposals—a terminological change that obliquely but decisively refocuses probation on control and monitoring functions. See Mair (2011) for the legal changes and Farrant (2006) for the atmospheric ones.

[7] These are: unpaid work (known as community payback); residence (requiring an offender to reside at a place specified in the court order); mental health treatment; drug rehabilitation; alcohol treatment; supervision (requiring an offender to attend appointments as instructed by a probation officer); attendance centre (requiring an offender aged under 25 to attend a particular centre at specified times); prohibited activity (requiring an offender to refrain from participating in certain activities as set out in the court order); curfew (confining an offender to a specified place for a specified number of hours per day); exclusion (prohibiting the offender from entering a place specified in the court order); programme (requiring the offender to participate in an accredited programme such as anger management courses); activity (requiring the offender to participate in certain activities such as basic skills classes); foreign travel prohibition requirement (see CJA 2003, sections 176 ff.). The Offender Rehabilitation Act (ORA) 2014 abolished the supervision requirement and the activity requirement and inserted a new 'Rehabilitation Activity Requirement' in their place. This was connected to the part-privatisation of probation-related services in the ORA 2014. The abolition of the supervision requirement was controversial (for discussion, see Robinson and Dominey 2019). The ORA reforms have been unsuccessful, and new organisational structures are being put in their place. At the time of writing it is unclear whether the supervision requirement will be reinstated.

to decide in the case before it. The court may refrain from imposing such a requirement only in exceptional circumstances (section 177 (2B) CJA 2003, also inserted in 2013).

When suspended sentences were introduced into English law in 1967, their legislative construction was remarkably similar to the model still in force in Germany today. Any term of imprisonment of up to and including two years was capable of being suspended, with the operational period lasting for between one and three years. In order to suppress the imposition of short sentences of imprisonment, the law required sentences of imprisonment of up to six months to be suspended, unless the case fell within relatively narrow exceptions. This legislative provision was quickly interpreted by the Court of Appeal as making suspended sentences available only in cases that had, on their specific facts, crossed the custody threshold, requiring sentencing courts to first consider and dismiss all non-custodial options, then determine which term of imprisonment to impose, before going on to consider whether that term of imprisonment could be suspended (*R v O'Keefe* [1969] 2 Q.B. 29).

Empirical research on the use of the suspended sentence quickly showed, however, that the suspended sentence was employed in a somewhat different manner by the courts. A Home Office study that analysed sentence patterns up to 1970 estimated that of all offenders given suspended sentences, 'only somewhere between 40 per cent and 50 per cent ... would, but for the new provisions, have been sentenced to imprisonment for the original offence' (Oatham and Simon 1972, quoted in Bottoms 1981: 5); the remainder would have been given fines or probation instead. There were also indications that magistrates' courts had '[begun] to impose longer sentences in those cases where they suspended imprisonment than they did in cases in which they actually imposed imprisonment' (Bottoms 1981: 6). Moreover, sentencers clearly disliked the injunction to suspend all sentences of imprisonment of up to six months, and an analysis of sentence patterns suggested that some of them would rather opt to impose a slightly longer prison term which they did not have to suspend (Bottoms 1981: 7).

Since the intention behind the introduction of the suspended sentence had been to reduce levels of imprisonment, these effects were viewed as malfunctions. Corrective action by the legislator enshrined in law the Court of Appeal's interpretation that sought to limit the imposition of suspended sentences to cases that would otherwise have attracted immediate imprisonment and abolished the six-month rule (Bottoms 1981: 12). A distinctive hiatus in the use of suspended sentences occurred after 1991, when the Criminal Justice Act 1991 made these sentences available only in exceptional circumstances. The 1990 White Paper preceding this Act explicitly endorsed desert-based sentencing (Home Office 1990). The reason for the introduction of the exceptional circumstances clause was that suspended sentences were seen as basically incompatible with a desert framework, because an allegedly onerous penalty—a suspended sentence of *imprisonment*—usually resulted in the offender walking free from the court with no further controls or restrictions imposed on his behaviour,[8] carrying only what Australian criminologist David Tait (1995) memorably dubbed an 'invisible sanction'. The 'exceptional circumstances' clause resulted in a very large decrease in the use of suspended sentences—a degree of judicial compliance with the statute which is perhaps surprising in light of the fact that, as pointed out above, the statutory requirement that sentencers should only pass a suspended sentence where otherwise they would send the offender to immediate custody has never been fully followed in the English courts.

The 'exceptional circumstances' restriction was abolished by the CJA 2003—a change which became effective from 2005 onwards. That Act also provided that the same requirements that can be imposed through a community order can also be attached to a suspended sentence. It was not originally possible after 2005 to pass a suspended sentence with no additional requirements—a radical change from the previous position, notwithstanding that sentencers were exhorted to use less onerous requirements in conjunction with suspended sentences than they would impose as part of a community order (see Mair et al. 2007: 19). The Legal Aid, Sentencing and Punishment of Offenders Act 2012 reintroduced the possibility of suspended sentences with no requirements, but in practice requirements are still attached to suspended sentences in the majority of cases (see Irwin-Rogers and Roberts 2019: 149–150).

Once the option to suspend a sentence of imprisonment was no longer limited to exceptional circumstances, the suspended sentence of imprisonment quickly gained ground. Scholars have drawn attention to the fact that whereas, in the Crown Court, suspended sentences were imposed in no more than 2 per cent of cases in 2004, by 2017 such sentences were imposed in 27 per cent of cases (see Irwin-Rogers and Roberts 2019: 143 and O'Malley 2018: 50). This provides some indication that suspended sentences

[8] Prior to 2005, the only possibility of a requirement added to a suspended sentence was the so-called Suspended Sentence Supervision Order, but in practice very few suspended sentences carried this additional requirement.

are being used in lieu of immediate imprisonment at the higher end of seriousness of cases in which suspended sentences are employed. That said, Irwin-Rogers and Roberts (2019: 144) also stress that the use of community sentences in Crown Court cases declined markedly during the same period, indicating that some of the rise in suspended sentences may have been due to courts preferring suspended sentences to community orders. Certainly, sentencing data strongly suggests that the growth of suspended sentences in magistrates' courts occurred mainly at the expense of community orders, despite the fact that the legislative construction in theory reserves suspended sentences for cases in which the custody threshold has been crossed (Roberts and Ashworth 2016: 314–315; see also Irwin-Rogers and Roberts 2019: 142 (Table 1)). This shift towards greater use of (suspended) sentences of imprisonment in preference to community orders could be indicative of an increase in punitiveness (as suggested by Mair et al. 2007: 19). It may, however, also in part be owing to the fact that, since 2012, it has been possible to impose a suspended sentence of imprisonment with *no* further requirement attached. Where sentencers fear that offenders may be unable to cope with even comparatively undemanding requirements, they may for this reason show a preference for a short suspended sentence without any further requirements over a community order.

It is clear from the legislative scheme that community orders are intended for offenders whose offending behaviour does not merit a sentence of imprisonment. They are freestanding disposals for cases located, in terms of their seriousness, between those that require imprisonment (including suspended imprisonment) and those that can be dealt with by a fine. A more difficult question is whether the suspended sentence should, in the English context, be categorised as an intermediate sanction, or as something else. In contrast to probation, which (even after it was, in 1991, turned into a sentencing option instead of an alternative to the imposition of a sentence) could conceivably be thought of as a non-punitive disposal, the suspended sentence is clearly not merely 'a punishment postponed'. But does it constitute an intermediate sanction, or is it (as the postulated sequence of decision-making for the sentencer in the *O'Keefe* judgment suggests) better analysed as a prison sentence whose enforcement has been modified? To answer this question, we first need to take a step back and ask ourselves: what exactly is the penal content of the suspended sentence of imprisonment?

In his evaluation of the operation of suspended sentences in England between 1967 and 1978, Bottoms (1981) made some prescient observations as to what might be the perceived punitive content of a suspended sentence (and thus account for its ready uptake by sentencers, and their understanding of it as an intermediate sanction). He suggested that the suspended sentence 'has acquired perhaps a special psychological attraction to sentencers in that they can feel they are being punitive and passing a severe sentence, while at the same time allowing themselves the warmth of recognising the humanity of their leniency' (Bottoms 1981: 20). Bottoms hypothesises that this two-sidedness of the suspended sentence may account for sentencers preferring it over probation or conditional discharges (which are merely lenient).

For this to be the explanation of the suspended sentence's attractiveness, the suspended sentence must, first, have a recognisable punitive content. This content appears to reside in its heightened denunciatory message (the reason why sentencers can 'feel they are being punitive'). A suspended sentence of imprisonment is, on the symbolic/communicative level, a prison sentence; while that does not make it equal to an actual prison sentence, its symbolic/communicative seriousness gives it the quality of a true sanction, and what Robinson (1994: 103) memorably calls 'punitive bite'.

Bottoms's second hypothesis concerning the popularity of suspended sentences with sentencers—that suspended sentences also allow sentencers to feel 'the warmth of recognising the humanity of their leniency'—picks up on another crucial feature of these sentences. The decision to suspend the sentence communicates that the sentencer views the offender as a fallible fellow human being, and is prepared to give him the benefit of the doubt that he is, at the end of the day (and after the shock and bother of the criminal trial and the shame of his conviction), able and willing to live in a law-abiding way, as a fully integrated member of society.

It is not unimportant in explaining the attraction of the sentence that it is not only less serious than prison in reality, but also able to express and communicate this lesser seriousness upfront—and not only lesser seriousness but a positive attitude towards the offender, a belief that 'I don't think you are a bad person at heart'. It is precisely the fact that the sentencer trusts the offender to remain in the community, that the sentencer in this way invests in the offender, that makes the suspended sentence a reintegrative tool that is potentially superior to a sentence of immediate imprisonment (which always also says to the offender 'you must be kept away from the rest of us, at least for a while'). Put differently, the attraction of the suspended sentence resides in part in the fact that the sentencer is able to say, at the same time, 'this is what your offending behaviour in principle deserves (to wit, a significant time in prison) but I do believe in you and believe that you don't quite deserve to have the full consequences of your wrongdoing rebound on you, so I'm giving you the chance to avoid the most serious of these consequences (and hence I'm suspending the sentence)'. Perhaps this second message should be thought of as an expression of benevolence. But that in my view distorts its true basis. Suspending the sentence is not about being nice to the defendant, punishing him less than he deserves, but about taking the stance that he *deserves to be treated in a lenient fashion* by reason of the fact that one should continue to place some trust, and hope, in him. This is an issue to which I will return in the final section of this chapter.

Advantages and limitations of a theorisation of suspended sentences and community-based disposals as intermediate sanctions

It is clear from experience in many countries that a system which only contains fines and immediate sentences of imprisonment as sentencing options is insufficiently nuanced (at least when it also excludes the option of very short prison sentences, such as one day). Imagine a system where the minimum length of a prison term is one month. Sentencers in such systems would surely feel that they cannot achieve proportionality in a fairly wide range of cases in the middle, where a fine seems not serious enough but imprisonment (let alone of this duration) should still be out of the question. It is unsurprising that sentencers would then happily turn to sentence alternatives that seem more appropriate for these cases, because they appear to sentencers to be more burdensome than a fine but still markedly less serious than imprisonment. It is also clear that, whatever the legislative conceptualisation of the alternative introduced (say, as a mere 'modification of the execution of a sentence of imprisonment', as the German legislator still insists), in practice it will be viewed, and used, as an intermediate punishment for cases which in seriousness sit between those appropriately dealt with by a mere fine, and those that require an immediate custodial sanction.

It should therefore not surprise us that, empirically, the introduction of 'a new or reformed alternative sanction [most commonly] reduces the use of custody (decarceration) while also increasing some of the community bound case-load (net-widening)' (Gazal-Ayal and Roberts 2019: iv; on net-widening effects see also Aebi et al. 2015). The most plausible explanation for this pattern of effects is that the alternative sanction responds to a felt need by sentencers to resort to a sanction which reflects, more accurately than the sanctions previously available, the seriousness of the sentenced behaviour, and which enables them to achieve, more precisely than other sanction types do, the impact on the offender which the sentencer wishes. That some offenders are now being punished more appropriately (in the sentencer's perception of what is deserved and what stands a good chance of achieving desired behavioural changes in the offender) is the most likely explanation for the phenomenon of net-widening (cf Tonry and Lynch 1996: 102).

Specifically as regards the suspended sentence, it is instructive that (as van Zyl Smit et al. 2015 have shown) both historically and in international policy documents prepared and adopted by United Nations bodies and in the Council of Europe from the 1950s onwards, suspended sentences as known in various Continental jurisdictions were seen as functional equivalents to English-style probation. While this was in important ways an over-simplification, it does remind us that the suspended sentence must, first and foremost, be made sense of as a custody-avoiding (and in that sense 'quasi non-custodial') sentence option—notwithstanding that the threat of imprisonment hangs over those who commit a breach.[9]

Against this background, it was only to be expected that, when suspended sentences were first introduced in England, their effect as a sentence that replaced immediate imprisonment was more muted, since the introduction of probation decades earlier had already swept up much of that effect and the clientele for suspended sentences were now drawn in part from those who would previously have been given probation, and only the remainder came from those who would have received immediate sentences of imprisonment. This led some (such as Radzinowicz 1999: 325, quoted in van Zyl Smit et al. 2015: 13) to categorically reject suspended sentences of imprisonment as a sentencing option in the English context. But, as Bottoms (and others, e.g. Sparks 1971) realised at the time, the introduction of suspended sentences in England still gave sentencers a valuable new disposal option, one that offered sentencers something that probation did not offer in the same way (see especially Bottoms 1981). The suspended sentence's displacement of probation as a penal disposal tells us something

[9] This analysis is confirmed by sentencers' views quoted in Mair et al. (2008): 27–28 (quoting judges as saying that 'in reality it's been regarded as a hybrid between the Community Order and a sentence of imprisonment' and describing the suspended sentence as 'an in-between sentence').

important about not just the practical but also the normative differences between suspended sentences and probation—and from which it follows that suspended sentences are more easily conceptualised as 'real' punishments than is classical probation (even after it became a sentence option rather than a diversion measure).

That said, international experience (both positive and negative) with suspended sentences also shows that the proper operation of this sentence option requires acceptance of the pure suspended sentence as a 'real punishment' by sentencers and public alike. Fortunately, it seems that the suspended sentence does not suffer from the same image problems in Europe that beset it in parts of Australia, where it came to be viewed by a politically important segment of the public as equivalent to 'no punishment'.[10] Both in England and in Germany, it is a sentence of high denunciatory content and is thus readily perceived by those inside and outside the system as more severe than a fine, thus functioning as a credible disposal option for fairly severe cases for which a fine would be perceived as 'too soft'.[11]

Serious implications for the proper theorisation of these sentences arise, however, from the fact that, in both systems, hardly anyone buys into the legislator's insistence that a suspended sentence of imprisonment is really a sentence of imprisonment, if by that we are meant to place it on the same rung of our imaginary severity ladder as imprisonment. It is overwhelmingly perceived, and used, as a less severe sanction than imprisonment (see Mair et al. 2008; Harrendorf 2017). As Bottoms (1981: 5) pointed out years ago, 'matters do not always work out in practice in the way that official dogma decrees that they should', and the evidence is now clear that, however much legislators in both jurisdictions still insist that suspended sentences must only be imposed if sentencers believe an immediate term of imprisonment of the stated length would also be deserved, Bottoms's (1981: 20) empirical conclusion that sentencers view and treat the suspended sentence as 'a measure of fairly general application, with a definite

[10] On these perceptions and attitudes, see Freiberg and Moore (2009); Freiberg (2019). The empirical findings reported in Bartels (2009) and Bartels and Bradfield (2015) strongly suggest that the demise of the suspended sentence in parts of Australia may have been influenced by politicians and the public becoming aware of the fact that even serious breaches were rarely followed up, and when followed up, would lead to the execution of the sentence in only a small minority of cases.

[11] For England, see, e.g., the findings of Mair et al. (2008). For Germany, similar interview-based studies with sentencers have apparently not been undertaken, but sentence patterns analysed by Harrendorf (2017) demonstrate the existence of clear practical sentence thresholds, in which suspended sentences occupy a rung above fines.

place in the tariff above the non-custodial sentences but below imprisonment', and moreover that they see it 'as a sentence in its own right, not as imprisonment momentarily suspended', stands firm.[12] Tellingly, in a sample of 21 English magistrates who were asked by Pina-Sanchez et al. (2019) to state, for a range of possible disposals, which of two different proposed punishments the sentencer considered more severe (an exercise used by the researchers to construe empirically plausible penal equivalents), opinions only started to split when a 12-month custodial sentence suspended for two years was compared to one, two, or three months of immediate imprisonment, with some magistrates believing the unsuspended but shorter sentences to be more severe than a suspended sentence between 12 and 4 times as long, whereas other magistrates took the opposite view. (For the data see Pina-Sanchez et al. 2019: 988 (Table 1)). These findings also imply that suspended and unsuspended sentences with a stated period of imprisonment of *equal* length (even when the operational period of the suspended sentence is longer) are perceived as significantly *different* in terms of their severity. This may well explain the observed tendency of magistrates to impose longer 'nominal' sentences of imprisonment when passing a sentence they suspend than when imposing a sentence of immediate imprisonment. (On the data, see Bottoms 1981: 15.)[13]

To the extent that decarceration occurs, it is less plausibly linked to a perception by sentencers that those no longer given a custodial sentence were punished too harshly under the previous system. Rather, the perception will more plausibly be either that the alternative sanction constitutes a convincing substitute for the custodial sentence (it punishes the offender in a different way but to the same extent), or that it punishes the offender

[12] For recent sentencing data analyses, see Harrendorf (2017) for Germany and Irwin-Rogers and Roberts (2019) for England.

[13] In Germany, the largest vignette-based empirical study of sentencing disparity (Streng 1984, with 522 professional participants) employed dividers of 2 (unsuspended sentence to suspended sentence) and 4 (unsuspended sentence to number of day-fines) to reflect, in an approximate way, the inherent differences in severity between these three disposal options. (Thus, a one-month unsuspended sentence weighs in as equivalent to a two-month suspended sentence or 120 day-fines.) While one may quibble with the translation rate, no one appears to have challenged the principle behind the researcher's attempt in this manner to factor in differences in severity between different types of disposal, let alone suggested that he should have used 1:1:1 instead. Hörnle (1999: 172–173), based on a comparison between fines and suspended and unsuspended sentences of imprisonment in respect of the kind and degree of penal hardship each sanction type involves, considers (for potentially suspendable sentences) actual imprisonment to be about three times weightier than suspended imprisonment of the same duration, while accepting equivalence between one day-fine and one day of suspended imprisonment.

less but that such 'underpunishment' is desirable in his case (say, on mercy grounds or on general policy grounds[14]). Indeed, less punishment is clearly what legislatures often want when introducing alternative sanctions with a view to reducing the prison population. It takes, however, a brave legislator to be sufficiently clear in her communication to sentencers that milder punishment of certain offender categories is what is intended.[15] Most legislatures, when introducing less severe alternative sanctions in order to reduce reliance on imprisonment, give in to the temptation to 'sell' the alternative sanction as 'differently constituted but equally severe', instead of coming clean and stating that it results from a conscious decision to *punish less severely* in this manner for the reasons that underpin the policy. These reasons may be as varied as a simple desire to reduce prison populations, a belief that the criminogenic and other harmful side effects of short prison sentences outweigh their possible penal advantages, and even—as one Home Secretary memorably suggested—that one should avoid where possible 'acclimatis[ing] people to prison' and thereby 'fritter[ing] away the deterrent effect of prison' (quoted in Dignan 1984: 189). Interestingly, this final concern is underscored by more recent research into the perceived severity of prison versus non-custodial options by offenders who have experienced both, and who often come to rate short sentences of imprisonment as 'easier' on them than certain types of non-custodial sentences requiring their active participation and/or involving intense behavioural monitoring and supervision (see van Ginneken and Hayes 2017 with further references).

[14] Consider, for instance, the Finnish scheme for replacing terms of imprisonment of up to eight months with community service, on a 'translation rate' of one day of imprisonment corresponding to one hour of community service. This commuted sentence of community service should be the standard sentence for all offenders in this category who consent to community service, are capable of performing it, are not first-time offenders (who presumably are meant to avoid a short prison sentence in the first place), and are also not prolific recidivists (Lappi-Seppälä 2019: 30). It appears implausible that this legislative scheme is grounded in an assumption that one hour of community work is as severe a punishment as one day of imprisonment. Rather, for the qualifying subgroup of offenders, the legislator has made a conscious choice to underpunish these offenders in this particular way, based on the undesirability on policy grounds of having these offenders serve the terms of imprisonment that have been imposed as deserved.

[15] Arguably, German law provides an example of this. Its offence definitions often specify a minimum punishment of 'no less than three months imprisonment' (which appears to rule out that the case can still be dealt with by a fine). In applying these provisions, though, judges are instructed by section 47 StGB to sentence an offender to a fine regardless of the minimum punishment of imprisonment specified for this offence if, in the concrete case, they are minded to impose a sentence of less than six months of imprisonment.

These observations, however, also suggest one reason why, despite the fact that these custody-avoiding disposals are located, as punishments, between fines and imprisonment, placing them in a hierarchy of available punishments may not be as simple as their often suggested classification as 'intermediate sanctions' would suggest. While it is true that, in one sense, these disposals occupy their defined place in the 'tariff' (such that it is possible to identify sentencing thresholds, linked to severity perceptions, which practitioners will use when negotiating or allocating punishments in particular cases), the very capacity of these disposals to replace significant periods of imprisonment cannot be explained by pointing to their supposedly lower place in the sanctions hierarchy as compared to imprisonment. (If simple equivalence or substitutability were the explanation, we would have to locate them on the same rung as imprisonment up to a certain duration.) For the ability to replace imprisonment to be made sense of while acknowledging the typically lesser severity of these sanctions compared to immediate imprisonment of 'suspendable' duration, we need to address certain further features of these sanctions, in particular the element of conditionality. We also need to get a better understanding of exactly how these sentences function as penal disposals, including how to make sense of the different bases (comparable burdensomeness or deliberate underpunishment) on which they may be employed as replacements for terms of immediate imprisonment.

These issues are further addressed in the next section, in the context of exploring further what makes these sanctions so resistant to being fitted neatly into a sanctions hierarchy.

Intermediate yet equivalent? Accommodating custody-avoiding sanctions in a sanctions hierarchy

What are the features of community-based disposals and suspended sentences of imprisonment that make it difficult to allocate these sanctions a defined rung on an imaginary penal ladder? This section starts with empirical research demonstrating wide interpersonal variations in the perception of the severity of these sanctions. It then turns to two key features of these sanctions which contribute to these large variations in perceptions of severity: their unstable content arising from the element of conditionality, and the fact that the same element in a given sanctions package may be deployed by sentencers in the service of a variety of concrete penal aims (what I will refer to as 'malleability of penal function'). The conclusion drawn from these findings is that a theorisation of these penal disposals as intermediate sanctions is insufficiently complex, in that it can block our understanding of the way in which these sanctions can and do function as penal equivalents to other sanctions. The final sub-section draws on Bottoms's (2017b) analysis of the limitations of a focus on punitive burdensomeness in the theorisation of community punishments to help us understand in which way these sanctions are equivalent to other sanctions, and what therefore enables these disposals to successfully operate as alternatives to other types of sanctions.

Interpersonal variation in the perception of sanction severity

As we have just seen, there is an obvious tension between viewing community-based disposals and suspended sentences of imprisonment as located, in terms of their severity, *between* fines and imprisonment and utilising them (as empirical studies confirm they are being utilised) as *substitutes* for not insignificant periods of the latter, and on occasion for the former. In particular, these observations put pressure on the assumption that fines are always less severe than community orders, and suspended sentences always more severe than both.

This pressure point is familiar from empirical research into penal equivalency. As numerous studies have shown, perceptions of the degree of hardship imposed by these sanctions compared to other types of sanctions differ quite widely, and those differences obtain in respect of different sentencers, different defendants, and different members of the public alike (see, e.g., Leclerc and Tremblay 2016; Crouch 1993; Harlow et al. 1995; van Ginneken and Hayes 2017; Wood and Grasmick 1999; Wood and May 2003). Moreover, Leclerc and Tremblay (2016) discovered in their analysis of data collected in a large vignette-based study in Canada in the 1980s that views about the absolute severity of non-custodial sanctions, and about their severity compared to other sanctions, differ more profoundly between individuals than do their perceptions of the severity of custody—and, interestingly, this is the case for professional and non-professional respondents alike (Leclerc and Tremblay 2016: 361–363). Whereas for imprisonment Leclerc and Tremblay were able to identify a clear majority or mainstream view among respondents, such that strongly differing views could be conceptualised as outliers, the response patterns in respect of non-custodial sanctions did not permit such a construction. Rather, for these kinds of disposals, response patterns suggested that

> there are, in fact, three to four different scales, which capture idiosyncratic divergences. Differences are found principally in the relative severity of the penalty and in the evaluation of long or excessive penalties. None of the profiles [constructed by grouping similar responses together] reach the mark of a simple majority [of respondents]. The group size varies from 7% to 49% and is generally in the vicinity of 30%. (Leclerc and Tremblay 2016: 367)

Respondents profoundly disagreed about the intrinsic severity of fines, community work, and what Leclerc and Tremblay refer to as probation. Leclerc and Tremblay (2016: 365–366) further observe that:

> Respondents disagree about both marginal severity and intrinsic severity ... Certain individuals judge the severity of non-custodial penalties to be trivial no matter what penalty is imposed, whereas others judge the deprivations or restrictions they impose to be sizeable, even in small amounts. Between these two extremes are one or two intermediate groups that see non-custodial penalties as being moderately severe.

Indeed, qualitative studies with small groups of offenders demonstrate that such disagreement is not only prevalent amongst those who merely imagine the punishment instead of experiencing it. Among those being punished in these different ways, van Ginneken and Hayes (2017), who conducted qualitative interviews with, respectively, prisoners and offenders given a community-based punishment, encountered a number of respondents who were explicit that they perceived fines to be a more severe punishment than some community-based punishments, specifically community orders imposing unpaid work requirements, and others who made it clear that they viewed many community-based disposals (particularly those that required ongoing self-management) as distinctly more onerous than a short prison sentence. As regards the views of sentencers, Pina-Sanchez et al. (2019: 988 (Table 1)) found that, in their responses given to a questionnaire asking them to rate different penal disposals as more or less severe than another, the magistrates split when rating one-month custody suspended for six months against community orders and when rating community orders against fines, confirming that fines may be perceived in some contexts as more severe, and suspended sentences as less severe, than certain community orders.

This not only carries important lessons for the interchangeability of sanctions. It also challenges assumptions about sanction severity that underpin the construction of suspended sentences of imprisonment and community-based disposals and measures as intermediate sanctions more broadly.

Instability of content arising from conditionality

The most intractable obstacles to penalty-scaling community sanctions and suspended sentences, however, arise from what may be termed the instability of these sanctions. That instability is rooted in their conditionality: unlike fines or periods of immediate imprisonment, the custody-avoiding sanctions discussed in this chapter are in a sense preliminary sanctions, subject to the condition of the offender's successful compliance with their demands.[16]

Indeed, Gazal-Ayal and Roberts (2019: v) have gone as far as suggesting that, by reason of the 'wide range of optional conditions' and the fact that 'courts often enjoy wide discretion in responding to wilful breaches of these

[16] Problematically, fines—while not explicitly conditional—may in the case of poor defendants in practice also operate as a 'preliminary sanction', in that non-payment of a fine can lead to further burdensome consequences which can, in their totality, quickly constitute overpunishment for the original offence. Extreme and, in its effects, clearly discriminatory against poorer people is the 'replacement sanction' for unpaid criminal fines used in the German system (of a number of days of actual imprisonment equivalent to the number of day-fines by which the fine in a criminal case is specified). Empirical studies show that the clientele of fine defaulters serving prison sentences is almost exclusively drawn from the ranks of the dysfunctional, the destitute, and the desolate, with outstanding fines for offences such as using public transport without a valid ticket (see Bögelein et al. 2014: 285). While efforts are being made by the enforcement authorities to substitute community service for replacement imprisonment, replacement imprisonment is still served by a fairly large number of offenders. The author recalls that the City of Hamburg had at one point instituted a system by which, practically on arrival at the prison door of an offender brought there to serve a period of replacement imprisonment, a pardon would be issued to this offender by the City's Senator of Justice (so as to avoid clogging up the City's jails with people who neither the courts nor the enforcement agencies believed should be imprisoned). This pragmatic and morally defensible practice was subsequently shot down by political posturing. It is surely a disgrace for a nation that prides itself on its constitutional guarantees of human rights that politicians of nearly every hue appear to have found it too difficult to grasp the thought that a state that cannot punish a person proportionately must not punish that person at all.

conditions', the 'severity of a suspended sentence order or a conditional sentence cannot therefore be specified in advance'. This is correct to the extent that the ultimate sentence (in case of breaches) cannot be foreseen with exactitude. At the same time, the requirements of the order can—and must—of course be specified fully at the point of its imposition, meaning that it *is* known at this point what burdens the order will impose on the offender, if he complies with it. The unquantifiability claim pertains only to the unknown nature of the total severity of the sentence in case of a breach.[17] *That* element of unknowability does not prevent a sentencer from assessing the burdensomeness of the order on the assumption that it will be complied with. But to rest matters here would be to ignore the element of conditionality altogether, and that would distort the nature and severity of the sentence that has been imposed.

What, then, is the significance of conditionality for the theorisation of these sentences? The German scholar Ellscheid (2001: 207) contends in respect of suspended sentences (whether or not with further conditions attached) that they exist on a different ontological plane from fines and imprisonment, representing 'possible' rather than 'actual' penal hardships. This is, however, too extreme. It misses the extent to which suspended sentences are readily understood as actual penal hardships. The research into sentencing patterns that we have already analysed clearly shows that practical thresholds exist that are in an important sense generated by drawing an imaginary line between sentence suspension and non-suspension (see, e.g., Harrendorf 2017 for the German context). It would not be possible for such conventions among practitioners to develop unless the imposition of a suspended sentence was perceived to carry some actual penal hardship. Most likely, the perceived hardship pertains to the denunciatory weight of the sanction, and the legal and social status reductions associated with its imposition. As Freiberg has noted, '[t]he recording of a criminal conviction is a . . . judicial act by which a person's legal status is officially . . . altered', the alteration consisting in 'a diminution of the offender's legal rights and capacities' (Freiberg 2014: 85). While these effects, according to Freiberg, 'follow automatically from the fact of conviction and are not necessarily tied to the sanction that follows it', it is important to note that legal consequences are frequently additionally tied to the sanction passing certain thresholds. For instance, in German law, the obligation to disclose a prior

[17] Also explored by Wasik (1994) and von Hirsch (1990).

conviction to prospective employers depends on whether the imposed sanction exceeded a certain threshold, and similarly the period of time that needs to expire before a conviction is expunged from the record depends in part on the type of sanction that was imposed.[18]

What is important in the present context is that the strength of the denunciatory message is not uniform but is influenced both by the label of the offence for which an offender is convicted[19] and by the type and amount of punishment imposed for it. Both elements form one integrated communicative package. To put the point precisely, the denunciatory message is constituted by the conviction for an offence bearing a certain label that is met with a certain sanction. Once one sees this, it should be evident that the denunciatory message of an unsuspended sentence of imprisonment is harsher than the denunciatory message of a suspended sentence, because of the further messages it sends about how the sentencer has evaluated the offender's attitudes to his offending behaviour and prospects for future good behaviour (see my discussion of what the suspended sentence says at the end of the second section of this chapter).[20] It is therefore unsurprising that Marinos (2005) has found that sentences of immediate imprisonment are sometimes demanded by members of the public (and possibly preferred by sentencers) for denunciatory reasons, in that the public may perceive other types of sentences as equally hard to undergo but as less denunciatory, and thus insist on immediate imprisonment as the only response of sufficiently high denunciatory content (even if equally severe hardship for the offender could be brought about in other ways).

While this helps us to understand the extent to which a conditional sentence is an actual punishment, it does not yet help us to answer the question of how the conditionality of these sentences affects their theorisation. In order to resolve this issue we have to address the connection between the instability of these sanctions in consequence of a breach—hinted at by Ellscheid's insistence that suspended sentences are located in the realm of 'possible' as opposed to 'actual' punishment—and the manner in which

[18] Bundeszentralregistergesetz (Federal Central Criminal Register Act), sections 32 and 46.

[19] I owe this point to discussions with Khomotso Moshikaro, who is conducting research into criminal labels as punishments, and who argues that they constitute legal and social status reductions which, as such, meet the criteria for penal hardship.

[20] Hence it isn't really possible, contrary to what O'Malley (2018: 44–45 ff.) appears to accept, to see the censuring or denunciatory message as simply contained in the nominal length of a suspended sentence. Such a perspective implies that the censuring message sent by suspended and unsuspended sentences of the same length are the same. But, as I argue in the text, the decision to suspend does affect the strength of the denunciation.

penal aims are pursued by the imposition of these sentences. Before addressing this question, however, we need to explore another feature which contributes to the unstable and divergent severity perceptions of custody-avoiding sanctions—the fact that some elements in a given sanctions package are perceived as rehabilitative or reparative in contrast to punitive, and that the same elements may, depending on the context and purpose of their imposition, be viewed as either.[21]

Malleability of penal function

As numerous writers have noted, the main custody-avoiding sanctions are notoriously difficult to fit into a system of punishment that conceives of punishment simply as a hardship imposed on the offender in response to the crime (see, e.g., Tonry 1994, and—for valiant attempts to develop normatively based criteria for assessing the severity of non-custodial sanctions—von Hirsch et al. 1989, Rex and von Hirsch 1998, Hayes 2016). What Canton (2018: 254) says in respect of probation is true for many of the more reform-oriented measures and instructions that can be imposed through a community order:

> Probation may certainly involve hardships ... but this is not all that probation amounts to, and far from their being intended, it is the policy of many probation agencies to do all they can to mitigate those effects – for instance, by making it easier for people to comply with the requirements of a community order.

Canton therefore insists that: 'To regard probation supervision simply as an imposition of hardship would be to misunderstand its aims and aspirations, as well as how it is experienced by practitioners and probationers'

[21] The points made in the text reflect empirical findings established by Sue Rex's research into how the main elements of community sentences are perceived. Rex (2005) asked study participants (professionals, offenders, and victims) to assign primary and secondary purposes to the main elements of custody-avoiding sentences. As to their primary purpose, the main options were stably associated with different distinct purposes (probation with rehabilitation, unpaid work with reparation, and curfew with incapacitation). As to their secondary purposes, answers showed that each of these disposals can be viewed as serving almost any of the other purposes as well (and may therefore be chosen by a sentencer in order to serve that purpose along with, or rather than, the primary purpose associated with the disposal). (For the data, see Rex 2005: 89–90.)

(Canton 2018: 254). He also observes that '[c]ommunity service ... has often brought a sense of personal achievement and enjoyment ... and yet it would seem odd to argue that this somehow disqualifies it as a punishment' (Canton 2018: 256). What is more, many of the conditions that may be imposed as part of a custody-avoiding disposal can serve different penal objectives depending on the context. Canton points to electronic monitoring, which can 'sometimes [be] imposed just to be burdensome' but 'in other circumstances [...] is used for surveillance, control or even as a contribution to rehabilitation' (Canton 2018: 255).

The upshot of this discussion is that not only do the motivations for which some of these sentencing options are imposed, and their intended and likely effects, appear to be in tension with their conceptualisation as penal hardships, but even when they do involve hardship, the degree of hardship appears more difficult to gauge for community orders than is the case for imprisonment and fines . For these reasons, custody-avoiding intermediate sanctions disrupt the uniformity of focus on the intended and expected burdensomeness as the primary reference point of the proportionality calculation, and thus (more widely) the justificatory framework for the imposition of the sentence. So, how should one go about fitting them into that justificatory framework?

A simple but unsatisfactory solution is given by the German legislator. Here, the legislative scheme insists that immediate imprisonment and suspended imprisonment are fully interchangeable sanctions up to the maximum suspendable sentence length, thus equally satisfying proportionality concerns and allowing the choice between them to be driven entirely by prospective (rehabilitative or special-preventive) concerns. (For details, see Harrendorf 2017: 516–518.) The reason why this is an unsatisfactory solution is that it suppresses the factual difference in severity between these different sentences. The logic of treating the choice between suspension and non-suspension as 'severity-neutral' is also in obvious tension with the assessment of additional conditions that may be imposed alongside a suspended sentence of imprisonment, where an explicit distinction is drawn between (positive or negative) requirements (*Auflagen*), on the one hand, and instructions (*Weisungen*), on the other hand. Whereas requirements (such as hours of socially beneficial unpaid work, victim compensation, a payment to a charitable or governmental organisation, and the like) can be imposed as part of a suspended sentence with the explicit aim of achieving an appropriately punitive overall sentence, instructions (e.g., to undergo drug treatment or drug testing) can only be imposed on rehabilitative or special-preventive grounds. The first problem here is that it remains unclear why it would be legitimate to increase the punitive element of a suspended sentence, if it is already equal in punitiveness to a non-suspended sentence of the stated length. The second problem arises because it appears that sentencers should only attach punitive weight to conditions which they impose by way of requirements. Obligations imposed by way of instructions are not necessarily less onerous for the offender to undergo than obligations imposed as requirements. Can instructions really drop out of the severity calculation completely, as the legislative scheme implies, by reason of the fact that they are imposed with a view to addressing the underlying causes of the offending behaviour and are thus rehabilitative or special-preventive in intention and effect?

The English system has gone down a different track. Here, the relevant legislation does make the imposition of custody-avoiding penal disposals subject to a severity calculation, with section 148(2) CJA 2003 (as originally passed) requiring that:

> Where a court passes a community sentence which consists of or includes a community order—(a) the particular requirement or requirements forming part of the community order must be such as, in the opinion of the court, is, or taken together are, the most suitable for the offender, and (b) the restrictions on liberty imposed by the order must be such as in the opinion of the court are commensurate with the seriousness of the offence, or the combination of the offence and one or more offences associated with it.

The Sentencing Guidelines Council's 2004 guideline on new sentences under the CJA 2003 inverted the order of these considerations by explaining that the court must,

> [w]hen deciding which requirements to include . . . be satisfied on three matters—i. that the restriction on liberty is commensurate with the seriousness of the offence(s); ii. that the requirements are the most suitable for the offender; and iii. that, where there are two or more requirements included, they are compatible with each other. (Sentencing Guidelines Council 2004: para. 1.1.12)

It also offered sentencers non-exhaustive lists of conditions that it would be commensurate with the seriousness of the offending behaviour to impose in cases located at the low, medium, and high end of seriousness. Beyond the provision of these somewhat impressionistic, experience-based lists, no attempt was made in the guideline to develop a general framework for calculating the severity of individual conditions based on some measurement of the restrictions on liberty involved. Indeed, this last point remains true in respect of the Sentencing Council's more recent definitive guideline on the imposition of community and custodial sentences (Sentencing Council 2016; guideline effective since February 2017), which in other respects provides some more detailed guidance.

The most sustained effort to develop a normative model for the assessment of the severity of non-custodial sentence elements was undertaken by the Victorian Court of Appeal in the case of *Boulton v The Queen* (2014) 46 VR 308. The relevant sentencing legislation merely provided that non-custodial sentence options were to be used even at the higher end of seriousness of cases where offenders were at risk of being sentenced to significant periods of imprisonment of three years and more. In this context, the appeals court needed to develop an approach which would enable the court to assess the proportionality of extensive non-custodial sanction packages of long duration. In an important first step, the court decided to take up the proposal made by von Hirsch and Ashworth (2005: 147–148) to focus the severity assessment on the effect which the conditions imposed on the offender have on his rights and interests (*Boulton* 2014: 331). It is clear from the court's statements that 'conditions of this kind, whether singly or in combination, [are] likely to interfere very significantly with the offender's freedom to live as he/she chooses', and that 'by attaching conditions prescribing where the offender must live, and which locations and persons he/she must avoid, the court can effectively require the offender to embark on a new life' (*Boulton* 2014: 332). Accordingly, the court viewed the punitive effect of these conditions as constituted by the extent to which they restrict the offender's freedom to conduct his life as he pleases (see also Maxwell 2017: 549). The similarity in approach to the English legislation's 'overall restrictions on liberty' reference point for the proportionality test is obvious, and was also stressed by one of the judges when writing extrajudicially (Maxwell 2017: 541 n.2).

This approach can measure the burdensomeness of a sentence package but it has trouble responding to the 'benevolent' dimension of some of these sentence elements. Rehabilitatively oriented conditions feature in this calculus only as a reductive distortion, by focusing on how they restrict the offender's freedom. While the *Boulton* court is by no means blind to the fact that these types of custody-replacing community sentences are importantly justified by their capacity to pursue rehabilitative objectives (see especially *Boulton* 2014: 335), it remains ultimately unclear how, if at all, the rehabilitative dimension enters the proportionality assessment. Thus, while the *Boulton* approach is satisfactory in how it proposes to assess the hardship element, it is unsatisfactory in that it lets only the hardship element count in the proportionality assessment. It also leaves unanswered the question of why it matters that an offender agrees to the imposition of certain restrictions and conditions, and how the existence of this agreement affects the legitimacy of the punishment. A framework focused on degrees of hardship constituted by restrictions on liberty is a scheme in which either the differences between agreed-to and not-agreed-to impositions on offenders do not register, or additional considerations need to be developed to make these differences relevant.

Reflecting on the *Boulton* judgment, Bottoms (2017b) has suggested that it is not proportionality as such that is put under pressure by 'bespoke' sentences, but rather the reductive focus on what legislatures and courts view as punitive (in contrast to rehabilitative and reparative) sentence elements. He proposes a reconceptualisation of these sentences which accepts that we should stop trying to place all sentence elements on a scale of punitiveness. Instead, we should allow them to factor differently in an overall proportionality assessment, depending on the penal aims and objectives served by these different sentence elements in the concrete case at hand (Bottoms 2017b: 584–587). Bottoms's proposal reflects the insight that, by focusing only on what could possibly still be viewed as the punitive content of a sentence element that is primarily not imposed for the hardship it generates, not only the penal content of that sentence element, but also the criteria for its justified imposition, are distorted. By concentrating only on how a particular condition may be onerous or burdensome for an offender to comply with, we are at risk of missing other dimensions of what stands in need of justification in relation to the imposition of that sentence element. Take probation supervision, in respect of which Canton (as quoted above) has insisted that 'to regard [it] simply as an imposition of hardship would be to misunderstand its aims and aspirations'. It also would be to misunderstand its legitimacy conditions. To be a just punishment (granting for the moment that we accept that classification), the intention must precisely *not* be to seek to bring about hardship, but rather to assist the offender in turning his life around so that he can avoid reoffending. Not only might the imposition of a particular condition not be legitimated by the hardship it involves; also, it may not be permissible to impose it simply so that the hardship is generated.

The analysis in this section has shown that one cannot adequately conceptualise non-custodial sanctions unless one conceives of them (a) as punishments, but also (b) as legitimated, in respect of some of their components, not by their onerousness but rather by their rehabilitative/restorative potential. These are therefore components that it would not be permissible for a sentencer to impose were she to impose them for the very reason that they create the burdens they inevitably bring with them, but which are permissible only when these burdens arise as inevitable features of a penal imposition legitimated by its reformatory/rehabilitative (or, as the case may sometimes be, recidivism-preventive) objective.

Conditionality is linked to the functionality of these sentences because it is linked to the achievement of their rehabilitative and recidivism-preventive objectives which, in turn, justify the imposition of many of the relevant sentence elements. The very reason why custody-avoiding sentences are, and should be, preferred by courts over sentences that impose immediate custody is, as the *Boulton* court put it,

> the ability to impose a sentence which demands of the offender that he/she take personal responsibility for self-management and self-control and (depending on the conditions) that he/she pursue treatment and rehabilitation, refrain from undesirable activities and associations and/or avoid undesirable persons and places ... [offering] the sentencing court the best opportunity to promote, simultaneously, the best interests of the community and the best interests of the offender and of those who are dependent on him/her. (*Boulton* 2014: 335)

This provides another reason why the focus on simply gauging the severity of these sentences (whether on scales of hardship or liberty deprivation) is misplaced. This focus is overly reductive and therefore elides the most important dimensions of these sentences. It leads us to ask the wrong questions pertaining to their justified imposition.

All this is an indication that assessments of the appropriateness of a custody-avoiding sentence have to be approached in a different way, a way that permits us to openly and coherently factor into that assessment the different aims that a particular sentence is intended to serve. This does not mean that proportionality drops out of the picture, only that it cannot be measured merely in light of the 'intentionally punitive' components of the sentence (where punitive is contrasted with rehabilitative or preventive components), nor (as von Hirsch and Rex 1998 have suggested) by directing and limiting attention to degrees of intrusiveness, and effects on the standard of living, represented by the various components of a given sentence package. Of course, checking that the overall burdensomeness of the punishment does not render the punishment inappropriate to the seriousness of the underlying offending behaviour is one important component of ascertaining that a sentence is justified. But it is only that: one aspect of this assessment. The principal criterion for the appropriateness and legitimacy of a particular sentence is whether a particular sentence is appropriate and proportionate in light of its aims; that assessment must take into account which particular objective is pursued through the imposition of particular requirements, and establish whether this requirement is appropriate in light of the legitimate sentence aims pursued by it.

The remaining issue which needs to be addressed is the theoretical framework most suited to the integration of custody-avoiding sanctions into a penal regime. While recognised sentence aims appear diverse, they can—as further explored in the next section—be assembled under a unifying underlying conception of punishment that aims to set appropriate terms for the offender's future life in the polity. This can, if one wishes to, be understood as a process of positive censure. But referring to it in these terms in my view focuses too much on the rational–moral appeal which punishment makes to offenders. Sometimes appropriate term-setting may take into account the extent to which a particular offender cannot be expected to be responsive to rational–moral appeal. Where this must be doubted given the particular behavioural drivers and environmental triggers, the conditions may appropriately aim to reconfigure the context in which the offender acts. This may not need offender consent if the trigger is external, circumstantial, and not deeply personal, but it may require the offender's consent in moral and not merely practical terms where the objective is to change a prominent component of an offender's habituated self, requiring efforts and involving degrees of personal change that cannot be mandated by third parties (including the state).

Integrating conditional custody-avoiding sanctions into the penal-theoretical framework

When a penal system goes down the route of treating suspended sentences of imprisonment, and community-based measures and impositions, as sanctions in their own right (and not as mere modifications of enforcement, as a conditional withholding of punishment, or—as regards some community sanctions and measures—as alternatives to punishment), it also commits itself to fitting these sanctions into its overall framework of justified punishment. Hence, it commits itself to providing answers to three problems that Bottoms (1998) identified in his discussion of the place of probation orders in a theory of deed-proportionate punishments, and which I restate here in my own words: the problem of conceptual accommodation (we need a perspective that enables us to understand, at the theoretical level, why these dispositions are sanctions); the problem of coherent application (we need a framework in which concrete applications of the sanction can be assessed as fitting); and the problem of theoretical integration (we need a theory that allows us to evaluate the application of these penal disposals as legitimate exercises of penal authority). While we have offered answers to the first two of these problems, we still need to take a closer look at the third: the problem of theoretical integration.

Tonry (1994) contends that non-custodial intermediate sanctions destabilise proportionality as the sole or dominant sentencing objective not merely at the practical but also at the theoretical level. He bases this argument on the features of these sanctions explored in the previous section: a focus on penal hardship commensurate with the seriousness of the offending behaviour forces a reductive conceptualisation of intermediate sanctions as hardship-imposing punishments, which means that most of the very elements that make these types of disposal attractive from a legislator's and sentencer's perspective are thereby removed from view or relegated to secondary significance. From a practical perspective, the reform-oriented and future-focused dimensions of many intermediate punishments are their primary attractions; hence resort to these types of sanctions is motivated by an understanding of the state as engaging in constructive intervention in an offender's life with a view to avoiding re-offending or making appropriate reparation. While the seriousness of what the state is doing is indeed marked by the degree of interference with an offender's freedom of choice, and with his rights, such interference is not engaged in for the sake of its onerousness.

Tonry (1994) argues that a theoretical framework that exhorts and allows sentencers to decide between disposals affecting the severity of the overall sentence based on considerations such as an offender's perceived receptiveness to therapy or drugs treatment, and/or his manageability in terms of supervisability in the community, must be justified by the value of parsimony (understood, as Tonry 2019 clarifies, as a separate and potentially competing principle of justice governing, along with proportionality, fairness, and equality, the imposition of punishment). But this leaves unexplained how parsimony can be a guiding rationale. In his reply to Tonry's position, von Hirsch (1994: 37) points out:

> Parsimony does not tell us why this individual should be selected for penalty reductions rather than some other. Why not choose ... the offender who has made no effort to learn a trade or otherwise improve his lot? ... There must be some guiding reason for the selection.'[22]

In other words, even after a penal disposal has been identified as parsimonious, we are left with the question of what justifies its imposition from a penal-theoretical point of view. As von Hirsch perceptively noted: 'If the fairness and appropriateness of the selection criterion is at issue, then there is no avoiding addressing ... when, if ever, is it proper to deviate from proportionality to favour certain offenders' (von Hirsch 1994: 37).

From a justificatory perspective, a morally coherent sentencing system cannot be underpinned by the bifurcated perspective (individualised-rehabilitative versus standardised-punitive) that developed, as a matter of fact, in the 1960s Court of Appeal jurisprudence in England (perceptively analysed by Thomas 1970), and for which Tonry's 'parsimony trumps proportionality' approach might provide a theoretical frame. Nor can it be underpinned by a proportionality-external perspective such as the construction chosen by the German legislator, where sentencers are told to select the type of punishment, within the legislatively defined areas of substitutability, for reasons other than desert-based considerations. This is so

[22] Lest von Hirsch's provocative question 'Why not be parsimonious to the person who has made no effort to improve his lot?' be dismissed as flippant, recall that under the Finnish and German 'underpunishing' penalty substitution regimes mentioned in notes 14 and 15, it is indeed the case that the person who has made no effort to improve his lot benefits just as much as the person who has made every effort.

because, when these conceptualisations of intermediate punishments are adopted, it is unclear how the sentencing decisions which are reached constitute outcomes that treat offenders who deserve punishment in equal measure alike, and thus deliver (in comparative terms) on the value of equality between offenders.

What we need at this juncture is, first, a more capacious understanding of punishments that incorporates more than just the notion of hard treatment, and secondly, a unified conception of the appropriate sentence, one that applies in all cases. That conception must be general enough to underpin custody-avoiding intermediate sanctions as well as other kinds of punishment. And it must allow us to conceive of these sanctions as punishments, thereby avoiding the impression that some offenders are given preferential treatment when compared to others of equal penal desert. Previously I have put forward a conceptualisation of punishment as setting, on behalf of the polity, reasonable terms for continued co-existence with an offender in response to his crime (du Bois-Pedain 2017). This conception of state punishment understands it as a practice in which we engage against a background assumption of continuing community with the perpetrator of the crime. We make the effort to punish the offender because a life in common will have to continue. Punishment, in this context, serves to set reasonable terms for the future relationship between the offender and the polity, with the ultimate objective of successful reintegration. I do not suggest that this is the only correct, true, or possible conception of punishment as a social practice. Quite clearly, it is not. Some practices—both historical and contemporary—that we readily understand as punishments are clearly destructive of any continuing relationship, and the permanent exclusion of the offender from a shared social world is indeed the very point of inflicting these types of punishments. But I do maintain that the term-setting conception of punishment is the only defensible way in which we can conceptualise *legitimate state punishment* in a modern constitutional state. This is so because we have made a commitment to relate to each other as co-citizens with certain inalienable, fundamental rights, and that commitment outlasts the commission of acts defined as criminal.

Based on this understanding of the overall purpose and justification of state punishment, I have addressed the question of what constitutes a proportionate punishment in such a setting. I have argued that these 'foundational constitutional commitments also suggest a particular understanding of the proportionality of a penal response: a proportionate punishment is one that has an inclusionary orientation, seeking to respond to the offender not just qua perpetrator of this crime but also as a fellow citizen whose prospects and interests still matter' (du Bois-Pedain 2017: 200). Consequently, the proportionality assessment must be 'bifocal': it must look not just at the gravity of the offending behaviour, but also at the question of how the punishment will affect the person of the offender. 'We should not think of rehabilitative considerations as leading to 'deviations' from a punishment that would otherwise be warranted at all—instead, we should recognise that considerations concerning the offender's humanity and personal interests are integral to the notion of proportionate punishment in the constitutional state' (du Bois-Pedain 2017: 220).

Suspended sentences of imprisonment and community sentences are illustrative of how bifocal proportionality assessments work in practice. The precise sanctions package imposed by these sentences responds to the nature of the crime and is sensitive to how the sentence is likely to impact on the offender. In relation to any sentence, it is only because both considerations have been made relevant that the sentence is a proportionate one. And when sentencers do make genuine efforts to make both considerations relevant and avoid imposing a sentence that needlessly overpunishes the offender, the result of their deliberations can, and will, often identify a community sanction or a suspended sentence of imprisonment as the most appropriate sanction in the case at hand.

This conception of legitimate state punishment also makes it clear that custody-avoiding sentencing options are not subject to different or more demanding justifications compared to other punishments, particularly immediate custody. From a bifocal proportionality perspective, an immediate sentence of imprisonment likewise speaks to the offender not only about his offence but also about his perception, by the sentencer, as a person. Where the prison term is too long to be open to suspension, it says: 'what you did was so serious that I cannot countenance you continuing to live in the community (even under onerous restrictions); as someone who did this sort of thing you need to be made to experience a very serious disruption in the flow of your life.' Where the sentence of imprisonment could, in principle, be suspended, it says: 'what you did was serious enough to merit a short prison sentence and I have considered whether I should suspend it, but I have concluded that you need to be made to feel the consequences of your wrongdoing because otherwise I see no hope that you'll understand, and change your ways.' It is readily apparent that a sentencer should be cautious indeed before sending the second, somewhat discouraging, message to an offender. In light of this, non-suspension of a suspendable sentence is at least as difficult to justify as is sentence suspension.

This continuity in the theorisation of different sentences is important in another respect, too. In response to the crisis of mass incarceration in the United States, various scholars have argued for second-look sentencing and similar schemes that enable the penal system to react with sentence reductions to constructive responses by prisoners to their ongoing punishment (see, e.g., Roberts and Dagan 2019). It is almost as if a necessary element of conditionality is being recognised even in apparently unconditional and definite sentences. The basis for this demand is the realisation that an initially appropriate sentence can be rendered inappropriately severe due to the inability of the system to respond to how the offender reacts to his sentence. It is worth noting that sentence review-based conditionality makes sense in light of the very rehabilitative objectives of sentencing that are legitimated by the term-setting conception of punishment. If this is right, then the conditionality of the custody-avoiding sanctions discussed in this chapter may no longer appear odd or irregular but instead may simply constitute an efficient way of recognising upfront the reactive dimension of appropriately responsive sanctioning practices—and perhaps a mechanism for doing so that is more straightforward and better integrated into the system than 'second looks'.

Tony Bottoms will readily appreciate how much my argument in this chapter owes to his previous work and to our frequent conversations about the best way to theorise, and justify, criminal justice practices. When he returned to the topic of non-custodial sentences in 2017, he stressed that, while '[t]here is clearly merit in the desert-based insight that proportionality is a concept that has relevance for non-custodial as well as custodial sentencing . . . the attempt to operationalise this insight through a single concept of 'restrictions on liberty' has failed' (Bottoms 2017b: 574). He furthermore suggested that, *within* the proportionality assessment, attention needed to be given to the fact that 'a sentencer's decision concerning the type of non-custodial penalty necessarily entails a degree of choice among different penal values' and objectives (Bottoms 2005: 586, drawing on some of the findings of Rex's 2005 research). For these reasons, Bottoms (2017b: 587) believed that 'the language of "punishment"' had stultified 'the creative development of community sanctions', whereas 'the threefold conceptualisation of reparation, rehabilitation and incapacitation might, if properly developed and set within appropriate boundaries of proportionality, have much more to offer'. As I hope to have shown in this chapter, a bifurcated understanding of proportionality allows sentencers to integrate attention to the objectives pursued by different sentence elements into the proportionality assessment of custody-avoiding punishments in the way that Tony envisaged in his 2017 article.[23]

[23] The text of this chapter was completed in August 2020 and legislation cited was current as of 30 August 2020. In connection with a comprehensive consolidation of all applicable sentencing laws in England and Wales, the Sentencing Act 2020 has, with effect from 1 December 2020, repealed inter alia the provisions of the Criminal Justice Act 2003 and of the Powers of the Criminal Courts (Sentencing) Act 2000 cited in this chapter, and replaced them with provisions of equivalent content.

PART IV
PUNISHMENT AND PENAL ORDER

11

What Is Penal Populism?

Public Opinion, Expert Knowledge, and Penal Policy-Formation in Democratic Societies

David Garland

It was Tony Bottoms—Britain's most observant and insightful penologist—who, in 1995, first drew our attention to 'populist punitiveness' and its growing importance in contemporary penal policy (Bottoms 1995b).[1] In the two and a half decades since then, commentators have never ceased talking about 'populist punitiveness' and its place in penal policy and political discourse, though the phrase 'penal populism' has come to be the more usual term of art in such discussions. But for all its familiarity and frequency of use, the exact meaning and implications of this concept—and

[1] This essay has been on the stocks for several years and in the interim penal populism has become a less pressing issue while nationalist-authoritarian political populism has become much more of one. I deal here only with the penal variant of the larger phenomenon. (For an insightful analysis of populist themes in contemporary politics, see Jan-Werner Muller, 'Populism and the People', London Review of Books 23 May 2019.) My chapter has its distant origins in a short preface written for a special issue of *The Japanese Journal of Sociological Criminology*. That preface was subsequently revised and expanded to form the text of a plenary lecture delivered at the British Society of Criminology Conference in Portsmouth, England in July 2012. It was delivered for a second time, in a suitably revised Scottish version, as the Annual Lecture of the Scottish Centre for Crime and Justice Research in May 2015. The author is grateful to Tom Ellis, the editor of the Special Issue and an organiser of the BSC Conference, for these invitations and for encouraging a reconsideration of penal populism. He is also grateful to David Brown, Stephen Holmes, Neil Hutton, Russell Hogg, the late James B. Jacobs, Richard Jones, Lisa Kerr, Julian Roberts, and Mike Rowan for helpful suggestions and to the D'Agostino Foundation of the NYU School of Law for research support. I would like to take this opportunity to acknowledge Tony's shaping influence on my own research and ideas. It was in Tony's postgraduate classes on Penology and Punishment and Society at Sheffield University that I first encountered the work of Michel Foucault, and it was Tony who set me off on the research that would eventually become *Punishment and Welfare* (Garland 1985). Then as now, his detailed grasp of penal practice, together with his searching interest in social theory and sociological explanation, are a model and an inspiration.

David Garland, *What Is Penal Populism?* In: *Crime, Justice, and Social Order.* Edited by: Alison Liebling, Joanna Shapland, Richard Sparks, and Justice Tankebe, Oxford University Press. © Alison Liebling, Joanna Shapland, Richard Sparks, and Justice Tankebe 2022. DOI: 10.1093/oso/9780192859600.003.0011

the phenomena to which it points—remain matters of contention and disagreement.

Some writers regard penal populism as a significant and disturbing element in the contemporary criminal justice landscape, attributing to it a causal efficacy in bringing about the 'new punitiveness' of the 1990s and since, pointing to its spreading influence around the globe, and suggesting counter-measures that might limit its impact. Others appear less convinced, viewing the concept as imprecise, its application overly general, and its normative status less clearly negative.[2] In light of this interest and dissension—and Tony Bottoms's role in provoking it—I want to reflect on our use of this term and to consider in more detail the phenomena to which it alludes and the issues to which it refers. At the same time, I want to reflect on some of the implicit biases that shape our discussions of 'penal populism' and consider whether they too ought to be subject to discussion and critique. And finally, I want briefly to consider the role of penological expertise in shaping penal policy in democratic societies, especially when that expertise runs up against majority public opinion.

The term 'penal populism' condenses a whole series of empirical, conceptual, and normative issues. It poses questions about the relations between the media, the public, and our political representatives—what these relations are and what they ought to be. It prompts us to consider the proper balance between professional expertise and community sentiment in the formulation of penal policy—especially in respect of measures where moral rather than instrumental considerations appear to predominate. It raises theoretical and empirical questions about the nature of 'public opinion' and how it changes over time, methodological questions about how best to take its measure, and political questions about its proper status in the democratic process. Finally, it raises historical questions about the conditions under which 'penal populism' comes to prominence, as well as institutional and comparative questions about its varying capacity to shape policy

[2] On penal populism, see Pratt (2007); Roberts et al. (2003); Freiberg and Gelb (2008). On 'populist punitiveness', see Bottoms (1995b). On the 'authoritarian populism' of Mrs Thatcher's 'law and order' policies, see Hall (1980). For a qualified defence of 'penal populism' as an aspect of democratic politics, see Ryan (2005). On the virtues of 'insulating' criminal justice policy from populist pressure, see Lacey (2008), Roberts et al. (2003), and Roberts and de Keijser (2014); for democratic arguments against such insulation see Dzur (2012) and Loader and Sparks (2011). Ryberg and Roberts (2014) provides arguments for and against. On populism more generally, see Muller (2016), Taggart (2000), Canovan (1981), Barker (2005), and Hogg (2012). As Laclau (2007: 1) notes: 'A persistent feature of the literature on populism is its reluctance—or difficulty—in giving the concept any precise meaning.'

in different jurisdictions and institutional settings. None of these questions is yet settled. Some of them have barely begun to be posed. And one suspects that the political implications of penal populism—which is the one issue upon which most penologists agree—may be more open-ended and indeterminate than is typically assumed.[3]

What is penal populism?

Penal populism is, first and foremost, a form of political discourse that, directly or by implication, denigrates the views of professional experts and liberal elites and claims instead the authority of 'the people' whose views about punishment it professes to express. (I would stress the distinction between *popular* and *populist*. Penal discourses that have the support of experts and elites may attain popular support, thereby bringing elite and popular opinion into alignment. In Scotland, for example, the 'Children's Panels' system of juvenile justice has, at various times, commanded the support of expert elites and a majority of the Scottish public. In contrast, populist discourses set up an opposition between elites and 'the people'—i.e. the non-elite, 'ordinary' people—and purport to represent the views of the latter.) Penal populism typically has a punitive, reactionary cast—which is why we often think of it as a synonym for 'populist punitiveness.' As I will go on to suggest, however, this may be a contingent consequence of recent penal politics rather than an essential feature.

The implicit contrast that is drawn whenever commentators discuss penal populism is between newly politicised (and implicitly or explicitly anti-expert) forms of discourse and policy formulation on the one hand, and older, expert-led, evidence-based, criminologically sophisticated approaches on the other. Instead of attending to the views of penological experts and practitioners—as they once, apparently, did[4]—populist

[3] As Russell Hogg—another student of Tony Bottoms—notes: 'that crime and punishment is very difficult ground for left and progressive politics is hardly in doubt. It is nevertheless a mistake to conflate populism with punitiveness (as analyses of penal populism invariably do.) Rather, it is necessary ... to consider the very different ways in which (populist) politics and the penal might be articulated' (Hogg 2012).

[4] Loader (2006) discusses that earlier era under the rubric of liberal elites and 'Platonic Guardians.' And in his foreword to a book on penal populism, Nigel Walker (2003: v) remembers 'an era when the only feature of penal policy that politicians discussed was capital punishment, and even that was forgotten at election time.' According to Loader, Home Office civil servants in the 1960s and 1970s aimed to 'manage' public opinion on crime, their 'governing disposition' being that 'untutored public sentiment towards crime is a dangerous thing—an object to be monitored and contained, steered down appropriate paths, taken on and argued

politicians and law-makers claim to take their lead from the long-suffering, ill-served people, above all from victims, whose preferences are usually said to be for more punitive (or protective) measures. Where public opinion previously operated as a boundary constraint on policy initiatives, it is now said to function as a privileged source.[5] Empirical research and criminological knowledge are downgraded and in their place is a new deference to the voice of 'popular experience', of 'common sense', of 'what everyone knows' (Garland 2001).[6]

Penal populism goes hand in hand with a politicisation of policy-making, a reduction in expert influence in policy formation, and reduced managerial control of the penal process.[7] It involves a reversal of what Foucault (1977: 247) referred to as the 'declaration of carceral independence', a curtailment of the discretionary powers of penal professionals, and an expansion of direct political control over penal matters such as sentence length, conditions of confinement, and decisions about release. It also involves a change in the emotional tone of the penal process, replacing the cool detachment of professional decision-makers with a more expressive emotivism that claims to communicate the sentiments of an aroused and angry public.[8] California's Three Strikes Law—a voter ballot initiative statute enacted in 1994 following an emotive public campaign by the fathers of murder victims—might serve as paradigmatic of the genre.

with where necessary . . . but not to be followed, still less given governmental endorsement or expression' (2006: 568). In contrast, populist punitive policies 'are political stances, normally adopted in the clear belief that they will be popular with the public' (Bottoms 1995b: 40).

[5] For an example of the brakes being applied by public opinion in an otherwise expert-led policy environment, see the report 'Sentences of Imprisonment: A Review of Maximum Penalties' issued by the Advisory Council on the Penal System in 1978. Because of press criticism and reports of public outrage, the Council's recommendations for sentence length reductions were not taken up by the Labour government. The following year, the newly elected Conservative government effectively disbanded the Council.

[6] Ryan (2005: 141) summarises the shift as follows: 'It was "the people of Britain", Mrs. Thatcher once famously said, that she was listening to on crime and punishment, not to the academy, administrative élites running the Home Office Research Unit, or self-interested pressure groups, like the Howard League for Penal Reform.'

[7] In a recent memoir, former Home Office civil servant David Faulkner (2014: 14–15) remarks on this shift: 'Traditional sources of advice such as commissions, committees and civil servants themselves gave way to consultants and politically aligned think-tanks . . . issues became more matters of political than departmental or professional judgement.'

[8] On the distinction between 'cool' and 'hot' approaches to crime and punishment, see Garland (2001: 10–11) and Loader and Sparks (2011). On the need to recognise the emotional aspects of non-punitive penal measures, such as rehabilitation and restoration, see Sparks (2001) and Brown (2005).

Finally, populism involves an increased role for the mass media, which—in concert with populist politicians and high-profile victims—represents itself as the voice of the people. Tabloid headlines and editorials take on an increased importance in the shaping of penal decisions, and, conversely, penal measures are designed to play well in the popular press. Penal *representations* take on a new significance, and policy measures are presented to the public in idiomatic, tabloid-friendly, image-conscious language—the 'short sharp shock', the 'boot camp', 'three strikes', 'prison works!', 'Megan's law'.

In a political world characterised by penal populism, political debate about punishment plays to the crowd and takes less care to attend to criminological evidence or align itself with expert opinion. Populist measures are rarely 'evidence-led,' nor are they justified by cost–benefit analysis or kitted out with evaluative criteria and performance metrics. Their goal is the immediacy of public support and political advantage, not the long-term accumulation of penological results. And while they claim to represent 'public opinion' and 'the will of the people', populist measures are geared to respond to media headlines and vivid expressions of public mood rather than the social scientific findings of public opinion research (Pratt 2008; Green 2008). The 'people' they invoke are imagined and their supposed views assumed—not established by empirical evidence or extensive consultation.

How to think about penal populism

Conceived in these terms, penal populism is not a policy, whether punitive or otherwise. It is, instead, a way of *arguing for* or *representing* policy, a distinctive form of political discourse (and practice) that claims to represent 'the people' and is designed to appeal to popular audiences.[9] In recent times, penal populism has tended to move penal law towards harsher, more punitive measures—to what Bottoms termed 'populist punitiveness'—but it is possible to imagine populist policies that embrace more lenient measures if these happen to resonate with popular sentiments.[10] The connection

[9] Cf. Laclau (2007: xi): 'populism has no referential unity because it is ascribed not to a delimitable phenomenon but to a social logic ... Populism is quite simply, a way of constructing the political.'

[10] See Hogg (2012) for discussion of what a progressive penal populism might look like. See also Sparks (2001: 198), who raises the question: 'Can there be a populist penal politics of the

between populist policies and 'punitiveness' is a contingent rather than a necessary one. Penal populism can take a variety of forms, some punitive, some not. 'Populist punitiveness' and 'penal populism' ought not, therefore, to be viewed as exact synonyms. Instead, we should regard populist punitiveness as one specific instantiation of the more general phenomenon of penal populism.

Nor are punitive populist politics necessarily conservative or 'rightist' in their political alignments. When former London Mayor Ken Livingstone suggested to a London audience that we should 'hang a banker a week' until the financial industry improved, he was engaging in a leftist version of penal populism.[11] Demands for harsh punishment against bankers, financiers, and capitalist 'fat cats' are familiar examples of the same thing—and are, in fact, more in keeping with the prior history of populist politics (Kazin 1998).

Finally, we should note that not all punitive policies are populist. Authoritarian rulers in non-democratic societies—like absolutist sovereigns in early-modern Europe—impose harsh punishments in complete disregard of public preferences. Penal populism is a characteristic of societies in which public opinion matters, and especially of democratic societies with a commercialised, competitive mass media. It is particularly characteristic of the USA, which has populist political institutions such as voter ballot initiatives, party primaries, and elected prosecutors and judges, though similar institutions and practices are becoming important elsewhere and may soon become a feature of most democratic systems.

Populism, the people, and public opinion

The relationship between populist discourse and the 'will of the people' that it purportedly expresses raises two quite separate issues, each of them somewhat philosophical in nature.

The first question concerns the identity of the people being invoked. The categories of 'the people' and 'the public' that are inscribed in populist

left?' Jones (2010) discusses examples of 'populist leniency' of a more reactionary, conservative cast.

11 http://www.huffingtonpost.co.uk/2012/02/17/ken-livingstone-hang-a-banker-week_n_1284362.html

discourse are, like all interpellated entities, constructed and open to contestation. However confident populists appear when they invoke these terms—when the Tea Party purports to be the voice of 'true American patriots' or Occupy Wall Street claims the authority of 'the 99%'—the actual existence of a 'public' holding the views ascribed to them always remains to be determined. Perhaps such people exist, perhaps not. Perhaps they form a majority of the population or the electorate, or constitute the 'real people' or the 'silent majority'—perhaps they don't. But their existence will always be, in some part, a product of the very political representations that purport to represent them and call them forth.[12] In other words, the people whose 'will' supposedly grounds and legitimates populist positions are typically assembled, mobilised, and identified *in and through these very practices* of representation and political construction. Here is how Gareth Stedman Jones (1983: 23–24) puts the point:

> Political discourses are addressed to particular constituencies, indeed at certain formative turning points are able to constitute or reconstitute such constituencies. There is an intimate connection between what is said and to whom. Yet it cannot be said that such a connection can be conceived in terms of a recognition of the pre-existence of the common social properties of the addressees. It should rather be thought of as the construction, successful or unsuccessful, of a possible representation of what such common properties might be. Of course, the almost definitional claim of political discourse is to be a response to a pre-existing need or demand. But in fact the primary motivation is to create and then orchestrate such a demand, to change the self-identification and behaviour of those addressed. The attempted relationship is prefigurative, not reflective.

Ernesto Laclau (2007: 224) makes much the same point when he insists that 'the people' is a *political* category, not a reference to a pre-existing group or a datum of social structure, and that the populist invocation of that category always involves an active, instituting, constructive attempt to forge a new and singular agency out of a plurality of heterogeneous elements.

[12] As David Brown (2012) puts it, the category of 'the people' invoked by populist discourses is a 'floating signifier', an idealised, imaginary subject constructed in the process of representation. On the relation of political practices of representation to the thing represented, see Stedman Jones (1983) and Laclau (2007).

To put the matter plainly, populist discourse works to 'create and orchestrate' the popular opinion it claims to express. This *does not* mean that such opinions are conjured out of thin air. Populist discourses become mere demagoguery if they strike no chords, if they fail to resonate, if they do not succeed in interpellating a mass of actual subjects. And they can only succeed in these respects if the populist's positions are, in fact, popularly shared to some extent. Like all successful ideologies, populist discourses need to connect with the experience of real people and represent that experience in a usable form. But it *does* mean that these particular 'people', identifying with these particular representations, organised into these particular political positions, do not pre-exist the political practices of representation and organisation that work to bring them into existence. As Stuart Hall (1980: 2) remarks, populist politicians first form public opinion, and then, disingenuously, consult it.

Before leaving this analysis of how 'the people' are invoked and interpellated by populist discourses, we should note one characteristic that distinguishes *penal* populism from populism in its other forms. When social historians and political analysts analyse populism, they are usually dealing with political *movements* and the mobilization of popular forces. Whether the analysis is of the US People's Party, Peronism in Argentina, the Russian Narodniks, the English Chartist Movement, or the current wave of anti-establishment populism—the Tea Party and Donald Trump in the USA, the National Front in France, Italy's Five Star Movement, the Freedom Parties in Austria and the Netherlands, Podema in Spain, Fidesz in Hungary, Law and Justice (PiS) in Poland, and UKIP in Britain—that is currently sweeping across the western landscape, the political process being analysed is one of mobilisation, organisation, and action—manifested in demonstrations, rallies, social protest, party formation, and political conduct.[13] In contrast, the 'populism' of *penal populism* is not (or not primarily) about the mobilisation of social forces, the organisation of popular demands, or the formation of a popular movement. It is instead about the invocation of 'the people' and their (supposed) penal demands by political figures in the service of electoral campaigns or legislative reforms. Penal populism usually invokes 'the people' as electoral support and as legitimating authority without seeking to organise or mobilise them beyond this. Over the past few decades there have been many *discourses* of penal populism but few instances of popular

[13] See Tomasky (2014) and Muller (2016).

movements formed around penal demands, and fewer still that mobilise mass popular action that goes beyond signing a petition.[14]

The second issue concerns the nature of the beliefs and attitudes that supposedly constitute 'popular sentiment' and 'public opinion'. Liberal commentators often suggest that the linkage between populism and punitiveness is based on a misreading of popular sentiment, which is, they claim, less harshly retributive than is suggested either by the tabloid press or by opinion poll data.[15] But this issue is more complex than is sometimes appreciated. Criminologists insist that the responses that lay people give to 'superficial' opinion-poll surveys are generally more punitive than the responses they give to more fine-grained, interactive forms of inquiry, such as focus group research or deliberative polling.[16] And the critical conclusion usually drawn from this is that populist politicians are misrepresenting the true nature of public opinion, which is 'in reality' less harsh than the standard polls suggest. The problem with this standard account is that it assumes the existence of a 'real' or 'true' public opinion, to which some methods have better access than others, instead of viewing representations of public opinion as so many artifacts of the processes of inquiry that generate them.[17] It also assumes that 'deeper' forms of inquiry produce a more 'authentic' or more 'legitimate' account of public opinion. But neither assumption will withstand close scrutiny.

[14] The victims' movement might appear to be an exception, but it was initially a grass-roots movement and was subsequently co-opted by populist politicians rather than organised and mobilised by them—see Garland (2001).

[15] See, for instance, Frost (2010); Roberts et al. (2003); Applegate et al. (1996); Cullen et al. (1988). Hutton (2005: 246) summarises this pattern of findings as follows: 'Survey questions, issued in a structural way and the absence of information tend to generate more punitive responses, while methods which allow respondents to interact and engage in dialogue, issues framed in individual cases and the provision of more information, tend to generate more liberal attitudes.'

[16] '[An] extensive body of evidence ... has convincingly shown that people who seem to be punitive when asked for "top-of-the-head" responses to simplistic, abstract questions, become far less punitive when allowed to provide a considered, thoughtful response to more detailed information about a specific case.' Frieberg and Gelb (2008: 4). See also Green (2008) and Rowan (2012).

[17] Of course, these artefacts may be more or less robust: some public attitudes can be altered by the provision of more information. Others—such as support for the death penalty—are more tenaciously held. For a nuanced, insightful discussion, see Hutton (2005), who stresses the difficulty of producing a clear account of what the public thinks about sentencing and punishment: '[The public's] views appear to be complex and contradictory. They are dependent on the methods used to try to measure these views, on whether the accounts used in these methods are structural or individualized and on the nature of any additional information presented to respondents at the time of the data collection. Their views also reproduce more general social narratives about risk, insecurity and anxiety, which exist in a context wider than the personal experience or knowledge of the respondents.'

It is not just that, as Pierre Bourdieu (1993) bluntly states, 'public opinion does not exist'—though he is correct to insist that the thing we describe as 'public opinion' does not pre-exist the processes whereby it is primed by media cues, framed by survey questions, and flattened out by the numerical forms in which the heterogeneous phenomena of knowledge, belief, attitude, opinion, and preference are aggregated and represented.[18] The more important point is that *for the purposes of electoral competition* the public attitudes and preferences generated by opinion polls cannot be discounted just because they are 'superficial'. Nor can they be dismissed in favour of the more considered and more lenient attitudes that are sometimes generated by deeper forms of inquiry. Why? Because, when voters go to the polls and vote for one candidate or another, they mostly take with them the superficial attitudes reported to pollsters, not the more informed, more reflective understandings that can be produced by involvement in discussion groups or deliberative polling. From the point of view of the vote-seeking politician, what matters most is where voters stand on an issue, not where they might stand if subjected to an intense and transformative research protocol.

Statements about public opinion are generalisations based on various kinds of evidence—mostly produced by surveys, in response to set interview questions—about the opinions of individuals. These 'opinions' may be coded as 'for'/'against'/'don't know' or 'too much'/'too little'/'just right', but the underlying forms of knowledge, opinion, preference, and belief that these codifications represent are usually much more heterogeneous. Generalising about these heterogeneous phenomena, and giving them singular numerical values, necessarily occludes these variations. So, if our

[18] Cf. Bourdieu (1993: 149–150): 'Every opinion survey assumes that everyone can have an opinion; in other words, that producing an opinion is something available to all. At the risk of offending a naively democratic sentiment, I would contest this first premise. [This political competence is not universally distributed. It varies, roughly speaking, with education.] Secondly: it is assumed that all opinions are of equal value. I think it can be shown that this is untrue and that the cumulation of opinions that do not all have the same strength leads to the production of meaningless artefacts. The third implicit premise is this: putting the same question to everyone assumes that there is a consensus on what the problems are, in other words, that there is agreement on the questions that are worth asking ... The "public opinion" that is manifested on the front page of newspapers ("60% of French people are in favour of...") is a pure and simple artefact whose function is to disguise the fact that the state of opinion at a given time is a system of forces, tensions and that nothing more inadequately expresses the state of opinion than a percentage.' Johnstone (2000: 163) says of opinion polls: 'They fail to distinguish clearly between different aspects of "public opinion"—such as knowledge, attitudes and sensibilities—and also fail to tell us much of value about why people adhere to specific attitudes or how strongly they adhere to them.'

concern is to understand what people think and feel, these findings may be too crude to carry much weight. Nevertheless, summary representations of public opinion do approximate to something that may very well matter for the outcome of popular elections (or for patterns of consumer behaviour) and often prove to be good predictors of these outcomes. Consequently, critics of populism ought not to dismiss the 'reality' of the attitudes generated by opinion polls, nor ought they underestimate their predictive value (and hence importance) from a political point of view.

To some extent, the divisions between experts and politicians—even liberal experts and liberal politicians—on matters of penal policy are a consequence of the different lines of accountability, incentive, and reward affecting the different actors in the policy-making process. And if we are to understand the forces that shape penal politics we need to appreciate the distinctive pressures brought to bear on the differently situated actors involved in the process of policy-making and legislation. Progressive—and potentially unpopular—penal measures such as parole, remission, furlough schemes, or open prisons might accord with the professional ideology of progressive penologists and corrections department officials, and bring professional rewards and prestige to those concerned. But such programmes are often viewed with suspicion by the general public and bring few immediate benefits to the elected politician. And when things go wrong, it is often the politician's job that is most immediately on the line. For politicians facing electoral challenge, a series of negative tabloid headlines may carry more weight than a whole shelf of research reports. And where elected officials are exposed to frequent election cycles and the threat of primary challenges, as they are in the US political system, the prospects for progressive penal policy are often severely limited, particularly when questions of crime and punishment are in the public spotlight.[19] The challenge for penologists and penal policy advisers is to find ways to represent their preferred policies in forms that might resonate with public opinion and political narratives—and to help educate the public and politicians in such matters. Expressing disdain for popular sentiment and the political process is of little help in this regard.

[19] On the importance of political institutions in shaping penal outcomes, see Garland (2013).

Populism and penal expertise

Populist discourse about punishment has probably always existed, at least as a minor current, wherever democratic institutions allow the general public a voice in penal policy-making.[20] There have always been politicians, or judges, or newspaper editors willing to embrace a populist stance and rail against 'the establishment' in the name of 'ordinary people'. What seems different today, at least to some commentators, is that this style of penal–political discourse has become much more prominent and has been adopted not just by mavericks and outsiders but by government ministers and state legislatures.[21]

Although it is something of an overstatement to claim that penal populism now dominates official penal discourse, it is easy to see why commentators might form this impression.[22] What is striking about the penal populism of the past 20 years is that it stands in sharp contrast to the earlier correctionalist era in which penological experts and professionals played a dominant role.[23] Having been a marginal, reactionary current in the penal-welfare period, it subsequently moved to centre stage in the 'culture of control' that followed. What explains these developments?

The processes of professionalisation, rationalisation, and bureaucratisation that shaped criminal justice for much of the twentieth century worked to empower trained experts and professional administrators. That power was further entrenched by the rise of correctionalist ideas (stressing the treatment rather than the punishment of offenders) and by the indeterminate sentencing regimes that accompanied them. These regimes allowed

[20] A century ago, Max Weber (1948a) was already lamenting the passing of an intellectually rational, fact-based politics and the increasing resort to emotional means of persuasion. Democracy was, for him, 'a dictatorship resting on the exploitation of mass emotionality'.

[21] The populist insurgency (against the 'liberal elite' and its progressive notions) has, in recent decades, installed itself as the new establishment. And who knows? Perhaps we will one day see a progressive reaction against the current 'law and order' regime of punitive sentencing and mass imprisonment—a reaction that will embrace populist themes and representations: Michele Alexander's best-selling book The New Jim Crow (2010) proposed something of this sort, and a decade later popular movements such as Black Lives Matter embody such sentiments.

[22] Bottoms (1995b) was careful to suggest that populist punitiveness was one of several competing currents shaping recent sentencing policy. See Matthews (2005) for the claim that the 'punitiveness' of contemporary penal policy has been greatly exaggerated.

[23] For first-hand accounts of that earlier era, see Radzinowicz (1999), Blom-Cooper (1975), and Faulkner (2014). For histories of its emergence and decline, see Garland (1985, 2001). For discussions of the changing role of criminological expertise, see Garland and Sparks (2000) and Loader and Sparks (2011).

parole boards, prison wardens, and probation officers to control decisions about time served, treatment applied, and conditions of custody or supervision, and to do so in a discretionary manner that was largely hidden from public view. Up until the 1980s, officials and policy-makers tended to avoid engagement with public opinion because they assumed that most members of the public (together with many judges and politicians) held retributivist views that had long since been discredited among penal professionals. For penal progressives, public opinion was an obstacle to good decision-making, not a necessary component of it.[24]

That era of professional control has now passed. Penal policy and penal practice have been brought out into the open, politicised, subjected to media scrutiny, and increasingly controlled by legislatures who no longer delegate sentencing decisions to others. Discretionary powers are less frequently allocated to behind-the-scenes decision-makers.[25] The public and their elected representatives no longer trust penal professionals to make the right decisions or to use their powers wisely. Judicial discretion in sentencing is curtailed by mandatory sentence laws and by sentencing guidelines; in the USA, parole has been abolished in many states, and even where it continues to operate, the expert powers of the parole board are greatly reduced by 'truth-in-sentencing' policies. Political actors have reversed the 'declaration of penal independence' and taken more direct control of the power to punish.

Why this unexpected reversal? Did an insurgent penal populism emerge because of public concern about increased crime and the perceived failure of the expert-dominated penal-welfare system? Because of reduced trust in government?[26] The rise of the New Right? The new power of the tabloid media? Choosing between these hypotheses depends, in part, on how we

[24] See Cowperthwaite (1988) describing how Scottish Office officials sought to keep legislative proposals for a Children's Hearing System away from the press and public consultation for fear of a negative reaction to what they regarded as radically progressive proposals.

[25] In the US, prosecutors are an important exception to this trend, their powers having been increased by the new sentencing structures. But of course, most district attorneys in the US are elected, and their offices can usually be relied upon not to be 'soft on offenders' and to use their discretion in the interests of public safety.

[26] Zimring and Johnson (2006: 276–277) note: 'Much of the punishment hardware that facilitates leniency depends on trust in government's expertise and benevolence. Citizens are restrained from acting on emotions and "throw away the key" sentiments when they believe that there are principles of punishment—legal proportionality, predictions of dangerousness, responsiveness to treatment—that require government expertise. As soon as the claim of expertise is discredited, people on the street (or their state representatives) are every bit as expert as judges, parole boards, or correctional administrators.'

judge penal populism as a historical phenomenon. Is it a surface shift in political tactics and public sentiment or a more profound shift in the nature of government? Is its rise merely a mutation in political discourse or does it express deeper changes in the collective experience of crime and the popular attachment to punishment?

Initially, much of the discussion about penal populism was historical in nature, explaining the emergence of populist themes by reference to high crime rates, increased fear of crime, the rise of a victims' movement, late-modern insecurities, and so on (Garland 2001; Simon 2009). But in recent years the turn to comparative analysis has pointed to institutions that make the emergence of penal populism more likely in some jurisdictions than in others.

To take one notable comparison, the structure of criminal justice in the USA—with its state-based criminal law, its elected county prosecutors and state judges, and its local community juries—is designed to ensure local popular control of prosecution and punishment.[27] And the institution of ballot initiatives in many states enables direct law-making by voters, provided sufficient popular support can be mobilised around a proposition: witness California's Three Strikes Law and its Victims' Bill of Rights. In contrast, the structure of criminal justice in Germany or the Netherlands embodies an institutional design that more effectively insulates penal decision-making from pressure of popular opinion and gives a greater role to ministry officials and professional civil servants. Little wonder, then, that these two nations exhibit levels of punishment and imprisonment that are very different from those of the USA and respond quite differently to increased rates of crime and victimisation (Downes 1988; Savelsberg 1994).

Comparative studies of the political and social institutions that shape penal policy in various countries suggest that susceptibility to populist pressures is a variable that is differentially distributed across political systems.[28] The authority of the civil service relative to the political branch;

[27] Cf. Zimring and Johnson (2006: 278): 'What has always distinguished the governance of punishment in the United States from other advanced democracies is a structural vulnerability to democratic pressures that arise out of federalism, the election of prosecutors and judges, and high levels of life-threatening violence.' By contrast, many post-war European constitutions were drawn up, in the wake of fascism, in order to limit popular power and to multiply liberal safeguards (Muller 2016).

[28] See Zimring and Johnson (2006: 274) and their table distinguishing factors that facilitate severity from those that push towards restraint. See also Downes (1988); Roberts et al. (2003); Cavadino and Dignan (2005); Barker (2005); Savelsberg (1994); Pratt (2007); and Garland (2013).

the relative strength and cohesion of political parties; the frequency and competitiveness of elections; the relative accountability of individual representatives; the possibility of popular legislation by means of voter ballot initiatives; the character of the media—all of these have a bearing on the fate of penal populism, quite apart from the vicissitudes of rates of crime and violence, victims' movements, and public fears. Comparative work is just beginning to trace these differences and ascertain their impact on penal policy-making, just as it is beginning to explore whether the spread of penal populism is primarily the result of policy transfer and political emulation or of internal developments occurring in several societies simultaneously.

Evaluating penal populism: Empirical and normative issues

Penal populism is usually characterised as a political force of great effectiveness that has played a prominent role in moving penal practice in a more punitive direction. It is also characterised as having misrepresented public opinion, understating the nuanced and ambivalent aspects of collective penal sentiments and exaggerating their harsher, more vindictive aspects.

But these general characterisations are based on empirical assumptions that have not always been fully demonstrated, nor even carefully specified and differentiated. At least some populist measures have had much less impact on penal practice than is implied by the publicity that accompanied their introduction and by the critical attention they have received. A case in point is the 'three strikes' sentencing laws of many American states—other than California—which, despite the hoopla, have had little impact on the actual pattern of incarceration.[29] Indeed, penal populism is probably predisposed to gestural acts and symbolic legislation, since a primary concern is with audience effects rather than policy outcomes. Of course, even where penal populism amounts to little more than discourse, it still has effects of a sort—denigrating expert opinion, affirming the sovereignty of public opinion, reinforcing a tabloid-friendly political idiom. But we should not confuse these effects with the wholesale transformation of penal practice.

Turning to the normative issues, we might begin by observing that most commentators who talk about penal populism do so in a critical fashion.

[29] Zimring et al. (2003); Matthews (2005).

Indeed, in its current usage the phrase has mostly negative connotations.[30] But as I noted above, most commentators are criminological experts who worry that they are being marginalized in the policy-making process or liberals who associate populism with illiberal policies. Since their audiences are mostly other criminologists and other liberals, these writers rarely feel the need to defend their preferences. Nor do they explain why the public ought to defer to penological experts, especially in an era when penal policy is often framed as a question of expressive or retributive justice and not as an instrumental form of crime control. But making the case for penal expertise is, it seems to me, an important task for penologists today, and one to which too little effort has been devoted.

We should notice that it is primarily with respect to *penal* policy—and above all to sentencing questions—that populist discourses and policy-making processes are operative, rather than other areas of crime policy such as policing, prosecution, or crime prevention. This may be because, given the shift from rehabilitative to retributive sentencing, penal questions now focus on what kind of sentence is 'deserved', or 'appropriate', or 'expressive'—and these are often seen as matters of convention rather than of expert knowledge. In other words, populist politics have focused on those elements of crime control and criminal justice where community sentiments and intuitions appear most relevant to policy formation and decision-making. (No doubt too, the public is especially focused on questions of confinement and release insofar as these bear upon public safety: and in common sense thinking, longer terms of imprisonment make for less public risk of victimisation.)

When we think about the relation of policy to public preferences, there a distinction is often drawn between knowledge and opinion—between empirical claims about what *is* the case and preference statements about what *ought* to be the case. And that distinction is often brought to bear by assuming that the expert's proper role is to provide the public with accurate knowledge, not to seek to change its opinions. So, if public attitudes towards penal policy are based on false information—having being shaped by media sensationalism, political lies, or ideological distortions—it is the task

30 Some writers, such as Stuntz (2011), embrace the popular control of punishment and insist that local members of the community are better able to impose justice and control crime than are criminological experts or detached professionals. But they don't describe themselves as 'penal populists', preferring to talk of popular sovereignty, of democratic process, and of community control. For the most part, the phrase 'penal populism' is deployed in a critical or derogatory sense.

of academics and experts to counter these misrepresentations with more accurate, balanced, and contextualised information. But if public attitudes are based on beliefs and intuitions about 'proportional' or 'expressive' punishments, then the expert must simply defer to these moral judgements. On this view, the role of the scientific expert stops where normative judgement begins.

But matters are rarely so simple, and the centrality of normative questions about retributive or expressive punishment need not render penological expertise redundant. Perhaps there are penal questions that turn solely on matters of moral judgement and with regard to which penological experts have little to offer. But most of the time, normative evaluations and choices are constructed on a platform of factual information about how the world works, why offenders break the law, what effects punishments have, and what the alternative options are. And expert knowledge plays a vital role in building that scaffolding.

Take, for instance, the question of capital punishment, which in penal policy is often regarded as the moral issue *par excellence*. American politicians, and occasionally United States Supreme Court Justices, justify the continued use of the death penalty on the grounds that its deployment as a retributive punishment is a matter of moral judgement and that in a democratic society it is up to the people to decide such matters. But this is a misleadingly simple way of framing the issue. It is true that moral justifications can be offered for capital punishment. And it is true that, when asked 'do you support the death penalty for the crime of murder?', most Americans say they do. But capital punishment laws are not self-executing, and capital punishment is always a legal and administrative practice rather than an abstract moral question. Consequently, death penalty law and practice always entail factual issues about which experts have important things to say. So, for example, empirical research demonstrates that capital punishment is administered in an arbitrary and racist manner, that it involves lengthy delays and inordinate expense, and that the process of execution is prone to unintended cruelty and suffering. Experience also shows that there are feasible alternative punishments available; that other nations (and many American states) choose other ways of punishing murderers (without experiencing adverse consequences for murder rates); and that moral intuitions tend to change along with institutional arrangements and the expectations they establish. So even where debates about choice of punishment pivot around moral intuitions and beliefs, there remains an important role for penal expertise and penological wisdom.

Populism and democracy

Critical commentary about penal populism is often accompanied by reform proposals designed to 'insulate' penal practice from popular sentiments or create some kind of 'buffer' between penal policy and public opinion, such as an expert sentencing commission or an independent research brokerage.[31] But some critics draw back from condemning penal populism on the basis that we ought to trust the people, be sceptical of élites, and seek to engage ordinary people in the penal policy process. For these commentators, a commitment to democratic values means that majoritarian sentiment ought not to be dismissed merely because some experts find it unhelpful or misinformed.[32]

Concerns such as these have prompted increased interest in the relationship between democracy and punishment and a literature has emerged addressing these issues (Johnstone 2000; Zimring and Johnson 2006; Miller 2008, 2013; Barker 2009; Rowan 2012). A basic principle that informs this scholarship is that 'democracy' cannot be understood in any singular, essential way. There are many conceptions of democratic rule, and many distinct ways of institutionalising democratic principles—as Barker (2009) shows in her comparison of three US states and their distinctive democratic cultures.

Moreover, our generalised commitment to democracy always exists in tension with other values—such as liberalism or rationality—which are also held sacred in contemporary political culture. So although we often talk today as if 'liberal-democracy' is a single political form, the traditions of liberalism and democracy are historically and conceptually distinct and often pull penal policy in quite different directions.

The contrasting implications of democracy and liberalism for penal policy can be observed in the history of capital punishment (Garland 2010). By and large, it was liberal political forces—above all, liberal élites - that brought about the abolition of the death penalty. Liberal demands for restraints on state power, for legal process, and for the rights and dignity of individuals brought liberalism into principled opposition to capital punishment. Democracy, by contrast, has had a more ambivalent relation to state killing, and democratic forces have sometimes worked to conserve capital punishment as an expression of majority preferences. In the USA, for

[31] See Green (2008: 273); Roberts et al. (2003) chapter 10; Lacey (2008).
[32] Loader (2005); Ryan (2003, 2005); Johnstone (2000).

example, a radically local, populist form of democracy sustains the death penalty at the local level, and an avowed respect for the democratic process has led the Supreme Court to uphold the legal validity of capital statutes and practices.

When foreign observers criticise the politicised character of American criminal justice, and when they describe the popular election of prosecutors, judges, and police chiefs as a threat to impartial justice, they are expressing classical liberal values. Contrastively, when Justice Scalia characterised the 'finger-wagging' of European abolitionists as lofty élitism and a haughty disregard for the views of ordinary people, he was expressing a robustly American—and an altogether illiberal—commitment to popular democracy (Garland 2010).

If democratic and liberal commitments sometimes come into conflict, so too do (popular) public opinion and (élite) expertise. However robust one's commitment to democracy, there are few who would argue that government policy ought to be an unmediated expression of majority opinion. Majoritarian principles are powerful norms for deciding elections, but they are hardly a sufficient basis for enacting good law or making effective policy. In the electoral context, rules such as 'one-person-one-vote' and 'the majority prevails' make no operative distinction between deeply considered, fully informed views on the one hand and arbitrary whims or mistaken understandings on the other. In general elections, in referenda, or in legislative debates, the same weight is given to votes cast by knowledgeable experts and votes cast by uninformed ignoramuses. And we do not impose literacy tests or knowledge requirements as a condition of participation. Our guiding principle in this context is that every citizen should have a vote and that each vote should count equally.[33] But the process of policy-making is a different undertaking. Insofar as it involves the selection of effective means to promote desired ends, the weighing of costs and benefits, the anticipation of consequences, and the scrutiny of alternatives, it will benefit from the application of administrative expertise, research evidence, and institutional experience. Insofar as penal policy involves the deliberate infliction of human suffering, a careful weighing of liberal principles and ethical constraints is also required. And because penal institutions are dark places largely unknown to the general public, the voices of offenders, inmates, and correctional practitioners ought always to feature in conversations about

[33] I leave to one side the point that free, universal, public education is an enabling condition of this principle.

the design, use, and management of these institutions. Majoritarian norms that seem compelling for some purposes seem altogether inadequate for others.

Populism and popular consent

The problem with penal populism is not that it is 'popular'. The problem is that it uses intemperate political speech and demotic popular appeals to generate policies that have little relation to penological wisdom and decency. But the desired alternative is not to silence public opinion or to exclude the public from the processes of policy-making. In contemporary western democracies, where concern about crime is widespread and trust in criminal justice institutions often lacking, there is no likelihood that penal policy will be fully entrusted to an unaccountable civil service or to liberal élites. Nor is it likely that questions of crime and punishment will be kept out of the tabloid press or out of electoral competition.

Whichever penal laws and policies are enacted, and however these laws and policies are arrived at, they ultimately require public approval or acquiescence. But this need for public acceptance does not preclude a policy-making process that is grounded in reliable evidence, shaped by experienced experts, and attentive to social values.[34] Indeed, there are many examples of institutions that facilitate public engagement—England's lay magistracy, the Scottish children's hearing panels, deliberative democracy processes, consultative inquiries—that are not populist in temper and do not give rise to especially punitive practices.

But what if a 'rational penal policy' designed by policy-makers and expert penological advisers is in conflict with majority sentiment? How, in a decent, liberal democratic society, ought that conflict be managed? Not, I would suggest, by seeking to hide or deny the conflict. One reason why correctionalist policies so quickly lost political credibility in the 1980s and 1990s was that experts had rarely explained to the public why a rehabilitative approach to the treatment of offenders was preferable to common-sense retribution—preferring to develop their correctional policies away from the glare of public attention (Garland 2001).

[34] Cf. Lappi-Seppala (2008: 116): 'we should apply the normal rules of political accountability also in penal discourse. Nowhere else in political life plans and proposals can be presented without estimation of costs, benefits and alternatives.'

In a democracy, government officials are obliged to engage with public opinion. The preferences of citizens cannot be shut out of the policy-making assemblies or treated as the rantings of a disorderly mob.[35] Nor is it productive to pretend that somehow, when properly interpreted, majority opinion is actually progressive and 'on our side'—since this is, in effect, another way of ignoring it.

But democratic engagement between the electorate and elected officials—and between expert élites and both of these groups—needs to be dialogic and interactive. Politicians must attend to the views of the electorate and take account of settled public preferences. But, aided by their advisers and policy experts, they must also seek to educate citizens by providing information and facilitating deliberative debate. Those who occupy positions of authority, administer policies, and run institutions are in a position to develop knowledge and understanding that are not commonly available. And by explaining these perspectives they can enhance public understanding of the problems being faced and the relative efficacy of the solutions on offer. Rather than dismiss the public as incorrigibly punitive or ignorant, policy-makers and their penological advisers ought to engage public opinion and seek to improve public understanding. Those who occupy positions of leadership and authority in a democratic society have an obligation to explain, to communicate, to give reasons, and to respect the intelligence of the electorate.[36] The task of the expert in a democracy is not merely to acquire and apply high-level technical competence—it is also to communicate and explain these technical issues to the public in ways that they can readily understand.

Whenever popular preferences are resisted in the formulation of penal policy or the administration of justice, that resistance needs to be explicitly argued for and justified. Policies that are at odds with majority preferences need to be specially justified, for example by reference to constitutional or human rights and the (undemocratic) minority protections they entail. The values and traditions of liberalism—due process, minority rights, constitutional protections, restraints on state power, the sacredness of human life, and the importance of doubt—provide important resources for such

[35] Ryan (2005:147–148): '[D]espairing about 'populism' in learned academic journals ... suggests, in the British case at least, an enduring social snobbery: a last-ditch defence mounted by an increasingly isolated academic and administrative élite against the idea that ordinary people are entitled to have their say.' For accounts of efforts to incorporate public opinion in sentencing, see Hutton (2008) and Indermauer (2008).

[36] On the role of the criminologist as a public intellectual, see Loader and Sparks (2011).

arguments. So too do Enlightenment values of science, rationality, and empirically grounded knowledge.

In our kind of society, democracy is a sacred value and *vox populi vox dei* is a guiding principle, so counter-majoritarian positions always have to be defended and justified. Lacking broad public support, their principles have to be explained and the grounds of their legitimate authority established—if not in majority public opinion then in supportive coalitions of experts, government officials, and cultural élites. Without such engagement and the legitimacy it brings, counter-majoritarian measures will not survive the scrutiny they will sooner or later attract.

Conclusion: Penal policy and penological expertise

The relationship of punishment to democracy is a complex one and my review of the topic has touched on only a few of the important issues at stake. But in the end, the questions raised by penal populism are actually less profound and less difficult than these discussions of democracy would suggest.

A critique of penal populism is not the same as a critique of popular participation in shaping penal policy. The problem with penal populism is *not* that it permits the views of citizens to shape penal policy. Indeed, as David Indermaur points out: 'populism, even though it appears to deliver power to the people, does not engender any process of political debate or deliberation and effectively deals the public out of a role in policy formation' (Indermaur 2008: 58). The problem with penal populism is that it embodies a kind of politics in which reductive representations of public opinion are allowed to dominate public debate. The problem is that it facilitates a kind of know-nothing politicised policy-making that ignores pertinent information and fails to address relevant values. Penal populism tends to drive out evidence, experience, and expertise and replace these with crudely politicised representations of popular sentiment. Over the past two decades, many of us have railed against its influence and criticised its deleterious effects. But perhaps we penologists ought also to use it as an occasion to reflect on the nature of our own expertise, the sources of our expert power and authority, and the contribution our knowledge can make to public debate about punishment and penal policy.

If penological experts are be regarded as credible, if we are to be accorded public trust, if we are to be respected by officials and listened to by legislators, then we must take care to uphold the integrity of our knowledge and the sources of its legitimacy. Our public pronouncements must be carefully grounded in evidence and experience, and not merely expressions of political preference.[37] Our statements, *qua* experts, ought to stay within the confines of what can be knowledgeably discussed and what is confidently known. We ought to reflect on the ways in which our moral intuitions and value preferences shape our understandings and to acknowledge that other normative beliefs could be brought to bear on penal practices and our evaluations of them. And we ought to be willing to revise our presumptions and scrutinise our values in the light of new evidence or contrary arguments.

Importantly, we ought to admit that there are some things we just don't know. And, where our knowledge is probabilistic rather than certain, we ought to explain the reasoning that underpins our recommendations. Sometimes the difference between expert opinion and public opinion is not a matter of right versus wrong, but instead a disagreement about how to weigh risk and how to decide who should bear the costs of a mistaken risk assessment. For instance, an expert might take the view that releasing an offender from prison carries a low risk of further violent offending and may urge the granting of parole. A member of the public might regard even the smallest risk of further violence as unacceptable and insist that the offender should remain in custody. In such cases, experts should aim to focus the debate and improve its rationality by clarifying the basis on which they have reached their conclusions and distinguishing differences of opinion from competing factual claims. If a public preference proceeds on the basis that offenders' lives don't matter, then that value judgement and its implications should be exposed and subjected to debate.

Above all, we ought to separate our work as penological experts from our involvements as penal reformers and political activists, and make it clear when our arguments in favour of this or that penal measure are grounded in established evidence as opposed to political preference. I do not mean by this that we penologists must confine ourselves to discussing 'just the

[37] Cf. Max Weber's admonition: 'it is one thing to state facts, to determine mathematical or logical relations or the internal structure of cultural values ... it is another thing to answer questions of the value of culture and ... the question of how one should act ... [T]he prophet and the demagogue do not belong on the academic platform' (Weber 1948b: 146). And recall James Q. Wilson's provocative criticism of American criminologists who, when asked for advice by policy-making bodies, 'could not respond with suggestions derived from and supported by their scholarly work' so instead offered advice that 'tended to derive from their general political views' (Wilson 1983: 42). That Wilson's policy recommendations were no less politically tendentious does not detract from the force of his observation.

facts', such as rates of recidivism, deterrence research findings, comparative imprisonment rates, or the relative costs of this or that penal measure. Penological expertise also includes experiential wisdom about how penal institutions work, about the values embodied in penal measures, about how sentences are likely to be used, about previously unanticipated consequences, about the lessons of penal history, about how other nations deal with similar problems, and about the norms embodied in domestic and international law. All of these are forms of knowledge and understanding that provide legitimate bases for expert authority and their relevance to penal policy ought to be vigorously and repeatedly asserted.

One of the most effective antidotes to penal populism is an impressive showing of competence, wisdom, and integrity on the part of penologists, such that policy-makers and their public audiences develop a willingness to trust their judgment and accept their advice. And if we need a model of the kinds of professional and personal qualities required to win this respect and trust, the career of Tony Bottoms can serve as a powerful exemplar.

12

Penal Legitimacy, Well-Being, and Trust

The Role of Empirical Research in 'Morally Serious' Work

Alison Liebling

> [T]he acquiescence or otherwise of prisoners to the kinds of authority claimed or exercised over them by officials is a variable matter. The ways in which such acquiescence or consent (or resistance) varies centre, in our analysis, on a complex matrix of interactions between prisoners' expectations of their captivity and ... whether they come to see the behaviour of their custodians as being justifiable, comprehensible, consistent and hence, fair – or alternatively, unwarranted, arbitrary, capricious and overweening. (Bottoms and Sparks 1997: 22)

> [P]risons have moral and emotional climates, and ... these climates are shaped by values, ideas and relationships. What matters in prison ... is a set of values which are essentially *interpersonal* and *civic* ... Prisons are special moral environments in which how people feel treated (that is, how prisoners *and staff* feel treated) has serious consequences, first for what happens in them, and second, for the claims that can be made about them. (Liebling, assisted by Arnold 2004: 454)

Alison Liebling, *Penal Legitimacy, Well-Being, and Trust.* In: *Crime, Justice, and Social Order.* Edited by: Alison Liebling, Joanna Shapland, Richard Sparks, and Justice Tankebe, Oxford University Press. DOI: 10.1093/oso/9780192859600.003.0012

Introduction: Order, crisis, and the worth of persons in prison

To say that Tony Bottoms has acted as intellectual mentor and friend to me over more than 25 years is an understatement of the first order. He continues to do so, as he does for many others, since his recent freedom from university administration. My intellectual discussions with Tony throughout the various research projects I have conducted have been among the most satisfying and stimulating aspects of my own career to date. We have discussed ideas at his house, at mine, on benches, in gardens, in a variety of offices, on trains, over the telephone, in pubs, and in various College settings. His most regular informal talk time is five o'clock, with a mug of tea, at work. These conversations invariably become deeply serious, while remaining light, and lead to the purchasing of many books. His most important contributions to my professional life—beyond the intellectual—have been practical, political, and moral: he has acted as a witness to strange situations in the Home Office at my request, deliberated with me on the wisdom of resistance, and strengthened applications for small but critical funding contributions at precarious stages in my long research contract life, at times embodying the 'Platonic Guardian' (Loader 2006). Most of all, he has responded with enthusiasm to my interests in social order and the role of values in prison social life. His passion for the normative, in prisons and beyond, has seriously encouraged the work of others in this area. He is, as others in this volume suggest, a model criminologist, and an inspiration to others. It is fitting, therefore, that what follows is a set of ideas arising from and, in places, developing some of his. Its themes are social order, legitimacy, well-being, and trust.

This chapter is organised into three parts. First, I will briefly introduce selected strands of Tony's empirical and theoretical work which are most relevant to my research, with others, on prisons. His research interests are, of course, much broader than this, as is widely recognised and reflected in this volume. I will focus in particular on the interest we share in the links between social order and legitimacy in prison (among some other in-prison and after-prison effects) and broader socio-political ideas. Secondly, I shall reflect on where a sustained programme of prisons research, conducted with others and with strong roots in the original theoretical and empirical domains outlined in *Prisons and the Problem of Order* in particular, is taking us and how his continuing work (particularly with Justice Tankebe) resonates with our empirical explorations of contemporary prison life. Thirdly, I will show how Tony's theoretical instincts in relation to the prison, in his work with Richard Sparks and Will Hay, have been empirically verified, and also developed, in particular to incorporate notions of individual well-being and trust. I will attempt to outline, in this section and in the conclusions, why his preoccupation with the virtues, and how they might be grown, matters. The 'crisis of trust and social order' in prisons and in modern communities is, as Tony recently put it, 'morally serious'.

There have, of course, been penal crises before. In his introductory essay in the edited volume *The Coming Penal Crisis* (Bottoms and Preston 1980), Tony Bottoms identified several difficulties which together constituted something of a crisis for the penal system: overcrowding, an increasingly tense atmosphere in high-security prisons, a 'crisis of penological resources', and considerable 'uncertainty of role in the probation service' (p. 1). He could have been talking more recently, although now the scale of the population crisis is significantly greater, the tension more widespread and yet hidden from view, the resource constraints unprecedented, and the uncertainty in the probation service stems from external scrutiny and reform efforts rather than from internal qualms about casework. In the same chapter, Tony outlines the growing opposition to the treatment ethic characteristic of the 1970s, arguing after C. S. Lewis that 'the "humanity" which (this theory) claims' may be 'a dangerous illusion'. Without a moral framework, however, penological pragmatism, or a 'heavy preoccupation with the urgent practical problems of the moment' (p. 4), he argues, is 'no adequate basis on which to rethink the shape of the penal system of the future' (p. 5). His reservations about the 'justice model'—the alternative to a treatment model—concerned the limited conception of justice characteristic of discussions about punishment and sentencing. The term 'justice' has a far broader meaning than the elimination of disparities in sentence length. The somewhat chilling phrase 'secure and humane containment' represented the 'abandonment of hope' and made care for the offender unlikely (p. 20). In their concluding essay to the volume, Bottoms and Preston draw on what they recognise as Christian values but express as having a broader basis and appeal, stressing the 'importance to every civilised penal system' of demonstrating 'its respect for the persons it deals with', and of affirming the possibilities of individual human potential and fulfilment 'even within a necessarily coercive penal system'. Any penal system should build in procedures and practices which reflect respect for persons and hope for the future of unique individuals. This is not an instrumental but a normative requirement.

Tony returned to these themes of hope, care, and justice in his 'end of decade' publication *The Aims of Imprisonment* (Bottoms 1990; and see Nellis, this volume, on the importance of its timing), in which he set out the longstanding conflict between these ideals, their realisation, their abandonment, and their reappearance in an important official policy debate which culminated in a still functioning Statement of Purpose for the Prison Service of England and Wales, which reads:

> Her Majesty's Prison Service serves the public by keeping in custody those committed by the courts. Our duty is to look after them with humanity and help them lead law-abiding and useful lives in custody and after release.

These themes of humanity and justice (and the difficulties of their translation into practice: e.g., the difference between narrowly conceived concepts of 'reintegration' in policy and practice, and a humanitarian concern for individual potential and personal fulfilment) lay at the heart of Tony's interest in penal policy and practice. Underlying his attraction to these concepts lies an abiding concern with three value domains. One represents a conviction and two can be formulated as both normative and empirical questions. They are: (a) the intrinsic worth of persons; (b) the kind of society we should be living in (which should at least be orderly); and (c) the proper use of power and authority (which should be legitimate; that is, among other things, there are limits to, and different conceptions of, power).

Tony's interests in order have their foundation in broader questions of civic and political values. In his unpublished Nigel Walker lecture given in 1999, *Criminology and the Problem of Order*, he referred to a brilliant depiction of the difference between good and bad power in art, arguing that criminologists should concern themselves with the problem of order as well as the problem of crime. In his allegorical 'Frescoes of Good and Bad Government and their effects' painted in fourteenth-century Siena[1]—a complex depiction of the functions and responsibilities of political power, or the benefits of good government and the dangers of bad government—Ambrogio Lorenzetti portrayed how the virtues necessary for the proper

[1] These frescoes decorate the interior of the Palazzo Pubblico or city hall in Siena. See https://artsandculture.google.com/asset/effects-of-good-government-in-the-city/WAFg-CSkcQJsMw?hl=en. Prints of them were presented to Tony on his retirement from the Wolfson Chair of Criminology at Cambridge in 2006.

administration of power—justice, magnanimity, perseverance, carefulness, and temperance—led to peace, prosperity, and well-being, or the common good. The virtues are personified by six female characters and 'pass through the hands of the citizens, symbolising a voluntary political order'. The effects of good government are depicted here: the 'town is thriving, with prosperous markets and citizens happily going about their business' (see also Mulgan 2007: 2). This is 'a version of benign order, based on reciprocity between rulers and ruled, on equity and concord' (ibid). Bad government or tyranny, on the other hand, is characterised by greed, pride, deceit, and boastfulness, and leads to violence, famine, war, divisiveness, and misery. These paintings constituted both a vision and an argument about the state respecting the freedom of its citizens, and about what makes authority legitimate. Lorenzetti's murals capture in artistic form an enduring political truth: that moral values matter in durable social arrangements. He inscribes at the foot of his paintings that justice induces unity, and that in order to govern, leaders need to keep their eye on the virtues. These paintings appealed to Tony when he saw them in Siena, and I hope to show below how right he is, empirically, to take justice and social order so seriously.

It is not surprising that his contributions to the Research and Advisory Group on the Penal System (RAG), established in 1984, reflected these value-commitments. The Control Review Committee (CRC), which recommended the establishment of RAG, was itself created following a series of major disturbances in long-term prisons throughout the 1970s and early 1980s—so the 'problem of order' (or 'control', as it was then usually articulated) was urgent (Home Office 1984). There were also questions about the limited potential for 'human becoming' in a penal system aimed at very serious offenders, whether housed in small units[2] or in maximum security prisons.[3] RAG recommended a programme of research on several

[2] The newly conceived CRC small units for control-problem prisoners opened at Parkhurst, Lincoln, and Hull in 1984 as a direct result of the deliberations of the CRC (Bottoms 1992). They were disbanded in 1990 as a result of 'siltage' (prisoners becoming unwilling to move back to mainstream conditions), the accumulation of a list of difficult-to-place prisoners who were languishing in segregation units rather than finding places in CRC units, and the changing penal climate which could no longer sanction apparently 'special' treatment of difficult and challenging prisoners (see Liebling 2001; Bottomley et al. 1994a). They were replaced by the initially controversial Close Supervision Centres in 1992 (Clare and Bottomley 2001). These units have undergone a number of transformations in order to achieve an acceptable balance between control, humane containment, and progression (HMCIP 2000). Their future purpose and development is under review.

[3] The term 'dispersal prison' reflects the policy choice of accommodating the highest-security category of prisoners among slightly lower-security category prisoners, in order to provide a more 'liberal' and humane regime, 'within a secure perimeter'. See Sparks et al. 1996. The

complementary aspects of the problem of control problems in long-term prisons. One of these research projects was a study of the nature of control problems in dispersal prisons, including the conditions leading to their emergence. Tony directed this research, with Richard Sparks and Will Hay, and the team elaborated their terms of reference to include the goal of 'deepening theoretical understanding of the conditions of order in dispersal prisons' (Sparks et al. 1990). The study was conceived by the authors as a descriptive and explanatory project, and it was based on the assumption that social 'events' occur in the context of underlying patterns of social relations' (p. B). Their key research questions included the following: Are different forms of order observable in different prisons, and how and why is order disrupted or challenged by prisoners? How is a prison's handling of control problems linked to the conception of order to which staff adhere? Their work also had a normative dimension, so they asked: Are certain forms of order more desirable and defensible than others? The language in which these ideas were eventually expressed in the book-length version of the project is the language of legitimacy.[4]

The background to this research was that by the mid-1980s, only two of the five existing high-security dispersal prisons had escaped serious disorder. The others had experienced several major breakdowns, leading to various restrictions to the regimes in those prisons but also to a more overt preoccupation with control among staff. The nature of the relationships between staff and prisoners were thought to be a key factor in the relative stability of those two establishments which had avoided a major disturbance. Here was the key research question that became the core of the authors' analysis in *Prisons and the Problem of Order*. The question their book addresses is whether different forms of order can be identified in prison, and which, if any, are more legitimate, and sustainable, than others.

dispersal system for housing maximum security prisoners was established following a Report by the Advisory Council on the Penal System led by Sir Leon Radzinowicz in 1968. This system of placing the highest-security prisoners among those requiring a slightly lower level of security would enable a more constructive and 'liberal' regime within a secure perimeter to be operated than a single 'fortress' prison might offer, combining security with humanity and offering alternatives for prisoners who became difficult to place. The arguments in favour were both moral and pragmatic. See further, Dunbar (1970); Liebling (1992, 2016, 2020) on the history of dispersal prisons and their reformulation as High Security Prisons in the 2000s.

[4] The book addresses other important issues too—such as the nature of prisons, the role of routines in reproducing order, and the relevance of 'practical consciousness' and structuration theory to the work of prison officers.

The research was conducted in the 'dispersal prison system',[5] at a time when these prisons were the subject of considerable management and moral concern. The official policy (it would be wrong to say consensus), thanks to a Committee chaired by Sir Leon Radzinowicz, was that regimes in long-term prisons should be relatively open and relaxed, within a secure perimeter. The structure of the long-term prison system should be designed to encourage cooperation throughout the sentence rather than the reverse, but the Control Review Committee felt that the stability of regimes in relatively relaxed long-term prisons would depend on a supplementary system of small specialised units for persistently troublesome prisoners of various kinds. The model of order on which dispersal prisons had been conceived, then, was humane and based on close and non-abrasive relationships between staff and prisoners (Home Office 1984: 6). In the event, the five dispersal prisons operating by 1987 varied considerably in their approach to order, and this became the foundation for their study.

The empirical research was carried out in two establishments with deliberately distinctive identities and histories. Albany had a history of control problems, whereas Long Lartin did not. Albany had a particularly 'restricted' regime, largely related to its experiences of disorder, whereas Long Lartin was self-consciously the most 'liberal' regime within the dispersal system (Dunbar 1970). In this sense, the two prisons represented 'polar extremes', each having a distinct 'ethos'. Long Lartin paid explicit attention to 'choice, responsibility and self-respect' (Dunbar 1970). Its stable history was attributed, more than a decade later, to its 'good relationships, good foundations, good training and its innovation' (Jenkins 1987; although see HMCIP 1992). Senior staff at the establishment referred to its regime as representing the 'last Radzinowicz prison': it operated a 'liberal regime within a secure perimeter' (Home Office 1968; Liebling 1992). Albany, on the other hand, had a less stable history and emerged, in the late 1980s, with 'control, safety and supervision' as its key preoccupations. Its distinctive 'restricted regime' was linked to the restoration of staff confidence following three major disturbances, in 1973, 1983, and 1985. This became an 'ethos' to which staff referred. The culture at Albany was linked to the regime and services being predictably delivered. Its staff emphasised respectful interpersonal behaviour, good service delivery, and consistency of treatment. Long Lartin had higher levels of freedom of movement, and a 'soft-policing' approach to the

[5] See footnote 3.

regulation of prisoner behaviour. The forms of order existing at the two establishments could be broadly characterised as situational at Albany versus social at Long Lartin.[6]

Prisoners generally felt the regime at Long Lartin was fairer, or more legitimate, but this was complicated by the socially embedded nature of underground incidents of violence in the prison. Albany had higher levels of disciplinary incidents, illustrating a certain level of frustration and a high number of rubbing points in the daily routine, as well as a tighter policing strategy. Long Lartin attracted higher levels of basic consent, but this was not universal, as highly troublesome prisoners were regularly 'ghosted out' (transferred) and weaker prisoners felt somewhat unsafe. Levels of interpersonal violence were 'deeper' and involved more complex and embedded disputes between prisoners. The black economy thrived. Prisoners were trading a degree of autonomy for safety: which meant that weaker prisoners were more vulnerable.

The key idea in this study—the concept of legitimacy—emerged inductively at the writing stage as the authors analysed their empirical data. Others had identified the significance of the term in explanations of prison disorders (Useem and Kimball 1989), but here the authors were concerned less with the 'special' problem of disorder than with the more 'perennial problem of securing and maintaining order in prison', and what forms of order were possible (Sparks and Bottoms 2008: 92). It was significant that the book was written around the time of the publication of the Woolf report, following a series of major disturbances in prisons in England and Wales (Home Office 1991). One of Woolf's most significant conclusions was that prisoners felt a sense of grievance about their treatment, by staff, and by impoverished regimes and disrespectful staff cultures.[7] Sparks et al. (1996) suggested that what Woolf was outlining, albeit implicitly, was in fact 'something akin to a theory of legitimacy' (p. 304). Legitimacy in prison included the perceived fairness of staff, the perceived fairness of the regime, and procedural justice. Legitimacy required that authority is legally valid, that prison officers and other staff act fairly, that they justify what they do to

[6] See also Sparks and Bottoms (1995).

[7] Legitimacy is a concept concerned mainly with authority and power relations. It includes the nature and status of the formal rules, the existence of shared beliefs which support these rules, and the *manner* of one's treatment (Sparks and Bottoms 1995; Bottoms 2002b: 36–38). It is essentially a political–theoretical term. For a thorough analysis of the concept and its application in criminal justice, see Bottoms and Tankebe (2012), and the edited collection by Tankebe and Liebling (2013).

those affected by their decisions, and that prisoners perceive their actions as fair (Bottoms 1999a: 255; also Tyler 1990; Paternoster et al. 1997; Jost and Major 2001; and Bottoms and Tankebe 2012).

The explanatory part of their analysis was inevitably tentative but plausible: prisoners were more likely to assent to the regime at Long Lartin and to resist it in various ways at Albany, because of the importance given to concepts of human choice, dignity, and development at Long Lartin and the more overt deprivations and restrictions, which were experienced as more punishing, at Albany. Stated more generally, there were different and identifiable conditions 'which make it more or less likely that prisoners will accept the authority of their custodians' (p. 304). Their empirical evidence base consisted of sustained observation and interview data, supplemented by various less accessible figures on head injuries, transfers out of the prison, alarms, and adjudications.

Prisons and the Problem of Order identified and clearly articulated, for the first time, some of the most important conceptual, analytic, moral, and political problems of imprisonment (e.g., the question of what emphasis is given to different approaches to the use of coercion and authority and the inherent link between legitimacy and order). It revised 'the conceptual terms in which prisons were studied and described' (Sparks and Bottoms 2008: 91) and corrected some limiting errors, for example, the assumption by some 'radical pessimists' that prisons could only be run by coercion (p. 96). Prisons could, the authors argued, generate normative commitments towards compliance, and the actions and demeanour of prison staff were key variables in this framework. Prisons accomplished this partially, in different ways, and to varying degrees. The important questions, then, included the extent to which different prisons achieved this, their methods, and the impact of such varying forms of 'orderliness' on prisoner compliance and conflict. How do prisoners respond or adjust to different types or degrees of legitimacy deficit? What does sufficient legitimacy look like? How do different forms of concern with legitimacy (or order) shape practice? Their analysis made a considerable impact, on senior managers in the Prison Service and on new scholars of the prison, including me. What engaged audiences most about the book was this emphasis on the 'perennial problem of order' rather than on specific instances of disorder. Why should prisons be orderly at all? What happens when the maintenance of social order becomes an end in itself? How does power flow, or legitimacy matter, in the day-to-day practice and experience of imprisonment? Their analysis resonated with broader criminological questions about why people obey the law, as well as with broader political theoretical questions about the kind of society in which we wish to live, the proper use of authority, and the responses of citizens to different, including improper, versions of it.

A PhD student of Tony's, Suhail Ahmad (Ahmad 1996), explored this emerging analysis further, following discussions with Tony about potential research topics. He argued, on the basis of his empirical work in three prisons, that fairness in prison had three main components: the fairness of staff; the fairness of the regime; and the fairness of procedures (for example, disciplinary and grievance procedures). In a secondary analysis of his data from three prisons, Bottoms and Rose found that staff fairness was seen as the main determinant of perceived overall regime fairness. Perceptions of fairness in prison were 'substantially more dependent' on perceptions of staff fairness and staff–prisoner relationships than they were on 'the objective quality of various specific regime features' (i.e., material provision), or prisoners' evaluations of the fairness of these regime features (see Figure 12.1). In Tony's words: 'In a very real sense, therefore, it would seem that staff actually embody, in prisoners' eyes, the regime of a prison, and its fairness' (Bottoms and Rose 1998: 227).

This is a crucial insight, and it has significant implications for our understanding of prisons, the way in which they are evaluated by prisoners (as well as prison scholars), and our thinking about the work of prison officers (see further below). How a prison feels is shaped, as Goffman and others

	Local	Training	Dispersal	Young Offender	Womens Open	All Cases
Behaviour	↓	↑				
Order		↑↑	↑		↓	
Relations with Staff	↓			↓	↓↓	↓
Staff Fairness	(↓)	↓	↓	↓	↓	↓
Regime Fairness	↓	(↓)	↓	↓	↓	↓
Woolf Dimension	↓	(–)	↓	↓	↓	↓
Making Progress	↓	↓	(↓)	↓ (↓)	↓	↓
Participation	↓	↓		↓		↓

Figure 12.1 Overview of outcome effects of IEP policy change in five prisons 1995–1996

would have argued, by the daily interactions that constitute that prison: 'the face-to-face relationship is the most central dimension of the social world' (Schutz 1962: 318).

As a scholar who had by this time had spent a number of years observing prison life, and who had a background in political theory, it was inevitable that these themes would resonate with me. I show next how these important ideas have shaped and connected with my work, undertaken with others, providing a theoretical backdrop and point of comparison for a programme of empirical research which is ongoing. It was never my intention to 'test the legitimacy hypothesis', but I was drawn to the PPO study again and again, to help me think about and analyse data emerging from my own studies. The account below shows how right the authors were in their original theoretical formulations, but also that there is more to be said and learned about the role of legitimacy and fairness in prison life, as well as in the life trajectory of individuals.

Incentives, relationships, and power in prison

The 'bridging study' between *Prisons and the Problems of Order* and what became my own major study of *Prisons and Their Moral Performance* was an evaluation of a newly introduced system of incentives and earned privileges (IEP) into 5 of 32 first-phase prisons in 1995–1996, and all subsequent prisons thereafter, which I led, and to which Tony acted as academic advisor. The policy was introduced by the then Home Secretary, Michael Howard, as part of an attempt to reverse the liberalisation of regimes after Woolf and a consequent increase in the quantity of drug use and the rate of assaults in prison. The central idea was that privileges had to be 'earned' by good behaviour; and, since the privileges on offer were valued by prisoners, the expectation was that, on average, prisoner behaviour would improve. The five prisons included in the evaluation were of different types: one prison for women, one for young offenders, one category C training prison, one local prison, and one dispersal or high-security prison (the latter three all for adult men). We had to devise our 'before' questionnaires almost overnight, given the speed at which the policy was implemented and the research commissioned. Gerry Rose acted as statistical advisor to the project and taught us how to make composite variables—or dimensions—instead of single-item measures of complex concepts, such as fairness and staff–prisoner relationships. Below in Figure 12.2 are some results from

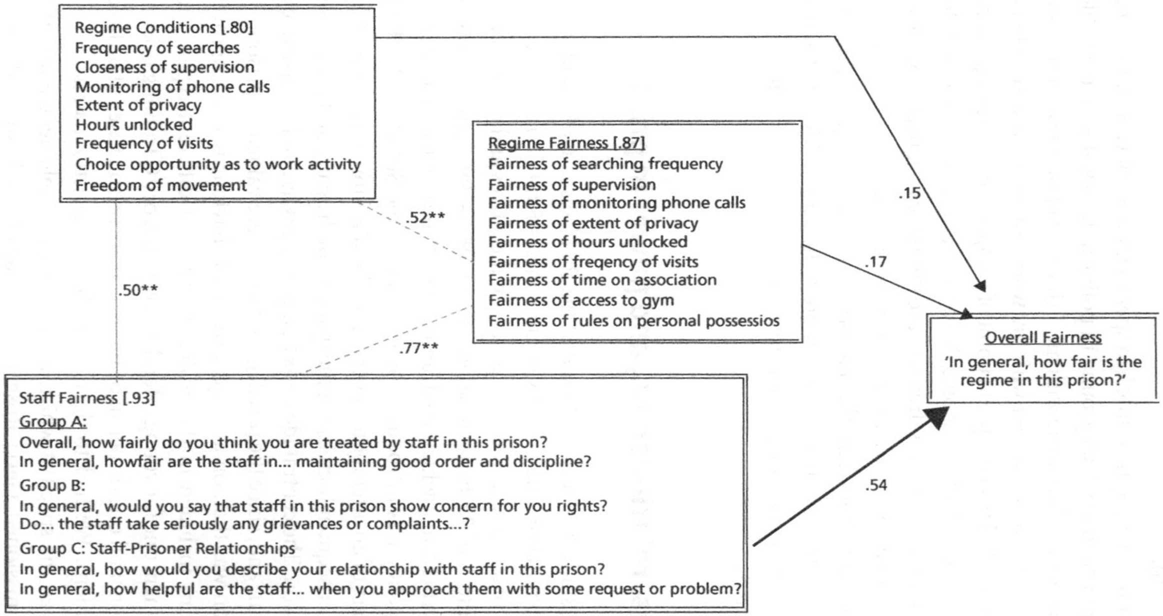

1 Adapted from Bottoms and Rose 1998, and further discussions with the authors. Alpha values (reliability scores) are given in square trackets. Beta-values (effect sizes on the dependent variable "Overall Fairness") are shown under each arrow. All are statistical significant, but the value for "staff fairness" is much higher than the values for "regime conditions" and "regime fairnss". Relationships between the three key independent variables are shown on dotted lines. They are all significant at the p<01 level (see further Bottoms Rose 1998).

Figure 12.2 Fairness in prison: a multivariate analysis

that study, showing 'the arrows all pointing in the wrong direction', as one of our research sponsors put it at the time. That is, the evaluation found few improvements to prisoner behaviour and widespread perceptions of unfairness. The full story of the policy and its effects is complex and can be found in various publications (e.g., Liebling 1992, 2008; Bottoms 2003), so I refer only briefly to this study here. My main points here are: (a) that perceptions of unfairness seemed to lead to a worsening of prisoner behaviour; and (b) that these complex but important concepts can be operationalised and measured in prisons with relative ease.

During the IEP evaluation, the research team (myself and Grant Muir, with others[8]) witnessed staff–prisoner relationships decline dramatically at Full Sutton, the dispersal prison in our sample, as a direct result of a shift away from the 'liberal' model of order then in place at several dispersal prisons, as described above. This period witnessed a move away from a reward-based and informal mode of power—which by this stage had become politically and managerially unpopular, as well as somewhat risky if taken too far—to a much more formal and punishment-based mode of power, which prisoners resented, especially when it came about too abruptly. We observed, using our empirical survey data, that a major disturbance on one wing in the prison—a reaction to the implementation of IEP, among other restrictive policies—was linked to the distant nature and quality of staff prisoner relationships on that wing, compared to others (Liebling 2000). Staff on E Wing, as it then was, were distant from prisoners, stayed in their offices, and resorted to formal rather than informal methods of discipline—unlike officers on other wings, who cajoled, reasoned, and persuaded prisoners into compliance. When the IEP policy was first introduced, E Wing staff placed relatively large numbers of prisoners on 'basic'—the lowest and somewhat punitive level of privileges—rather than using 'tactics of talk and persuasion' characteristic of the best prison officer work. On other wings where staff had better relationships with prisoners, and where they resorted to 'basic' less often, prisoners were more inclined to accept the new policy. This was a rather dramatic illustration of the fairness–compliance nexus.[9] It was clear that what constituted fairness in prisoners' eyes was mainly *relational*. Prisoners felt treated fairly when staff treated them respectfully and

[8] Gerry Rose, Andy Barclay, George Gilligan, Kirsty Windeyer, Marie Howes, Kate Alexander, and Nancy Loucks: all outstanding colleagues.

[9] It is possible that prisoners on E Wing were 'more difficult' and challenging than prisoners elsewhere in the establishment, but as in the Albany example, these differences, where found, rarely explain enough.

courteously; when they knew them as individuals, gave reasons for decisions, and rationally exercised 'mercy', or used their discretion intelligently. Formal power operated through informal means: via decent relationships. When staff withdrew into offices, resorted to formal methods of discipline, and then demanded compliance with new and unwelcome policies, prisoners withdrew their consent. The research team was present throughout this process of deteriorating and differential relationships and began to feel the tension building on E Wing as prisoners and staff retreated into conflict. This was a fraught and informative fieldwork experience which formed the basis of my first reflective article on 'Doing Prisons Research' (see Liebling 1999).

A year later, with my colleague Helen Arnold, I became preoccupied with the question of how one might identify, describe, and measure these relational matters in prison, largely as a result of complaints heard continually from prison staff, as we went about our research, that the newly emerging management technology of key performance indicators failed to reflect the true quality of life in a prison. This was 1999, a period in which an apparently valueless managerialism had taken hold—in prisons in particular, but also elsewhere in criminal justice. Prison staff were complaining that in an apparently poorly performing prison, good work was often being done and yet went unrecognised. The picture painted by performance data (unlike the artistic representations of good and poor states described above) was uninformative and conceptually and sociologically impoverished, and therefore misleading and unfair. To have meaning and purpose, a better conception of 'quality' was required. We were already engaged by this stage in an attempt to describe and capture the quality of staff–prisoner relationships, and prison quality, empirically.

There were tense disputes going on, at the time of our research interest, between the then Chief Inspector of Prisons, Sir David Rambotham, and the then Director General of the Prison Service, Martin Narey, about what the Prison Inspectorate's term 'a culture of brutality' (used about Wandsworth prison) might mean, and how reliable their evidence base was. With the benefits of a Home Office Innovative Research Challenge Scheme Award, Helen Arnold and I[10] spent a year in five local prisons in deep deliberation with staff and prisoners about what *should* be measured in prison. Our research questions were: What matters most when evaluating a prison? Is it

[10] With the assistance of Charles Elliott.

possible to reflect a prison's social climate or moral quality in figures? If a team of staff or prisoners were asked to go to a nearby prison to compare it with this one, where would they look? We drew on the method of Appreciative Inquiry,[11] looking for examples of peak experiences and interactions, and on what Charles Taylor would call 'strong evaluation' techniques[12] to structure our conversations with staff and prisoners about what mattered most. We were permitted to work closely with staff for several days, and with prisoners for shorter periods, to develop an insightful account of 'where the energy is' in this prison; of what kinds of activities and relationships brought about life, vigour, and hope, and of the institutions' 'best memories' and experiences. While these deliberations covered different ground in each prison, there emerged an agreed set of dimensions, or 'things that matter most' (see Liebling, assisted by Arnold 2004).

During one of our many conversations about this project, Tony observed that it was remarkable, given the complex social conditions of late modernity, that such a strong consensus arose from our varied deliberations about what the most important dimensions of prison life were.[13] He also commented that together they constitute the values of any consensual community.[14] We were finding that the characteristics of good prisons were the characteristics of good government: what distinguished one prison from another was authority used carefully and legitimately, and, linked to this,

[11] Appreciative Inquiry (AI) is a methodology based on strengths rather than weaknesses, and on a vision of what is possible rather than what is not (see Liebling et al. 2001; Liebling 2014). It has similarities with symbolic interactionism and grounded theory, as a creative and qualitative method concerned with theory generation and 'lived experience', narrative, and meaning. It includes an explicit use of *generative questions*, which are few in number, generate emotion as well as experience, and are based on real memories of specific experiences. They involve a deliberate focus on emotion and best experiences (see further Elliott 1999; Liebling et al. 1999a).

[12] Charles Taylor suggests that as human agents we have a deep and often inarticulate sense of what is important, and that it is possible to bring this deep sense of what matters to definition. These kinds of evaluations engage the whole self. They take concentration, for we have to bypass the distortions, compulsions, and deceptions of our shallow evaluations (Taylor 1985: 41). Appreciative Inquiry seeks and works with this deep sense of 'what matters'.

[13] They were: respect, humanity, staff–prisoner relationships, support, trust, order, fairness, safety, personal development, family contact, and well-being. Specific aspects of prison life that concerned prisoners most were: boredom, being locked up, staff having a lot of power and control over them, slow responses to requests and applications, the feeling of 'doing rather than using' time, staff never apologising to prisoners when they got things wrong, not being given reasons for decisions, prison feeling like punishment, not being involved in decisions, a lack of order and organisation, and the presence of drugs. The material conditions of imprisonment were less pressing: a quarter of the prisoners in our study strongly agreed that they were 'given adequate opportunities to keep themselves clean and decent'.

[14] He has recently returned to these themes of recognition and reciprocity: see his chapter in this volume, and Bottoms (2014).

the quality of interpersonal treatment. We talked with prisoners and staff at great length about what these dimensions looked like in practice (see Liebling, assisted by Arnold 2004).

It was deeply rewarding to be identifying and describing humanity and respect, then trying to measure them, rather than diagnosing a whole establishment as deficient in them. The reality was more complex and interesting. Prisons with poor cultures contained outstanding staff, exceptional wings, meaningful activities: micro-climates in which humanity 'seeps in'. It was important to reflect these exceptional places in evaluations. This was achieved via the construction of a many-item questionnaire. Staff and prisoners participated in the identification of items thought to reflect each dimension, and following an exploratory factor analysis this became a 14-dimension 'tick-box' questionnaire (which the Prison Service has routinely used since 2004). The survey became known as 'Measuring the Quality of Prison Life' or MQPL (see further Liebling 2011b; Liebling et al. 2011). It has been significantly revised over time, and we continue to develop it in ongoing studies.

This 'prison quality' survey has value for two reasons: first, because we engaged in a detailed attempt to involve staff and prisoners in the generation of the framework (i.e., the dimensions) and in the identification and wording of many of the items in the questionnaire; secondly, because the Appreciative Inquiry method captures aspects of peak human experiences of being treated with trust, respect, and fairness, and thereby helps to explore and clarify their meaning in practice. The survey is grounded in both real experience and highly valued aspects of human life ('ultimate concerns'; see Ludema et al. 1997: 1044). The relationship between the moral–philosophical literature and empirical exploration has been interactive and sustained. These, we claim, are two of the reasons why the survey 'works' empirically in a way that other attempts to measure prison quality, and relate these measures to important outcomes, have tended not to. As MacIntyre argued, in *After Virtue*: 'The notion that the moral philosopher can study the concepts of morality by merely reflecting, Oxford armchair style, on what he or she and those around them say or do is barren' (MacIntyre 1981, p. vii).

Moral concepts can be productively studied empirically, perhaps paradoxically, in a prison.

The dimensions identified *matter* for five main reasons. First, they are seriously under threat in the prison. The basic conditions of imprisonment (a stark imbalance of power and an ideology of punishment) make it highly likely that these issues, of authority used wisely and unwisely, will arise. Secondly, they have practical consequences: when staff *respect prisoners*, they unlock them on time, respond to calls for assistance, and try to solve prisoners' problems. Thirdly, the *absence* of respect and fairness is *psychologically painful*. Being treated disrespectfully, or without dignity, generates negative emotions (such as anger, frustration, indignation, defiance, humiliation, and rage: see Scheff and Retzinger 2001; Sherman 1993) and is damaging to character and identity (Ahmed et al. 2001; Jacobs 2013). Fourthly, and related to the arguments of Sparks et al. (1996), these dimensions constitute *a set of principles* to which we aspire in law and in contemporary moral and political philosophy. They are 'first virtues', the foundation of our social life (e.g., Jacobs 2004, chapter 5[15]). Fifthly, they are also, as MacIntyre has argued, *virtues that human beings need* (MacIntyre 1999). As vulnerable and dependent (as well as fallible) creatures (see, e.g., Bottoms 1998), we depend on acknowledgment, recognition, trust, and justice, or the virtues, as a condition of human flourishing (see, inter alia, Annas 2011; Jacobs 2004). Their opposites—disrespect, cynicism, neglect, and indifference—cause pain and damage to well-being and, we might argue, character (see, e.g., Jacobs 2013).

The framework outlined in *Prisons and Their Moral Performance* represents a conceptual scheme, which attracts considerable consensus among staff and prisoners, against which a prison can be empirically examined. It resonates with the moral–philosophical literature on how good societies function, despite the facts of imprisonment. We argued in retrospect that many of the dimensions included in the framework together constitute something of an approximation to, or operationalisation of, the concept of 'legitimacy' used by Sparks et al. (1996) in their analysis of the prison. We also argue, as the authors have, that there are some difficulties with the term: its meaning can shift, and more goes on in prison than the use of power. I shall return to this matter below.

These dimensions of prison quality were rated significantly differently in prisons of the same type, although there were also some patterns, so that fairness and personal development were always rated lower than order and decency (where decency has a mainly material meaning). How morality worked in each prison was related to an identifiable emotional climate, sometimes shared between staff and prisoners, but sometimes in direct

[15] Titled 'Politics and Human Excellence'.

opposition. These distinctive 'moral economies' (a complex term used by Socrates, Rousseau and E. P. Thompson, among others, but here meaning 'the extent and balance of interpersonal and other human values present in a prison's culture and environment')[16] were recognised by staff and prisoners once translated into empirical figures. The results from the surveys had high face validity.

Because we shifted from the descriptive and exploratory to the structured and standardised in this research, we were able to show in the analysis that followed that the dimensions were empirically related to each other in ways that were highly consistent with the Sparks et al. legitimacy thesis. Respect was highly correlated with fairness, which in turn was highly correlated with order. Where there was less respect and fairness, there was a higher risk of disorder, as we saw somewhat dramatically in one of the prisons in our study shortly after we had evaluated it. The relatively low levels of respect found at Holme House, an otherwise good 'service delivery prison', were linked to two major disturbances (on the house block with the lowest levels of respect) when population pressure meant that prisoners' relatively generous access to activities was curtailed. Staff were described by prisoners as 'confrontational' and 'in your face', despite high access to goods and services. The disturbances were confined to wings with the lowest respect scores, in a fine illustration of the distinction Tony has drawn between instrumental and normative compliance (see Bottoms 2002b).[17] We have seen further examples of links between moral quality of life (MQPL) scores and important outcomes in other studies (see further below and, e.g., Auty and Liebling 2019).

Beyond legitimacy: Well-being and trust

The Sparks, Bottoms, and Hay legitimacy thesis—that fairness, relationships, and respect are related to compliance with regimes, and general levels of order in prison—received considerable empirical support in this work. There have been other developments that together may take us beyond legitimacy, and in this part of the chapter I provide two specific examples.

[16] See Gotz (2015), who argues that the term should be 'a dynamic analytical tool that can illuminate the workings of [civil] society in the modern world' (p. 21).

[17] Prisoners said 'they talk down to you', 'some staff talk to you as if they want you to retaliate', 'they should recognise you more as an individual', 'it's a screw's jail'. On the wing where prisoners felt least respected, a stronger form of solidarity was found among prisoners (see Liebling, Elliott, and Arnold 2001).

First, I describe the important link between legitimacy and individual well-being, and secondly, I show how trust is related to social order in ongoing research.

Turning to well-being, an important new development in our empirical analysis was the relationship between perceived treatment in prison and psychological survival or its opposite: suicide. In a study of a major suicide prevention initiative in 12 high suicide-risk local prisons, higher levels of perceived fairness, relationships, and order were correlated with higher self-reported well-being, via higher levels of perceived safety. Higher levels of *trust in the environment* (i.e., predictable and approachable staff, an expectation of responsiveness, and help and assistance with problems) were linked to lower levels of distress, which in turn were highly correlated with institutional suicide rates over a three-year period (see Liebling et al. 2005). Using mean levels of distress as a dependent variable in the analysis, and holding 'imported vulnerability' factors (such as previous suicide attempts, drug use, or psychiatric hospitalisation) constant, we identified which aspects of the quality of life contributed most to variations in levels of distress across 12 establishments.[18] Those aspects of a prison's social or moral climate that made the difference between survival or despair were: fairness, respect, staff–prisoner relationships, safety, and opportunities for growth or personal development. A prisoner who was 'not entitled to a pillow' when he asked for one ('you are not entitled to a pillow': officer) argued that indifferent treatment 'can turn you into a different person'.[19] What he meant was that poor treatment leads to negative emotions (as well as healthier, defiant ones). It is distressing and damaging for individuals (see, e.g., Harris 2001: 84–86; De Zulueta 1993; Scheff and Retzinger 2001).

These findings have been crucial to my subsequent work, undertaken with others, and add considerable power to the legitimacy thesis, moving it away from its consequences for social order in any narrow sense (i.e., from

[18] The prison quality measures explained 45% to 50% of the variance in distress; imported vulnerability variables explained 8% to 15% of the variance in distress (see Liebling et al. 2005). This analysis supports the 'prison environment' or deprivation thesis in explaining suicide rates, showing how differences between prisons can generate significantly different levels of distress.

[19] Conversely, difficult prisoners in small units saw 'being treated fairly' and as a 'human being' as the most significant factor in their progress and personal development—a number mentioned specifically that they 'came to see staff in a completely different light as a consequence of their time in the [Barlinnie Special] unit' (Scottish Prison Service 2002: 4). See also Bottomley et al. (1994b) and Nellis, this volume.

arguments relating primarily to prisoner compliance) and towards broader political–theoretical arguments about the importance of proper governance in human flourishing, where it properly belongs.

The results were highly congruent with the argument that good government, or the careful and self-critical use of authority, supports our psychological as well as our social survival. Low levels of respect and fairness in prison have many consequences besides the loss of cooperation, including damaging effects on individual well-being. Legitimate treatment in prison may be literally a matter of life and death.

It is important to note that throughout these empirical studies, prisoners have been enthusiastic participants in moral conversation. One of the unexplored directions our various projects might have taken (and which we hope might be possible in the future) is to explore the implications of prisoners' identification of 'what matters' to them in evaluating the prison environment for their own future behaviour, or value priorities, more generally. Generating some commitment to civic values, even in a prison, is surely better than 'crowding them out' (Tyler 1998) and would be consistent with the important recent finding in the desistance literature that offenders who begin to desist from crime are 'growing the virtues' or starting to live a more determined 'ethical life' (Shapland and Bottoms 2011; Bottoms 2006; see also Mattingly 2014). It is significant that prisons with better moral climates 'grow virtues', and that prisoners are more likely to survive and flourish in places where human values can be found (see Auty and Liebling 2019).

Finally, we come to trust. I shall aim below to say a little about how exploring prison settings can begin, at least, to help to 'disentangle the problematics of trust' (Sztompka 1999: x) in contemporary society despite, or even because of, the upper limits to trust that are an inherent and perhaps, in places, necessary feature of prison communities. This project constitutes ongoing work, and continues to draw Tony in.[20]

[20] The following section draws on several studies, including a Home Office-funded 'return to Whitemoor', with Helen Arnold and Christina Straub (Liebling et al. 2011), and an ESRC-funded project: *Locating and building trust in high security settings*, conducted by Alison Liebling, Ruth Armstrong, Ryan Williams, and Richard Bramwell in the period 2013–2015. See Liebling et al. (2015); Liebling and Williams (2018), Liebling et al. (2020); and Williams and Liebling (2018).

The paradox of trust and modern prison societies

Trust emerged at the foundation or deliberation stages of our work as a dimension that mattered considerably to staff and prisoners, and as more central to prison life than some might think (Liebling, with Arnold 2004: 240–251; Liebling and Price 1999). Critics and scholars of the prison assume that they are low-trust environments, which they are. The lack of trust extended to prisoners, and the constraints experienced in feeling trust in others, are experienced as among the key pains of imprisonment, despite their almost complete absence from this literature. But some trust flows—sometimes in unexpected places and directions, and to different degrees—and these variations have major consequences for life in these prisons (see Liebling and Price 1999). Above a minimum threshold, cooperative relations seem possible. Below it, 'violent strife' erupts (Wrong 1994: 36; and see Liebling et al. 2011). Trust is, like many of the other dimensions in the prison quality study, an *asymmetric* concept: it may be built in one way, and slowly, and yet destroyed in another and in an instant. Respectful treatment built trust, whereas failure to act on commitments, inconsistent practices, or indifferent attitudes could destroy it. Beneath the façade of one of the basic rules of jail craft—'never trust a con'—we found that trust existed, but unevenly, and it was guarded. There are structural limits to trust, given the lack of equality, democracy, and autonomy in prison and the level of risk involved in prison life and management, but in fact acts of trust and distrust are found everywhere in prison, and tell us much about it. It is, like elsewhere, a fragile commodity, but some trust is essential if prison life is to flow at all. Onora O'Neill's concept of 'intelligent trust' is a helpful way to think about its flow and distribution (O'Neill 2002; 2009). As she puts it:

> The central problem in thinking about trust is that it can be misplaced: the trustworthy may be mistrusted, and the untrustworthy may be trusted. Both sorts of mismatch lead to practical anxiety as well as intellectual complexity. When we refuse to trust the trustworthy we incur needless worry and cost in trying to check them out and hold them to account, while those who find their trustworthiness wrongly questioned may feel undermined, even insulted—and ultimately less inclined to be trustworthy . . . The central practical aim in placing and refusing trust is to do so well, that is to *align the placing of trust with trustworthiness*. The central practical question is how we can *place trust intelligently*, despite the inevitable incompleteness of evidence that others' words are true of the world, or that their acts will live up to their words. (O'Neill 2009: 1)

Using the results of our Measuring the Quality of Prison Life survey in the first five prisons studied, supplemented by observational and interview data, we were able to describe the distribution and flow of trust in prison empirically, for the first time (Liebling, with Arnold 2004: 240–251). The sites included three public sector local prisons[21] (Belmarsh, Holme House, and Wandsworth); one public sector prison recently rerolled to a Category C training prison, but which continued to operate (and self-identify) primarily as a local (Risley); and one newly built private sector private local prison (Doncaster). Belmarsh and Wandsworth were London locals, with 'traditional' cultures (see Liebling and Kant 2016). In two of the prisons in our study (Belmarsh and Doncaster), staff reported—to their own surprise, as they completed the questionnaires—that they trusted prisoners significantly more than they trusted their senior managers (see further below). This finding had important sociological implications for life in those prisons. Where staff trust prisoners more than their senior managers, they tell prisoners things they might be wiser not to, collude with them, rely on them for protection, and encourage resistance to unpopular policies. These dynamics can have dangerous consequences. Where staff trust both prisoners and senior managers 'just enough', they become skilled negotiators of order and fairness. They can speak back in both directions and try to secure a workable deal for prisoners in their charge while fulfilling the obligations or efforts of those above them to run safe and orderly prisons.

In our structured survey, the exploratory dimension 'trust' consisted of four statements:

1.	[Statement 58]	I feel that I am trusted quite a lot in this prison [.793]
2.	[Statement 15]	I trust the officers in this prison [.777]
3.	[Statement 45]	This prison is good at placing trust in prisoners [.773]
4.	[Statement 71]	Staff in this prison often display honesty and integrity [.753]

Table 12.1 shows the percentage of prisoners who agreed or strongly agreed with each statement. It is interesting to note that prisoners did not trust staff much at Risley, a benign but disorganised prison, despite reporting

[21] Local prisons serve the courts, so tend to have a high turnover and a mixture of prisoners awaiting trial and recently sentenced prisoners.

Table 12.1 Percentage of prisoners who agree/strongly agree with statements about trust

	Belmarsh	Holme House	Risley	Doncaster	Wandsworth
1. I trust the officers in this prison.	31.3	28.7	21.8[b]	39.5[a]	25.0
2. This prison is good at placing trust in prisoners.	12.0[b]	22.4	23.8	37.7[a]	20.0
3. I feel that I am trusted quite a lot in this prison.	28.9[b]	35.1	30.7	36.8[a]	36.7
4. Staff in this prison display honesty and integrity.	22.9[b]	34.1	31.7	43.9[a]	31.7

a = highest score; b = lowest score.

Table 12.2 Scores on the overall dimension 'Trust'

Prisons	Reliability	Mean score (of 5)
Doncaster	0.78	3.16
Wandsworth	0.73	2.81
Holme House	0.76	2.72
Risley	0.81	2.72
Belmarsh	0.72	2.64

relatively high levels of respect. Trust was related to predictability as well as 'friendliness', so that Risley was experienced as a prison in which little confidence about outcomes was possible. Belmarsh had the lowest scores on prisoners feeling trusted (which corresponds with its high security status and ethos). Prisoners likewise felt that staff were least trustworthy at Belmarsh (see question 4). Doncaster, a private prison, clearly had higher than average levels of trust, in both directions.

Three of the four statements discriminated significantly between the prisons, with only the statement 'I feel that I am trusted quite a lot in this prison' not attracting significantly different answers.

The overall internal reliability score of the dimension 'trust' across all prisons was high, at 0.78. As regards the mean scores for the overall dimension, only one of the five prisons (Doncaster) scored above three (an overall positive score: see Table 12.2). The trust score for this prison was significantly higher than at Holme House, Risley, and Belmarsh (but not Wandsworth). This was, it turned out, a dangerously high score, as staff became careless in some of their security procedures in a series of events leading to two escapes. Levels of trust needed to be at the golden mean 'between excess and deficit': a narrow and fragile compromise between cynicism and laxity that characterises most of the best prison officer work (Liebling 2011b).[22] Without trust, life for prisoners was brutal and unfair. Too much trust, however, became 'blind faith' (D'Cruz 2019). Scepticism should be distinguished from cynicism. I shall return to this below.

Trust was significantly positively correlated with all other dimensions. It was most highly correlated with: Humanity [.76]; Respect [.75]; Fairness

[22] As Aristotle put it: virtue is a mean state between two vices, one of excess and one of deficit (Aristotle, *Ethics* Book II vi 15).

[.74]; Support [.73]; and Relationships [.70]. In turn, these dimensions were significantly correlated with well-being.

Trust was important in the professional lives of prison officers too. Where they trusted their senior managers more, better work was done. New policies were enthusiastically embraced and implemented, and prisoners felt treated more fairly (see Liebling 2008a).

These figures, while imperfect, tell us much about the context in which staff–prisoner relationships 'go on'. The high levels of trust in senior managers at Holme House, combined with lower levels of trust in prisoners, captured an important dimension of the social climate at this prison (a 'control model'), in which prisoners felt distanced and regarded with disdain ('it's them and us') on some wings in particular, rather like the model described by Sparks et al. in the Vulnerable Prisoner Unit at Albany (Sparks et al. 1996). There can be too much trust—as we found at privately run Doncaster prison (and see Gambetta 1990), where two escapes were linked to staff having a somewhat naïve relationship with or view of prisoners (Liebling 2004). One officer (in a different prison) told us in the course of a long interview, 'if I was on my own and something happened, I believe [the prisoners on this wing] would look after me ... In some cases, I trust prisoners enough to give them my keys'. He quickly added, 'obviously I never would', but we have witnessed incidents that suggest that the prohibitions against trust are occasionally breached in prison. The right or 'intelligent' use of trust is one of the most pressing and complex problems of contemporary prison work, particularly in light of changing prisoner demographics, where staff report difficulties in relating to, recognising, or understanding their population (see Liebling et al. 2011).

Table 12.3 Staff perceptions of trust in senior managers

Statement	Belmarsh	Holme House	Risley	Doncaster	Wandsworth
1. How much do you trust senior managers in here?	15.8[b]	41.7[a]	30.6	33.4	35.3
2. How much do you trust prisoners?	57.9	25.0[b]	49.0	60.6 [a]	47.1

Figures in 1 show those agreeing 'very much' and 'quite a lot'; and in 2 those agreeing 'very much', 'quite a lot', and 'a little'; a = highest; b = lowest.

The question of how to balance competing values in prison settings—how to trust 'just enough', find the mean between excess and deficit, or weigh 'security' against 'harmony values' in a professional manner—is, as I have argued elsewhere, one of the key problems both of the prison and of moral decision-making more generally (see Liebling, with Arnold 2004: 435–439; and Crewe et al. 2011). There is an important distinction between a 'theory of the moral' and a theory of 'being nice', as Thomas and others have argued (2003), and as illustrated in the Prison Service's misappropriation of the term 'justice' as 'care' in the early 1990s (Liebling, with Arnold 2004, chapter 1). Justice is not the same as care, just as humanity is not the same as laxity. Intelligent trust is not the same as naivety. Jason D'Cruz suggests that 'Trust loses its power to signal respect when it is indiscriminate' (D'Cruz 2019: 16). As Hollis argues (and many others have suggested): 'All errors in politics and morals are based on philosophical errors and these in turn are connected with scientific errors' (Concordet, p. 163, in Hollis 1998: 7).

My main point here is to argue that if trust is so central to social co-operation and well-being, as so many argue that it is (including Tony: see Bottoms 2014), then we should enquire about it empirically, developing reliable methods for doing so. Trust has become a major preoccupation of contemporary social theorists, for good reason (see, e.g., Baier 1986; Barbalet 2009; Seligman 1997; Misztal 1996; Hollis 1998; Sztompka 1999), partly because of its apparent decline in modern societies. Without it, we feel discomfort and uncertainty as individuals (Erickson 1995), but if the 'peculiar features of human society at the end of the twentieth century' lead to its decline, then the shared meanings and expectations that make society work begin to break down. Understanding 'the rationality of trust' is central to 'political understanding in any society of the modern world' (Dunn 1984: 281). To say that prison is a low-trust environment is not to say enough—prisons differ significantly, and in 'survivable' prisons there is often more trust operating than most would imagine. We should be asking: How much trust is there, of what kinds, to do what, between whom, and with what effects? How much trust, of what kind, is enough? What are the dynamics, and consequences, of *distrust* (see D'Cruz 2019)? The answers to these questions are analytically important (see O'Neill 2002).[23] I have continued to pursue these questions in ongoing work.

[23] Feelings of trust and safety among prison staff, for example, are important indicators of staff culture more generally. Traditional staff culture (as we have measured it) is a key variable in the provision or withholding of care for prisoners, willingness to implement suicide

Trust can decline in certain types of prisons over time, with serious consequences for life in those establishments. In a repeated sociological study of a single maximum security prison (Whitemoor), for example, we found that the low but workable levels of 'guarded trust' exchanged at 'Time 1' (1998–1999) made life in the prison flow relatively smoothly. Talk, and relationships, oiled the flow of life in the prison. By 'Time 2' (2009–2010) the prison had become 'paralysed by mistrust' (Liebling et al. 2011). There were special reasons for this decline, outlined more fully elsewhere (see, e.g., Liebling 2013), but the post-9/11 context, in which an increasing number of prisoners had been convicted of terrorism-related offences, formed part of the explanation (see Liebling 2015b; Liebling and Williams 2018). A high rate of in-prison conversions to Islam, linked with a major preoccupation with risk and poor understandings of Islam, had squeezed out the ordinary relationships on which penal order is built. Levels of fear and violence in the prison were, as a result of the new distance between staff and prisoners, and their fear-infused assumptions about each other, high. The question of who is 'us' and who is 'them' had fundamentally changed, so that only a minority of older, white, 'respectable' prisoners were trusted by staff (Liebling and Arnold 2012). Another explanation was related to the more general alienation of long-term prisoners, whose extremely long sentences were increasingly unexpected and barely comprehensible, leading to a loss of trust or faith in 'the system'. A lack of access to sources of identity, and the lack of hope or meaning brought about by a resurgent punishment ideology, made 'doing time' intensely difficult and hazardous (see also Liebling et al. 2020).

The staff culture at Whitemoor had changed from 'heavy-present' to 'heavy-absent' (Crewe et al. 2012) in the ten years between our two studies: staff had moved away from prisoners, and their orientation was towards security and control rather than personal development or humanity. There had been a kind of narrowing or misrecognition of the changing prisoner community. In the terms of Martin Buber, the prison staff (as well as the Prison Service organisation) had shifted from '*I–Thou*' to '*I–It*' relations with prisoners: prisoners were regarded as 'experienced objects' rather than 'experiencing subjects' (Buber 2010). The complementary relationship between trust and familiarity (Luhmann 1979: 20) was no longer emphasised in policy or practice.

prevention strategies, and day-to-day delivery of the socially reproduced practice of a prison regime (see Liebling 2008b, 2011b).

Whitemoor in 2019–2010 was both a 'new penological' and a 'failing state' prison, with officer alienation and retreat, a relative absence of management presence, and, for prisoners, a lack of purpose, safety, fairness, or opportunities for growth and meaning. There were new and unexplored moral and religious challenges in the prison, and because of heavier security intelligence activity, and the links between this and risk or progress out (among other things, such as fear of 'conditioning'), a new mood that regarded talk as dangerous. The prison was more difficult to penetrate for us as researchers, and power was being fought over by prisoners, some of whom were converting to Islam because it was both appealing and poorly understood and therefore its practices were difficult to police. There were high levels of fear in the prison. We used Axel Honneth's analysis of 'the struggle for recognition' to describe what we saw. Staff no longer knew, or recognised, their prisoners, but experienced them as dangerous and unfathomable. This was understandable but damaging (Liebling et al. 2011).

The important message for us in this heartbreaking study (see Liebling 2014) was that, despite structural limits, trust in prison officers, in criminal justice, in other prisoners, in prisoners by staff, and in senior managers by staff, is fundamental to legitimate prison functioning. Just as is the case outside prison, it acts as a lubricant, smoothing the flow of power, encouraging social cooperation, and making intelligent distinctions possible. But it requires familiarity, recognition that personhood is not reducible to a role, and civility, in order for it to grow. Modern societies have brought with them, as Tony has argued, threats and disruptions to the building of trust. Sources of trust have shifted and declined (Giddens 1990) and some argue that there is a 'crisis of trustworthiness' in addition (Seldon 2009)—an argument of particular (but by no means exclusive) relevance to the prison. This decline is linked to growing fearfulness and anxiety, and to low social well-being (e.g., Putnam 2000; Fukuyma 1995; Sztompka 1999; Uslaner 2002; Seldon 2009). We might argue, as Sztompka 1999 and others have, that trust becomes *more* important in complex modern (as opposed to traditional) societies, where the 'risk profile' as well as the 'risk perception' is greater (Giddens 1990; Luhmann 1990). Long-term prisoners certainly recognised the importance of the concepts of 'intelligent trust' and the building of trustworthiness to their futures, as subsequent correspondence and in-prison seminars on the topics of trust and recognition, for example, confirm.

The work described above has shown that empirical differences in levels of trust in prison have major consequences for life in those prisons. As Tony observed when first discussing the 'return to Whitemoor' results with me, some of the characteristics of modern societies that have brought about a decline in trust are showing themselves very clearly in long-term, closed prison settings. Explorations of 'the emergence or decay' of trust cultures in such settings (Sztompka 1999: x) have much to offer those seeking to understand its growth or decay in modern societies more generally. The work I have done subsequently with others has attempted to do just this, exploring the effects as well as the processes of the decline or building of trust in high security prisons (Liebling et al. 2015). The lowest levels of trust were found to be associated with higher levels of 'political charge' (anger and alienation among prisoners), and steeply hierarchical and power-infused, instead of open-minded or exploratory, faith-based religious identities (Williams and Liebling 2018). The relationship between such empirical explorations in prison and broader sociological inquiry lies at the heart of my own aspiration in scholarship. Tony's continuing work in these areas, and in this manner, has inspired and shaped this quest. If order is 'the most fundamental problem of social theory' (Wrong 1994: 1) then trust is surely a key component or building block of that fundamental problem of social life—underlying or supporting legitimate social order, however invisibly.

Conclusion: Prisons as a special case of social cooperation

> [O]rder and safety are essential not just for life to carry on but also for people to live well. The available data suggest that political stability and order, the rule of law and justice, are decisive to happiness ... It is hard to overestimate the value of strong, stable and protective and legitimate governance to human well-being. (Mulgan 2007: 45)

Prisons constitute a 'special case' of the problem of social cooperation, and the associated problems of action, structure, power, and authority (Sparks et al. 1996: 29 and 300). Better models of order, with sustainable foundations, lead to better outcomes, including prisoner well-being. One of the things that governments and prisons have in common is that they have to—or should aspire to—remain legitimate while sometimes taking unpleasant actions in the interests of social order. When the organisation and management of prisons is driven by politics rather than principle, the consequences for legitimacy are serious. A climate of austerity, implemented within a punitive ideological framework (so more, larger, no-frills prisons, with longer, risk-based sentences, rather than better prisons, used judiciously), places considerable moral and operational strain on career-minded governors who manage prison establishments (see Liebling and Crewe 2016).

The empirical research to which I have referred in this chapter supports the argument that Tony made several decades ago—that efficiency and utility are insufficient as foundations for penal policy and practice—and yet we find ourselves in an era where civil servants insist that morality is a costly luxury, and the market takes precedence over justice (an 'economic rationality': see Liebling 2011b).[24] The question 'what should our prisons be like' might be reformulated to ask 'what should our democracy be like?' (Karstedt 2013) and 'how legitimate are our power holders?' (Bottoms and Tankebe 2013).[25] As Mulgan says in his book *Good and Bad Power*, 'from afar power looks mysterious and full of conspiracies. From close up the people involved look reasonable, humane and constrained.' This is a problem with which Ben Crewe and I have grappled in an empirical project on public–private sector prison comparisons and the professional identities of senior prison managers (Mulgan 2007: 4; Liebling and Crewe 2012). We have found that men and women in power vary and that, despite the policy climate, their translation of policies into practice can shape the model of order on which an institution operates, sometimes drastically altering the fates of individual prisoners. As Tony has argued in his essay on the relationship between theory and research, there needs to be a continuing dialogue between theory and empirical observation, and normative reflection, in our 'ongoing cumulative search for the truth' (Bottoms 2008b: 83).

[24] According to Mulgan, civil servants are both servants of the public and of ideals (2007: 44).

[25] Apparently the British Prime Minister Harold Macmillan was asked what the collective noun was for heads of government. He replied: a 'lack' of principals! (Mulgan 2007: 4).

In our search for underlying causes, then, and for explanations of social order, empirical detail is essential. I have benefited a great deal from regular conversations with Tony about emerging findings and conceptual frameworks relating to social and normative order. I end with a definition of the well-known verb 'to Tonify': it means to 'improve; to deepen and stretch theoretically; and to clarify'. This is a highly appropriate term to reflect the continuing influence of Tony Bottoms on the work of others.

13

Creative Arts, Offender Rehabilitation, and Penal Reform

Remembering the Early Years of the Barlinnie Special Unit

Mike Nellis

Introduction

In 1973, a therapeutically oriented 'Special Unit' opened in D-wing of HMP Barlinnie, Glasgow's old Victorian prison, to house a small number of life-sentence prisoners who had been deemed at that time to be the most dangerous and difficult in the Scottish penal system. The Unit was formally operational until 1996 and although it has remained a significant touchstone of debate in Scottish penal policy, it has been remembered ambivalently (Sparks 2002: 563). To some it became a legendary institution, which, through the use of creative arts, enabled the rehabilitation of some of Scotland's most violent prisoners, particularly a man called Jimmy Boyle (b. 1944). After his departure in 1980, it seemingly became a mere shadow of its former self, a lost opportunity to reform the wider penal system.

To others its early years represented a moment when penal authority was inadvertently ceded to critical and manipulative prisoners—Boyle especially—and their unduly liberal champions in Scotland's social work and arts communities, which was fortunately retreated from, never to be allowed to happen again, and considered best forgotten. In between, some late-in-the-day comment and research quietly accepted that the Unit had effected a useful reduction in the erstwhile violent behaviour of its inmates, but mostly without *capturing what was truly 'special' about it*, least of all in respect of its early use of creative arts (Whatmore 1987, 1990; Stephen 1988; Cooke 1997; Sparks 2002). To many, perhaps most, turn-of-the-century

Mike Nellis, *Creative Arts, Offender Rehabilitation, and Penal Reform*. In: *Crime, Justice, and Social Order*.
Edited by: Alison Liebling, Joanna Shapland, Richard Sparks, and Justice Tankebe, Oxford University Press.

DOI: 10.1093/oso/9780192859600.003.0013

practitioners in the Scottish penal system the Special Unit had faded from memory, although belated attempts to commemorate it are now beginning to occur.

This chapter concentrates mainly on the early years of the Unit, from 1973 to 1982—the era which gave it its lasting association with creative arts and its controversial public identity, whose legacy remains uncertain. It is simultaneously an exposition and a celebration of the Special Unit's extraordinary early achievements and contemporary impact, a conscious act of remembrance, and a call for it be given an informed and prominent place in the Scottish—indeed, British—penal heritage. It detours to consider responses to the Unit by the Anglo-Welsh Control Review Committee (CRC) shortly afterwards, in which Committee's research agenda on managing difficult prisoners Tony Bottoms became deeply involved (Home Office 1984, 1987; Bottoms and Light 1986; Bottomley and Hay 1991).

Historically, however, the Special Unit's story has been most enduringly memorialised through the testimony of two prisoners who experienced it (Boyle 1977, 1985; Collins 1997, 2000) rather than through any official (or professional) account, although academic Joe Sim has tirelessly championed it (Macdonald and Sim 1978; Scraton, Sim, and Skidmore 1991) and professional penal reformers wrote supportively of it at the time (for example Wright 1982: 132–133). Popular penal histories of HMPs Barlinnie and Peterhead acknowledge it appreciatively (Jeffreys 2009, 2013).

Important and influential as Special Unit prisoner testimonies have been, they do not entirely explain how creative arts came to underpin and sustain the Unit in its controversial early period. Their take on the penal and political context in which this occurred, while never less than astute, is necessarily subjective. Early academic accounts were similarly vague on the origin of the arts in the Unit and gave the erroneous impression that their use was always intended (Short 1979). In England, the CRC's attention to the artistic aspects of the regime was negligible, despite the availability of a book edited by a Glasgow art gallery director and an art therapist (Carrell and Laing 1982) that celebrated the first eight years of the Unit's 'evolution though its art'. The book, arguably as much a landmark in Scottish penological writing as in arts writing, contained thoughtful commentary from a wide range of people involved, including prisoners—although the Scottish Office shortsightedly forbade contributions from *some* serving prison staff—as well as vividly depicting some of the artwork produced there.

This chapter draws extensively on that book, focusing on the same formative period in the Unit's history, and seeks to show how creative arts briefly but spectacularly became integral to the concept of offender rehabilitation and, by dint of that, to the always 'cultural' politics of penal reform in Scotland—a politics inseparable from the fixed and shifting senses of what a country thinks it is, what its people are like, and what they aspire (or don't aspire) to be. It is undeniably a heartfelt account on my part, reflecting a longstanding interest in the work—and legend—of the Special Unit and the practical and political lessons which could be drawn from Jimmy Boyle's (1977) autobiography, *A Sense of Freedom*. Like many of my generation I read the book when it first appeared, just prior to training as a social worker at the London School of Economics, on a 'generic' course which singularly neglected the specifics of knowledge necessary to work with young offenders. More than any academic book I had read at that point, *A Sense of Freedom* gave me some of that knowledge, and also the confidence to believe that if someone as deeply criminal as Boyle had once been could turn around, surely the somewhat less delinquent youngsters I was encountering in south London could also be enabled to do so. Alongside the ideas for practice that I took from it, Boyle's book roused my interest in the *place* in which he had changed and the kind of transformative culture which prevailed there.

Working with young offenders led me to the Cambridge Institute of Criminology in 1984 to undertake a PhD on the history of 'intermediate treatment'—the then current neologism for youth justice social work—which was linked to a government-funded national evaluation of such work, managed by Tony Bottoms. Tony, newly appointed as Director of the Institute, became my doctoral supervisor. I was immediately struck by his interest in and respect for practitioners, his insistence that while theory and research were vital, criminology was an *applied* discipline, relevant to policy-making and to life. Tony's high expectations of me, together with immersion in the milieu of the Institute as a whole, gave me my own experience of a transformative place and culture, opening up career possibilities that would not otherwise have come my way.

Coincidentally, I first heard Jimmy Boyle speak about his penal concerns, and experiences, in 1985, at the Institute of Criminology, where it was customary to hold guest seminars on Wednesday afternoons. The guest was usually an academic of some standing, with audiences of approximately 40 people. Boyle had been invited to speak on 'the crisis in the Scottish prison system'. Such was his celebrity at that time that attendance doubled. Tony introduced him, and I recall thinking as they sat together at the front table, waiting to begin, of the quite different life journeys that each had made to arrive in that particular moment. Their juxtaposition left a lasting impression, and I remain convinced that serious penal reform requires both of their types of expertise. When, years later, I became involved in the training of probation officers, the courses I developed consistently blended the theoretically informed, applied criminology that Tony practised with more experiential, autobiographical accounts, exemplified by *A Sense of Freedom* (Nellis 2002). While it was quite serendipitous that I took up an academic post in Glasgow in 2005, it was probably inevitable, once there, that I would properly explore how the Special Unit had come into being.

Creating the Barlinnie Special Unit

In Scotland, in the aftermath of the abolition of capital punishment in the 1960s, 'special units' were developed to deal with particularly intractable prisoners, mostly long-sentence lifers perceived as having little or nothing to lose from violence towards staff—but in two very different ways (Coyle 1987). The Scottish Home and Health Department (1971) Working Party report *Treatment of Certain Male Long term Prisoners and Potentially Violent Prisoners* emerged from official anxieties about escalating violence between staff and a handful of particular prisoners who had demonstrably not been rendered manageable by the available repressive sanctions—beatings by squads of baton-armed prison officers, and/or solitary incarceration, often naked, for protracted periods in the prison-within-a-prison of 'the cages'—the first form of 'special unit'—in HMP Porterfield, Inverness. The Working Party proposed a new kind of unit, whose regime was influenced loosely by Maxwell Jones's and Dennie Briggs's conception of a therapeutic community (Jones 1968; Whitley, Briggs, and Turner 1972)—as practised at Dingleton Hospital in the Scottish borders— and by visits to HMP Grendon, the special hospitals Broadmoor and Carstairs, and the C-Wing special unit in HMP Parkhurst (Donnison 1978). It was intended to house up to ten prisoners, to have an explicitly psychiatric orientation, to make use of group counselling and drug therapy, and to create a therapist/patient relationship between staff and prisoners.[1] Such was the crisis of violence

[1] The development of therapeutic communities, usually in hospital settings in England after the Second World War, is described in Harrison (2000). Their use in British prisons, HMP Grendon notwithstanding, has been limited. Dennie Briggs (b. 1927), an American psychologist who had been particularly associated with those in California, worked at both Dingleton psychiatric hospital, Melrose, in Scotland (where Maxwell Jones had established a therapeutic

in Scottish prisons that this proposal had the full personal backing of the then (Conservative) Undersecretary of State for Scotland, Alick Buchanan-Smith, and the Controller of Scottish Prisons, Alex Stephen, both of whom were keen to import any lessons from the Unit into the wider prison system.

Peter Whatmore was appointed Consultant Psychiatrist to the Unit, visiting on a thrice-weekly basis. Links were established at the outset with the Douglas Inch Centre for Forensic Psychiatry and Ian Stephen, its Principal Clinical Psychologist, developed a lasting association with the Unit. Prison staff were volunteers, specially trained over 11 weeks in therapeutic techniques, although individual temperament remained important. Prisoner numbers were to be too small to make viable reliance on traditional prison work, other than routine cleaning duties (although unpaid 'work therapy' was integral to Maxwell Jones's conception of a therapeutic community (Jones 1968). From the start there was some uncertainty among those in charge as to what the daily routine might consist of. Jones had experimented successfully with psychodrama, but not the creative arts as such, and 'in the initial planning of the Special Unit, the arts had not been considered, at least not more than as a leisure pursuit for the occasional interested prisoner ... The arts do not have a high priority in the thinking of penologists' (Laing 1982: 56–57).[2]

The Special Unit opened in February 1973 in D-wing of HMP Barlinnie, a Victorian institution which otherwise mostly housed 1000 adult remand and short sentence prisoners. Architecturally, the Unit was unprepossessing, consisting of a foyer, two hallways, ten larger-than-average cells (some on an upper catwalk), a kitchen for communal cooking, the governor's office, an officer's meeting room, a surgery, the community meeting room, and several rooms which were subsequently to be identified by the arts that took place in them—the wood workshop, the painting studio, and the sculpture studio, the latter having originally been designated the Unit's solitary confinement cell for recalcitrant prisoners, but never being used. There

community) and the Henderson Hospital in England, as well as becoming a consultant for NACRO in this period.

[2] The idea that uneducated and violent men might benefit from creative art did not originate with the Barlinnie Special Unit. For example, former young offender and armed robber Rick Cluchey (1933–2015) developed an interest in performing Samuel Beckett's plays whilst in San Quentin in the 1950s and, after his release in 1966, became both a significant interpreter of Beckett's oeuvre and a drama-activist in US prisons (Esslin 1961). He brought his theatre group to Scotland in the 1970s at the behest of Richard Demarco and visited the Barlinnie Special Unit, returning again to HMP Barlinnie to perform *Krapp's Last Tape* in 2008.

was also a courtyard, where the sculpting of larger pieces was eventually to take place; a small garden; and a greenhouse.

Three of the first five[3] prisoners—Edinburgh-born Ben Conroy and Glaswegians Larry Winters and Jimmy Boyle, the latter two serving life for manslaughter and murder respectively—came from prisons in the far north of Scotland (Porterfield and Peterhead) where they had frequently been involved in violent confrontations with staff, accruing additional custodial sentences as a result, and experiencing long spells of solitary confinement in 'the cages'. Boyle's and Winter's trial for their participation in a particularly savage fight with officers in Porterfield in December 1972 was still pending at the time of their transfer. The excessive courtroom security reflected a police view that they were far too dangerous for, and undeserving of, the liberal regime of the new Unit. They each got six years. Boyle, aged 29 when he entered the Unit, already had a press profile—arguably warranted—as one of Scotland's most fearsome and violent criminals, but against all official expectations he was to become the Unit's most spectacular—and challenging—success.

The Special Unit in practice

The Unit inevitably began in an atmosphere of mistrust and suspicion: despite commitment to trying something new, prison staff and prisoners carried into the situation labels and expectations with which they were associated in the mainstream prison system. Some prison officers were also nurses, and the prisoners, for whom the informal, relaxed regime was undeniably disorienting, worried that they would be subdued by drugs and/or that the Unit was merely a step towards incarceration in the state mental hospital at Carstairs (where some of the Unit staff had indeed trained). One particular prison officer—Ken Murray, a member of the Executive Committee of the Scottish Prison Officers Association (SPOA), who had been on the Working Party that proposed the Special Unit—took

[3] The other two prisoners, both murderers, had not been involved in gangland criminality in the way that Boyle, Winters, and Conroy had, and were seemingly more in need of psychiatric support: see Short (1979: 140–141) for an account of Robert Wallace's background. When they first transferred to the Unit some prisoners feared they would be treated as 'mentally disturbed' and perhaps, after 'assessment', moved on to the Special Hospital (formerly for the criminally insane) at Carstairs—hence the nickname, 'Nutcracker Suite', that they bestowed on the Unit.

the lead in challenging the prisoners' (and his colleagues') perceptions. One prisoner—Jimmy Boyle, as it happened—responded in kind to the trust Murray showed, and to the hopes he had for the Unit. Kay Carmichael (1982a), a University of Glasgow social work lecturer who observed the Unit's development, said of the pair that they

> built a bridge of their friendship and trust in each other, which made possible communication between the staff group and the prisoners' group. These two men became the significant figures in the drama that was to follow ... The others, the Governor, the psychiatrist, the range of specialists and friends who worked in and around the Unit, interesting and helpful though they were, never functioned as more than bit players. The action was between prisoners and staff, and that, without intermediaries, was and is the way it has to be. (Carmichael 1982: 22)

Boyle (1985: 11) later agreed that prisoners and staff 'talking together' was 'the single most important factor of the Unit' and, while never subscribing to a fully psychiatric view of how the Unit functioned, regarded Peter Whatmore as a positive influence and formed a good relationship with him. In view of the significance that creative arts were subsequently to have there (which prison staff rarely initiated or participated in, other than helping to organise activities and events), this may seem to underplay the role of those who fostered the prisoners' artistic endeavours, but it is a useful reminder that the Unit was first and foremost a therapeutic community, however tentatively and ambivalently. Mutual hostilities between once antagonistic groups diminished—though there were awkward flashpoints along the way—and the milieu created by the changed relationships between prison staff and prisoners was critical in enabling individual prisoners to change. The regular community meetings, in which staff and prisoners learned painfully to communicate honestly, to see through each other's eyes, to express vulnerability, to confront unacceptable behaviour and resolve conflicts, to ponder past allegiances and to form new interpersonal alliances, were the basis of all the other changes that occurred in the Unit: the transformation in 'daily living', and the emergence of an environment which 'encourage[d] flexibility, spontaneity, confidence and tolerance', were the seedbed of its creativity (Carmichael 1982a: 23). Carmichael further suggests that the community meetings and general ethos were perhaps 'even more liberating for staff than prisoners'. Some of them, Ken Murray and Malky McKenzie in particular, learned to 'ask questions of their administrative masters and senior management'—no easy thing in a bureaucracy in which 'promotion prospects are dependent on conformity' (ibid).

The Unit was intentionally hospitable to visitors, beginning with extended visits from families and friends, mostly on weekends, without the barrier of the glass screen which had divided them in mainstream prison settings. This practice was abused: drink and drugs were smuggled in (as they were to some degree in most prisons), but when the press picked this up it was sensationalised and exploited by the Unit's political critics, creating problems for the prison authorities in publicly legitimating the Unit's work (Dowle 1982). Alex Stephen visited the Unit regularly. However, this was the first time that there had been such direct contact or such open discussion about the ills of the prison system between a senior civil servant and serving prisoners, and, crucially, he supported what the Unit became, though this was more troublesome than the original Working Party had envisaged.

As arts activities became important—the way this occurred is explained below— artists of various kinds also became regular visitors, and above and beyond the 'professional' contribution they provided—as Dr Sarah Trevelyan, a young psychiatrist who herself became a regular visitor to the Unit from 1978, noted—a useful means of dispelling the secrecy which had traditionally surrounded prisons (Boyle 1982). A significant number of visitors were to form 'a close relationship with the Unit or with individual residents' (Paterson 1982: 52). They never coalesced into a single force, acted in concert, or held a common view of the Unit, but individually they each exemplified instances of achievement with which inmates were unfamiliar, providing 'a reflective surface upon which [they] might view themselves' and develop 'aspects of [their] identity free from histories of offending in society and independent of allegiance to an offending culture' (ibid: 52).

Therapeutic communities in penal settings—anomalous at the best of times—are exceptionally vulnerable to changes in their wider political environment (Jones 1968). Everyone in the Special Unit was aware that the Scottish Office, ever mindful of 'public and political opinion ... might at any time, and without disclosure of reasons, act to modify [the Unit's] freedom and direction' (Paterson 1982: 52). Thus, when Alex Stephen was transferred to another post, the two men who replaced him did not have the same sense of 'ownership' of the Unit. When Ken Murray (who had become the most influential official in the Unit) was expelled from the Executive Committee of the SPOA for challenging criticisms of the Unit by its general secretary, the Unit lost a strong voice in a body still much in need of reform. In 1979, after a series of clashes with senior management, Murray was transferred out of the Unit to HMP Low Moss, and a 'proper' official hierarchy was imposed. Under such circumstances, it is not surprising that 'the residents feared for the survival of the Unit' (Paterson 1982: 54) and were wary of what they were being expected to invest in.

A consultant clinical psychologist in the Unit, Maxwell Paterson (1982: 55), was nonetheless adamant that most prisoners did want what the Unit offered. Acknowledging that in the community meetings and group therapy sessions the prisoners *did* 'identify their own sense of inadequacy and need' and *did not* 'present their histories with pride', he also understood why, in such a politically volatile situation, the task of personal transition was made doubly difficult. The prisoners were already 'dealing with paradox', he wrote, each individual seeking 'to reconcile a former identity, which is not to be denied, with an emergent identity—the same, yet another'. They should not in addition, he felt, be beset by uncertainty about the Unit's future.

Not all prisoners benefited equally or in the same way from the Unit: 'observation would suggest', wrote Paterson (1982: 52), 'that for some the experience has remained a game while for others there has been a movement from a peripheral, questioning response to a centre of commitment and personal representation of the ethos'. After 11 months, uncomfortable with the psychological pressures in the Unit, Ben Conroy (1982) transferred back to an ordinary prison at his own request. Duncan Bathgate, a relative newcomer, was transferred out after only four months for attacking another prisoner in March 1976—one of only two serious assaults in the Unit's entire 23-year-history (Cooke 1997). Larry Winters was a deeply intelligent man, sporadically creative, but too lost to prescription drugs (for depression) to benefit fully from the Unit's approach. Tragically and traumatically for all, he died alone in his cell of a (probably accidental) barbiturate overdose in September 1977, the drugs having been smuggled in by another prisoner. Both of these incidents intensified press criticism of the Unit's lax regime—particularly, but not only, in *The Daily Record*—but the definitive and lasting controversy about the Unit was less to do with specific organisational failings, and more to do with incontrovertible evidence of its success in transforming a man of violence into someone quite different (Dowle 1982).

The opening of Jimmy Boyle's play *The Hard Man*, co-written with Tom McGrath (McGrath and Boyle 1977), at the Traverse Theatre in Edinburgh, and the publication of his autobiography *A Sense of Freedom* (Boyle 1977), raised media debate to a new level. Both play and book showed how the enduring poverty of post-war Glasgow's slums bred a culture of extreme violence that was deeply appealing to young men for whom status and glamour were otherwise hard to come by. Far from challenging this violence when it had the opportunity to, Boyle claimed that traditional imprisonment compounded and reinforced it in Scotland's poor communities. Offenders had written memoirs before (see Broadhead 2006; Nellis 2012), but (in Scotland) none of them had been quite so violent or notorious as Boyle had been, nor as eloquent. Latent within this eloquence was a larger, unspoken indictment; how had modern Scotland's welfare state, the egalitarian and educational traditions of which it was supposedly so proud, failed a man of such evident intelligence and talent, and offered him so few prospects that he sank so early into crime and savagery? More awkwardly still, how many more men (and boys) like him were still being failed? Although the book's exposure of prison brutality was relatively new, overall the novelty was less in the message than the messenger, around whom opinion polarised. The Shadow Secretary of State for Scotland, Conservative Teddy Taylor, for example, demanded to know why Boyle had been 'allowed' to criticise the prison system. Even the fact that royalties from the book were later used to support the Gateway Exchange in Edinburgh to support ex-prisoners and young drug users was insufficient to placate Boyle's detractors.

There were other prisoners in the Unit whose artwork was rightly to be celebrated by Carrell and Laing (1982)—Bob Brodie, Tom Galloway, and Hugh Collins. Collins joined the Unit in early 1978, and published his own autobiography two decades later (Collins 1997). None had Boyle's energy, charisma, or artistic versatility, or his growing public profile as a critic of the penal system. After *A Sense of Freedom* appeared—it was also dramatised by Channel 4 in 1981 (Mackenzie 1981)—it was almost always around Boyle that the purpose and legitimacy of the Unit would be most intensely debated. The film—well made as it was—did not in fact cover Boyle's time in the Special Unit, ending at the point of his arrival there, and while the brutalities to which the 'old system' had subjected him still needed denunciation (and were more in keeping with the dramatic conventions of prison movies), the experience was, as renowned trade unionist Jimmy Reid (1981) noted at the time, a bit 'like filming the *Birdman of Alcatraz* without the birds'—it missed what was most interesting and important about Boyle, and the milieu in which he had changed.

The birth of art in the Unit

The single most important person in the establishment of creative arts in the Special Unit was Joyce Laing, a fine arts graduate who had subsequently trained as an art therapist. She set up Scotland's first art therapy department at the Ross Clinic in Aberdeen, and worked extensively in general and psychiatric hospitals, and in prison, with both young people and adults. The first governor invited her into the Unit a few months after it opened to provide weekly arts activities for the first five prisoners. Laing had no illusions about his modest intentions. 'Any activity which was considered time-consuming would have been a welcome resource during the early months of what was still a very uncertain experiment', she wrote: 'That on this occasion it was art was probably incidental' (Laing 1982: 57). For all that the men were polite and welcoming, she was immediately conscious of their suspicion of her as an artist and a woman, well aware of how unpromising an environment—artistically speaking—the Unit and its inmates were, but inwardly confident that in time the men's manifestly 'pent-up emotions . . . would bubble to the surface and, if not negated by other factors, would result in some form of art' (ibid: 58). Her initial efforts, over a period of weeks, to encourage the men to take up painting, drawing, and sculpting were to no avail. The arts materials she left for them each week went untouched, frustrating her, so on one occasion she simply sat on the floor and modelled a head out of clay. One prisoner joined her, getting the feel of the clay but not making anything. This was, however, the moment of breakthrough:

> On the following visit a few pieces of sculpture, mostly heads, had been made. Among them was one piece which completely captured my attention. It was the small model of a roughly fashioned figure crouched behind a few rods of wire which surrounded the figure. It was titled *Solitary*, one of the first sculptures by Jimmy Boyle. This, I believe was the birth of the arts in the Special Unit. Jimmy Boyle had not only made the small sculpture, he was filled with enthusiasm over the possibilities the clay offered. Two parallel emotions were engulfing him; he was bursting with enthusiasm for ideas he wanted to try with this material which was new to him and he was also experiencing a new concept of the self: the former hard man spending his time working on art. (Laing 1982: 58)

Several prisoners then took up clay modelling. Boyle showed particular talent and enthusiasm for it, and quickly moved to carving stone and working metal. His work was taken up by some of the artists whom Laing introduced to the Unit, and brought personal rewards. One such visitor, Richard Demarco, an eminent and pugnacious Scottish arts impresario and Edinburgh gallery owner, arranged an exhibition of the Unit's work (mostly Boyle's) at the Edinburgh Festival in August 1974 (Demarco 1995). Boyle was officially allowed out of the Unit, under escort, to see it. He soon had his first commissions—stone heads of the *Men of Jarrow* for the Bede Gallery in the north of England in 1975; a concrete *Gulliver* for the Craigmillar Festival Society in Edinburgh in 1976 (Crummy 1992). In that same year he had a one-man show in Edinburgh, and also at Glasgow's leading modern arts venue, the Third Eye Centre on Sauciehall Street (with whose director, playwright Tom McGrath, he had written his autobiographical play (McGrath and Boyle 1977). Alongside all this he was keeping a diary of events in the Special Unit, studying sociology and psychology, and writing an autobiography. He encouraged others to participate. Larry Winters, well-read because of long years already spent in prison, wrote and read poetry and prose, which eventually achieved recognition in its own right, albeit posthumously (Winters 1979). 'The advent of poetry reading and the pieces of sculpture appearing in the various rooms', wrote Joyce Laing (1982: 59), 'gave a college-like atmosphere to the Unit'.

Artistic attention quickly turned to the drabness of the Unit environment itself—iron bars and blank walls—and the idea of painting a large mural on the long wall opposite the cells emerged in a community meeting. A Glasgow street scene became the theme: 'the result was not great artistic achievement yet it captured the magic of childhood memories' (Laing 1982: 59). Creative cell decoration ran parallel to this, augmented by donations of curtains and ornaments by friends and relatives—creating necessary private spaces where prisoners could gain respite from the pressures of communal living, and rest, work, or study as the mood took them.

In addition, a Unit magazine containing writing, poetry, and drawings by both prisoners and visitors also developed, intended for distribution among the Unit's supporters and in other prisons. The production of *The Key* in 1974/1975—the symbolism of the name was not lost on the prisoners—actively involved both staff and prisoners. It circulated widely among the Unit's supporters, but the Prisons Department forbade its distribution to other prisons. *The Key* ran to only three published editions, the last in November 1975.

Despite occasional sentimentality, the many eminent 'arts' visitors to the Unit were central to the consolidation of its creative ethos and its reputation as a Scottish penal innovation. The 'dialogue' which Richard Demarco (1995: 6) 'was anxious to create between the worlds of the Edinburgh Festival goer and the prisoner and prison officer' did happen—to a degree (prison officers were not much involved). Impressed from the start, convinced that even deeper immersion in creative arts would further aid the men's rehabilitation, and hopeful that the public value of art itself would be enhanced in this way, the artist-visitors to Barlinnie spread word about the Unit in circles where prison was rarely mentioned. Jimmy Reid's (1981) proletarian view that some of them were 'carpetbaggers of good causes who search for a new social issue like entomologists trying to add to their bizarre collection of rare insects' contained a tiny grain of truth, later echoed by Hugh Collins (2000)—but it unfairly derides the role that the often middle-class visitors played in shielding the Unit from its more vociferous critics, and speaking out against occasional rumours that its regime was to be tightened up. Even Vladimir Bukovsky, a formerly imprisoned Soviet dissident who visited Boyle, defended the Unit in this way (*The Observer*, 11 March 1979).

Simply because most of the prisoners could not leave the Unit to visit theatres and galleries, artists of various kinds were invited into it, in a conscious effort to sustain and enlarge the prisoners' artistic horizons (Laing 1982: 60). One was filmmaker Bill Beech (who later scripted a dramatisation of Larry Winter's life and death, *Silent Scream (1990)*, directed by actor David Hayman—another visitor—who had earlier played Jimmy Boyle in the TV film of *A Sense of Freedom*). Another was Beth Shadur, a Chicago muralist who worked with the prisoners on a second mural, *Wall of Neglect*, depicting capitalist exploitation in the Third World (Carrell and Laing 1982: 40). A proposal for a three-day arts festival in the Unit emerged out of the visits, which, after some delays caused by ongoing uncertainty about the Unit's future, took place in September 1979. Among the events were poetry readings by Edwin Morgan (later Scotland's 'makar'/poet laureate), music by Alan Cameron (and by psychologist Ian Stephen), and performances by the Glasgow Citizens and the Easterhouse Theatre Companies (Laing 1982: 61). The festival was opened by the then Secretary of the Scottish Home and Health Department, whose 'opening remarks sealed official approval of the festivities and brought people of varied backgrounds closer together [and] also strengthened belief in this "special" penal unit' (Laing 1982: 61). Other arts events subsequently took place in the Unit, while in 1980 the Third Eye Centre curated a comprehensive exhibition, *The Special Unit, Barlinnie Prison: Its Evolution through Its Art*, accompanied by a book of the same name edited by Christopher Carrell (Tom McGrath's successor) and Joyce Laing.

This 'evolution' was unique. At no other point in Scottish (or British) penal history had a penal institution become so identified with the arts, or the rehabilitation of prisoners so tied to creative expression. Furthermore, the visible support and encouragement of significant individuals in the Scottish arts community gave the somewhat nebulous penal ideal of rehabilitation a tangibility which it often lacked, even among people who subscribed to the principle. And although 'arts' had not been part of the plan, this unexpected development gave those penal officials who did want to maintain the Unit some ammunition to do so. As the Unit's clinical psychologist put it: 'The early introduction of art materials and the un-enforced development of the Unit as a studio for the encouragement of the arts had the greater significance for the successful passage of the Unit through its early crises. It [gave] the Unit a purposeful and distinctive identity' (Paterson 1982: 54).

Too many subsequent accounts of the Barlinnie Special Unit's early years underplay its 'studio-like' character, and while it is true that the creative arts may never have flourished there had it not been for the underlying therapeutic ethos, it is equally true that artistic aspiration, once established, became a powerful catalyst for personal change in its own right. Sparks, Bottoms, and Hay (1996: 25) called the Unit 'the most "normalized" prison setting in the country', and while its permeability to outside influences was indeed distinctive, there was little in the regime with which its prisoners had previously been familiar—and in that sense it wasn't 'normal' at all. Without art—and a talented art therapist—the history of the Unit may have been very different. Joyce Laing fully understood the connection between its loose and relatively unmanaged structure and the flourishing of creativity on the scale that occurred:

> That the Unit was allowed to evolve without the limitations of time-tables, conventional routines or even all the usual prison rulings, undoubtedly saved its existence. Had the arts been programmed in as an educational pursuit not one of the inmates in th[o]se early days, would have agreed to embark on such a course. Any attempt to set up a teaching situation would have been viewed with the distaste that all the inmates had come to associate with their previous school experiences. The fragile embryo of creativity had to be left to grow at its own pace. It should not be overlooked that the Prisons Department did not insist, at

> this early and vital stage in the Special Unit's life, on pre-designed curricula or planned requisitions for equipment or art materials. This relaxed approach on how the inmates used their time was an important one, for it protected the precarious first steps of creativity. (Laing 1982: 57–58).

Creativity and rehabilitation

In post-war Britain (and in the USA), parallel to the growth of the therapeutic community movement, there had been much intelligent reflection on the relationship between creativity, aggression, and personal development (Schneider 1950; Westman 1961; Koestler 1964; Storr 1972; Liebmann 2000). This had largely taken place in the psychotherapeutic rather than the empirical criminological tradition, despite some intellectual overlap between them. As it aspired to become more 'scientific', criminology paid scant attention to the role that the arts might play in offender rehabilitation. As both artist and psychotherapist, and with more of a mental health perspective than a criminal justice one, Joyce Laing was open to the possibility that, with some individuals, creative activity in a place like the Special Unit could sometimes go beyond mere therapy—vital as that was to personal healing and wellbeing—to genuine artistic expression which communicated meaningful concepts and feelings to others. The one could segue into the other. Laing could also skilfully nurture creative stirrings in people, even those professing no talent for artistic expression, in a way that other workers in the Unit could not. She was, furthermore, a respected member of a Scottish creative arts community whose support for what was to happen in the Unit—outwith traditional penal reform networks—might not otherwise have been tapped. 'There are three ways the arts can be used in any institutional setting', Laing wrote:

> firstly as a pleasurable time filling occupation, secondly as an educational pursuit both in practical and theoretical terms, and thirdly as a living expression of thought, emotion and portrayal of images from the subconscious. The first two ways provide obvious benefits. Yet the arts will not engender change or growth for the individual, without the third way, which is the spontaneous expression of the inner psyche. (Laing 1982: 57)

The therapeutic and artistic aspects of the work produced in the Unit—and the often fine line between them—were regularly validated by the many artists and critics who visited the Unit, and commended at the 14 external exhibitions—including one at the Venice Biennale—of the Unit's work in the 1973–1981 period. Cordelia Oliver, an arts graduate, director of Glasgow's Third Eye Centre, and *The Guardian*'s art critic in Scotland, commented astutely on the prisoners' work, seeing their art primarily as expressions of recent or ongoing penal experiences, of solitary confinement and sexual frustration, but with potential beyond that. Thus, she described Bob Brodie's small clay models as needing 'little explanation simply because they are immediately accessible, eloquent of whatever situation Brodie is trying to express', and Tom Galloway's primitive figures simply as 'a *cri de coeur*, an attempt to maintain sanity in an alien environment' (Oliver 1982a: 91; 1982b: 103). Somewhat simplistically, she perceived the prisoners' past proclivity to violence in terms of thwarted creativity; while this seriously underplayed the historical, structural, and cultural factors underpinning violent criminality in Scotland, it led her to the view that, pragmatically, there was 'excellent sense in the theory [of diverting] the energy behind the overpowering need for violent behaviour into legitimate creative activity, using paint or clay or hammer and chisel on stone' (Oliver 1982c: 61).

Writing of Hugh Collins, Oliver noted the 'inexpertness' of his early paintings and drawings, even his poetry, and suggested that they 'amount[ed] to little more than a safety valve for himself' which helped him deal with violent and suicidal feelings within himself, and to understand the damage and humiliation that imprisonment had inflicted on him (Oliver 1982d: 81). A 'turning point' occurred in 1977/1978, when, in his own words: 'I was beginning to look at my own isolation, and realised that prison staff were just as isolated and damaged as I was by the system'. Oliver felt that this incipient empathy, kindled before Collins entered the Unit, was quickened by immersion in drawing, painting, and sculpture, and of the latter she said presciently that 'it was in a class by itself so far as the Special Unit is concerned' (ibid).

The fate of the Unit

As if events in the Special Unit had not been extraordinary enough, a relationship developed between Jimmy Boyle and Sarah Trevelyan while she was visiting the Unit, and they married in January 1980 (see Trevelyan

2017). In March Boyle reluctantly transferred out of the Special Unit to HMP Saughton as part of a 'planned' release process. He, and the many people in the arts community who were convinced of his complete rehabilitation, would have preferred his release direct from the Unit: legal action was taken unsuccessfully to prevent his transfer to Saughton, and Joseph Beuys went on hunger strike on his behalf.[4] Boyle finally left prison on life licence in November 1982, having served his full 15-year tariff (the additional custodial sentences being deemed concurrent). The Special Unit continued in existence for a further 16 years, and initially still did useful work, but with a lower public profile. This chapter is not concerned with the events and processes which led finally to its closure in 1994 (Bottomley, Liebling, and Sparks 1994b; Barlinnie Working Party 1994; Cooke 1997; Jeffrey 2009; Sparks 2000) but notes that in any case, after Murray and Boyle (and indeed most of the original staff group) had left a certain dynamism was lost, which Inspectorate reports quietly welcomed (Her Majesty's Inspectorate of Prisons for Scotland 1982; 1986, see also Collins 1992). Apart from Collins's sculpting, the Unit's later artwork was more akin to that of a traditional prison education department, and the Unit functioned more like the modest therapeutic community that it had first been envisaged as. Walter Davidson, who continued for a while as senior officer in the Unit, saw nothing to regret, and seemingly missed the point:

> the Unit of today and the Unit of six or seven years ago is a day and night situation. There aren't the same emotional involvements, people by and large have become more professional in their jobs and you have a nucleus of staff and inmates who have been there for sufficient time to settle down. (Davidson 1982: 48)

While Murray's and, especially, Boyle's departures eased the Unit's relationship with the Prison Department, opinion has inevitably varied as

[4] While the Special Unit had been intended to make difficult prisoners manageable enough to be transferred back to mainstream prisons, the nature of its regime, and the first cohort of prisoners selected for it, meant that it initially functioned uneasily as both a place of last resort and as a new beginning—'a place of resort beyond the last resort of permanent segregation' (Sparks 2002: 561)—with all the tension implied by that juxtaposition. It was never envisaged that prisoners would be released direct from the Unit, or indeed that they would stay there as long as Boyle did. The argument that sending people back to mainstream prisons risked them unlearning precisely what the Unit had taught them was a valid one and in Boyle's case it did look as though gratuitous punishment was being imposed on him, if only to assuage hostile public opinion. In the event, in HMP Saughton Boyle was exemplary: helpful to other younger prisoners, consolidating his supporters' faith in him, and confounding some of his detractors.

to whether the ending of their joint, charismatic, leadership was a good or bad thing for the remaining and subsequent residents. Maxwell Jones (1968) had always counselled against charismatic leadership in therapeutic communities and took steps to avoid his own leadership becoming so to preserve a democratic ethos. That was not what was restored (or created) by Boyle's and Murray's departures (and arguably never fully can be in a prison). Hugh Collins (1999), befriended and mentored by Boyle (although he was always touchy about being seen as too like him), struck a more despondent note than Davidson:

> After Jimmy Boyle's transfer the place deteriorated. People think I should keep things going but they just don't realize how much of a vacuum he has left. Jimmy had Ken, Malky and the staff to support his efforts. That's all changed now. No one is interested. (Collins 1997: 148)

Outside the Unit, earlier policy ambitions were reined in too. The Working Party which had first recommended it had anticipated that if it was 'successful it may indicate the way in which the penal system should be developed in future' (Scottish Home and Health Department 1971). Largely because of the controversy the Unit aroused and the departures of its early champions, Buchanan-Smith, Stephens, Murray, and Whatmore (who retired in 1980), this aspiration had been vanquished by the end of the decade: as MP Renee Short (1979: 142) noted, annual Prison Service reports were 'singularly uninformative' about this extraordinary initiative, coyly mentioning it only in a 'statistical appendix'. By then there were other modernising forces at work elsewhere in the Scottish Prison Service, which would come to fruition a decade or so later. A rising younger generation of reform-minded managers appreciated the Unit's achievements despite the controversy and official silence and took its lessons to heart—but in late 1979 one senior Prison Service official (unnamed) was expressing doubts about the Unit with ill-disguised derision:

> We do not really see the need for them.... Just because certain prisoners have gone to the Special Unit and *appear to have* responded to that sort of regime does not mean that there are many more prisoners in the system who would benefit from that sort of regime. (quoted in McClintock 1982: 10: emphasis added)

The condescension of this remark is disconcerting. The Unit had not been independently evaluated, but it was hard to argue from the evidence available that it had not fulfilled its purpose of reducing violence. Of the 19 prisoners (including 12 lifers) who had passed through it by 1981, 8 remained there, 5 had been released, 1 was on a release programme, 1 (Winters) had died, and 4, including Jimmy Boyle, had returned to mainstream prisons (Scottish Information Office, quoted in Carrell and Laing 1982: 7). Perceptions of what the Unit had achieved, however, were invariably refracted through polarised perceptions of Boyle. Mirroring Scottish opinion more generally, some penal administrators did not begrudge him his success, but others—like the unnamed official above —did, seeing him less as someone who had been reformed by the system, and more as someone who had beaten it.

The significance of Jimmy Boyle

The man that Jimmy Boyle became in the 1970s was undoubtedly a product of the Special Unit environment, but it is as true to say that the Special Unit environment was, in its early years, a product of him, and of the support of the Scottish arts community. The Unit gave him an opportunity for personal fulfilment that he would never otherwise have had—which he seized with both hands—and gave him a platform from which he was able to challenge the more iniquitous aspects of the penal system. Always a natural leader, nothing in his background had prepared him—or the prison authorities, or indeed anyone else—for the transformation that occurred in him in the Special Unit. Born in 1944 into the poverty of the Gorbals, and inexorably drawn into thieving and gang culture, he was from the age of 12 onwards an inmate of various penal institutions—remand homes, approved schools, and borstal (where he and Ben Conroy first became friends). As a young adult he became a vicious enforcer for moneylenders and protection rackets, served several prison sentences, and was prosecuted in two abortive murder trials (whose witnesses were terrorised into silence), before finally being sentenced in 1967 to life imprisonment, with a 15-year minimum tariff, for the murder of another criminal called William 'Babs' Rooney, for not paying his 'protection money'. While never denying his past involvement in atrocious violence (although *A Sense of Freedom* may not have catalogued everything he did, or all the institutional abuse that he experienced, particularly as a teenager—shame perhaps being the reason in both cases), he denied this murder, and has always done so.[5] In prison, Boyle never accepted the authority of prison staff, never saw them as fully human (any more than they did him), and fought them to a standstill at every opportunity, solo or in association with like-minded men from similarly harsh backgrounds.

Throughout the twentieth century, the most disadvantaged areas of Scottish cities had generated gang cultures and violent criminals, a phenomenon which had been an established object of journalistic and literary interest from the 1930s (McArthur and Long 1935: Burrowes 1998; Burgess 1998) and a recurrent theme in Glasgow police memoirs (McNee 1983). Until Boyle, history had been destiny for hardmen[6] from the Gorbals; prevailing Scottish, and especially Glaswegian, narratives allowed no positive outcomes for 'villains' like him—they were either executed; or became elderly 'crime boss' figures, evil to the end; or died young by violence amid their own kind; or became burnt-out non-entities in early middle age; or ended up drunk in the gutter. They were not thought to have the 'potential' to be otherwise. Even before he left prison, with his sculpting and writing and his marriage to Sarah Trevelyan Boyle had conspicuously broken the mould, in full view of a mesmerised Scottish media. Liberal, educated middle-class Scotland mostly encouraged and appreciated him for having had the courage to change, for exposing the shameful brutality of 'the cages', for his manifest articulateness and intelligence, and, indeed, for his charm.

[5] Because Boyle never appealed the conviction, this will never *formally* be resolved to anyone's satisfaction. He has always said it was a friend of his who killed Rooney, on whom he refused to 'grass' (Campbell 1999). Glasgow journalist George Forbes (2004), who is otherwise supportive of Boyle, still insists that the evidence incriminates him. Given Boyle's lifestyle and association in the 1960s, it is not *implausible* that he could have killed someone. *It is no less implausible* that the police hated him so much that they fitted him up and fooled the courts. Whether he killed Rooney or not, Boyle did appalling things as a young man—as his self-portrait in *The Hard Man* (Boyle and McGrath 1977) makes clear. In the course of the inward changes that are unavoidably entailed by the kind of transformation he put himself through, it is hard to believe that he has not had demons to deal with, which he was never under any obligation to share publicly—although some might conceivably be inferred from his surreal, allegorical novel *Hero of the Underworld* (Boyle 1999), a story conceived in part while he was still in the Special Unit, at his most introspective.

[6] There is room for argument about whether the term 'hard man' was rightly applied to Boyle. Spring (1990: 76) says it meant 'a tough guy, or at least someone who can't be taken advantage of' and while, at least since the Scottish crime novels of the 1930s, a gangster had been one embodiment of it, the term did not have fixed associations with criminality. The associations with fighting (fists more than knives), a taciturn masculine presence, and a cold self-possession were constants but 'hard men' could be good men—even policemen—who fought for decent principles. On the streets, Boyle's violence was as often crazed as it was self-possessed; in the Unit he discovered that some of his best qualities—creativity, intelligence, articulateness—were quite different from the 'hard' virtues to which he might once have aspired.

Almost from the start of his time in the Special Unit he was never without allies or champions, and the Scottish arts community—not a constituency that had traditionally engaged with penal reform—was at the heart of that.

There is no doubt that Boyle genuinely felt himself becoming an artist, and that he was taken seriously as one by other artists and critics. His early stone and metal sculptures were vivid, accessible expressions of thoughts and feelings that preoccupied him as a prisoner—about anger, survival, justice. There is simply no denying the insight and eloquence, as early as 1974, with which he wrote about discovering beauty and the pleasure of creation, the realisation of how much of his life he had wasted, the joy that had been missing from it, and the wrongs he had blindly done, as well as the burgeoning sense of concern to prevent the next generation of young men like himself from making the same mistakes (Boyle 1982). Art was not all he experienced in the Unit—education in social sciences also informed his self-understanding and transformation—but in his case, creating it and learning about it was part of what 'improved' him, giving him hope and prospects of which he could once barely have dreamed. That a man from Boyle's background should ever have encountered (at Richard Demarco's gallery on one of his day releases) the German sculptor and performance artist Joseph Beuys (Boyle 1977: 257)—at the time 'the most influential figure in the European art world' (Hughes 1980: 402)—was emblematic of the changed milieu in which he moved.[7] *Guardian* art critic Caroline Tisdall (1974: 6) was sufficiently impressed with Boyle's insight into Beuys's work that she dedicated her book on Beuys to him.

Nonetheless, what Boyle accomplished in the Special Unit also provoked anger and resentment. The media debates about him brought closer to the surface liminal assumptions about class, power, violence, and masculinity in Scottish life—and, by dint of that, exposed some deep-rooted constraints on progressive penal reform. After the screening of the Channel 4 movie, Jimmy Reid (1981) derided the fact 'that Jimmy Boyle is no longer viewed as an individual but as an issue'. In truth he *was* an issue, and a profoundly

[7] Joseph Beuys (1921–1986) was an exponent of German neo-Expressionism, so influential, according to Robert Hughes (1980: 402), that he 'was to no small degree responsible for the eighties upsurge of European confidence in its own art against New York's'. He believed that everyone had creative potential, and while not being conventionally left-wing, his view of art's politically transformative potential lent itself to at least some of the art produced in the Special Unit. 'Art', he declared, 'should be a real means, in daily life, to go in and transform the power fields of society' (quoted in Hughes 1980: 402–403). Boyle (1982) was thinking of himself as an 'Expressionist' as early as 1974. Richard Demarco (2016) was a prescient champion of Beuys's work and vision.

emblematic one which confronted Scotland with some harsh realities and awkward choices. Opposition to Boyle came from several quarters. Some was orchestrated by the Glasgow police and elements in the SPOA, for whom Boyle's past crimes were simply too grave to justify the liberties he had been accorded (Jeffrey 2009). For Conservative MP Teddy Taylor, and the newspapers who supported his party, hostility to Boyle ran deeper than an ingrained ideological preference for punishment over rehabilitation; the Special Unit violated their very conception of what a prison should be. Prisoners, Boyle especially, seemed no longer to know their place. The tabloid Labour press concurred: commenting on a sculpture in which Boyle invited society to think more imaginatively about crime and punishment, *The Daily Record* wrote contemptuously, 'Now why should a prisoner be addressing his mind to such problems?' (quoted in Dowle 1982: 114).

Historian Sydney Checkland (1981: 132) observed that 'the powerful moralism in Glasgow working class life' meant that 'working class opinion certainly contains a strong element that finds it hard to forgive [Boyle] his violence on the grounds that he was a victim of a vicious society, for they know the terror of such men'. True and important as this was, it neglected the equally powerful moralism embedded in Ken Murray's socialist sensibility, as authentically working class as the traditions articulated by the *Daily Record*, but more informed and hopeful. Ken Murray (who later attended the Cambridge Institute of Criminology's senior course for professionals) was himself an exceptional man, certainly an exceptional prison officer, and had he not had the personal faith to believe that Boyle was still not beyond the reach of ordinary human decency and the courage to trust him, both of their histories in the Unit may have been very different. It is to Boyle's great credit that he always acknowledged that: he knew a good man when he saw one.[8]

While accepting that Boyle's transformation posed some difficult, but not insurmountable, questions about the tension between justice and rehabilitation, and some dilemmas even for well-meaning penal administrators,

[8] When Ken Murray retired from the Prison Service in 1987 he became chair of the social work committee of the then Strathclyde Regional Council, and, in that role, a significant champion of work with people with alcohol and drug dependencies, the homeless, and ex-prisoners. He died in October 2007, aged 76. His death made headlines in national newspapers, and in the obituaries he could not have been praised more highly for his work in the Special Unit (Steven 2007; Wilson 2007). Even the Scottish Prison Service, which did not treat him well in 1979 or the years thereafter, conceded that he was a 'widely respected individual whose ideas were probably ahead of their time' and that 'contemporary ways of working with prisoners today are due in no small measure to people like Ken' (*The Herald*, 5 October 2007).

one must still conclude that even if he had been the Special Unit's only success, he would still have proved an important point. Over and above his personal attainments, he very publicly shattered an enduring Scottish cultural stereotype—that of the vicious and incorrigible hardman—and he made the case for civility, creativity, and intelligence in penal treatment more compellingly than any academic research could have done: he became the indisputable living proof of its worth. As it was, Boyle was not a one-off: other people in the Unit developed creatively, benefiting from Boyle's pace-setting and leadership even as his reputation continually eclipsed almost anything else that happened there. After this, as Barbara Wootton (1982: 12) pointed out, it was no longer possible for anyone to pretend that it was 'impossibly idealistic' to think that the behaviour of seriously recalcitrant prisoners could not be changed for the better. Culturally, this was indeed the Unit's great achievement.

Boyle himself undoubtedly had a network of supporters and was not to be without influence in the future, but it was clear even before he left prison in 1982 that some segments of Scottish society would never acknowledge the manifest changes in his behaviour or recognise his talent, or would cynically treat both as mere camouflage for latent malevolence. In Glasgow, Boyle and the Special Unit could have become powerful icons in a city so keen to transcend its crime-ridden past and its violent image, but media-stirred reminders of what he had *once been* constantly obscured perceptions of who he had *now become* (Spring 1990). Even Channel 4's well-intentioned film played into that. Notwithstanding his denial of the murder of which he was convicted, it was never the case that Boyle refused to admit remorse or regret for his past violence (Boyle 1977: 251): what his critics seemingly wanted from him—more than signs of repentance[9] —was a broken, penitential posture so abject that he would forever be shunned

[9] In Scotland in the 1970s, Boyle's transformation was so unique and surprising that many people struggled to find words to comprehend it, falling back on clichés or remaining baffled. Bit by bit, never explicitly, Boyle's story was quietly absorbed into diffuse, distinctively Scottish, egalitarian mythologies—a belated 'lad o'pairts', the poor kid with talent who should not be held back and who comes good in the end—and "democratic intellectualism", which, in one version at least, acknowledges that voices from the margins of the polity should be attended to, however discomfiting. Within such frameworks, Boyle slowly came to be seen as a more intelligible and acceptable figure—opinionated and controversial, perhaps unduly flamboyant, but not someone whose transformation was inherently implausible, or duplicitous, or un-Scottish. His detractors always had Jekyll and Hyde-style 'duality' to fall back on—the idea that an ostensibly respectable life in Edinburgh could still hide links with the criminal underworld. As it became clearer that Boyle had severed links with crime, those who clung to this view came to seem shamelessly vindictive.

because of his violent acts, rather than respected and learned from as someone who had transcended and repudiated them.

Official responses to the Special Unit in the 1980s

By the early 1980s, to a greater degree than any other British 'special unit', Barlinnie had registered in the national consciousness. Jimmy Boyle's manifest transformation, his book, and his own media presence after leaving prison, made it impossible for anyone with serious penological interests—official or otherwise—to disregard its existence. Even Leon Brittan, Minister of State at the Home Office, agreed that extending the model to England was an 'important and constructive subject which ought to be considered' (quoted in Light 1985: 17). *A Sense of Freedom* was running counter to the tendency of offender autobiographies and prisoner memoirs to have a short shelf-life, to captivate the public for only a brief period of time, if at all (Nellis 2012). Extracts had been serialised in several major newspapers, and it had remained in print for much longer than usual. Along with armed robber John McVicar's (1974) well-received account in England a few years earlier, it raised the status of working-class prisoner memoirs as sources of intelligent argument about the nature, purposes, and impact of imprisonment. They helped stimulate a reappraisal of such sources in official and academic contexts. Certainly the Home Office's Control Review Committee sensed the lacuna in prison research:

> Very little work of any kind has been done in this country to ascertain prisoners' perceptions of their experiences. We do not know what are the factors that most affect prisoners views of regimes and we clearly need to establish some facts on this if we are to develop a more considered approach to incentives or to move to a programme model for the delivery of regime activities. (Home Office 1984: para 100)

The Control Review Committee had been established in England and Wales in 1983 in the aftermath of several serious disturbances in its dispersal prisons, and the failure of a short-lived and notorious segregation unit at HMP Wakefield between 1974 and 1978 (not dissimilar to the Inverness 'cages') as a defensible means of controlling disruptive prisoners. 'Special units' were one of its three core concerns in (the other two were 'new generation architecture' and the overall 'structure of the system' for managing long-term prisoners). Its members went on a number of international visits, some to the Barlinnie Special Unit, although there are no specific references to its accomplishments in the final report, or to *A Sense of Freedom* (Home Office 1984). The CRC envisaged special units as being non-punitive in nature but at the same time emphasised 'sending the right signals' to prisoners in terms of their earning incentives to return to the mainstream penal system. 'Special Units' were not to be places of 'last resort', as the Barlinnie Unit had been in its early years—but even so, given the CRC's interest in Unit regimes, the absence of any reference to creative arts was telling, suggesting that only certain aspects of it were being attended to.

To carry forward the CRC's work, the Prison Service established a Research and Advisory Group (RAG) on the Long-Term Prison System to help develop policy on a cluster of existing and upcoming, and mutually complementary, special units in England and Wales (in HMPs Parkhurst, Lincoln, and Hull). Tony Bottoms was a member of this group, which, among other visits, 'spent a very useful day with officials and Governors of the Scottish Home and Health Department discussing the Scottish experience of small units' (Home Office 1987: para 29). 'RAG', Bottoms (1991: 10) wrote, 'was very conscious that neither prior experience nor prior research pointed to any very obvious "ideals" or particular kinds of prisoners [amenable to such units]; it would be necessary, therefore, to proceed on a "trial and error" basis'. This was, of course, precisely how the Barlinnie Special Unit itself had developed, although for the upcoming English units RAG anticipated a sounder articulation of foundational principles and more rigorous evaluation of outcomes.

RAG anticipated all future units developing in terms of three sets of variables—'degree of structure', the nature and extent of 'specialist professional assistance', and 'the nature of interactions between staff and inmates' (Home Office 1987: paras 83–86). Looking back on it, Bottoms (1991) created a typology from its reflections which compared and contrasted the characteristics of the Parkhurst, Lincoln, and Hull units and the Barlinnie Special Unit, which clearly showed how distinct from them it actually was. 'Degree of staff involvement with prisoners' was 'high' for the first three, and 'very high' for Barlinnie. 'Promotion of opportunities for prisoners to become involved in finding ways of modifying their own problem behaviour' was rather nondescript ('some opportunities') in the English units (greatest in Lincoln) but registered to a 'very high degree' in Barlinnie. 'Inmate participation in the running of the unit' registered as 'none' in all the others, but as 'high' in Barlinnie. The most marked (and misleading) divergence came under the heading 'use of specialism to inform principles and practice of the unit's regime'. The English units were characterised as 'psychiatric' and/or 'psychological', while Barlinnie was characterised, uniquely in the typology, as 'sociological and social psychological', to denote its roots in the philosophy of therapeutic communities (Bottoms 1991: 8).

Its most obvious sociological aspect—its 'very liberal visiting arrangements' (for families and friends)—was nonetheless considered 'inappropriate' for any future English unit housing maximum security prisoners (Home Office 1987: para 132). Other sociological aspects of the Unit's formative years went unremarked, notably the part played by Joyce Laing and Richard DeMarco in building links with external artistic networks and venues, or the links Boyle made with the prestigious community arts project the Craigmillar Festival Society. Similarly, Joseph Beuys's (and Demarco's) distinctive 'social' vision of art, his belief that everyone had latent artistic capacities and that iconoclastic art could and should have socially transformative consequences—which became part of the Unit's early ethos via Jimmy Boyle—was underplayed (Demarco 1997; Harlan 2004). In more contemporary parlance, serious creative endeavour gave the prisoners both human and social capital, fostering skill and exposing them to a succession of artist-visitors whom they would never otherwise have encountered. The neglect of this fact by RAG may be explained by the fact that by the time it visited the Unit the undeniably intense artistic ethos of its early days had been diluted, with even the Scottish prison inspectorate portraying that as an anomaly, irrelevant to its future (Her Majesty's Inspectorate of Prisons for Scotland 1982, 1986). That ethos, however, had been part of what first brought the Unit to public prominence, made it controversial, and helped give hope and confidence to its inmates.

Experience of the Barlinnie Special Unit helped convince Tony Bottoms personally of the importance of encouraging 'creativity'—crafts and hobbies as much as sculpture—in Unit regimes (personal communication 30 November 2011), and the RAG as a whole was sufficiently impressed to recommend experimentation along these lines in England (Home Office 1987: para 133)—but not strongly, and the CRC did not take it up. Even in the subsequent Institute of Criminology Cropwood conference on 'Problems of long-term imprisonment', convened to explore issues raised by the CRC, neither of the two papers dealing with the Special Unit addressed the place of creative arts in offender rehabilitation as a topic warranting further research, despite their *de facto* centrality to much of what the Unit in its first 'phase' had achieved (Bottoms and Light 1987; Whatmore 1987; Coyle 1987). The conference did re-open important questions about therapeutic communities in prison, and highlighted the profound, foundational importance of relationships between prisoners and staff, but what Joyce Laing (1982: 56–57) had said five years previously sadly still held: 'The arts do not have a high priority in the thinking of penologists.'

Conclusion: The Special Unit and penal heritage

Compared to those aspects of a country's past around which a valued 'national heritage' can be built (art and culture, industry, military achievement, and so on)—and notwithstanding a handful of prison museums (Welch 2015)—there are several reasons why the penal past rarely figures prominently in contemporary social memory.[10] At root, the less that registers in popular and professional memory about penal measures that have *failed* in the past, the easier it is to continue doing the same thing, to bestow an aura of innovativeness on such measures and perennially reintroduce them in new guises. Almost any penal present can be made to seem like an improvement on the carceral horrors of the more distant past. Paradoxically, measures which have simultaneously been both successful *and unduly challenging* to established forms of penal practice, or which have exposed the contradictions and limits of penal systems, are far less likely to be officially commemorated. Such has been the fate—formally and officially—of the Barlinnie Special Unit overall, and especially of its early years with which this chapter has been concerned. It is true that the Unit survived for 16 years longer, despite the political embarrassment its early years caused the penal authorities—albeit in more muted form, therapeutically, and with less artistic focus and less public profile. It was, however, never 'beyond repair'

[10] I mean by 'penal heritage' all the ways we have of remembering the penal past, from prison museums and official histories, to journalistic reminiscence, historical true crime, obituaries, and everyday folk memory (Misztal 2003). All signs of the Unit's former presence in D Wing have been obliterated in HMP Barlinnie itself. A small section of the Glasgow People's Palace museum is devoted to crime and punishment, and within that—around a display of an edition of *The Key*—the Special Unit is lightly commemorated. Journalist Robert Jeffrey (2002, 2009) has celebrated the Unit's achievements under the sombre rubric 'so successful they shut it down', but there remains an uglier side to some of contemporary Glasgow's other true crime and local history writing in this respect, which shamelessly vilifies Boyle the young thug from 40 years ago, without ever mentioning what it was that truly made him memorable and distinctive in later life: the Special Unit and his rehabilitation within it.

(Sparks 2002: 572), rendering its eventual closure by the Scottish Prison Service—a calculated, if misjudged, attempt to erase its record—lamentable. Boyle's high profile as a penal commentator in the 1980s, and *A Sense of Freedom*'s print run of more than two decades, nonetheless ensured that the Unit's memory was kept alive—ambivalently—for longer than might otherwise have been the case.

A certain generation in Scotland, interested in arts and penal reform, has in fact remembered it well, and taken its achievements to heart. Nonetheless, the Unit has never become unequivocally totemic and nation-defining in the way that, say, its near-contemporary innovation the Children's Hearing System has done. It never came to signify the kind of penal enlightenment in which national pride could be invested. Because of the embarrassment it had caused, discussion about it was dampened down—evidenced by the constraints on speaking about it imposed on Ken Murray and the Scottish Office's unwillingness to co-operate fully with Carrell and Laing's art book. The lessons that might have been drawn from it, while never wholly disregarded, were never proudly learned or owned. The implications of *A Sense of Freedom* for the reform of the Scottish school system—arguably as great as its implications for the adult penal system—and the challenge it posed to complacency about the culture of violence in the west of Scotland were noted by journalists but not pursued by policy-makers. The subsequent laudatory insider accounts of the Special Unit's work (Whatmore 1987, 1990; Stephen 1988; Cooke 1989a, 1989b, 1997; Coyle 1989) belatedly give it penological legitimacy, but none captured the tension or exuberance of life in the Unit as well as the contributors to Carrell and Laing's book, coy as it sometimes was about key moments.

By 1982 the specific premises on which the Special Unit's practice was founded were becoming dissonant with emerging trends in penal politics and organisation, and would have required special efforts to preserve them, or re-articulation to survive intact within new policy frameworks. Very little of what the Unit stood for—the therapeutic community ideal and the models of personal change implicit in it, reliance on experientially informed faith in people rather than a 'scientific' evidence base, the stimulation of creativity, openness to haphazard and unpredictable external influences, the encouragement of argumentativeness—sat comfortably with the nascent managerialism of the 1980s—even the milder forms of it articulated by the Anglo-Welsh Control Review Committee (Adler and Longhurst 1994). The Special Unit's key lessons lived on, however, in the minds of a rising generation of younger prison managers who had seen with their own eyes that—however serendipitously it had been brought about—facilitating personal change in violent men was, to use Sparks, Bottoms, and Hay's (1996: 32) somewhat coy phrase, 'not actually impossible'. Tony Bottoms's personal end-of-decade reflections on 'the aims of imprisonment' were more emphatic: 'respect, care and hope' were duties *owed* to prisoners everywhere (Bottoms 1990). He argued that penal regimes which merely attend to the *present and immediate* needs and rights of prisoners, however thoroughly, were 'ontologically incomplete'. 'Surely', he wrote, "the prison service at its best has always wanted to recognize . . . a future dimension, which sees hope and possibilities even in the most unlikely individuals and social situations' (Bottoms 1990: 23). This certainly captures the 'therapeutic community' vision to which some of the Special Unit's founders and champions were committed, although they could never have anticipated how potent a catalyst for personal change hope would become for Unit residents, once they realised that a future different from the one to which they had felt destined was within their grasp.

Integrating the Special Unit into the Scottish penal heritage—getting it commemorated as the milestone that it was—is not primarily a question of asking its key players to recall or reaffirm their achievements. Many are old, and several have died.[11] Joyce Laing, who serendipitously helped the arts to flourish in the Unit, subsequently ran a gallery devoted to 'outsider art' in Pittenweem, Fife (Cox 2006). Richard Demarco still promotes the arts in Edinburgh, and continues to celebrate the visionary qualities of Joseph Beuys's work (Demarco 2016): the photographic exhibition which formed part of Demarco's eightieth birthday celebrations included iconic images from the Unit (*The Herald*, 11 November 2011). Boyle, in his seventies, lives abroad and still sculpts. Having, through choice and circumstance, lived in the public eye as a 'reformed ex-con' for far longer than most prison authors choose or get to, he manages a degree of anonymity, periodically returning to the limelight on his own terms (as a property developer in Morocco, or having one of his sculptures marked up at £20,000 in a sale), without the 'Killer Boyle' headline that taunted him in the media for years after he left

[11] Several key people associated with the early years of the Barlinnie Special Unit have died, among them Ken Murray (1931–2007); playright Tom McGrath (1940–2009); arts journalist Cordelia Oliver (1923–2009), social work academic Kay Carmichael (1925–2009), artist Caroline McNairn (1955–2010)—later Hugh Collins's wife—and John MacKenzie (1928-2011), director of the 1981 film of *A Sense of Freedom*. I wish I had found time to interview them. As it was, Joyce Laing, Richard Demarco, Sarah Trevelyan, Meg Murray, and latterly Bill Beech have all been exceedingly helpful. Thanks too to journalist Rachelle Money, and to Tony Bottoms for advice on RAG.

prison (*The Herald*, 10 July 2010). Boyle and Sarah Trevelyan divorced in 2001, but her own memoir of their life together and her current work as a therapist, along with his own recent reminiscences, testify to continuing mutual respect (Trevelyan 2017; Boyle 2016).

A powerful and moving French documentary film, *La Rage et le Reve Condamnes* (Krief 2002)—about the use of creative arts in French prisons, structured around a lengthy and eloquent interview with Boyle (with cameos from Ken Murray and Joyce Laing)—won a major award at the Montreal Film Festival, although it has been little shown in Scotland. Hugh Collins, also still sculpting, followed up his *Autobiography of a Murderer* (Collins 1997) with a partially revisionist account of the Unit, *Walking Away*, which, while possibly helpful at the time to his continuing quest for an authentic post-prison identity, somewhat denigrated its achievements and key people associated with it (Collins 2000). There have been people enough in Scotland prone to doing this without the Unit's beneficiaries joining in, although in fairness to Collins it could be seen as a misjudged response to the sentimentality in which some of its public champions might once have mired it.

The task of remembrance and commemoration is for a new generation, who are mindful that a country's penal achievements and failures reflect deeper cultural sensibilities and invite judgement upon it (Scottish Government 2008). Past penal successes, vividly drawn, can ground and shape future possibilities in a field where political courage and optimism are often in short supply. They can signal to the present how near or far we might be from realising new aspirations, and can condition our sense of whether or not they are feasible. The price of forgetting, or misremembering, is a desultory continuity, diminished hope, or wrongheaded change, or all three. The praise rightly bestowed on Ken Murray in his obituaries in October 2007—which openly acknowledged his part in creating the Special Unit (Steven 2007; Wilson 2007)—*tentatively* suggests that sufficient time may now have elapsed for the Unit (even its earliest years) to be officially commemorated in the way it deserves. Its image, of course, will forever be tied to what Jimmy Boyle achieved there. No history could pretend otherwise. Interestingly, when a series of short-term arts-based projects were introduced into Scottish prisons in 2010, the broadsheet media frequently made sense of this by comparing it to the Barlinnie Special Unit and reminding readers of Boyle's artistic achievements. There was no direct connection between the Special Unit and the new projects, but the press comment indicated that the Unit had remained a framing device—a touchstone, even—for appraising the worth of arts-in-prison initiatives (see Anderson et al. 2010 for a brief evaluation of these).

A prestigious touring production of *The Hard Man*—eventually considered by theatre historians to be 'one of the most powerful of recent Scottish dramas' (Gifford, Dunnigan, and McGillivray 2002: 820)—was revived in Scotland in 2011 (Breen 2011; Lichtenfels 2011). It did not publicly resurrect the old controversies about Boyle (although he was consulted about the production) but was reviewed well (MacMillan 2011). Its themes of violence and poverty were explored in an accompanying Educational Resource Pack (for schools) and effectively related to both past and contemporary aspects of Scottish life (Traverse Theatre 2011). Ironically, the Resource Pack made only cursory mention of the Special Unit, but the fact that McGrath and Boyle's 44-year-old narrative could still be thought relevant to debate about crime and punishment in contemporary Scotland testifies both to its intrinsic dramaturgical qualities and to the more occasional propensity of 'the culture industries' to mobilise progressive concern about penal reform and contribute to debate about offender rehabilitation. These latter points have been given greater penological recognition in recent years, but it is extraordinary that almost half a century on, no rounded academic history of the Special Unit has yet been written.

But the Unit needs a more tangible commemoration than a book. Some seeds have been sown. 'A Way Out of a Dark Time'—a temporary, three-month exhibition and lecture series about the Unit in Glasgow's Kelvingrove Museum in spring 2017, curated by Claire Coia from personal archive material donated by Joyce Laing and supported by the Education Department in HMP Barlinnie (whose then class of prisoners had undertaken a research project on the Special Unit)—may yet be the basis of something more permanent. A second, four-month exhibition, built around Bill Beech's personal archive and focused on the way in which the Unit had embodied Joseph Beuys's ideas (including a new video of Boyle and Demarco reminiscing), was held at the University of Hull library in autumn 2019. Whether or not it finds its way to Glasgow in time for the 50th anniversary of the opening of the Barlinnie Special Unit in 2023 is uncertain, but the persistent sense that *this* Unit, uniquely among such units, actually warrants public commemoration is part of what now sustains its 'specialness' in the Scottish penal imagination.

14

Rightful Authority

Exploring the Structure of Police Self-Legitimacy

Justice Tankebe

Legitimacy is not conventionally viewed as embracing power-holders' own need to believe in the moral validity of their authority.[1] The main focus on legitimacy has been on its audience dimension; that is, legitimacy as perceived by those over whom power is exercised. However, legitimacy cannot be sufficiently understood from the perspective of power-audiences alone; a fuller analysis necessarily requires a focus on power-holders' self-confidence in the moral validity of their own claims to power. Max Weber argued that *self or power-holder legitimacy* was a precondition for cultivating *audience legitimacy.* Yet in their empirical analysis of legitimacy to date, police scholars have not given power-holder legitimacy the importance Weber indicated it deserved. Using data from Ghana, this chapter examines the conditions associated with self-legitimacy among a sample of frontline police officers.

Legitimacy and self-legitimacy

Anthony Kronman refers to Max Weber's argument that legitimation is an attempt to 'still *a voice within* as well as the sometimes louder but no more pressing *voices without*' (1983: 41). Weber meant by the 'voices without'

[1] It is now fifteen years since I first encountered legitimacy and procedural justice during my graduate studies at Cambridge. Tony Bottoms has been key in shaping my thinking on the subject, and I am delighted to have the opportunity to contribute to this edited volume in honour of his unique influence in criminology. I am deeply grateful to Tony Bottoms and Alison Liebling for their detailed comments on more developed version of the chapter. I also received helpful feedback from Barak Ariel, Kofi E Boakye, Tim Coupe, Amy Nivette, and Tal Jonathan-Zamir on an initial draft.

Justice Tankebe, *Rightful Authority*. In: *Crime, Justice, and Social Order*. Edited by: Alison Liebling, Joanna Shapland, Richard Sparks, and Justice Tankebe, Oxford University Press. © Alison Liebling, Joanna Shapland, Richard Sparks, and Justice Tankebe 2022. DOI: 10.1093/oso/9780192859600.003.0014

what Bottoms and Tankebe (2012) call 'audience legitimacy'; that is, the recognition by citizens of the rightness of a claim to legitimacy. This dimension is the focus of much fruitful criminological analysis today. Without doubt, the reference point for the current interest in legitimacy is Tom Tyler's seminal work *Why People Obey the Law.* Based on analysis of panel data on citizens' interactions with legal authorities in Chicago, the study demonstrated the centrality of normative considerations, in particular procedural justice, in shaping reactions to these authorities. Tyler's legitimacy arguments have been studied in different contexts, focusing principally on everyday interactions between criminal justice agents—such as prison and police officers—and citizens. The results from these studies consistently show that public perceptions of police legitimacy shape general compliance with the law (Jackson et al. 2012a; Papachristos et al. 2012; Sunshine and Tyler 2003), cooperation with legal authorities (Murphy and Cherney 2012; Reisig et al. 2012; Tankebe 2013), recidivism in spousal assault (Paternoster et al. 1997) and support for vigilante violence (Tyler et al. 2012; Tankebe 2009).

While a good deal is now known about *audience legitimacy*, work on the structure and predictive utility of the dimension of legitimacy that relates to the 'voices within' remain undeveloped (see, e.g., Bradford and Quinton 2014; Nix and Wolfe 2016; Tankebe 2019; Tankebe and Meško 2015). Yet, according to Kronman (1983), Max Weber placed a greater weight on this dimension, arguing that the powerful have a need to 'persuade *themselves* that their fates are deserved and therefore rightful' and that self-legitimation is prior to, and indeed a necessary precondition for, claiming legitimacy among citizens (Kronman 1983: 41). As he put it: 'to the extent that he anticipates and understands the criticism of those who are less fortunate, the man of good fortune must already be a critic himself' (Kronman 1983: 41). The key passage from Max Weber on self- legitimacy is worth quoting:

> The fortunate is seldom satisfied with the fact of being fortunate. Beyond this, he needs to know that he has a *right* to his good fortune. He wants to be convinced that he 'deserves' it, and above all that he deserves it in comparison with others. He wishes to be allowed the belief that the less fortunate also merely experiences his due. Good fortune thus wants to be 'legitimate' fortune (Weber 2009: 271).

Weber's point is that the fortunate rarely consider their mere advantage a sufficient basis to wield power, and that they seek to consolidate that power by convincing themselves that it is rightful. This need to cultivate legitimacy for their power and positions is not for the purposes of securing the cooperation of their power-subjects, but primarily to satisfy themselves that they have a legitimate right to hold power (Wrong 1995). In *Beyond Procedural Justice,* we described this dimension of legitimacy as 'power-holder legitimacy' or 'self-legitimacy' (Bottoms and Tankebe 2012). It refers to power-holders' recognition of, or confidence in, their own individual entitlement to power. In other words, self-legitimacy concerns the self-recognition of entitlement to power (Bottoms and Tankebe 2012, 2013). This focus on the individual power-holder's self-constructions of their own claims sets power-holder legitimacy apart from assessments of organisational legitimacy as made by police officers and managers. Questions about organisational legitimacy concern the extent to which police officers and managers recognise the police organisation's activities, whereas self-legitimacy focuses on the belief of such officers and managers that the power they wield over other citizens is rightful or valid. As Barker (2001) puts it, this dimension of legitimacy is self-referential.

Sociologists and political scientists have long recognised the duality of legitimacy (see, e.g., Wrong 1995; Holmes 1993; Sternberger 1968). Beetham's (2013) recent definition—itself a reflection of his journey beyond an exclusive focus on audience legitimacy (see Beetham 1991)—captures the current understanding of the nature of legitimacy: legitimate power is 'power that is *acknowledged as rightful* by relevant agents, who include power holders and their staff, those subject to the power and third parties whose support or recognition may help confirm it' (Beetham 2013: 19, emphasis original). However, analysis of power-holder legitimacy in the political science literature tends to focus almost exclusively on the ruling elite (e.g., presidents, kings and queens, and prime ministers), thereby potentially missing the significant role in social order played by more junior power-holders (such as basic-grade police and prison officers), who are in direct contact with citizens and often exercise a significant degree of local power on a daily basis (Bottoms and Tankebe 2013).

Power-holder legitimacy among police officers was first explored in my doctoral work at Cambridge, under the supervision of Tony Bottoms. Yet the major statements on the subject came much later in two papers we jointly authored: 'Beyond procedural justice' (2012) and 'Voices within: Power-holders' perspectives on legitimacy' (2013), in which we discussed some of the factors that might account for variations in the degrees of confidence that officers have in their individual legitimacy. The aims of this chapter, then, are two-fold. First is to discuss hypothesised sources of any such variations. Drawing on the literature on self-concept, I focus, in particular, on the treatment officers received from their *supervisors*, and the relations they have with *colleagues* and with *citizens*. I also examine the role of perceived police *effectiveness* in maintaining social order. Second, I examine empirically whether and to what extent these factors shape officer self-legitimacy perceptions. Although I have recently conducted a series of studies seeking to examine self-legitimacy empirically (e.g., Tankebe 2019; Tankebe and Meško 2015), I focus in this chapter on re-analysing data from my doctoral work. The data constitute the first attempt to explore our theoretical arguments empirically, using survey data from frontline officers in Ghana.

Sources of confidence in self-legitimacy

Practically and theoretically, the problem of understanding the conditions associated with producing and nourishing police confidence in self-legitimacy is of immense importance. However, empirically, not much is known about those conditions. Part of the reason for this is that this dimension of legitimacy has been undeveloped. In this section, I discuss a number of hypotheses that link self-legitimacy to officers' social interactions and to their perceptions of effectiveness. These hypotheses are then tested using survey data from frontline officers in Accra, Ghana.

Social interactions

Police exercise of power generates information with the potential to shape confidence in self-legitimacy. To explore this, we need to connect our analysis to the social-psychological literature on self- concept. Of particular interest here is the notion of *possible selves* (Markus and Nurius 1986). In their highly influential paper, Markus and Nurius defined a possible self as the type of 'self- knowledge [that] pertains to how individuals think about their potential and about their future. Possible selves are the ideal selves that we would very much like to become . . . the selves we could become and the selves we are afraid of becoming' (1986: 954).

On their analysis, officer Sara might see herself currently as someone who doubts the legitimacy of her authority or role, but she may see herself in the future with a more developed sense of confidence in her legitimacy. However, she might also be *anxious* or *fearful* that she might turn out to be a diffident and worthless officer, prone to impulsive reactions to situations. Viewed this way, self-legitimation may be understood as a process of constructing, affirming, or resisting certain self-images of identity. Immediately relevant for our present purposes is Markus and Nurius's claim that possible selves are 'representations of potential' and that this makes them 'particularly sensitive to those situations that communicate new or inconsistent information about the self'; in other words, they are provisional until verified or confirmed in a person's social experience (pp. 955–956). This also means that the possible self is dynamic, constantly in flux, and perhaps never emerges from any social interaction the same.

Markus and Nurius's analysis connects well with Bottoms and Tankebe's dialogic conception of legitimacy. According to this view, legitimacy is 'more like a perpetual discussion' (Bottoms and Tankebe 2012: 129), 'which begins with power-holders making a *claim* to exercise legitimate authority. That claim is responded to by one or more audiences; power-holders might perhaps adjust their claims in the light of audience responses, and so on' (Bottoms and Tankebe 2013: 60). In other words, and in the language of Markus and Nurius (1986), power-holders (such as police and prison officers) enter the legitimacy dialogue with a certain estimation of their identity as rightful powerholders. The interactions officers have with colleagues, supervisors, and the wider community are—to borrow a phrase from Tyler (2011)—a *teachable moment* for self-legitimacy, in the sense that those interactions present an opportunity for the officers to confirm or verify their constructed possible selves. According to Barker, the claiming of legitimacy

> is carried out in a series of concentric circles. It takes place first at the centre, and for the benefit of the immediate ruler or rulers. Then it takes place at one remove from the centre, both *between ruler and staff* and *among the staff themselves*. Next it takes place in an exchange between the ruling group as a whole or some of its members, and ... the mighty subjects who stand nearer to the throne or the presidential palace than do ordinary subjects or citizens, and at some distance from the street, the factory, or the forum (2001: 70, emphasis added).

What is involved in an officer's interactions with different audiences is a continuous claim–response dialogue in which she projects and seeks to confirm a certain self-image or identity, an identity of confidence in her rightful entitlement to power. The feedback or reactions of these audiences can be measured in terms of the quality of the social relations between them and the officer. Thus, the key to understanding variations in self-legitimacy may reside in the continuous reciprocal dialogues in which officers engage (Muir 1977). In this way, the roots of self-legitimacy are to be found in the various relationships in which officers find themselves, and how they evaluate their standing in those relationships.

A key question remains: Which of the multiple interactions has the greatest consequence for the attempts by officers to build a desired identity as confident claimants to legitimate power? Barker offers us a lead with what might be called a *concentric model of self-legitimacy* (CMS). According to this model, 'at each stage out from the centre [legitimation] is likely to be carried out with less time, attention, energy and intensity' (Barker 2001: 70–71), reflecting the weight that each circle of legitimation has on the power-holder's constructed self. Starting, as he does, from the power-holder at the top of the system of governance (that is, a ruler), we will expect the reactions of the immediate powerful subordinates to exhibit the greatest influence on the ruler's sense of rightful entitlement. As we move further away from the power-holder, the impact of feedback or reactions on the constructed self declines, with the least impact being exerted by citizens. However, when our focus is on low-level power-holders (e.g., frontline police or prison officers) things assume a more complex posture; here legitimation is upwards to supervisors, sideways to their colleagues, and downwards to citizens. The concentric model should lead us to expect the views or actions of colleagues, with whom officers spend most of their time, to have the greatest impact of self legitimacy. This should be followed by supervisors, and with citizens to having the least impact for self-confidence.

Interactions with supervisors

Confidence, as Barbalet argues, 'arise[s] from acceptance and recognition in social relationships' (2001: 87). The greater the feeling of acceptance and recognition, the greater an actor's feeling of confidence, and the more inclined the actor will be to engage in (successful) future interactions. In this regard, first, self-legitimacy might be nourished or damaged, depending on the quality of interactions between officers and their supervisors. This implies the potential influence of procedural justice. As is now well established, procedural justice concerns the perceived fairness of the process employed in dealing with citizens (Jonathan-Zamir, Mastrofski, and Moyal 2013; Paternoster et al. 1997; Tyler 1990). In more developed work, procedural justice has itself been shown to comprise two separate elements: namely, *quality of decision-making* (e.g., did the citizen have a fair opportunity to state his/her point of view? Was the power-holder neutral?) and *quality of interpersonal treatment* (e.g., how far was the citizen treated as a person with human dignity and respect? Was the power-holder trustworthy, or did he/she show care for the person?) (Reisig, Bratton, and Gertz 2007; Tyler and Blader 2000; Tyler 2003).

Thus, when officers interact with supervisors they will look for evidence of fairness and care for their well-being not only because such evidence communicates information about their status in the 'governing community'; also, it may be a source of self-confirmation or self- verification. The research evidence appears mixed. In England, an unexpected finding emerged from Bradford and Quinton's (2014) study showing that perceived supervisory fair treatment was associated with a reduction in self-legitimacy. However, among a sample of police officers from Slovenia, Tankebe and Meško (2015) found a positive association between perceived fair treatment by supervisors and expressions of self-legitimacy.

Interactions with colleagues

According to Coleman (1988: 101), 'a group within which there is extensive trustworthiness and extensive trust is able to accomplish much more than a comparable group without that trustworthiness and trust'. Such a group is characterised by so-called relational social capital, and is considered 'an aid in accounting for different outcomes at the level of individual actors' (Coleman 1988: 101). Among police officers, the police subculture literature suggests the presence of relational social capital among officers, which is as much a resource for getting police work done as it is a possible facilitator of misconduct among officers. The concern of the present analysis is to extend the notion of relational social capital to the legitimacy discussion by exploring its influence on officers' understandings of their own legitimacy. As previously argued, following Barbalet (2001), feelings of confidence have their foundation in social relations; thus, we expect officers' self-confidence in their legitimacy to arise from situations of high relational social capital. This is consistent with Muir's (1977) study, which emphasised the role of social capital (attachment to and views of one's peers) in the cultivation, maintenance, and reproduction of officers' self-legitimacy.

The salience of relational social capital in promoting self-legitimacy would be even stronger in contexts in which face-to-face interactions between management or supervisors and frontline officers are infrequent. One of the remarkable developments in policing over the past several decades is the use of technology. It has allowed police managers and supervisors to communicate to, and to access information (e.g., data on performance targets) from, frontline officers without much warrant for recurrent face-to-face interactions. As Cain (1973) found in her detailed ethnographic work in England, low visibility and infrequent interactions with senior officers were the seedbed of trust and camaraderie among frontline officers. It is thus the quality of relationships among these officers rather than the quality of interactions with 'virtual supervisors' that might prove crucial in promoting self-legitimacy among police officers.

Interactions with citizens

Police officers engaged in daily routine patrol are low-ranked actors in the hierarchy of their organisation. Yet, to the citizen, they are in possession of enormous power, including the power to arrest and detain; and, as power-holders, they regularly engage in legitimacy dialogues as their authority is challenged by citizens in one way or another (Bottoms and Tankebe 2013). In the various empirical studies of audience legitimacy, police–citizen interactions constitute a 'teachable moment' in the sense that citizens are likely to form their views about the legitimacy or otherwise of the police on the basis of their perceptions of how fairly they have been treated.

On Barker's analysis, we should expect citizens' responses to exhibit the least impact on confidence in self-legitimacy. Barker argues that 'rulers do not need subjects, or citizens, to enable them to legitimate themselves or to cultivate their governing identities. Their first mirror is themselves, and subjects are at the edge of the outer circle' (2001: 125). This is a consistent theme throughout Barker's discussion: power-holders have little regard for the approval and support of the wider population, and they are 'not in the first instance concerned about what those whom they rule think, nor whether their cultivated image themselves is recognised and approved of by ordinary people' (2001: 106).

However, low-level patrol officers are not like rulers. They are sometimes the least powerful group within a large criminal justice agency. The decisions of police managers set limits and create opportunities for them. Yet the nature and outcome of everyday police–public interactions may lead to outcomes that necessitate a recalibration of the modes of external legitimacy and a transformation of police practices and procedures. Many of the scandals that have resulted in major organisational changes have emanated first and foremost from the action or inaction of ordinary officers, which police chiefs then fail to correct (e.g., incidents such as those relating to Stephen Lawrence in London, or Rodney King in Los Angeles).

Given this, interactions with citizens are likely to be the critical site for cultivating and verifying a possible self of confidence in legitimacy. Evidence from England (Bradford and Quinton 2014), the USA (Nix and Wolfe 2016) and Slovenia (Tankebe and Meško 2015) shows that officers' impressions of how citizens view them affect their sense of self-legitimacy. Specifically, the more officers believe citizens perceived them to be legitimate power-holders, the more confident the officers are in their own legitimacy.

Performance in maintenance of social order

The legitimacy–effectiveness relationship is the subject of much confusion across the social sciences. Rothschild (1977) argues that both 'interact organically': on the one hand, legitimacy 'can compensate for ... for erroneous, inefficient, and ineffective performance' (1977: 488); on the other hand, a legal and political order, 'though fully legitimate, is subject to erosion and delegitimation over the long run if it becomes chronically incompetent or ineffective', and 'no system stands still, forever legitimate, without being effective' (1977: 488). In criminology, in particular the literature on criminal justice legitimacy, effectiveness is often seen as a purely instrumental consideration which has little to do with the more normative issue of legitimacy (see, e.g., Jonathan-Zamir and Weisburd 2013; Tankebe 2009; Sunshine and Tyler 2003). However, there is recent evidence to show that, together with lawfulness, distributive justice, and procedural justice, effectiveness is a key dimension of attributions of legitimacy by audiences of power (Tankebe 2013; Liebling, with Arnold 2004).

What is not known empirically is whether and to what extent effective performance, actual or perceived, might contribute to the construction and confirmation of confidence in self- legitimacy. Bottoms and Tankebe (2013) argue that power-holders can gain a real sense of their own legitimacy from carrying out their responsibilities efficiently and effectively, believing that the system as a whole fulfils vital public functions. Extrapolating from Denis Wrong (1994), Bottoms and Tankebe (2013) argue that since order and governance are a 'transhistorical necessity for human groups, it makes perfectly good sense for some individuals to seek to serve the general good by becoming leaders in a government or other public service' (2013: 71). Thus, we should expect power-holders to draw upon evidence or perception of effectiveness to 'still the voice within', and therefore to contribute to developing a sense of confidence in their own legitimacy. This may come from police assessments that, as individual power-holders, they are effective in contributing to social order or preventing disorder. The assessments may also be based on evidence of the organisation's effectiveness, the latter being the empirical focus of the Ghana study.

Data and methods

The data for the study came from a survey in the Accra Metropolis from June to August 2006. The research participants were selected through a multi-stage sampling technique. The Metropolis has four main police divisions with a total of 32 police stations. Seven police stations were randomly selected, and at each of these police stations a complete list of all police officers from the rank of constable to inspector was obtained. The reason for targeting police officers within these ranks was that they constitute the 'primary determinant of policing where it really counts: on the street' (Reiner 2000: 86). Before the sampling was conducted, the list of officers was cleaned to exclude officers on United Nations peacekeeping missions and those on leave. In total, 220 police officers were randomly selected and targeted for the study. The questionnaires were sealed in envelopes and given to all of the selected police officers. Officers were asked to complete the questionnaire and to return it within one week to their various stations, from where they were collected. Out of the 220 questionnaires sent out, 181 were returned, representing a response rate of 82.3%. The items used to operationalise each of the variables in the study are shown in Appendix A.

About a third of the research participants were female; most were of the rank of corporal (35%), with constables forming the smallest constituency (16%); the majority had attained up to secondary school education (80.1%). These were of the ranks of constable to sergeant, but inspectors had higher educational attainment: polytechnic or university degree. With the exception of gender and rank, the Ghana Police Service does not have any readily available statistics on background characteristics to enable comparison of the sample with the larger police population. Official statistics on the gender composition of police officers from the ranks of constable to inspector indicate that two thirds of police officers are males (i.e., 75.4%). In other words, in terms of gender, the sample was representative of the larger population of police officers in the Accra Region.

Findings

Table 14.1 displays results from ordinary least squares (OLS) regression of self-legitimacy on individual characteristics, relations with citizens, relations with colleagues, treatment by supervisors, and perceived police effectiveness. Results from Model I reveal that, in comparison with officers who were relatively new on the job, officers with at least 20 years of service were more confident in their own legitimacy. More substantively, we found a moderate but positive association between perceptions of citizens' reactions and confidence in self-legitimacy ($\beta = .30$, $p < .001$). However, the model explained merely 7.8% of the variation in self-legitimacy.

The results in Model II indicate that relations with citizens continued to influence self- legitimacy when controlling for relations with colleagues, with the latter also exhibiting a statistically significant association with self-legitimacy. Interestingly, though, there was a 40% reduction in the strength of the citizen–legitimacy association. Introducing treatment by supervisors into the model (Model III) appears to wash out the influence both of colleagues and of citizens. Sobel tests confirmed supervisors mediated the effect of colleagues ($z = 4.55$, $p < .001$) and citizens ($z = 3.75$, $p < .001$) on self-legitimacy. In other words, we cannot adequately explain the influence colleagues and citizens have on self-legitimacy without reference to the quality of the professional relations between officers and supervisors. This makes supervisors key to nurturing frontline officers' belief in the moral rightness of their authority.

Table 14.1 OLS Regression showing the influence of effectiveness, supervisors, colleagues and citizens on self-legitimacy

	Model I	Model II	Model III	Model IV
	β (s.e)	β (s.e)	β (s.e)	β (s.e)
Female	.08 (.10)	.07 (.10)	.08 (.09)	.08 (.09)
Education	.07 (.12)	.06 (.11)	.04 (.10)	.05 (.10)
Length of Service∞				
10-19 years	−.07 (.12)	−.05 (.11)	−.03 (.10)	−.02 (.11)
≥ 20 years	−.17* (.10)	−.15 (.10)	−.13 (.09)	−.13 (.09)
Citizens	.30*** (.06)	.18* (.07)	.12 (.06)	.11 (.06)
Colleagues		.27*** (.09)	.10 (.09)	.09 (.09)
Supervisors			.41*** (.07)	.40*** (.07)
Effectiveness				.06 (.06)
N	180	179	179	179
Adj. R^2	7.8%	13.9%	25.9%	25.8%

Note: ∞ reference category is "less than 10 years"; standard errors in parenthesis; *p<.05 (two-tailed test), ***p<.001 (two-tailed test)

Finally, in Model IV, perceived police effectiveness was incorporated into the model. The results show it has no influence on self-legitimacy. The reason why effectiveness was the last entry was based on a concern with Barker's CMS hypothesis, which was more focused on how others reacted to the constructed self. In a separate analysis, police effectiveness was examined on its own and found to be associated positively with officer self-legitimacy (β=.23, p<.01), but explained only 5% of the variance among officers. It remained statistically significant after controlling for 'relations with citizens', but this diminished when 'relations with colleagues' was introduced into the model.

An implicit assumption in Barker's analysis is that power-holders are homogeneous, so that his concentric circle thesis will hold across all power-holders. Yet some might argue that his thesis would vary across various demographics, such as gender and length of service and rank. Further analysis showed that perceived treatment by supervisors was the only factor shaping self- legitimacy among male (b =.34 {s.e. = .09}, p<.001) and female (b =.52, {s.e. = .12}, p<.001) officers, and its influence was similar across both groups (z = .15, p >.05). In terms of length of service, we found that supervisors had no influence on the self-legitimacy of officers who had been with the organisation the longest, that is, those serving at least 20 years (p =.10); among these officers, it was reactions from colleagues (p = .04, one-tailed) that seemed critical. Supervisor influence was more pronounced among officers having served less than ten years (b =.54 {s.e. = .12}, p<.001) and those having served 10–19 years (b =.40 {s.e. = .14}, p<.001); its effects were similar across both groups (z =.76, p>.05). One reason why those with less than 20 years of service appear sensitive to supervisors' reactions to their constructed self-image of legitimate power-holders might be linked to the wide powers supervisors hold over officers' career progression (see Cain 1983).

The general methodology employed so far assumes that a unit increase in perceived effectiveness, treatment by supervisors, relations with colleagues, and reactions from citizens will produce a corresponding increase in self-legitimacy. However, it is possible that some of the relationships are non-linear, and that these explanatory variables matter more at one end of the distribution than at the other. In order to assess this non-linearity, the four explanatory variables that were measured on continuous scales were divided into four quartiles and related to self-legitimacy. The question is then how much more confidence in self-legitimacy is felt by an officer whose views fall within the second, third, or fourth quartiles compared with those who fall within the first quartile (the reference category).

Table 14.2 shows the results when the continuous measures of relations with supervisors, colleagues, and citizens and effectiveness in crime prevention are replaced by dummy variables indicating quartiles of each predictor. The main comparison is Model IV of Table 14.1. We find that some of the overall findings in the linearity relationships are replicated. However, we also find some evidence of non-linearities in the influence of effectiveness. Moving from the second quartile of perception of effectiveness to the

Table 14.2 Multiple Regression exploring non-linearity in Predicting Self-legitimacy

	(s.e)	B	*p*-values
Female	(.10)	.12	.090
Education	(.11)	.04	.537
Length of Service			
10-19 years	(.11)	-.03	.712
20 years or more	(.10)	-.15	.042
Citizens			
Quartile 2	(.11)	.07	.426
Quartile 3	(.11)	.14	.112
Quartile 4	(.15)	.20	.015
Colleagues			
Quartile 2	(.13)	.03	.773
Quartile 3	(.16)	.05	.553
Quartile 4	(.13)	-.04	.695
Supervisors			
Quartile 2	(.11)	.26	.003
Quartile 3	(.13)	.23	.004
Quartile 4	(.12)	.53	.000
Effectiveness			
Quartile 2	(.12)	.01	.929
Quartile 3	(.13)	.17	.041
Quartile 4	(.13)	.02	.852
Adj. R^2	24%		
N	180		

Note: reference category for length of service is "less than 10 years"; standard errors in parenthesis

third quartile was associated with gains in self-legitimacy; however, those gains disappeared in the fourth quartile. In other words, there was no difference in self-legitimacy between officers who rated police effectiveness very poorly and those who rated it most favourably. This will mean there is an inflection point in effectiveness, after which any further increase in perceptions of effectiveness does not translate into greater confidence in self-legitimacy. Once the inflection point is reached, police managers relying on effectiveness to nurture or promote self-legitimacy among frontline officers may find that their efforts yield very little return.

However, there was no such inflection in the influence of relationship-based factors; thus, for example, in the case of relationship with supervisors, we find that every improvement in perception of the quality of relationships between officers and their supervisors matters for the former's self-legitimacy. As exemplified by the regression coefficient, the highest improvements in expressions of confidence in self-legitimacy are associated with moving from the third quartile ($b = .23$) to the fourth ($b = .53$). In the case of their relationships with citizens, the gains in self-legitimacy are associated with views in the fourth quartile. In other words, to the extent that the recognition of citizens has an influence on officers' self-legitimacy, that recognition needs to be unequivocal.

In terms of individual-level variables, we find officers who have been on the job for more than 20 years to be less confident in self-legitimacy than relatively new officers.

Conclusion

Criminology has, in recent years, witnessed a *legitimacy turn* (Tankebe 2013). However, conceptually and empirically, this turn has been engineered and sustained by a disproportionate focus on the views of power-audiences. Our concern in this chapter was to explore the conditions associated with officers' confidence in their self-legitimacy, with an empirical focus on Ghana. To accomplish that task we sought to connect the self-legitimacy literature to the literature on self-concept, in particular the notion of possible selves (Markus and Nurius 1986). We argued that when officers legitimate power to themselves, what they have done is to construct a possible self of confident power-holder. This self-image is however perpetually vulnerable until verified or confirmed through interactions with others. As low-level power-holders, frontline officers are routinely engaged in multiple legitimation dialogues. It might be argued that the reactions of the different parties in these dialogues would have different meanings for officers' confidence in their constructed legitimacy.

In an empirical paper, Jonathan-Zamir and Harpaz (2014) reported a gap between police perception of the grounds on which citizens would recognise their claim to legitimacy and what citizens actually thought those grounds to be. Officers thought citizens prioritised police effectiveness when in fact citizens were more concerned with procedural justice. The authors argue that unless power-holders understand what nourishes audience legitimacy, the reciprocal impact of audience reactions on self-legitimacy will be lacking. However, even if power-holders read the bases of their audience legitimacy correctly, we are still left with the question of how they respond to those reactions. Social psychologists have documented a variety of ways through which people react to challenges to, or feedback that is incongruent with, the constructed self. Extrapolating from the evidence from these studies, police officers would seem to have a range of choices available to them in managing the effects of reactions from others on their constructed self.

First, officers might choose to limit themselves to interacting with people whose responses affirm the cultivated view of confidence in the rightful entitlement to power (cf. Marks and Wurf 1987: 318). In this way, officers might seek to avoid supervisors, teams/units, or even neighbourhoods that constantly challenge their conception of themselves. Second, they could engage in what Greenberg and Pyszczynski (1985) refer to as 'compensatory self-inflation'; this involves an attempt to bolster self in one domain due to challenges confronted in another domain by 'increasing the favourability or perceived value of self-image, perhaps without any real positive changes in self' (1985: 274). For example, an officer may say: 'My colleagues might not like me, but citizens on my beat value what I do and what I stand for'; or 'My supervisor might not value who I am, but my colleagues do'. In both cases, the aim is to minimise the threat to the self-conception of confidence in legitimacy. However, there is a third possible response: to understand, evaluate, and incorporate information from social interactions in a way that will 'enhance the possibility that they will receive positive feedback' in future interactions (Markus and Wurf 1987: 318).

The data from Ghana offered us an opportunity to explore whether and to what extent officers' confidence in their legitimacy is influenced by reactions of, or quality of interactions they have with, supervisors, colleagues, and citizens. Two key results emerged from the data. First, interactions with supervisors appeared to have the most critical consequence for the self-legitimacy of the officers studied. This finding about the influence of supervisors building legitimacy has since been replicated in other studies (see, e.g., Tankebe and Meško 2015; Nix and Wolfe 2015), although other studies have found either no evidence or negative supervisory influence on self-legitimacy (e.g., Bradford and Quinton 2014; Tankebe 2019). In terms of length of service, however, it was irrelevant to officers who had served for at least 20 years; for these officers, the reactions of colleagues mattered more.

Second, we found evidence of non-linearity in the relationship between, on the one hand, citizens' reactions, perceived effectiveness, and reactions of supervisors, and, on the other, self-legitimacy. It appeared that the reactions of supervisors and citizens must be rated extremely favourably in order to shape self-legitimacy; this was especially the case with the latter. Regarding the effectiveness–self-legitimacy relationship, there was evidence of an inflection point beyond which the influence of perceptions of effectiveness on self-legitimacy drops off.

A number of questions await further empirical investigation. First, there is a good deal of research on crisis in (audience) legitimacy (e.g., Friedrichs 1980; Habermas 1973; Reus-Smit 2007; Zhong 1996); we need to know how *self-legitimacy* in crisis manifests itself. How is it repaired and what are the implications of a self-legitimacy crisis for officer behaviour? Second, we have focused here on understanding what creates confidence in self-legitimacy. Such a focus leaves unattended a critical question: in what ways do individual officers legitimate themselves and what kinds of 'counter-legitimations' are prevalent among those who challenge officer authority (Barker 2001: 23)? Third, the literature on self-concept suggests that how people view themselves influences their perception of others and situations, and their decisions. Thus, might variations in self-legitimacy correlate with officers' readiness to use force against citizens? To answer these questions will require methodological diversity, since survey-based data alone cannot help satisfactorily to investigate these questions. It would be necessary for future tests to use data from systematic social observations (Mastrofski et al. 1998) and interviews of the kind that Rydberg and Terrill (2010) employed in their investigation of the effects of educational attainment on police behaviour.

Finally, as an activity, legitimation entails 'creation, modification, innovation, and transformation' (Barker 2001: 28). As we have also noted, self-conception of legitimacy is a continuous activity. There is a need for longitudinal studies that attempt to measure changes in the levels of self-legitimacy over time, and the conditions that might be antecedent to stability and change in levels of self-legitimacy through time. Fifth, there are prior studies of officers' perceptions of organisational legitimacy (e.g., De

Angelis and Kupchik 2009; Tyler, Callahan, and Frost 2007a). These studies have identified procedural justice as the primary antecedent of perceived organisational legitimacy. To what extent might self-legitimacy relate to assessments of organisational legitimacy? There are presently no systematic attempts to address this question, but it might be worth attention because the answer could offer an additional pathway to enhance organisational legitimacy.

Criminology is now returning to an emphasis on normative mechanisms for citizens' reactions to law and legal institutions (see Bottoms, this volume). It is a return to what Bottoms contended, in his inaugural lecture, to be the central analytical focus of criminology; as he put it, 'criminological inevitably involves analyses of social values and normative choices' (Bottoms 1987b: 261). This welcome development must focus as much on normativity in ordinary citizens' behaviour and perceptions as it does on normativity in the decisions and behaviour of police officers. A study of self-legitimacy can provide an insight into the motivations and decisions of officers. Work on self-legitimacy is only just beginning. By highlighting and clarifying some of the potential correlates of self-legitimacy, this chapter has sought to lay the groundwork for further research.

Appendix A Descriptive Statistics for Scales and Items

Scales and Items	Mean	S.D.
CONFIDENCE IN SELF-LEGITIMACY[a] ($\alpha = .71$)	4.03	.61
1. Putting on my police uniform makes me feel that I have a special kind of authority.	3.99	1.05
2. It is right that the police have been given special authority over their fellow citizens (e.g. to stop, search, or make arrests).	4.24	.87
3. I have confidence in the authority vested in me as a police officer.	4.37	.72
4. As a police officer, I believe I occupy a position of special importance in society.	4.26	.85
5. I believe people should always do what I tell them as long as my orders are lawful.	3.79	1.11
6. I am confident that I have enough authority to do my job well.	3.96	1.03
7. I believe the police are capable of providing security for all Ghanaians	3.80	1.15

Appendix A *Continued*

Scales and Items	Mean	S.D.
TREATMENT BY SUPERVISORS[a] (α = .74)	4.14	.64
1. I am valued as a member of the police service by my station commander.	4.33	.79
2. I am trusted by senior officers in this police station.	4.23	.74
3. The senior commander in this station is approachable when I need to discuss an issue with him/her	4.33	.71
4. I am treated fairly by the senior officers in this station	4.12	.92
5. The station commander takes interest in my welfare	3.87	.1.00
RELATIONS WITH COLLEAGUES[a] (α = .81)	4.01	.54
1. I feel supported in my work by my colleague officers.	4.10	.82
2. I feel a sense of loyalty to my colleagues.	4.07	.73
3. I trust my colleagues in this police station.	3.60	.95
4. My colleagues in this station trust me.	3.82	.83
5. I feel respected by colleagues in this police station.	4.17	.65
6. There is a good communication among my colleagues.	4.11	.76
7. I have a good relationship with my colleagues.	4.28	.62
REACTIONS CITIZENS[a] (α = .63)	3.47	.70
1. I have good relationship with most people in this community.	3.97	.75
2. Most people in this community are decent.	3.06	1.12
3. Most people in this community respect the police.	3.30	1.16
4. I have come to like most people in this community.	3.66	.86
EFFECTIVENESS[b] (α = .81)	3.40	.68
1. How would you rate the performance of the police in fighting crime?	4.03	.81
2. How would you rate the police response to public calls for assistance?	3.73	.90
3. How would you rate the level of security in the neighbourhood where you mainly work?	3.82	.84
4. How good a job are the police doing in fighting armed robbery?	4.22	.78

Appendix A *Continued*

Scales and Items	Mean	S.D.
5. How good a job are the police doing in tackling problems of illegal drug use?	3.57	1.08
6. How good a job are the police doing in detecting reported crimes?	4.07	.74

a. Response set ranged from 1 – *'strongly disagree' to 5 = 'strongly agree'*

b. Response set ranged from 1 = *'very poor' to 5= 'very good'*

Bibliography

Abbey, R. (2000) *Charles Taylor*. Teddington: Acumen.

Adelman, L. (2016) 'How Congress, the U.S. Sentencing Commission and Federal Judges Contribute to Mass Incarceration'. 7 December. http://dx.doi.org/10.2139/ssrn.3070489

Adler, M., and Longhurst, B. (1994) *Discourse, Power and Justice: Towards a New Sociology of Imprisonment*. London: Routledge.

Aebi, M. F., Delgrande, N., and Marguet, Y. (2015) 'Have Community Sanctions and Measures Widened the Net of the European Criminal Justice Systems?' *Punishment and Society*, 17 (5): 575–597.

Aertson, I., Daems, T., and Robert, L. (eds) (2006) *Institutionalizing Restorative Justice*. Cullompton: Willan.

Ahmad, S. (1996) *Fairness in Prisons*. PhD thesis, University of Cambridge.

Ahmed, E., Braithwaite, J., Braithwaite, V., and Harris, N. (2001) *Shame Management through Reintegration*. Cambridge, UK: Cambridge University Press.

Alexander, Michelle (2010) *The New Jim Crow: Mass Incarceration in the Age of Colorblindness*. New York: The New Press.

American Friends Service Committee (1971) *Struggle for Justice*. New York: Hill and Wang.

American Probation and Parole Association (APPA) and National Center for State Courts (NCSC) (2013) *Effective Responses to Offender Behavior: Lessons Learned for Probation and Parole Supervision*. Lexington, VA: APPA.

Ames, A., Di Antonio, E., Hitchcock, J., Webster, S., Wong, K., Ellingworth, D., Linda Meadows, L., McAlonan, D., Uhrig, N., and Logue, C. (2018) *Adult Out of Court Disposal Pilot Evaluation: Final Report*. London: Ministry of Justice.

Ancel, M. (1971) *Suspended Sentence*. London: Heinemann.

Anderson, E. (1999) *Code of the Street: Decency, Violence, and the Moral Life of the Inner City*. New York: W.W. Norton and Company.

Anderson, E. (2006) 'The Epistemology of Democracy', *Episteme*, 3 (1–2): 8–22.

Anderson, K., Colvin, S., McNeill, F., Nellis, M., Overy, K., Sparks, R., and Tett, L. (2010) *Inspiring Change: End of the Project Report of the Evaluation Team*. Motherwell: Motherwell College.

Andrews, D., Bonta, J., and Hoge, R. (1990) 'Classification for Effective Rehabilitation: Rediscovering Psychology', *Criminal Justice and Behavior*, 17: 19–52.

Annas, J. (2011) *Intelligent Virtue*. Oxford: Oxford University Press.

Ansell, C (2011) *Pragmatist Democracy: Evolutionary Learning as Public Philosophy*. Oxford: Oxford University Press.

Applegate, B., Cullen, F., Turner, M., and Sundt, J. (1996) 'Assessing Public Support for Three Strikes and You're Out'. Crime and Delinquency, 42 (4): 517–534.

Ariel, B., and Farrar, J. (2013) *The Effects of Body-Worn Video on Police Citizen Encounters: An RCT. Presentation to the 2013 Conference on Evidence-based Policing*. Cambridge: Institute of Criminology, 11 July 2013.

Ariel, B., Farrar, W. A., and Sutherland, A. (2014) 'The Effect of Police Body-Worn Cameras on Use of Force and Citizens' Complaints Against the Police: A Randomized Controlled Trial', *Journal of Quantitative Criminology*, 31 (3): 509–535.

Ariel, B., Sherman, L., and Vila, J. (2012) 'Random Assignment without Tears: How to Stop Worrying and Love the Cambridge Randomizer', *Journal of Experimental Criminology*, 8 (2): 193–208.

Auty, K. M., and Liebling, A. (2019) 'Exploring the Relationship between Prison Social Climate and Reoffending', *Justice Quarterly*: 1–24.

Aristotle (2000) *Nichomachean Ethics*, trans. Roger Crisp. Cambridge: Cambridge University Press, *Book II*.

Badinter, Robert (2008) *Abolition: One Man's Battle against the Death Penalty*. Boston: Northeastern University Press.

Baier, A. (1986) 'Trust and Antitrust', *Ethics*, 96 (2): 231–260.

Baldwin, J., and Bottoms, A. E. (1976) *The Urban Criminal*. London: Tavistock Publications.

Barbalet, J. (2009) 'A Characterization of Trust, and Its Consequences', *Theory and Society*, 38: 367–382.

Barker, R. (2001) *Legitimating Identities: The Self-Presentation of Rulers and Subjects*. Cambridge, UK: Cambridge University Press.

Barker, R. (2003) 'Legitimacy, Legitimation, and the European Union: What Crisis?' in P. Craig and R. Rawlings (eds) *Law and Administration*. Oxford: Oxford University Press.

Barker, V. (2009) *The Politics of Punishment: How the Democratic Process Shapes the Way America Punishes Offenders*. New York: Oxford University Press.

Barker, Vanessa (2005) *The Politics of Imprisonment*. Oxford: Oxford University Press.

Barlinnie Working Party (1994) *Small Units in The Scottish Prison System: Report of the Barlinnie Working Party on Barlinnie Special Unit*. Edinburgh: Scottish Prison Service.

Bartels, L. (2009) 'Sword or Butter Knife? A Breach Analysis of Suspended Sentences in Tasmania', *Current Issues in Criminal Justice*, 21: 219–241.

Bartels, L., and Bradfield, R.. 2015. *Phasing Out of Suspended Sentences Background Paper*. Hobart (Tasmania): Sentencing Advisory Council (Tasmania).

Bazemore, G., and Erbe, C. (2004) 'Reintegration and Restorative Justice: Towards a Theory and Practice of Informal Social Control and Support' in S. Maruna and R. Immarigeon (eds) *After Crime and Punishment: Pathways to Offender Reintegration*. Cullompton: Willan, pp. 27–56.

Bedford, L., and Neyroud, P. W. (2018) Organisational Learning from Field Research in Policing: How Police Can Improve Policy and Practice by Implementing Randomised Controlled Trials, *European Journal of Police Studies*, 5: 1–28.

Beetham, D. (1991) *The Legitimation of Power*. Basingstoke: Palgrave.

Beglan, M. (2013) 'The 218 Experience' in M. Malloch and G. McIvor (eds) *Women, Punishment and Social Justice*. London: Routledge.

Belenky, M., Clinchy, B., Goldberger, N., and Tarule, J. (1986) *Women's Ways of Knowing*. New York: Basic Books.

Bell, M. C. (2016) 'Situational Trust: How Disadvantaged Mothers Reconceive Legal Cynicism', *Law and Society Review*, 50: 314–347.

Bernstein, R. J. (2010) *The Pragmatic Turn*. Cambridge: Polity.

Blanchette, K., and Brown, S. (2006) *The Assessment and Treatment of Women Offenders: An Integrated Perspective*. Chichester: Wiley.

Blom-Cooper, Louis (1975) *Progress in Penal Reform*. Oxford: Oxford University Press.

Bögelein, N., A. Ernst and F. Neubacher. 2014. 'Wie kann die Vermeidung von Ersatzfreiheitsstrafen gelingen? Zur Lebenssituation der Verurteilten und zur Zusammenarbeit staatlicher und nichtstaatlicher Organisationen', *Bewährungshilfe*, 61 (3): 282–294.

Bonger, W. (1905) *Criminalité et conditions économiques*. Amsterdam: G. P. Thierie.

Bonta, J., Rugge, T., Scott, T., Gourgon, G., and Yessine, A. (2008) 'Exploring the Black Box of Community Supervision', *Journal of Offender Rehabilitation*, 47 (3): 248–270.

Bottomley, A. K. (1991) 'Implications for Future Policy and Research' in A. K. Bottomley and W. Hay (eds) *Special Units for Difficult Prisoners*. Hull: Centre for Criminology and Criminal Justice, University of Hull.

Bottomley, A. K., and Clare, E. (2001) *An Evaluation of Close Supervision Centres*. London: Home Office.

Bottomley, A. K., and Hay, W. (eds) (1991) *Special Units for Difficult Prisoners*. Centre for Criminology and Criminal Justice, University of Hull.

Bottomley, A. K., Jepson, N., Elliott, K., and Coid, J. (1994a) *Managing Difficult Prisoners: The Lincoln and Hull Special Units*. London: Home Office.

Bottomley, A. K., Liebing, A., and Sparks, R. (1994b) *Barlinnie Special Unit and Shotts Unit: An Assessment*. Scottish Prison Service Occasional Paper No 7. Edinburgh: Scottish Prison Service.

Bottoms, A. E. (1977) 'Reflections on the Renaissance of Dangerousness', *Howard Journal of Penology and Crime Prevention*, 16: 70–96.

Bottoms, A. E. (1978) 'Promise and Performance in British Criminology: A Comment', *British Journal of Sociology*, 29 (4): 503–505.

Bottoms, A. E. (1980) *The Suspended Sentence after Ten Years: A Review and Reassessment*. Leeds: University of Leeds Centre for Social Work and Applied Social Studies.

Bottoms, A. E. (1981) 'The Suspended Sentence in England, 1967-1978', *British Journal of Criminology*, 21 (1): 1–26.

Bottoms, A. E. (1987a) 'Limiting Prison Use: Experience in England and Wales', *The Howard Journal of Criminal Justice*, 26 (3): 177–202.

Bottoms, A. E. (1987b)'Reflections on the Criminological Enterprise', *Cambridge Law Journal*, 46 (2): 240–263.

Bottoms, A. E. (1989) 'The Concept of Intermediate Sanctions and Its Relevance for the Probation Service' in R. Shaw and K. Haines (eds) *The Criminal Justice System: A Central Role for the Probation Service*. Cambridge: Institute of Criminology, pp. 84–102.

Bottoms, A. E. (1990) 'The Aims of Imprisonment' in D. Garland (ed.) *Justice, Guilt and Forgiveness in the Penal System*. University of Edinburgh Centre for Theology and Public Issues, Occasional Paper No. 18, 3–36.

Bottoms, A. E. (1991) 'The Control of Long Term Prisoners in England: Beyond the Control Review Committee Report' in A. K. Bottomley and W. Hay (eds) *Special Units for Difficult Prisoners*. Hull: Centre for Criminology and Criminal Justice, University of Hull, pp. 1–15.

Bottoms, A. E. (1993) 'Recent Criminological and Social Theory: The Problem of Integrating Knowledge about Individual Criminal Acts and Careers and Areal Dimensions of Crime' in D. P. Farrington, R. J. Sampson, and P.-O. H. Wikström (eds) *Integrating Individual and Ecological Aspects of Crime. BRÅ Report* 1993: 1. Stockholm: Allmänna Förlaget.

Bottoms, A. E. (1995a) *Intensive Community Supervision for Young Offenders: Outcomes, Process and Cost* [includes economic study by Martin Knapp and Andrew Fenyo]. Cambridge: Institute of Criminology, University of Cambridge.

Bottoms, A. E. (1995b) 'The Philosophy and Politics of Punishment and Sentencing' in C. M. V. Clarkson and R. Morgan (eds) *The Politics of Sentencing Reform*. Oxford: Clarendon Press, pp. 17–49.

Bottoms, A. E. (1998) 'Five Puzzles in von Hirsch's Theory of Punishment' in A. Ashworth and M. Wasik (eds) *Fundamentals of Sentencing Theory*. Oxford: Oxford University Press, pp. 53–100.

Bottoms, A. E. (1999a) *Criminology and the Problem of Order: Nigel Walker Lecture*. Institute of Criminology, University of Cambridge.

Bottoms, A. E. (1999b) 'Interpersonal Violence and Social Order in Prisons', *Crime and Justice: A Review of Research*, 26: 205–281.

Bottoms, A. E. (2001) 'Compliance and Community Penalties' in A. E. Bottoms, L. Gelsthorpe, and S. Rex (eds) *Community Penalties: Change and Challenges*. Cullompton: Willan, pp. 101–130.

Bottoms, A. E. (2002a) 'The Divergent Development of Juvenile Justice in England and Scotland' in M. K. Rosenheim, F. E. Zimring, D. S. Tanenhaus, and B. Dohrn (eds) *A Century of Juvenile Justice*. Chicago: University of Chicago Press, pp. 413–504.

Bottoms, A. E. (2002b) 'Morality, Crime, Compliance and Public Policy' in A. E. Bottoms and M. Tonry (eds) *Ideology, Crime and Criminal Justice: A Symposium in Honour of Sir Leon Radzinowicz*. Cullompton, Devon: Willan, pp. 20–51.

Bottoms, A. E. (2003) 'Theoretical Reflections on the Evaluation of a Penal Policy Initiative' in L. Zedner and A. Ashworth (eds) *The Criminological Foundations of Penal Policy*. Oxford: Oxford University Press.

Bottoms, A. E. (2006) 'Desistance, Social Bonds and Human Agency: A Theoretical Exploration' in P.-O. H. Wikström and R. J. Sampson (eds) *The Explanation of Crime: Context, Mechanisms and Development*. Cambridge: Cambridge University Press, pp. 243–290.

Bottoms, A. E. (2007) 'Place, Space, Crime and Disorder' in M. Maguire, R. Morgan, and R. Reiner (eds) *Oxford Handbook of Criminology*, 4th edition. Oxford: Oxford University Press, pp. 528–574.

Bottoms, A. E. (2008a) 'The Community Dimension of Community Penalties', *The Howard Journal of Criminal Justice*, 47 (2): 146–169.

Bottoms, A. E. (2008b) 'The Relationship between Theory and Empirical Observations in Criminology' in R. D. King and E. Wincup (eds) *Doing Research on Crime and Justice*, 2nd edition. Oxford: Oxford University Press, pp. 75–116.

Bottoms, A. E. (2011) *Foreword to An Evaluation of the Diamond Initiative: Year Two Findings*. London: London Criminal Justice Partnership.

Bottoms, A. E. (2012) 'Developing Socio-Spatial Criminology' in M. Maguire, R. Morgan, and R. Reiner (eds) *The Oxford Handbook of Criminology*, 5th edition. Oxford: Oxford University Press, pp. 450–489.

Bottoms, A. E. (2013) 'Learning from Odysseus: Self-Applied Situational Crime Prevention as an Aid to Compliance' in P. Ugwudike and P. Raynor (eds) *What Works in Offender Compliance: International Perspectives and Evidence-Based Practice*. London: Routledge, pp. 67–89.

Bottoms, A. E. (2014) 'Civil Peace and Criminalisation' in R. A. Duff, L. Farmer, S. E. Marshall, M. Renzo, and V. Tadros (eds) *Criminalization: The Aims and Limits of the Criminal Law*. Oxford: Oxford University Press.

Bottoms, A. E. (2017a) 'Crime Specifics, Offender Residences, and Social Change: Developing the Criminology of Place', *Jerusalem Review of Legal Studies*, 15: 1–11.

Bottoms, A. E. (2017b) '"Punishment' in Non-Custodial Sentences: A Critical Analysis', *Criminal Law Forum*, 28 (3): 563–587.

Bottoms, A. E. (2018a) 'The Importance of High Offender Neighborhoods within Environmental Criminology' in Gerben Bruinsma and Shane Johnson (eds) *The Oxford Handbook of Environmental Criminology*. Oxford: Oxford University Press, pp. 119–149.

Bottoms, A. E. (2018b) *The Sentencing Council in 2017: A Report to Advise on How the Sentencing Council can Best Exercise its Statutory Functions*. London: Sentencing Council.

Bottoms, A. E. (2019a) 'Penal Censure, Repentance and Desistance' in A. du Bois-Pedain and A. E. Bottoms (eds) *Penal Censure: Engagements Within and Beyond Desert Theory*, Oxford: Hart Publishing, pp. 109–139.

Bottoms, A. E. (2019b) 'Understanding Compliance with Laws and Regulations: A Mechanism Based Approach' in M. Krambia-Kapardis (ed.) *Financial Compliance: Issues, Concerns and Future Directions*. Cham: Palgrave Macmillan, pp. 1–45.

Bottoms, A. E., and Light, R. (eds) (1987) *Problems of Long-Term Imprisonment*. Aldershot: Gower.

Bottoms, A. E., and McClintock, F. H. (1973) *Criminals Coming of Age: A Study of Institutional Adaptation in the Treatment of Adolescent Offenders*. London: Heinemann Educational Books, 1973.

Bottoms, A. E., Mawby, R. I., and Xanthos, P. (1989) 'A Tale of Two Estates' in D. Downes (ed.) *Crime and the City: Essays in Memory of John Barron Mays*. London: Macmillan, pp. 36–87.

Bottoms, A. E., and Pratt, J. (1989) 'Intermediate Treatment for Girls in England and Wales' in M. Cain (ed.) *Growing Up Good: Policing the Behaviour of Girls in Europe*. London: Sage.

Bottoms, A. E., and Pratt, J. (1990) *Intermediate Treatment and Juvenile Justice: Key Findings and Implications from a National Survey of Intermediate Treatment Policy and Practice*. London: H.M. Stationery Office.

Bottoms, A. E., and Preston, R. H. (eds) (1980) *The Coming Penal Crisis: A Criminological and Theological Exploration*. Edinburgh: Scottish Academic Press.

Bottoms, A. E., and Rose, G. (1998) 'The Importance of Staff–Prisoner Relationships: Results from a Study in Three Male Prisons' in D. Price and A. Liebling (eds) *Staff–Prisoner Relationships: A Review of the Literature*, unpublished report submitted to the Prison Service.

Bottoms, A. E., and Shapland, J. (2011) 'Steps towards Desistance amongst Male Young Adult Recidivists' in S. Farrall, R. Sparks, M. Hough, and S. Maruna (eds) *Escape Routes: Contemporary Perspectives on Life after Punishment*. London: Routledge, pp. 43–80.

Bottoms, A. E., and Shapland, J. (2016) 'Learning to Desist in Early Adulthood: The Sheffield Desistance Study' in J. Shapland, S. Farrall, and A. E. Bottoms (eds) *Global Perspectives on Desistance: Reviewing What We Know, Looking to the Future*. London: Routledge, pp. 99–125.

Bottoms, A. E., and Sparks, R. (1997) 'How Is Order in Prison Maintained?' in A. Liebling (ed) *Security, Justice and Order: Developing Perspectives*. Cambridge: Institute of Criminology.

Bottoms, A. E., and Stelman, A. (1988) *Social Inquiry Reports: A Framework for Practice Development by Anthony Bottoms and Andrew Stelman*. Aldershot: Wildwood House.

Bottoms, A. E., and Stevenson S. (1992) '"What Went Wrong?" Criminal Justice Policy in England and Wales, 1945–70' in D. Downes (ed.) *Unravelling Criminal Justice*. London: Palgrave Macmillan, https://doi.org/10.1007/978-1-349-22044-1_1

Bottoms, A. E., and Tankebe, J. (2012) 'Beyond Procedural Justice: A Dialogic Approach to Legitimacy in Criminal Justice', *Journal of Criminal Law & Criminology*, 102: 119–170.

Bottoms, A., and Tankebe, J. (2013) '"Voice Within": Powerholders' Perspectives on Authority and Legitimacy' in J. Tankebe and A. Liebling (ed.) *Legitimacy and Criminal Justice: An International Exploration*. Oxford: Oxford University Press, 60–82.

Bottoms, A. E., and Tankebe, J. (2017) 'Police Legitimacy and the Authority of the State' in A. du Bois-Pedain, M. Ulväng, and P. Asp (eds) *Criminal Law and the Authority of the State*. Oxford: Hart Publishing, pp. 47–88.

Bottoms, A. E., and Wiles, P. (1986) 'Housing Tenure and Residential Community Crime Careers in Britain', *Crime and Justice: A Review of Research*, 8: 101–162.

Bottoms, A. E., and Wiles, P. (1995) 'Crime and Insecurity in the City' in C. Fijnaut, J. Goethals, T. Peters, and L. Walgrave (eds) *Changes in Society, Crime and Criminal*

Justice in Europe, vol. 1: Crime and Insecurity in the City. The Hague: Kluwer Law International, pp. 1–38.

Bottoms, A. E., and Wiles, P. (1996) 'Understanding Crime Prevention in Late Modern Societies' in T. H. Bennett (ed.) *Preventing Crime and Disorder: Targeting Strategies and Responsibilities*. Cambridge: University of Cambridge Institute of Criminology, pp. 1–41.

Bottoms, A. E., and Xanthos, P. (1981) 'Housing Policy and Crime in the British Public Sector' in P. J. Brantingham and P. L. Brantingham (eds) *Environmental Criminology*. London: Sage.

Bottoms, A. E., Brown, P., McWilliams, B., McWilliams, W., and Nellis, M. (1990) *Intermediate Treatment and Juvenile Justice: Key Findings and Implications from a National Survey of Intermediate Treatment Policy and Practice*. London: H.M.S.O.

Bottoms, A. E., Claytor, A., and Wiles. P. (1992) 'Housing Markets and Residential Community Crime Careers: A Case Study from Sheffield' in D. J. Evans, N. R. Fyfe, and D. T. Herbert (eds) *Crime, Policing, and Place*. London: Routledge.

Bottoms, A. E., Gelsthorpe, L. R., and Rex, S. (eds) (2001) *Community Penalties: Change and Challenges*. Cullompton: Willan.

Bottoms, A. E., Rex, S., and Robinson, G. (2004a) *Alternatives to Prison: Options for an Insecure Society*. Cullompton: Willan.

Bottoms, A. E., Shapland, J., Costello, A., Holmes, D., and Muir, G. (2004b) 'Towards Desistance: Theoretical Underpinnings for an Empirical Study', *The Howard Journal of Crime and Justice*, 43 (4): 368–389.

Bourdieu, Pierre (1993) 'Public Opinion Does Not Exist' in *Sociology in Question*. London: SAGE., pp. 149–157.

Boyle, J. (1977) *A Sense of Freedom*. London: Pan.

Boyle, J. (1982) 'Thoughts: 1974—Reprinted from the Catalogue to Jimmy Boyle's Exhibition at Third Eye Centre, 1976' in C. Carrell and J. Laing (eds) *The Special Unit: Its Evolution through Art*. Glasgow: Third Eye Centre.

Boyle, J. (1984) *The Pain of Imprisonment*. London: Pan.

Boyle, J. (1999) *Hero of the Underworld*. London: Serpent's Tale.

Boyle, J. (2016) Afterword in *A Sense of Freedom*: new edition, with an introduction by novelist Irvine Welsh. London: Ebury Press.

Boyle, S. (1982) 'The Special Unit and the Outside World' in C. Carrell and J. Laing (eds) *The Special Unit: Its Evolution through Art*. Glasgow: Third Eye Centre.

Bradford, B., and Quinton, P. (2014) 'Self-Legitimacy, Police Culture and Support for Democratic Policing in an English Constabulary', *British Journal of Criminology*, 54: 1023–1046.

Bradley, D., and Nixon, C. (2009) 'Ending the "Dialogue of the Deaf": Evidence and Policing Policies and Practices. An Australian Case Study', *Police Practice and Research*, 10 (5–6): 423–435.

Braga, A. A., Welsh, B. C., Papachristos, A. V., Schnell, C., and Grossman, L. (2014) 'The Growth of Randomized Experiments in Policing: the Vital Few and the Salience of Mentoring', *Journal of Experimental Criminology*, 10: 1–28.

Braithwaite, J. (1989) *Crime, Shame and Reintegration*. Cambridge: Cambridge University Press.

Braithwaite, J. (1992) 'Reducing the Crime Problem: A Not So Dismal Criminology', *Australian and New Zealand Journal of Criminology*, 25 (1): 1–10.

Braithwaite, J., and Mugford, S. (1994) 'Conditions of Successful Reintegration Ceremonies: Dealing with Juvenile Offenders', *British Journal of Criminology*, 34: 139–171.

Braithwaite, J., and Pettit, P. (1990) *Not Just Desserts: A Republican Theory of Criminal Justice*. Oxford: Clarendon Press.

Braithwaite, J., and Pettit, P. (2000) 'Republicanism and Restorative Justice' in H. Strang and J. Braithwaite (eds) *Restorative Justice: Philosophy to Practice*. Burlington, Vermont: Ashgate, pp. 145–163.

Brantingham, P. J., and Brantingham, P. L. (1981) 'Introduction: The Dimensions of Crime' in P. J. Brantingham and P. L Brantingham (eds) *Environmental Criminology*. Beverly Hills, CA: Sage.

Brantingham, P. J., and Brantingham, P. L. (1984) *Patterns in Crime*. New York: Macmillan.

Brantingham, P. J., and Brantingham, P. L. (1993) 'Environment, Routine and Situation. Toward a Pattern Theory of Crime' in R. V. Clarke and M. Felson (eds) *Routine Activity and Rational Choice*. New Brunswick, NJ: Transaction Publications.

Brantingham, P. J., and Brantingham, P. L. (2008) 'Crime Pattern Theory' in R. Wortley and L. Mazerolle (eds) *Environmental Criminology and Crime Analysis*. Abingdon: Routledge.

Breen, P. (2011) 'Thoughts on the First Production' in T. McGrath and J. Boyle, *The Hard Man*. Edinburgh: Capercaille Press.

Broadhead, J. (2006) *Unlocking the Prison Muse: The Inspirations and Effects of Prisoners' Writing in Britain*. Cambridge: Cambridge Academic.

Bronfenbrenner, U. (1979) *The Ecology of Human Development*. Cambridge, MA: Harvard University Press.

Brown, David (2005) 'Continuity, Rupture, or Just More of the "Volatile and Contradictory"?' in J. Pratt and D. Brown (eds) *The New Punitiveness: Trends, Theories, Perspectives*. Collumpton: Willan.

Brown, David (2012) 'Imprisonment Rates, Social Democracy, Neo-Liberalism and Justice Reinvestment' in K. Carrington et al (eds) *Crime, Justice and Social Democracy: International Perspectives*. London: Palgrave Macmillan.

Brown, David (2013) 'Mapping the Conditions of Penal Hope', *International Journal for Crime, Justice and Social Democracy*, 2 (3): 27–42.

Brown, Elizabeth (2011) 'Constructing the Public Will: How Political Actors in New York State Construct, Assess and Use Public Opinion in Policy-Making', *Punishment & Society*, 13 (4): 424–450.

Buber, M. (2010) *I and Thou*. Mansfield Centre, CT: Martino Publishing.

Buckley, K., and Wilson, C. (1989) 'Empowering Women', *Probation Journal*, 36 (4): 165–170.

Burgess, E. W. (1925) *The City*. Chicago: University of Chicago Press.

Burgess, M. (1998) *Imagine a City: Glasgow in Fiction*. Glendaruel: Argyll.

Burnett, R. (1992) *The Dynamics of Recidivism*. Oxford: Centre for Criminological Research.

Burnett, R., and Maruna, S. (2006) 'The Kindness of Prisoners: Strengths-Based Resettlement in Theory and in Action', *Criminology and Criminal Justice*, 6 (1): 83–106.

Burrowes, J. (1998) 'No Mean City' in J. Burrowes, *Great Glasgow Stories*. Edinburgh: Mainstream Publishing.

Bursik, R. J., and Grasmick, H. G. (1993) *Neighborhoods and Crime*. New York: Lexington.

Cain, M. (1973) *Society and the Policeman's Role*. London: Routledge & Kegan Paul.

Calverley, A. (2009) *An Exploratory Investigation into the Processses of Desistance amongst Minority Ethnic Offenders*. PhD thesis. Keele: Keele University.

Campbell, D. (1999) Hand Over Fist: An Interview with Jimmy Boyle. *The Guardian Weekend* 23 January 1999.

Campbell, C., Devlin, R., O'Mahony, D., Doak, J., Jackson, J., Corrigan, T., and McEvoy, K. (2005) *Evaluation of the Northern Ireland Youth Conference Service*. NIO Research and Statistical Service Report No. 12. Belfast: Northern Ireland Office.

Canovan, Margaret (1981) *Populism*. New York: Harcourt Brace.

Carlen, P. (1989) 'Feminist Jurisprudence—or Women-Wise Penology?', *Probation Journal*, 36 (3): 110–114.

Carlen, P. (1990) *Alternatives to Women's Imprisonment*. Milton Keynes: Open University Press.

Carlen, P. (2002) 'Carceral Clawback: The Case of Women's Imprisonment in Canada', *Punishment & Society*, 4 (1): 115–121.

Carmichael, K. (1982a) 'Daily Living' in C. Carrell and J. Laing (eds) *The Special Unit: Its Evolution through Art*. Glasgow: Third Eye Centre.

Carmichael, K. (1982b) 'Postscript to Daily Living' in C. Carrell and J. Laing (eds) *The Special Unit: Its Evolution through Art*. Glasgow: Third Eye Centre.

Carrell, C., and Laing, J. (eds) (1982) *The Special Unit: Its Evolution through Art*. Glasgow: Third Eye Centre.

Cavadino, Mick, and Dignan, James (2005) *Penal Systems: A Comparative Approach*. London: Sage.

Checkland, S. G. (1981) *The Upas Tree: Glasgow 1875–1975 ... and after 1975–80*. Glasgow: University of Glasgow Press.

Chigwada, R. (1989) 'The Criminalisation and Imprisonment of Black Women', *Probation Journal*, 36 (3): 100–105.

Choi, J., and Severson, M. (2009) 'What! What Kind of Apology Is This? The Nature of Apology in Victim Offender Mediation', *Children and Youth Services Review*, 31: 813–820.

Christie, N. (1977) 'Conflicts as Property', *British Journal of Criminology*, 17: 1–15.

Claes, B., and Shapland, J. (2016) 'Desistance from Crime and Restorative Justice', *Restorative Justice*, 4 (3): 302–322.

Clarke, R. V. (1997) *Situational Crime Prevention: Successful Case Studies*. New York: Harrow and Heston.

Clarke, J., and Newman, J. (1997) *The Managerial State: Power, Politics and Ideology in the Remaking of Social Welfare*. London: Sage.

Clarke, R. V., and Cornish, D. B. (1985) 'Modelling Offenders' Decisions: A Framework for Research and Policy', *Crime and Justice*, 6: 147–185.

Clarke, R. V., and Felson, M. (1993) *Routine Activity and Rational Choice. Advances in Criminological Theory*, Vol. 5. Piscataway, NJ: Transaction.

Cohen, L. E., and Felson. M. (1979) 'Social Change and Crime Rate Trends: A Routine Activity Approach', *American Sociological Review*, 44: 588–608.

Cohen, S. (1985) *Visions of Social Control*. Cambridge: Polity Press.

Coicaud, J-M. (2002) *Legitimacy and Politics: A Contribution to the Study of Political Right and Political Responsibility*. Cambridge, UK: Cambridge University Press.

Coleman, J. (1988) 'Social Capital in the Creation of Human Capital', *American Journal of Sociology*, 94: 95–120.

Collins, H. (1997) *Autobiography of a Murderer*. London: Macmillan.

Collins, H. (2000) *Walking Away*. Edinburgh: Canongate.

Commonwealth of Massachusetts Superior Court. 2016. *Criminal Sentencing in the Superior Court: Best Practices for Individualized Evidence-Based Sentencing*. March. Online version available at https://www.mass.gov/doc/criminal-sentencing-in-the-superior-court-best-practices-for-individualized-evidence-based/download

Conroy, B. (1982) 'Inmates' Impressions of the Special Unit' in C. Carrell and J. Laing (eds) *The Special Unit: Its Evolution through Art*. Glasgow: Third Eye Centre.

Cooke, D. (1989a) 'Containing Violent Prisoners: an analysis of the Barlinnie Special Unit', *British Journal of Criminology*, 29 (2): 129–143.

Cooke, D. (1989b) *The Barlinnie Special Unit. in Scottish Prison Service. Current Issues in Scottish Prisons: systems of accountability and regimes for difficult prisoners. Occasional Paper No 2*. Edinburgh: HMSO.

Cooke, D. (1997) 'The Barlinnie Special Unit: The Rise and Fall of a Therapeutic Experiment' in E. Cullen, L. Jones, and R. Woodward (eds) *Therapeutic Communities for Offenders*. Chichester: Wiley.

Corston, Baroness J. (2007) *The Corston Report: A Review of Women with Particular Vulnerabilities in the Criminal Justice System*. London: Home Office. https://webarchive.nationalarchives.gov.uk/20130206102659/http://www.justice.gov.uk/publications/docs/corston-report-march-2007.pdf.

Covington, S. (1998) 'The Relational Theory of Women's Psychological Development: Implications for the Criminal Justice System' in R. Zaplin (ed.) *Female Offenders: Critical Perspectives and Effective Interventions*. Gaithersburg, MD: Aspen.

Cowperthwaite, David (1988) *The Emergence of the Scottish Children's Hearing System*. Southampton: Institute of Criminal Justice, Southampton University.

Cox, R. (2006) 'Creativity Is All in the Mind.' *The Scotsman* 6 May 2006.

Coyle, A. (1987) 'The Scottish Experience with Small Units' in A. E. Bottoms and R. Light (eds) *Problems of Long Term Imprisonment*. Aldershot: Gower.

Coyle, A. (1989) 'Incidents in the Scottish Prison Service: Incident and Response' in Scottish Prison Service, *Current Issues in Scottish Prisons: Systems of Accountability and Regimes for Difficult Prisoners*. Occasional Paper No 2. Edinburgh: HMSO.

Crawford, A., and Goodey, J. (2000) *Integrating a Victim Perspective within Criminal Justice*. Abingdon: Routledge.

Crewe, B., Liebling, A., and Hulley. S. (2014) 'Heavy/Light, Absent-Present: Re-thinking the "Weight" of Imprisonment', *British Journal of Sociology*, 65 (3): 387–410.

Crouch, B. M. (1993) 'Is Incarceration Really Worse? Analysis of Offenders' Preferences for Prison over Probation', *Justice Quarterly*, 10 (1): 67–88.

Crummy, H. (1992) *Let the People Sing: The Story of the Craigmillar Festival Society*. Glasgow: Hyperion Press.

Cullen, F. T. (2017) 'Choosing our Criminological Future: Reservations about Human Agency as an Organizing Concept', *Journal of Developmental and Life-Course Criminology*, 3: 373–379.

Cullen, F. T., and Gilbert, K. E. (1982) *Reaffirming Rehabilitation*. Cincinnati, OH: Anderson Publishing.

Cullen, Francis, Cullen, John, and Wozniak, John (1988) 'Is Rehabilitation Dead? The Myth of a Punitive Public', *Journal of Criminal Justice*, 16 (4): 303–317.

Cullen, F. T., Jonson, C. L., and Mears, D. P. (2017) In M. Tonry and D.S. Nagan (eds), *Reinventing American Criminal Justice* (Crime and Justice Vol. 46): 27–93. Chicago: Chicago University Press.

D'Cruz, J. (2019) 'Humble Trust', *Philosophical Studies*, 165 (3): DOI 10.1007/s11098-018-1220-6.

Demarco, R. (1995) *A Life in Pictures*. Ellon, Aberdeenshire: Famedram Books.

Demarco, R. (1997) *Kunst = Capital: Art = Wealth. The Adam Smith Lecture 1995*. Kingston University; Kingston Business School Occasional Paper Series

Demarco, R. (2016) *A Unique Partnership: Richard Demarco and Joseph Beuys*. Edinburgh: Luath Press.

Dengate, C. (1978) *The Use of Suspended Sentences in South Australia*. Adelaide: Department of Correctional Services.

Department of Justice (2010) *Women's Offending Behaviour in Northern Ireland: A Strategy to Manage Women Offenders and Those Vulnerable to Offending Behaviour 2010–2014*. Belfast, Department of Justice.

Dewey, J. (1918) 'Philosophy and Democracy' in J. Boydston (ed.) *The Middle Works of John Dewey, 1889–1924*. Carbondale: Southern Illinois University Press.

Dewey, J. (1927) *The Public and Its Problems*. Athens: Shallow Press.

Dewey, J., and Tufts, J. H. (1908) *Ethics*. San Francisco: University of California Libraries.

De Zulueta, F. (1993) *From Pain to Violence: The Traumatic Roots of Destructiveness*. London: Whurr.

Dignan, J. (1984) 'The Sword of Damocles and the Clang of the Prison Gates: Prospects on the Inception of the Partly Suspended Sentence', *Howard Journal of Criminal Justice*, 23 (3): 183–200.

Dignan, J., Atkinson, A., Atkinson, H., Howes, M., Johnstone, J., Robinson, G., Shapland, J., and Sorsby, A. (2007) 'Staging Restorative Justice Encounters against a Criminal Justice Backdrop: A Dramaturgical Analysis', *Criminology and Criminal Justice*, 7: 5–32.

Donnison D. (1978) 'Special Unit'. *New Society* 12 January 1978 60–61.

Dooley, B., and Goodison, S. (2019) 'Falsification by Atrophy: The Kuhnian Process of Rejecting Theory in US Criminology', *British Journal of Criminology*, https://doi.org/10.1093/bjc/azz026

Dowle, M. (1982) 'A Bold Reform or a Cracking Good Yarn: The Press and the Special Unit' in C. Carrell and J. Laing (eds) *The Special Unit: Its Evolution through Art*. Glasgow: Third Eye Centre.

Downes, David (1988) *Contrasts in Tolerance* (Oxford: Oxford University Press).

du Bois-Pedain, A. 2017. 'Punishment as an Inclusionary Practice: Sentencing in a Liberal Constitutional State' in A. du Bois-Pedain, M. Ulväng, and P. Asp (eds), *Criminal Law and the Authority of the State*. Oxford: Hart Publishing, pp. 199–227.

du Bois-Pedain, A., and Bottoms, A. (eds) (2019) *Penal Censure: Engagements Within and Beyond Desert Theory*. Oxford: Hart Publishing.

Duff, R. A. (1991) 'Punishment, Expression, and Penance' in H. Jung and H. Müller-Dietz (eds), *Recht und Moral. Beiträge zu einer Standortbestimmung*. Baden Baden: Nomos.

Dunbar, I. (1970) Long Lartin: The Development of a Concept, *Prison Service Journal* (April).

Dunn, J. (1984) *The Politics of Socialism*. Cambridge: Cambridge University Press.

Durkheim, E. (1897/2006) *On Suicide*, ed. R. Sennett, trans. R. Buss. London: Penguin Classics.

Dzur, Albert (2008) *Democratic Professionalism: Citizen Participations and the Reconstruction of Professional Ethics, Identity and Practice*. University Park, PA: Penn State University Press.

Dzur, A. (2013) *Punishment, Participatory Democracy and the Jury*. Oxford: Oxford University Press.

Dzur, A. (2019) *Democracy Inside: Participatory Innovation in Unlikely Places*. Oxford: Oxford University Press.

Dzur, A. W. (2012) Participatory Democracy and Criminal Justice, *Criminal Law, Philosophy*, 6: 115–129.

Dzur, A., Loader, I., and Sparks, R. (eds) (2016) *Democratic Theory and Mass Incarceration*. Oxford: Oxford University Press.

Easton, H., and Matthews, R. (2011) *Evaluation of the Women's Inspire Project*. London: London South Bank University.

Elliott, C. (1999) *Locating the Energy for Change: An Introduction to Appreciative Enquiry*. Winnipeg, MB: International Institute for Sustainable Development.

Ellscheid, G. (2001) 'Tatproportionale Strafzumessung und Strafaussetzung zur Bewährung – Bemerkungen zu einem kategorialen Irrweg' in G. Britz, H. Jung, H. Koriath, and E. Müller (eds) *Grundfragen staatlichen Strafens. Festschrift für Heinz Müller-Dietz zum 70. Geburtstag*. Munich: Beck, pp. 201–212.

Emirbayer, M., and Mische, A. (1998) 'What is Agency?' *American Journal of Sociology*, 103: 962–1023.

Engel, R. S., and Henderson, S. (2013) 'Beyond Rhetoric: Establishing Police Academic Partnerships that Work' in J. Brown (ed.) *The Future of Policing*. London: Routledge.

Erickson, R. J. (1995) 'The Importance of Authenticity for Self and Society', *Symbolic Interaction*, 18: 121–144.

Ericson, R. (2005) 'Publicizing Sociology', *British Journal of Sociology*, 56 (3): 365–372.

Ericson, R., Baranek, P., and Chan, J. (1987) *Visualizing Deviance: A Study of News Organizations*. Toronto: University of Toronto Press.

Esslin, M. (1961) *Theatre of the Absurd*. New York: Anchor Books.

Farrall, S. (2002) *Rethinking What Works with Offenders*. Cullompton: Willan.

Farrall, S., Bottoms, A. E., and Shapland, J. (2010) 'Social Structures and Desistance from Crime', *European Journal of Criminology*, 7 (6): 546–570.

Farrall, S., Hunter, B., Sharpe, G. H., and Calverley, A. (2014) *Criminal Careers in Transition: The Social Context of Desistance from Crime*. Oxford: Oxford University Press.

Farrant, F. (2006) 'Knowledge Production and the Punishment Ethic: The Demise of the Probation Service', *Probation Journal*, 53 (4): 317–333.

Farrington, D. P. (2019) 'The Duration of Criminal Careers: How Many Offenders Do Not Desist up to Age 61?', *Journal of Developmental and Life-course Criminology*, 5 (1): 4–21.

Farrington, D. P., and Welsh, B. (2006) 'A Half Century of Randomized Experiments on Crime and Justice', *Crime and Justice*, 34 (1): 55–132.

Farrington, D. P., Coid, J. W., Harnett, L., Jolliffe, D., Soteriou, N., Turner, R., and West, D. J. (2006) *Criminal Careers up to Age 50 and Life Success up to Age 48*, Home Office Research Study No. 299. London: Home Office.

Faulkner, D. (2014) *Servant of the Crown: A Civil Servant's Story of Criminal Justice and Public Service Reform*. Eastbourne: Waterside Press.

Feder, L., Jolin, A., and Feyerherm, W. (2000) 'Lessons from Two Randomized Experiments in Criminal Justice Settings', *Crime and Deliquency*, 46 (3): 380–400.

Felson, M. (2008) 'Routine Activity Approach' in R. Wortley and L. Mazerolle (eds), *Environmental Criminology and Crime Analysis*. Oxford: Routledge.

Felson, M., and Boba, R. (2010) *Crime and Everyday Life*. 4th edn. London: Sage.

Felson, M., and Clarke, R. V. (1998) *Opportunity Makes the Thief. Practical Theory for Crime Prevention*. Police research series paper 98. Home Office.

Felson, M., and Eckert, M. A. (2019) *Crime and Everyday Life*. 6th edn. Los Angeles: SAGE.

Festenstein, M. (2014) 'Dewey's Political Philosophy' in E. N. Zalta (ed.) *The Stanford Encyclopaedia of Philosophy* (Spring 2014 edition) http://plato.stanford.edu/archives/spr2014/entries/dewey-political/

Forbes, G. (2004) *Such Bad Company: True Tales of Glasgow's Underworld*. Glasgow: LangSyne Publishing.

Foucault, Michel (1977) *Discipline and Punish*. London: Allen Lane

Freiberg, A. (2014) *Fox and Freiberg's Sentencing: State and Federal Law in Victoria*. 3rd edn. Sydney: Thomson.

Freiberg, A. (2019) 'Suspended Sentences in Australia: Uncertain, Unstable, Unpopular, and Unnecessary?' *Law and Contemporary Problems*, 82 (1): 81–109.

Freiberg, A., and Gelb, K. (eds) (2008) *Penal Populism, Sentencing Councils and Sentencing Policy*. Annandale: Hawkins Press.

Freiberg, A., and Moore, V. (2009) 'Disbelieving Suspense: Suspended Sentences of Imprisonment and Public Confidence in the Criminal Justice System', *Australian & New Zealand Journal of Criminology*, 42 (1): 101–122.

Frost, Natasha (2010) 'Beyond Public Opinion Polls: Punitive Public Sentiment and Criminal Justice Policy', *Sociology Compass*, 4 (3): 156–168.

Fukuyama, F. (1995) *Trust: The Social Virtues and the Creation of Prosperity*. New York: The Free Press.

Fung, A. (2006) *Empowered Participation: Reinventing Urban Democracy*. Princeton: Princeton University Press.

Fixsen, D. L., Naoom, S. F., Blase, K. A., Friedman, R. F., and Wallace, F. (2005) *Implementation Research: A Synthesis of the Literature*. Tampa, FL: University of South Florida.

Fortes, M. (1983) *Rules and the Emergence of Society*. London: Royal Anthropological Society.

Friedrichs, D. O. (1980) 'The Legitimacy Crisis in the United States: A Conceptual Analysis', *Social Problems*, 27: 540–555.

Gambetta, D. (1990) 'Can We Trust Trust?' in D. Gambetta (ed.) *Trust: Making and Breaking Cooperative Relations*. Oxford: Blackwell.

Garland, David (1985/2018) *Punishment and Welfare: A History of Penal Strategies* Reprint edition, New Orleans: Quid Pro Books.

Garland, D. (1992) 'Criminological Knowledge and Its Relation to Power: Foucault's Genealogy and Criminology Today', *British Journal of Criminology*, 32 (4): 403–422.

Garland, D. (1995) 'Penal Modernism and Post-Modernism' in T. Blomberg and S. Cohen (eds) *Punishment and Social Control*. New York: Transaction, pp. 45–73.

Garland, D. (2001) *The Culture of Control*. Oxford: Oxford University Press.

Garland, D. (2011) 'Criminology's Place in the Academic Field' in M. Bosworth and C. Hoyle (eds) *What Is Criminology?* Oxford: Oxford University Press, pp. 298–317.

Garland, David (2013) 'Penality and the Penal State', *Criminology*, 51 (3): 475–517.

Garland, David, and Sparks, Richard (2000) 'Criminology, Social Theory, and the Challenge of our Times' in *Criminology and Social Theory*. Oxford: Oxford University Press, pp. 1–22.

Gazal-Ayal, O., and J. V. Roberts. 2019. 'Foreword. Alternatives to Imprisonment: Recent International Developments', *Law and Contemporary Problems*, 82 (1): i–ix.

Gelb, Karen (2008) 'Myths and Misconceptions: Public Opinion versus Public Judgement about Sentencing' in A. Freiberg and K. Gelb (eds) *Penal Populism, Sentencing Councils and Sentencing Policy*. Annandale: Hawkins Press.

Gelsthorpe, L. (2001) 'Accountability: Difference and Diversity in the Delivery of Community Penalties' in A. E. Bottoms, L. Gelsthorpe, and S. Rex (eds) *Community Penalties: Change and Challenges*. Cullompton: Willan Publishing.

Gelsthorpe, L. (2004) 'Back to Basics in Crime Control: Weaving in Women', *Critical Review of International Social and Political Philosophy*, 7 (2): 76–103.

Gelsthorpe, L. (2010) 'Anthony E Bottoms' in K. Hayward, S. Maruna, and J. Mooney (eds) *Fifty Key Thinkers in Criminology*. London: Routledge.

Gelsthorpe, L. (2020) 'What Works with Women Offenders? An English and Welsh Perspective' in P. Ugwudike, H. Graham, F. McNeill, P Raynor, F Taxman, and C. Trotter (eds) *The Routledge Companion to Rehabilitative Work in Criminal Justice* , Abingdon: Routledge.

Gelsthorpe, L., and Morris, A. (2002) 'Women's Imprisonment in England and Wales: A Penal Paradox', *Criminal Justice*, 2 (3): 277–301.

Gelsthorpe, L., and Russell, J. (2018) 'Women and Penal Reform: Two Steps Forwards, Three Steps Backwards?' *Political Quarterly*, 89 (2): 227–236.

Gelsthorpe, L., Sharpe, G., and Roberts, J. (2007) *Provision for Women Offenders in the Community*. A report for the Fawcett Society.

Geuss, R. (1981) *The Idea of a Critical Theory*. Cambridge: Cambridge University Press.

Giblin, M. J. (2002) 'Using Police Officers to Enhance the Supervision of Juvenile Probationers: An Evaluation of the Anchorage CAN Program', *Crime & Delinquency*, 48 (1): 116–137.

Giddens, A. (1984) *The Constitution of Society*. Cambridge: Polity.

Giddens, A. (1987) *Social Theory and Modern Sociology*. Cambridge: Polity.

Giddens, A. (1990) *The Consequences of Modernity*. Cambridge: Polity.

Gifford, D., Dunnigan, S., and McGillivray, A. (2002) 'Modern Scottish Drama' in D. Gifford, S. Dunnigan, and A. McGillivray (eds) *Scottish Literature in English and Scots*. Edinburgh: Edinburgh University Press.

Giordano, P. (2016) 'Mechanisms Underlying the Desistance Process: Reflections on "A Theory of Cognitive Transformation"' in J. Shapland, S. Farrall, and A. E. Bottoms (eds) *Global Perspectives on Desistance: Reviewing What we Know, Looking to the Future*, London: Routledge, pp. 11–27.

Gottfredson, D. C., McNeill III, R. J., and Gottfredson, G. D. (1991) 'Social Area Influences on Delinquency: A Multilevel Analysis', *Journal of Research in Crime and Delinquency*, 28: 197–226.

Gottschalk, M. (2015) *Caught: The Prison State and the Lockdown of American Politics*. Princeton: Princeton University Press.

Gotz, N. (2015) '"Moral Economy": Its Conceptual History and Analytical Prospects', *Journal of Global Ethics*, 11 (2): 147–162, DOI: 10.1080/17449626.2015.1054556

Green, C. (1990) *Bonhoeffer: A Theology of Sociality*, revised edition. Michigan: Wm. B. Erdmans Publishing Co.

Green, David (2008) *When Children Kill Children: Penal Populism and Political Culture*. Oxford: Oxford University Press.

Greenberg, I., and Pyszczynski, T. (1985) 'Compensatory Self-Inflation: A Response to the Threat to Self-Regard of Public Failure', *Journal for the Society of Personality and Social Psychology*, 49: 273–280.

Greene, J. (2014) 'New Directions in Policing: Balancing Prediction and Meaning in Police Research', *Justice Quarterly*, 31 (3): 193–228.

Grenz, S. (1990) *Reason for Hope: The Systematic Theology of Wolfhart Pannenberg*. Oxford: Oxford University Press.

Grierson, J. (2021) 'Ministers Criticised for Plans to Create 500 New UK Prison Places for Women'. *The Guardian* 23 January 2021.

Habermas, J. (1973) *Legitimation Crisis*. Boston: Beacon Press.

Hall, Stuart (1980) *Drifting into a Law and Order Society* London: Cobden Trust.

Hammond, J. L. (1973) 'Two Sources of Error in Ecological Correlation'. *American Sociological Review*, 38: 764–777.

Harlan, V. (2004) *What Is Art? Conversations with Joseph Beuys*. Forest Row, East Sussex: Claireview Books.

Harlow, R. E., Darley, J. M., and Robinson, P. H. (1995) 'The Severity of Intermediate Penal Sanctions: A Psychophysical Scaling Approach for Obtaining Community Perceptions', *Journal of Quantitative Criminology*, 11 (1): 71–95.

Harrendorf, S. (2017) 'Sentencing Thresholds in German Criminal Law and Practice: Legal and Empirical Aspects', *Criminal Law Forum*, 28 (3): 501–540.

Harris, N. (2001) 'Shaming and Shame: Regulating Drink-Driving' in A. Eliza et al., *Shame Management through Reintegration*. Victoria: Cambridge University Press.

Harris, N., Walgrave, L., and Braithwaite, J. (2004) 'Emotional Dynamics in Restorative Conferences', *Theoretical Criminology*, 8: 191–210.

Harrison, T. (2000) *Bion, Rickman, Foulkes and the Northfield Experiments: Advancing on a Different Front*. London: Jessica Kingsley.

Hart, H. L. A. (1963) *Law, Liberty and Morality*. London: Oxford University Press.

Hawken, A., and Kleiman, M. (2009) *Managing Drug-Involved Probationers with Swift and Certain Sanctions: Evaluating Hawaii's HOPE. Evaluation Report*. NCJ 229023. Washington DC: National Institute of Justice.

Hawkins, J. D., and Catalano Jr., R. F. (1992) *Communities that Care: Action for Drug Abuse Prevention*. Jossey-Bass.

Hay, C. (1996) *Re-Stating Social and Political Change*. Buckingham: Open University Press.

Hay, A., and Stirling, A. (1998) 'Practice Note: Women Need Women', *Probation Journal*, 45 (1): 36–38.

Hayes, D. J. (2016) 'Penal Impact: Towards a More Intersubjective Measurement of Penal Severity', *Oxford Journal of Legal Studies*, 36 (4): 724–750.

Hedderman, C. (2004) 'Why Are More Women Being Sentenced to Custody?' in G. McIvor (ed.) *Women Who Offend*. London: Jessica Kingsley.

Hedderman, C., Palmer, E., Hollin, C., Gunby, C., Shelton, N., and Askari, M. (2008) *Implementing Services for Women Offenders and Those 'At Risk' of Offending: Action Research with Together Women*. Ministry of Justice, August 2008.

Hedderman, C., Gunby, C., and Shelton, N. (2011) 'What Women Want: The Importance of Qualitative Approaches in Evaluating Work with Women Offenders', *Criminology and Criminal Justice*, 11 (1): 3–19.

Heinz, W. (2005) 'Kriminalprävention auf justizieller Ebene: Hilft weniger mehr? Alternativen zu "klassischen" Sanktionen – Erfahrungen aus Deutschland', Paper given at the International Conference 'Kriminalität und Kriminalprävention in Ländern des Umbruchs', 9–14 April 2005, Baku, Azerbaijan. http://www.uni-konstanz.de/rtf/kis/Heinz_Alternativen_zu_klassischen_Sanktionen.pdf

Henry, D., Gorman-Smith, D., Schoeny, M., and Tolan, P. (2014) 'Neighborhood Matters'. Assessment of Neighborhood Social Processes. *American Journal of Community Psychology*, 54: 187–204.

Her Majesty's Inspectorate of Prisons for Scotland (1982) *Report on HM Special Unit Barlinnie*. Edinburgh: Scottish Home and Health Department.

Her Majesty's Inspectorate of Prisons for Scotland (1986) *Report on HM Special Unit Barlinnie*. Edinburgh: Scottish Home and Health Department

Her Majesty's Inspectorate of Probation.(HMIP) (1996) *Report on Women Offenders and Probation Service Provision for Women Offenders*. London: Home Office.

Hirschman, A. (2013) 'Political Economics and Possibilism' in J. Adelman (ed.) *The Essential Hirschman*. Princeton: Princeton University Press, pp. 1–34.

Hitlin, S., and Elder, G. H. (2007) 'Time, Self and the Curiously Abstract Concept of Agency', *Sociological Theory*, 25: 170–191.

HMCIP (1992) *Report on HM Prison Long Lartin [13–18 January 1992]* London: The Stationery Office.

HM Chief Inspector of Prisons (HMCIP) (2000) *Inspection of Close Supervision Centres: August–September 1999: A Thematic Review by HM Chief Inspector of Prisons for England and Wales*. HM Inspectorate of Prisons.

HMIC (2014) *State of Policing: The Annual Assessment of Policing in England and Wales 2012/3*. London: Her Majesty's Inspectorate of Constabulary.

https://pure.southwales.ac.uk/files/1345742/report.pdf

Hobsbawm, E. (1994) *Age of Extremes: The Short Twentieth Century, 1914–1991*. London: Abacus.

Hogg, Russell (2012) 'Punishment and "The People": Rescuing Populism from Its Critics' in K. Carrington et al (eds) *Crime, Justice and Social Democracy: International Perspectives*. London: Palgrave Macmillan.

Hollin, C., and Palmer, E. (2006) 'Criminogenic Need and Women Offenders: A Critique of the Literature', *Legal and Criminological Psychology*, 11 (2): 179–195.

Hollis, M. (1998) *Trust within Reason*. Cambridge: Cambridge University Press.

Hollis, M. (2002) *The Philosophy of Social Science*, revised edition. Cambridge: Cambridge University Press.

Hollis, M., Felson, M., and Welsh, B. (2013) 'The Capable Guardian in Routine Activities Theory: A Theoretical and Conceptual Reappraisal', *Crime Prevention & Community Safety*, 15: 65–79.

Holloway, K., and Brookman, F. (2010) *An Evaluation of the Women's Turnaround Project*.

Holmes, L. (1993) *The End of Communist Power: Anti-Corruption Campaigns and Legitimation Crisis*. Cambridge, UK: Polity Press.

Holmes, J. (2003) *John Bowlby and Attachment Theory*. Abingdon: Routledge.

Home Office (1968) *Advisory Council on the Penal System (1968) The Regime for Prisoners in Conditions of Maximum Security (The Radzinowicz Report)* London: HMSO.

Home Office (1984) *Managing the Long-Term Prison System (The Control Review Committee Report)* London: HMSO.

Home Office (1987) *Special Units for Long Term Prisoners: A Report by the Research and Advisory Group on the Long Term Prison System*. London: HMSO.

Home Office (1990) *Crime, Justice and Protecting the Public*. Cm. 965. London: H.M. Stationery Office.

Home Office (1991) *Prison Disturbances April 1990: Report of an Inquiry by the Rt. Hon. Lord Justice Woolf (Parts I and II) and his Honour Judge Stephen Tumim (Part II)*. London: HMSO.

Home Office (2000), *The Government's Strategy for Women Offenders*. London: HMSO.

Hörnle, T. (1999) *Tatproportionale Strafzumessung*. Berlin: Duncker & Humblot.

Hope, T., and Sparks, R. (eds) (2000) *Crime, Risk and Insecurity: Law and Order in Everyday Life*. London: Routledge.

Hoppe, R. (1999) 'Policy Analysis, Science and Politics: From "Speaking Truth to Power" to "Making Sense Together"', *Science and Public Policy*, 26 (3): 201–210.

Hughes R. (1991) *The Shock of the New: Art and the Century of Change*. London: Thames and Hudson.

Hurwitz, S., and Christiansen, K. (1983) *Criminology*. London: George Allen & Unwin.

Hutton, Neil (2005) 'Beyond Populist Punitiveness', *Punishment & Society*, 7 (3): 243–258.

Hutton, Neil (2008) 'Institutional Mechanisms for Incorporating the Public' in A. Freiberg and K. Gelb (eds) *Penal Populism, Sentencing Councils and Sentencing Policy*. Annandale: Hawkins Press, pp. 205–223.

Indermaur, David (2008) 'Dealing the Public In: Challenges for a Transparent and Accountable Sentencing Policy' in A. Freiberg and K. Gelb (eds) *Penal Populism, Sentencing Councils and Sentencing Policy*. Annandale: Hawkins Press, pp. 45–67.

Inspire (2017) *Re-offending behaviour after participation in the Brighton Women's Centre Inspire programme*. Ministry of Justice, April 2017. https://assets.publishing.service.gov.uk/government/uploads/system/uploads/attachment_data/file/608283/brighton-womens-centre-report.pdf

Institute for Criminal Policy Research, School of Law, King's College, London (2009) *Statistics on Women and the Criminal Justice System*. https://lx.iriss.org.uk/sites/default/files/resources/women-criminal-justice-system-07-08.pdf

Irwin-Rogers, K., and Roberts, J. V. (2019) 'Swimming Against the Tide: The Suspended Sentence Order in England and Wales, 2000–2017', *Law and Contemporary Problems*, 82 (1): 137–162.

ISIS (2012) *ISIS Women's Centre and the Nine Lessons of Desistance*. Gloucester: Nelson Trust. http://www.isiswomenscentre.com/

Jackson, J., B. Bradford, M. Hough, A. Myhill, P. Quinton, and T. Tyler (2012a) 'Why Do People Comply with the Law? Legitimacy and the Influence of Legal Institutions', *British Journal of Criminology*, 52 (6): 1051–1071.

Jackson, J., Bradford, B., Stanko, E. A., and Hohl, K. (2012b) *Just Authority? Trust in the Police in England and Wales* . Oxford: Routledge.

Jacobs, J. (2001) *Choosing Character: Responsibility for Virtue and Vice*. Ithaca: Cornell University Press.

Jacobs, J. (2002) *Dimensions of Moral Theory: An Introduction to Metaethics and Moral Psychology*. Malden, MA: Blackwell.

Jacobs, J. (2004) *Aristotle's Virtues: Nature, Knowledge, and Human Good*. New York: Peter Lang.

Jacobs, J. (2013) 'The Fact/Value Distinction and the Social Sciences', *Society*, 50: 560–569.

Jacobs, J. (2016) 'Character, Punishment and the Liberal Order' in A. Masala and J. Webber (eds) *From Personality to Virtue: Essays in the Philosophy of Character*, Oxford: Oxford University Press, pp. 9–34.

Jeffrey, R. (2002) *Glasgow's Hard Men*. Edinburgh: Black and White Publishing.

Jeffrey, R. (2009) *The Barlinnie Story*. Edinburgh: Black and White Publishing.

Jeffrey, R. (2013) *Peterhead: The Inside Story of Scotland's Toughest Prison*. Edinburgh: Black and White Publishing.

Jenkins, M. (1987) 'Control Problems in Dispersals' in A. E. Bottoms and R. Light (eds), *Problems of Long-Term Imprisonment*. Aldershot: Gower.

Johnstone, Gerry (2000) 'Penal Policy-Making: Elitist, Populist or Participatory?' *Punishment & Society*, 2 (2): 161–180.

Jolliffe, D., Hedderman, C., Palmer, E., and Hollin, C. (2011) *Re-Offending Analysis of Women Offenders Referred to Together Women (TW) and the Scope to Divert from Custody*. Ministry of Justice, December 2011. https://justiceacademy.org/iShare/Library-UK/women-offenders-referred-together-women.pdf

Jonathan-Zamir, T., and Harpaz, A. (2014) 'Police Understanding of the Foundations of their Legitimacy in the Eyes of the Public: The Case of Commanding Officers in the Israel National Police', *British Journal of Criminology*, 54: 469–489.

Jonathan-Zamir, T., and Weisburd, D. (2013) 'The Effects of Security Threats on Antecedents of Police Legitimacy: Findings from a Quasi-Experiment in Israel', *Journal of Research in Crime and Delinquency*, 50: 3–32.

Jonathan-Zamir, T., Mastrofski, S. D., and Moyal, S. (2013) 'Measuring Procedural Justice in Police–Citizen Encounters', *Justice Quarterly*. DOI:10.1080/07418825.2013.845677

Jones, M. (1968) *Social Psychiatry in Practice: The Idea of a Therapeutic Community*. Harmondsworth: Penguin.

Jones, Richard (2010) 'Populist Leniency, Crime Control and Due Process', *Theoretical Criminology*, 14 (3): 331–347.

Jones, M., Mordecai, M., Rutter, F., and Thomas, L. (1991) 'The Miskin Model of Groupwork with Women Offenders', *Groupwork*, 4 (3): 215–230.

Jost, J., and Major, B. (2001) *The Psychology of Legitimacy: Emerging Perspectives on Ideology, Justice, and Intergroup Relations*. Cambridge: Cambridge University Press.

Judt, T. (2010) *Ill Fares the Land*. Harmondsworth: Penguin.

Karstedt, S. (2013) 'Trusting Authorities: Legitimacy, Trust and Collaboration in Non-Democratic Regimes' in J. Tankebe and A. Liebling (eds) *Legitimacy and Criminal Justice: An International Exploration*. Oxford: Oxford University Press, pp. 127–156.

Kazin, M. (1998) *The Populist Persuasion: An American History*. Ithaca: Cornell University Press.

King, R. D. (1994) 'Order, Disorder and Regimes in The Prison Services of Scotland, and England and Wales' in E. Player and M. Jenkins (eds) *Prisons after Woolf: Reform through Riot*. London: Routledge.

Kleiman, Mark (2009) *When Brute Force Fails: How to Have Less Crime and Less Punishment*. Princeton: Princeton University Press.

Knight, J., and Johnson, J. (2014) *The Priority of Democracy: The Political Consequences of Pragmatism*. Princeton: Princeton University Press.

Koestler, A. (1964) *The Act of Creation*. London: Hutchinson

Kornhauser, R. R. (1978) *Social Sources of Delinquency*. Chicago: University of Chicago Press.

Krief, J-P. (2002) *La Rage et le Reve Condamnes*. Paris: KS Films.

Kronman, A. (1983) *Max Weber*. London: Edward Arnold Publishers Ltd.

Lacey, Nicola (2008) *The Prisoners' Dilemma: Political Economy and Punishment in Contemporary Democracies*. Cambridge, UK: Cambridge University Press,

Laclau, Ernesto (2007) *On Populist Reason*. London: Verso

Laidlaw, J. (2014) *The Subject of Virtue: An Anthropology of Ethics and Freedom*. Cambridge: Cambridge University Press.

Laidlaw, J. (2017) 'Ethics/Morality'. In F. Stein (ed) *The Cambridge Encyclopedia of Anthropology* 1–24.

Lamb, M. C. (2015) 'A Return to Rehabilitation: Mandatory Minimum Sentencing in an Era of Mass Incarceration', *Journal of Legislation*, 41 (1): 126–150.

Lambek, M., Das, V., Fassin, D., and Keane, W. (2015) *Four Lectures in Ethics: Anthropological Perspectives*. Chicago: HAU Books.

Lanctot, N., and Smith, C. a. (2001) 'Sexual Activity, Pregnancy, and Deviance in a Representative Urban Sample of African American Girls', *Journal of Youth and Adolescence*, 30: 349–372.

Lappi-Seppala, Tapio (2008) 'Explaining National Differences in the Use of Imprisonment', *Japanese Journal of Sociological Criminology*, 33: 93–120.

Lappi-Seppälä, T. (2019) 'Community Sanctions as Substitutes to Imprisonment in the Nordic Countries', *Law and Contemporary Problems*, 82 (1): 17–50.

Lart, R., Pantazis, C., Pemberton, S., Turner, W., and Almedia, C. (2008) *Interventions Aimed at Reducing Re-Offending in Female Offenders: A Rapid Evidence Assessment (REA)*. Ministry of Justice Research Series 8/08 May 2008.

Lasch, C. (1991) *The True and Only Heaven: Progress and Its Critics*. New York: Norton.

Latimer, J., Dowden, C., and Muise, D. (2005) 'The Effectiveness of Restorative Justice Practices: A Meta-Analysis', *The Prison Journal*, 85: 127–144.

Latour, B. (2004) *Politics of Nature: How to Bring the Sciences into Democracy*. Cambridge: Cambridge University Press.

Laub, J. H., and Sampson, R. J. (2003) *Shared Beginnings, Divergent Lives*. Cambridge, MA: Harvard University Press.

Law Reform Commission (Ireland) (2017) *Issues Paper: Suspended Sentences*. LRC IP 12-2017. Dublin: Law Reform Commission.

Laycock, G. (2013) 'Happy Birthday?' *Policing*, 6 (2): 101–108.

Laycock, G., and Tilley, N. (2002) *Working Out What to Do: Evidence-Based Crime Reduction. Crime Reduction Series Research Paper 11*. London: Home Office.

Leclerc, C., and Tremblay, P. (2016) 'Looking at Penalty Scales: How Judicial Actors and the General Public Judge Penal Severity', *Canadian Journal of Criminology and Criminal Justice*, 58 (3): 354–384.

Lichtenfels, P. (2011) 'Thoughts on the First Production' in T. McGrath and J. Boyle, *The Hard Man*. Edinburgh: Capercaille Press.

Liebling, A. (1992) *Suicides in Prison*. London: Routledge.

Liebling, A. (1999) 'Doing Research in Prison: Breaking the Silence', *Theoretical Criminology*, 3 (2): 147–173.

Liebling, A. (2000) 'Prison Officers, Policing and the Use of Discretion', *Theoretical Criminology*, 4 (3): 333–357.

Liebling, A. (2001) 'Policy and Practice in the Management of Disruptive Prisoners: Incentives and Earned Privileges, the Spurr Report and Close Supervision Centres' in E. Clare and A. K. Bottomley (assisted by A. Grounds, C. Hammond, A. Liebling, and C. Taylor) *An Evaluation of Close Supervision Centres*, Home Office Research Study: 219, London: Home Office.

Liebling, A. (2004) *Prisons and Their Moral Performance*. Oxford: Oxford University Press.

Liebling, A. (2008a) 'Incentives and Earned Privileges Revisited: Fairness, Discretion and the Quality of Prison Life', *Journal of Scandinavian Studies in Criminology and Crime Prevention*, 9: 25–41.

Liebling, A. (2008b) 'Why Prison Staff Culture Matters' in J. M. Byrne, D. Hummer, and F. S. Taxman (eds) *The Culture of Prison Violence*. Boston: Allyn and Bacon Publishing, pp. 105–122.

Liebling, A. (2011a) 'Distinctions and Distinctiveness in the Work of Prison Officers: Legitimacy and Authority Revisited', *European Journal of Criminology*, 8: 484–499.

Liebling, A. (2011b) 'Moral Performance, Inhuman and Degrading Treatment, and Prison Pain', *Punishment and Society*, 13 (5): 530–550.

Liebling, A. (2013) '"Legitimacy under Pressure" in High Security Prisons', in J. Tankebe and A. Liebling (eds) *Legitimacy and Criminal Justice: An International Exploration*. Oxford: Oxford University Press.

Liebling, A. (2014) 'Postscript: Integrity and Emotion in Prisons Research', *Qualitative Inquiry*, 20 (4): 481–486.

Liebling, A. (2015a) 'Appreciative Inquiry, Generative Theory, and the "Failed State" Prison' in J. Miller and W. Palacios (eds) *Advances in Criminological Theory*. Transaction Publishers, pp. 251–270.

Liebling, A. (2015b) 'Description at the Edge: I-It/I-Thou Relations and Action in Prisons Research', *International Journal for Crime, Justice and Social Democracy*, 4: 18–32.

Liebling, A. (2016) 'High Security Prisons in England and Wales: Principles and Practice' in Y. Jewkes, J. Bennett, and B. Crewe (eds) *The Handbook on Prisons*, 2nd edition. London: Routledge, pp. 477–496.

Liebling, A. (2020) 'The Changing "Regime of the Custodians": Visions of Order and Authority in High Security Prisons in England and Wales, 1988–2019' in B. Crewe, M. Halsey, and A. Goldsmith (eds) *Revisiting the Society of Captives*. Oxford: Oxford University Press.

Liebling, A., with H. Arnold (2004) *Prisons and Their Moral Performance: A Study of Values, Quality and Prison Life*. Oxford: Oxford University Press.

Liebling, A., and Arnold, H. (2012) 'Social Relationships Between Prisoners in a Maximum Security Prison: Violence, Faith, and the Declining Nature of Trust', *Journal of Criminal Justice*, 40 (5): 413–424.

Liebling, A., and Crewe, B. (2012) 'Prisons beyond the New Penology: The Shifting Moral Foundations of Prison Management' in J. Simon and R. Sparks (eds), *The SAGE Handbook of Punishment and Society*. London: SAGE Publications Ltd.

Liebling, A., and Crewe, B. (2016) 'Why Moral Values Matter' in R. van Eijk and T. de Wit (eds) *For Justice and Mercy: International Reflections on Prison Chaplaincy*. Oiserwijk: Wolf Legal Publishers.

Liebling, A., and Kant, D. (2016) 'The Two Cultures: Correctional Officers and Key Differences in Institutional Climate.' *The Oxford Handbook of Prisons and Imprisonment. Oxford Handbooks Online.*

Liebling, A., and Williams, R. J. (2018) 'The New Subversive Geranium: Some Notes on the Management of Additional Troubles in Maximum Security Prisons', *The British Journal of Sociology*, 69 (4): 1194–1219.

Liebling, A., Arnold, H., and Straub, C. (2011) *An Exploration of Staff-Prisoner Relationships at HMP Whitemoor: Twelve Years On*. London: National Offender Management Service.

Liebling, A., Elliott, C., and Arnold, A. (2001) 'Transforming the Prison: Romantic Optimism or Appreciative Realism?' *Criminal Justice*, 1 (2): 161–180.

Liebling, A., Maruna, S., and McAra, L. (eds) (2017) *The Oxford Handbook of Criminology*, 6th edition. Oxford: Oxford University Press.

Liebling, A., Price, D., and Elliott, C. (1999a) 'Appreciative Inquiry and Relationships in Prison', *Punishment & Society*, 1, 71–98.

Liebling, A., Williams, R. J., and Lieber, E. (2020) 'More Mind Games: How "the Action" and "the Odds" Have Changed in Prison', *The British Journal of Criminology*, azaa046, https://doi.org/10.1093/bjc/azaa046

Liebling, A., Armstrong, R., Williams, R. J., and Bramwell, R. (2015) *Locating Trust in a Climate of Fear: Religion, Moral Status, Prisoner Leadership, and Risk in Maximum Security Prisons—Key Findings from an Innovative Study*. Prisons Research Centre, Institute of Criminology: University of Cambridge.

Liebling, A., Laws, B., Lieber, E., Auty, K., Schmidt, B.E., Crewe, B., Gardom, J., Kant, D., and Morey, M. (2019) 'Are Hope and Possibility Achievable in Prison?' *Howard Journal of Crime and Justice*, 58: 104–126.

Liebling, A., Muir, G., Rose, G., and Bottoms, A. E. (1999b) *Incentives and Earned Privileges for Prisoners: An Evaluation*, Home Office Research Findings *No.* 87. London: Home Office.

Liebling, A., Tait, S., Stiles, A., and Durie, L. (2005) 'Revisiting Prison Suicide: The Role of Fairness and Distress' in A. Liebling and S. Maruna (eds), *The Effects of Imprisonment*. Cullompton: Willan.

Liebmann, M. (2000) 'The Arts Therapies' in B. Gates, J. Gear and J.Wray (eds) *Behavioural Distress: Concepts and Strategies*. London and Edinburgh: Bailliere Tindall/Royal College of Nursing.

Light, R. (1985) 'The Special Unit—Barlinnie Prison', *Prison Service Journal*, October, 14–17.

Loader, I. (2006) 'Fall of the "Platonic Guardians": Liberalism, Criminology and Political Responses to Crime in England and Wales', *British Journal of Criminology*, 46 (4): 561–586.

Loader, I., and Sparks, R. (2004) 'For an Historical Sociology of Crime Policy in England and Wales since 1968', *Critical Review of International Social and Political Philosophy*, 7 (2): 5–32.

Loader, I., and Sparks, R. (2011) *Public Criminology?* Abingdon: Routledge.

Loader, I., and Sparks, R. (2012a) 'Situating Criminology: On the Production and Consumption of Knowledge About Crime and Justice' in M. Maguire, R. Morgan, and R. Reiner (eds), *The Oxford Handbook of Criminology*, 5th edn. Oxford: Oxford University Press.

Loader, I., and Sparks, R. (2012b) 'Beyond Lamentation: Towards a Democratic Egalitarian Politics of Crime and Justice' in T. Newburn and J. Peay (eds) *Policing: Politics, Culture and Control*. Oxford: Hart.

Loader, I., and Sparks, R. (2013a) 'Unfinished Business: Legitimacy, Crime Control and Democratic Politics' in A. Liebling and J. Tankebe (eds) *Legitimacy and Criminal Justice: An International Exploration*. Oxford: Oxford University Press.

Loader, I., and Sparks, R. (2013b) 'Knowledge Politics and Penal Politics in Europe' in T. Daems, S. Snacken, and D. van Zyl Smit (eds) *European Penology?* Oxford: Hart.

Loader, I., and Sparks, R. (2016) 'Ideologies and Crime Control', *Global Crime*, 17 (3–4): 314–330.

Loeber, R., and Wikström P.-O. H. (1993) 'Individual Pathways to Crime in Different Types of Neighborhoods' in D. P. Farrington, R. J. Sampson, and P.-O. H. Wikström (eds) *Integrating Individual and Ecological Aspects of Crime*, BRÅ Report 1993: 1. Stockholm: Allmänna Förlaget.

Ludema, J. D., Wilmot, T. B., and Srivastva, S. (1997) 'Organizational Hope: Reaffirming the Constructive Task of Social and Organizational Inquiry', *Human Relations*, 50 (8): 1015–1052.

Luhmann, N. (1979) *Trust and Power*. New York: Wiley.

Luhmann, N. (1990) 'Familiarity, Confidence, Trust: Problems and Alternatives' in D. Gambetta (ed) *Trust: Making and Breaking Cooperative Relations*. Oxford: Blackwell.

Lum, C., Hibdon, J., Cave, B., Koper, C., and Merola, L. (2011) 'License Plate Reader (LPR) Police Patrols in Crime Hot Spots: An Experimental Evaluation in Two Adjacent Districts', *Journal of Experimental Criminology*, 7: 321–345.

Lum, C., and Koper, C. (2017) *Evidence-based Policing: Translating Research into Practice*. Oxford: Oxford University Press.

Lynam, D. R., Caspi, A., Moffitt, T. E., Wikström, P.-O. H., Loeber, R., and Novak, S. (2000) The Interaction Between Impulsivity and Neighborhood Context on Offending: The Effects of Impulsivity are Stronger in Poorer Neighborhoods. *Journal of Abnormal Psychology*, 109: 563–574.

Macdonald, D., and Sim, J. (1978) *Scottish Prisons and the Special Unit*. Glasgow: Scottish Council for Civil Liberties.

MacIntyre, A. (1981) *After Virtue: A Study in Moral Theory*. London: Duckworth.

MacIntyre, A. (1999) *Dependent Rational Animals: Why Human Beings Need the Virtues*. Chicago: Open Court.

MacKenzie J. (1981) *A Sense of Freedom*. London: Channel 4 films

MacMillan J. (2011) 'Theatre Reviews: The Hard Man'. *The Scotsman* 8 April 2011.

Mair, G. (2011) 'The Community Order in England and Wales: Policy and Practice', *Probation Journal*, 58 (3): 215–232.

Mair, G., Cross, N., and Taylor, S. (2007) *The Use and Impact of the Community Order and the Suspended Sentence Order*. London: Centre for Crime and Justice Studies.

Mair, G., Cross, N., and Taylor, S. (2008) *The Community Order and the Suspended Sentence Order: The Views and Attitudes of Sentencers*. London: Centre for Crime and Justice Studies.

Marinos, V. (2005) 'Thinking about Penal Equivalents', *Punishment and Society*, 7 (4): 441–455.

Matthews, Roger (2005) 'The Myth of Punitiveness', *Theoretical Criminology*, 9 (2): 175–201

Maxwell, C. (2017) 'Non-Custodial Dispositions and the Politics of Sentencing', *Criminal Law Forum*, 28 (3): 541–562.

McArthur, A., and Long, H. K. (1935) *No Mean City*. Neville Spearman.

McBarnet, D. (2004) *Crime, Compliance and Control*. Farnham: Ashgate.

McClintock, F. (1982) 'The Penological Significance of the Special Unit' in C. Carrell and J. Laing (eds) *The Special Unit: Its Evolution through Art*. Glasgow: Third Eye Centre.

McGloin, J. M., and Thomas, K. J. (2013) 'Experimental Tests of Criminological Theory' in B. C. Welsh, A. A. Braga, and G. J. N. Bruinsma (eds) *Experimental Criminology: Prospects for Advancing Science and Public Policy*. Cambridge: Cambridge University Press, pp. 15–42.

McGrath, T., and Boyle, J. (1977) *The Hard Man*. Edinburgh: Canongate.

McNee, D. (1983) *McNee's Law*. London: Collins.

McVicar, J. (1974) *McVicar by Himself*. London: Arrow.

Maguire, M., in collaboration with Bennett, T. (1982) *Burglary in a Dwelling*. London: Heinemann.

Manning, P. (2011) *Democratic Policing in a Changing World*. Boulder, CO: Paradigm Press.

Markus, H., and Nurius, P. (1986) 'Possible Selves', *American Psychologist*, 41: 954–969.

Markus, H., and Wurf, E. (1987) 'The Dynamic Self-Concept', *Annual Review of Psychology*, 38: 299–337.

Marshall, T. (1999) *Restorative Justice: An Overview*. Home Office Occasional Paper. London: Home Office.

Martinson, R. (1974) 'What Works? Questions and Answers about Prison Reform', *The Public Interest*, Spring Issue, 22–54.

Maruna, S. (2000) *Making Good*. Washington, DC: American Psychological Association.

Matthews, R. (2010) 'The Construction of "So What?" Criminology: A Realist Analysis', *Crime, Law and Social Change*, 54 (2): 125–140.

Mattingly, C. (2013) 'Moral Selves and Moral Scenes: Narrative Experiments in Everyday Life', *Ethnos*, 78: 301–327.

Mattingly, C. (2014) *Moral Laboratories: Family Peril and the Struggle for a Good Life*. Cambridge: Cambridge University Press.

Maxwell, G., and Morris, A. (2001) 'Family Group Conferences and Reoffending' in A. Morris and G. Maxwell (eds) *Restorative Justice for Juveniles: Conferencing, Mediation and Circles*. Portland, OR: Hart Publishing, pp. 243–266.

Mazerolle, L. W., Eggins, E., and Higginson, A. (2019) *The Role of Randomized Experiments in Developing the Evidence for Evidence-Based Policing*. Presentation to the Drapkin Seminar, Hebrew University, June 2019.

Mazerolle, L. W., Lum, C., and Braga, A. A. (2014) 'Using Experimental Designs to Study Police Interventions' in M. Reisig and R. J. Kane (eds) *Police and Policing*. Oxford: Oxford University Press.

McCold, P. (2004) 'What Is the Role of Community in Restorative Justice Theory and Practice?' in H. Zehr and B. Toews (eds) *Critical Issues in Restorative Justice*. Monsey, NY: Criminal Justice Press, pp. 155–171.

McNeill, F. (2006) 'A Desistance Paradigm for Offender Management', *Criminology and Criminal Justice*, 6 (1): 39–62.

Melossi, D. (2008) *Controlling Crime, Controlling Society: Thinking About Crime in Europe and America*. Cambridge: Polity Press.

Messner, S. F. (2012) 'Morality, Markets and the A.S.C.: 2011 Presidential Address to the American Society of Criminology', *Criminology*, 50: 5–25.

Miller, Lisa (2008) *The Perils of Federalism*. New York: Oxford University Press.

Miller, L. (2013) 'Power to the People: Violent Victimization, Inequality, and Democratic Politics', *Theoretical Criminology*, 17 (3): 283–314.

Mills, C. Wright (1959) *The Sociological Imagination*. Harmondsworth: Penguin.

Ministry of Justice (2009) *Statistics on Women and the Criminal Justice System A Ministry of Justice publication under Section 95 of the Criminal Justice Act 1991*.

Ministry of Justice (2010) *Sentencing Statistics: England and Wales 2009*. Statistics Bulletin. https://assets.publishing.service.gov.uk/government/uploads/system/uploads/attachment_data/file/218034/sentencing-stats2009.pdf

Ministry of Justice (2017) *Offender Management Statistics*. London: Ministry of Justice. https://www.gov.uk/government/collections/offender-management-statistics-quarterly

Ministry of Justice (2018) *Female Offender Strategy 2018* (Cm 9642). London: Ministry of Justice. https://www.gov.uk/government/publications/female-offender-strategy.

Ministry of Justice (2021) Strengthening probation, building confidence. https://www.gov.uk/guidance/strengthening-probation-building-confidence.

Misak, C. (2000) *Truth, Politics, Morality: Pragmatism and Deliberation*. London: Routledge.

Mistry, T. (1989) 'Establishing a Feminist Model of Groupwork in the Probation Service', *Groupwork*, 2 (2): 145–158.

Misztal, B. A. (1996) *Trust in Modern Societies*. Cambridge: Polity Press.

Misztal, B. A. (2003) *Theories of Social Remembering*. Maidenhead: Open University Press.

Morris, A., and Maxwell, G. (1998) 'Restorative Justice in New Zealand: Family Group Conferences as a Case Study', *Western Criminology Review*, 1 (1): 1–17.

Morris, A., and Maxwell, G. (2000) 'The Practice of Family Group Conferences in New Zealand: Assessing the Place, Potential and Pitfalls of Restorative Justice' in

A. Crawford and J. Goodey (eds) *Integrating a Victim Perspective within Criminal Justice*. Aldershot: Ashgate, ch. 10.

Morse, J. M. (2007) 'Sampling in Grounded Theory' in A. Bryant and K. Charmaz (eds) *The Sage Handbook of Grounded Theory*. Thousand Oaks, CA: Sage, pp. 229–244.

Mortimore, G. W. (ed.) (1971) *Weakness of Will*. London: Macmillan.

Muir, W. K. (1977) *Police: Streetcorner Politicians*. Chicago: University of Chicago Press.

Mulgan, G. (2007) *Good and Bad Power: The Ideals and Betrayals of Government*. London: Penguin.

Muller, J-W (2016) *What Is Populism?* Philadelphia: University of Pennsylvania Press.

Mulvey, E. P., and Schubert, C. A. (2016) 'Issues to Consider in Future Work on Desistance from Adolescence to Early Adulthood: Observations from the Pathways to Desistance Study' in J. M. Shapland, S. Farrall, and A. E. Bottoms (eds) *Global Perspectives on Desistance: Reviewing What we Know and Looking to the Future*. London: Routledge.

Murdoch, I. (1970) *The Sovereignty of Good*. London: Routledge.

Murphy, K., and Cherney, A. (2012) 'Understanding Cooperation with Police in a Diverse Society', *British Journal of Criminology*, 52: 181–201.

Murphy, T., and Whitty, N. (2013) 'Making History: Academic Criminology and Human Rights', *British Journal of Criminology*, 53 (4): 568–587.

National Offender Management Service (2008) *National Framework for Female Offenders. The Offender Management Guide to Working with Women Offenders*. London: Ministry of Justice, May 2008. https://webarchive.nationalarchives.gov.uk/20081013091058/http://noms.justice.gov.uk/news-publications-events/publications/guidance/OM-Guide-Women

National Offender Management Service (2012) *A Distinct Approach: A Guide to Working with Female Offenders*. London: Ministry of Justice.

National Research Council (2014) *The Growth of Incarceration in the United States: Exploring Causes and Consequences*. Washington, DC: The National Academic Press.

Nelken, D. (2010) *Comparative Criminal Justice*. London: SAGE.

Nellis, M. (2002) 'Prose and Cons: Offender Autobiography, Penal Reform and Probation Training', *Howard Journal*, 41 (5): 434–468.

Nellis, M. (2011) 'Prose and Cons: British Prisoner Autobiography 1950–2009' in L. Cheliotis (ed) *The Arts of Imprisonment: Control, Resistance and Empowerment*. Chichester: Wiley.

Nelund, A. (2014) "Troubling Publics: A Feminist Analysis of Public Criminology', *Radical Criminology*, 4: 57–84.

New Economics Foundation (2008) *Unlocking Value: How We All Benefit from Investing in Alternatives to Prison for Women Offenders*. London: NEF. https://neweconomics.org/uploads/files/6533e0a823956802b3_10m6buwft.pdf

Neyroud, P. W. (2011) *Review of Police Leadership and Training*. London: Home Office.

Neyroud, P. W. (2017) *Learning to Field Test in Policing: Using an Analysis of Completed Randomised Controlled Trials Involving the Police to Develop a*

Grounded Theory of the Factors Contributing to High Levels of Integrity in Police Field Experiments. PhD Dissertation, University of Cambridge, at https://www.repository.cam.ac.uk/bitstream/handle/1810/268177/Neyroud-2017-PhD.pdf (accessed 2 November 2021).

Neyroud, P. W. (2019) 'De-Policing and Homicide: Applying evidence and ethics to the de-policing debate', *Criminology and Public Policy*, 18 (1): 81–88.

Neyroud, P. W., and Sherman, L. W. (2013) 'Dialogue and Dialectic: Police Legitimacy and the New Professionalism' in J. Tankebe and A. Liebling (eds) *Legitimacy and Criminal Justice: An International Exploration*. Oxford: Oxford University Press.

Neyroud, P. W., and Slothower, M. (2013) *Operation Turning Point: An Interim Report. Unpublished report*. Cambridge: Institute of Criminology.

Neyroud, P. W., and Weisburd, D. (2014) 'Transforming the Police through Science: Some New Thoughts on the Controversy and Challenge of Translation', *Translational Criminology*, Spring, 16–18.

Nicholles, N., and Whitehead, S. (2012) *Women's Community Services: A Wise Commission*. New Economics Foundation. http://www.womencentredworking.com/wpcontent/uploads/2014/08/Nef-report-Womens-Community-Services-A-Wise-Commission.pdf

Norman, R. J. (2005) 'Prescriptivism' in T. Honderich (ed.) *The Oxford Companion to Philosophy*, 2nd edition. Oxford: Oxford University Press.

Nix, J., and Wolfe, S. E. (2016) 'The Impact of Negative Publicity on Police Self-Legitimacy', *Justice Quarterly*, 34: 84–108.

Nutley, S. M., Walter, I., and Davies, H. T. O. (2007) *Using Evidence: How Research Can Inform Public Service*. Bristol: Policy Press.

Oliver, C. (1982a) 'Tom Galloway' in C. Carrell and J. Laing (eds), *The Special Unit: Its Evolution through Art*. Glasgow: Third Eye Centre.

Oliver, C. (1982b) 'Bob Brodie' in C. Carrell and J. Laing (eds) *The Special Unit: Its Evolution through Art*. Glasgow: Third Eye Centre.

Oliver, C. (1982c) 'Art at the Special Unit' in C. Carrell and J. Laing (eds) *The Special Unit: Its Evolution through Art*. Glasgow: Third Eye Centre.

Oliver, C. (1982d) 'Hugh Collins' in C. Carrell and J. Laing (eds) *The Special Unit: Its Evolution through Art*. Glasgow: Third Eye Centre.

O'Malley, P. (2008) 'Neo-Liberalism and Risk in Criminology' in T. Anthony and C. Cuneen (eds) *The Critical Criminology Companion*. Sydney: Federation Press, pp. 55–67.

O'Malley, P. (2010) *Crime and Risk*. London: Sage.

O'Malley, T. (2018) '"That measure of wise clemency": Defending the Suspended Sentence'. *Irish Criminal Law Journal*, 28 (2): 39–53.

O'Neill, O. (2002) *A Question of Trust: The BBC Reith Lectures 2002*. Cambridge: Cambridge University Press.

O'Neill, O. (2009) 'Perverting Trust'. *The clare hall ashby lecture of*.

Oatham, E., and F. Simon. 1972. 'Are Suspended Sentences Working?' *New Society* 3 August, pp. 233–235.

Orme, J. (1992) 'Women and the Criminal Justice Act', *Probation Journal*, 39 (2): 78–81.

Osborough, W. N. (1982) 'A Damocles' Sword Guaranteed Irish: The Suspended Sentence in the Republic of Ireland'. *Irish Jurist*, 17 (2): 221–256.

Papachristos, A. V., Meares, T. L., and Fagan, J. (2012) 'Why Do Criminals Obey the Law? The Influence of Legitimacy and Social Networks on Active Gun Offenders', *Journal of Criminal Law and Criminology*, 102: 397–440.

Park, R. E. (1961) 'The City. Suggestions for the Investigation of Human Behavior in Urban Environment' in G. A. Theodorson (ed) *Studies in Human Ecology*. Evanston, IL: Row, Peterson and Company.

Paternoster, R. (2017) 'Happenings, Acts and Actions: Articulating the Meaning and Implications of Human Agency for Criminology', *Journal of Developmental and Life-Course Criminology*, 3: 350–372.

Paternoster, R., and Bushway, S. (2009) 'Desistance and the "Feared Self": Toward an Identity Theory of Criminal Desistance', *Journal of Criminal Law & Criminology*, 99: 1103–1156.

Paternoster, R., Brame, R., Bachman, R., and Sherman, L. (1997) 'Do Fair Procedures Matter? The Effects of Procedural Justice on Spousal Assault', *Law & Society Review*, 31: 163–204.

Paternoster, R., Bachman, R., Kerrison, E., O'Connell, D., and Smith, L. (2015) 'Human Agency and Explanations of Desistance: Arguments for a Rational Choice Theory', *Journal of Developmental and Life-Course Criminology*, 1: 209–235.

Paterson, M. H. (1982) 'The Special Unit: An Experience of Learning' in C. Carrell and J. Laing (eds) *The Special Unit: Its Evolution through Art*. Glasgow: Third Eye Centre.

PERF (2014) *Future Trends in Policing*. Washington DC: Police Executive Research Forumss

Pina-Sanchez, J., Gosling, J. P., Chung, H., Bourgeois, E., Geneletti, S., and Marder, I. D. (2019) 'Have the England and Wales Guidelines Affected Sentencing Severity? An Empirical Analysis Using a Scale of Severity and Time-Series Analyses', *British Journal of Criminology*, 59 (4): 979–1001.

Piquero, A., Farrington, D. P., and Blumstein, A. (2007) *Key Issues in Criminal Career Research: New Analyses of the Cambridge Study in Delinquent Development*. Cambridge: Cambridge University Press.

Platt, A. M. (1991) '"If We Know, Then We Must Fight": The Origins of Radical Criminology in the US' in M. Oppenheimer, M. Murray, and R. Levine (eds) *Radical Sociologists and the Movement*. Philadelphia: Temple University Press, pp. 219–232.

Pratt, John (2007) *Penal Populism*. London: Routledge.

Pratt, John (2008) 'Penal Scandal in New Zealand' in A. Freiberg, and K. Gelb (eds) *Penal Populism, Sentencing Councils and Sentencing Policy*. Annandale: Hawkins Press.

Pratt, J., Brown, D., Brown, M., Hallsworth, S., and Morrison, W. (eds) (2005) *The New Punitiveness: Trends, Theories, Perspectives* Collumpton: Willan.

Pratt T. C., and Cullen F. T. (2005) 'Assessing Macro-level Predictors and Theories of Crime: A Meta-analysis', *Crime and Justice*, 32: 373–450.

Putnam, H. (1990) 'A Reconsideration of Deweyian Democracy', *Southern California Law Review*, 63: 1671–1697.

Putnam, R. D. (2000) *Bowling Alone: The Collapse and Revival of American Community*. New York: Touchstone.

Radcliffe, P., Hunter, G., and Vass, R. (2015) *The Development and Impact of Community Service for Women Offenders: An Evaluation*. London: ICPR, Birkbeck College.

Radzinowicz, L. (1999) *Adventures in Criminology*. London: Routledge.

Raynor, P. 2018. 'Back to the Future? The Long View of Probation and Sentencing', *Probation Journal*, 65 (3): 335–347.

Reid, J. (1981) 'Like the Birdman of Alcatraz Without the Birds. Glasgow Herald, 21 February 1981' in *As I Please: The Collected Journalism of Jimmy Reid*. Edinburgh: Mainstream Publishing.

Reiner, R. (2000) *The Politics of the Police*. Oxford: Oxford University Press.

Reiner, R. (2006) 'Beyond Risk: A Lament for Social Democratic Criminology' in D. Hobbs and T. Newburn (eds) *The Politics of Crime Control*. Oxford: Oxford University Press, pp. 7–49.

Reiner, R. (2010) 'New Theories of Policing: A Social Democratic Critique' in D. Downes, D. Hobbs, and T. Newburn (eds), *The Eternal Recurrence of Crime and Control*. Oxford: Oxford University Press, pp. 141–182.

Reiner, R. (2011) *Policing, Popular Culture and Political Economy: Towards a Social Democratic Criminology*. Aldershot: Dartmouth.

Reisig, M. D., Tankebe, J., and Meško, G. (2012) 'Procedural Justice, Police Legitimacy, and Public Cooperation with the Police among Young Slovene Adults', *Journal of Criminology and Security*, 14: 147–164.

Reiss, A. J. (1986) 'Why are Communities Important in Understanding Crime?' in A. J. Reiss and M. Tonry (eds) *Communities and Crime*. Chicago: University of Chicago Press.

Reus-Smit, C. (2007) 'International Crises of Legitimacy', *International Politics*, 44: 157–174.

Rex, S. (2005) *Reforming Community Penalties*. Cullompton: Willan.

Robbins, J., and Sommerschuh, J. (2016) 'Values'. *The Cambridge Encyclopedia of Anthropology* (online)

Roberts, J. (2002) 'Women-Centred: The West Mercia Community-Based Programme for Women Offenders' in P. Carlen (ed.) *Women and Punishment: The Struggle for Justice*. Cullompton: Willan.

Roberts, Julian (2008) 'Sentencing Policy and Practice: The Evolving Role of Public Opinion' in A. Freiberg and K. Gelb (eds) *Penal Populism, Sentencing Councils and Sentencing Policy*. Annandale: Hawkins Press, pp. 15–30.

Roberts, J. V., and Ashworth, A. (2016) 'The Evolution of Sentencing Policy and Practice in England and Wales, 2003–2015', *Crime and Justice*, 45 (1): 307–358.

Roberts, J. V., and Dagan, N. (2019) 'The Evolution of Retributive Punishment: From Static Desert to Responsive Penal Censure' in A. du Bois-Pedain and A. E. Bottoms (eds), *Penal Censure: Engagements Within and Beyond Desert Theory*. Oxford: Bloomsbury, pp. 141–159.

Roberts, J., and de Keijser, J. (2014) 'Democratising Punishment: Sentencing, Community Views and Values', *Punishment and Society*, 16 (4): 474–498.

Roberts, J., and Hough, M. (2005) *Understanding Public Attitudes to Criminal Justice*. Maidenhead: Open University Press.

Roberts, J., Hough, M, Jackson, J., and Gerber, M. (2012) 'Public Opinion towards the Lay Magistracy and the Sentencing Council Guidelines: The Effects of Information on Attitudes' *British Journal of Criminology*

Roberts, J., Stalans, L., Indermaur, D., and Hough, M. (2003) *Penal Populism and Public Opinion*. Oxford: Oxford University Press

Robinson, Paul H. (1997) *Justice, Liability and Blame: Community Views and the Criminal Law*. Boulder, CO: Westview Press.

Robinson, G., and Dominey, J. (2019) 'Probation Reform, the RAR and the Forgotten Ingredient of Supervision', *Probation Journal*, 66 (4): 451–455.

Robinson, G., and McNeill, F. (2010) 'The Dynamics of Compliance with Offender Supervision' in F. McNeill, P. Raynor, and C. Trotter (eds) *Offender Supervision: New Direction in Theory, Research and Practice*. Cullompton: Willan.

Robinson, G., and Shapland, J. (2008) 'Reducing Recidivism: A Task for Restorative Justice?' *British Journal of Criminology*, 48 (3): 337–358.

Robinson, P. H. 1994. 'Desert, Crime Control, Disparity, and Units of Punishment' in R. A. Duff, S. Marshall, R. E. Dobash, and R. P. Dobash (eds), *Penal Theory and Practice. Tradition and Innovation in Criminal Justice*, Manchester: Manchester University Press, pp. 93–107.

Roche, D. (2003) *Accountability in Restorative Justice*. Oxford: Oxford University Press.

Rock, P. (1988) 'The Present State of Criminology in Britain', *The British Journal of Criminology*, 28 (2): 58–69.

Rock, P. (2007) 'Sociological Theories of Crime' in M. Maguire, R. Morgan, and R. Reiner (eds) *The Oxford Handbook of Criminology*, 3rd edition. Oxford: Oxford University Press, pp. 3–42.

Roman, J. K., Reid, S. E., Chalfin, A. J., and Knight, C. R. (2009) 'The DNA Field Experiment: A Randomised Controlled Trial of Using DNA to Solve Property Crimes', *Journal of Experimental Criminology*, 5: 345–369.

Rosanvallon, P. (2008) *Counter-Democracy: Politics in an Age of Distrust*. Cambridge: Cambridge University Press.

Rose, G., and Hamilton, R. (1970) 'The Effects of a Juvenile Liaison Scheme', *British Journal of Criminology*, 10 (1): 2–20.

Rothschild, J. (1977) 'Observation on Legitimacy in Contemporary Europe', *Political Science Quarterly*, 92 (3): 487–501.

Rowan, Mike (2012) 'Democracy and Punishment: A Radical View', *Theoretical Criminology*, 16 (1): 43–62.

Rumgay, J. (2004) 'Scripts for Safer Survival: Pathways Out of Female Crime', *Howard Journal of Crime and Justice*, 43 (4): 405–419.

Runciman, W. G. (1972) *A Critique of Max Weber's Philosophy of Social Science*. Cambridge: Cambridge University Press.

Runciman, W. G. (1983) *A Treatise on Social Theory, vol. 1, The Methodology of Social Theory*. Cambridge: Cambridge University Press.

Ryan, Mick (2003) *Penal Policy and Political Culture in England and Wales*. Winchester: Waterside Press.

Ryan, Mick (2005) 'Engaging with Punitive Attitudes towards Crime and Punishment' in J. Pratt et al (eds) *The New Punitiveness*. Cullompton: Willan.

Ryberg, J., and Roberts, J. (eds) (2014) *Popular Punishment: On the Normative Significance of Public Opinion*. Oxford: Oxford University Press

Rydberg, J., and Terrill, W. (2010) 'The Effect of Higher Education on Police Behavior', *Police Quarterly*, 13 (1): 92–120.

Sabel, C. (2012) 'Dewey, Democracy, and Democratic Experimentalism', *Contemporary Pragmatism*, 9 (2): 35–55.

Sampson, R. J. (1988) 'Local Friendship Ties and Community Attachment in Mass Society: A Multilevel Systemic Model', *American Sociological Review*, 53: 766–779.

Sampson, R. J. (1997) 'Collective Regulation of Adolescent Misbehavior: Validation Results from Eighty Chicago Neighborhoods', *Journal of Adolescent Research*, 12: 227–244.

Sampson, R. (2010) 'Gold Standard Myths: Observations on the Experimental Turn in Quantitative Criminology', *Journal of Quantitative Criminology*, 25: 489–500.

Sampson, R. J. (2012) *Great American City: Chicago and the Enduring Neighborhood Effect*. Chicago: University of Chicago Press.

Sampson, R. J., and Bartusch, D. J. (1998) 'Legal Cynicism and (Subcultural?) Tolerance of Deviance: The Neighborhood Context of Racial Differences', *Law and Society Review*, 32: 777–804.

Sampson, R. J., and Wikström, P.-O. H. (2008) 'The Social Order of Violence in Chicago and Stockholm Neighbourhoods: A Comparative Inquiry' in I. Shapiro and S. Kalyvas, *Order, Conflict and Violence*. Cambridge: Cambridge University Press.

Sampson, R. J., Morenoff, J. D., and Earls, F. (1999) 'Beyond Social Capital: Spatial Dynamics of Collective Efficacy for Children. *American Sociological Review*, 64 (5): 633–660.

Sampson, R. J., Morenoff, J. D., and Gannon-Rowley, T. (2002) 'Assessing "Neighborhood Effects": Social Processes and New Directions in Research', *Annual Review of Sociology*, 28: 443–478.

Sampson, R. J., Raudenbush, S. W., and Earls, F. (1997) 'Neighborhoods and Violent Crime: A Multilevel Study of Collective Efficacy', *Science*, 277 (5328): 918–924.

Sanderson, I. (2009) 'Intelligent Policy-Making for a Complex World: Pragmatism, Evidence and Learning', *Political Studies*, 57: 699–719.

Sarat, A., and Vidmar, N. (1976) 'Public Opinion, the Death Penalty, and the Eighth Amendment: Testing the Marshall Hypothesis', *Wisconsin Law Review*, 171–207.

Savelsberg, J. (1994) 'Knowledge, Domination and Criminal Punishment', *American Journal of Sociology*, 99: 911–943.

Scheff, T. J., and Retzinger, S. M. (2001) *Emotions and Violence: Shame and Rage in Destructive Conflicts*. iUniverse.

Schneider, D. (1950) *The Psychoanalyst and the Artist*. New York: Mentor Books.

Schutz, A. (1962) *The Problem of Social Reality: Collected Papers I*. The Hague: Martinus Nijhoff.

Schwartz, M., Brown, D., and Boseley, L. (2012) *The Promise of Justice Reinvestment*. Available at SSRN: http://dx.doi.org/10.2139/ssrn.2078715

Scottish Government (2008) *Scotland's Choice: Report of the Scottish Prison Commission*. Edinburgh: Scottish Government

Scottish Home and Health Department (1971) *Treatment of Certain Long-term Prisoners and Potentially Violent Prisoners. Report of a Working Party*. Edinburgh: Scottish Home and Health Department.

Scraton, P., Sim, J., and Skidmore, P. (1991) *Prisons under Protest*. Buckingham: Open University Press.

Sebba, L., and Berenblum, T. (2014) 'Victimology and the Sociology of New Disciplines: A Research Agenda', *International Review of Victimology*, 20 (1): 7–30.

Seldon, A. (2009) *Trust: How We Lost It and How We Get It Back*. Biteback Publishing Ltd.

Seligman, A. (1997) *The Problem of Trust*. Princeton, NJ: Princeton University Press.

Sen, A. (2009) *The Idea of Justice*. Harvard University Press.

Sentencing Council (2016) *The Imposition of Community and Custodial Sentences: Definitive Guideline*. London: Sentencing Council.

Sentencing Guidelines Council (2004) *New Sentences: Criminal Justice Act 2003 Guideline*. London: Sentencing Guidelines Council.

Shadish, W. R., Cook, T. D., and Campbell, D. T. (2002) *Experimental and Quasi-Experimental Designs for Generalized Causal Inference*. Belmont, CA: Wadsworth Cengage Learning.

Shapiro, A., and Glicksman, R. (2003) *Risk Regulation at Risk: Restoring a Pragmatic Approach*. Stanford: Stanford University Press.

Shapland, J. (1981) *Between Conviction and Sentence: The Process of Mitigation*. London: Routledge & Kegan Paul.

Shapland, J. (2009) 'Restorative Justice Conferencing in the Context of Community Policing', *Journal of Police Studies*, 2: 119–138.

Shapland, J. M., and Bottoms, A. E. (2011) 'Reflections on Social Values, Offending and Desistance among Young Adult Recidivists', *Punishment and Society*, 13: 256–282.

Shapland, J. M., and Bottoms, A. E. (2017a) 'Desistance from Crime and Implications for Offender Rehabilitation' in A. Liebling, S. Maruna, and L. McAra (eds) *The Oxford Handbook of Criminology*, 6th edition. Oxford: Oxford University Press, pp. 744–766.

Shapland, J. M., and Bottoms, A. E. (2017b) 'Offending and Offence Patterns in the Early Stages of Desistance: A Study of Young Men in England' in A. Blokland and V. van der Geest (eds) *The Routledge International Handbook of Life-Course Criminology*. London: Routledge, pp. 301–323.

Shapland, J., Atkinson, A., Atkinson, H., Dignan, J., Edwards, L., Hibbert, J., Howes, M., Johnstone, J., Robinson, G., and Sorsby, A. (2008) *Does Restorative Justice Affect Reconviction? The Fourth Report from the Evaluation of Three Schemes*. Ministry of Justice Research Series 10/08. https://restorativejustice.org.uk/sites/default/files/resources/files/Does%20restorative%20justice%20affect%20reconviction%20-%20The%20fourth%20report%20from%20the%20evaluation.pdf

Shapland, J., Atkinson, A., Atkinson, H., Chapman, B., Colledge, E., Dignan, J., Howes, M., Johnstone, J., Robinson, G., and Sorsby, A. (2006) *Restorative Justice in Practice: The Second Report from the Evaluation of Three Schemes*. The University of Sheffield Centre for Criminological Research Occasional Paper 2 (on behalf of the Home Office) Sheffield: Faculty of Law. https://www.sheffield.ac.uk/polopoly_fs/1.783!/file/RestorativeJustice2ndReport.pdf.

Shapland, J., Bottoms, A. E., Farrall, S., McNeill, F., Priede, C., and Robinson, G. (2012) *The Quality of Probation Supervision: A Literature Review*. University of Sheffield: Centre for Criminological Research.

Shapland, J., Robinson, G., and Sorsby, A. (2011) *Restorative Justice in Practice*. London: Routledge.

Sharkey, P., and Faber, J. W. (2014) 'Where, When, Why, and For Whom Do Residential Contexts Matter? Moving Away from the Dichotomous Understanding of Neighborhood Effects', *Annual Review of Sociology*, 40: 559–579.

Shaw, C., and McKay, H. (1969) *Juvenile Delinquency and Urban Areas*, 2nd edition. Chicago: University of Chicago Press.

Shepherd, J. P. (2003) 'Explaining Feast or Famine in Randomized Field Trials: Medical Science and Criminology Compared', *Evaluation Review*, 27 (3): 290–315.

Sherman, L. W. (1993) 'Defiance, Deterrence and Irrelevance: A Theory of the Criminal Sanction', *Journal of Research in Crime and Delinquency*, 30: 445–473.

Sherman, L. W. (1998) *Evidence-Based Policing. Ideas in American Policing*. Washington, DC: Police Foundation.

Sherman, L. (2009) 'Evidence and Liberty: The Promise of Experimental Criminology', *Criminology & Criminal Justice*, 9 (1): 5–28.

Sherman, L. W. (2010) 'An Introduction to Experimental Criminology' in A. R. Piquero and D. Weisburd (eds) *Handbook of Quantitative Criminology*. New York: Springer, pp. 399–436.

Sherman, L. W. (2013) 'The Rise of Evidence-Based Policing: Targeting, Testing and Tracking' in M. Tonry (ed.) *Crime and Justice in America 1975–2025*. Chicago: Chicago University Press, pp. 377–451.

Sherman, L. W., Gartin, P. R., and Buerger, M. E. (1989) 'Hot Spots of Predatory Crime: Routine Activities and the Criminology of Place', *Criminology*, 27: 27–55.

Sherman, L., Neyroud, P., and Neyroud, E. (2016) 'The Cambridge Crime Harm Index: Measuring Total Harm from Crime Based on Sentencing Guidelines', *Policing: A Journal of Policy and Practice* 10 (3): 171–183.

Sherman, L. W., and Strang, H. (2007) *Restorative Justice: The Evidence*. London: Smith Institute.

Sherman, L., Strang, H., Mayo-Wilson, E., Woods, D., and Ariel B. (2015) 'Are Restorative Justice Conferences Effective in Reducing Repeat Offending? Findings from a Campbell Systematic Review', *Journal of Quantitative Criminology* 31: 1–24.

Short, R. (1979) *The Care of Long Term Prisoners*. London: Macmillan.

Shover, N. (1996) *Great Pretenders: Pursuits and Careers of Persistent Thieves*. Boulder, CO: Westview Press.

Simcha-Fagan, O., and Schwartz, J. E. (1986) 'Neighbourhood and Delinquency: An Assessment of Contextual Effects', *Criminology*, 24: 667–703.

Simester, A. P., and Von Hirsch, A. (eds) (2006) *Incivilities: Regulating Offensive Behaviour*. Oxford: Hart Publishing.

Simon, J. (2009) *Governing through Crime* (New York: Oxford University Press).

Slothower, M. P. (2014) 'Strengthening Police Professionalism with Decision Support: Bounded Discretion in Out-of-Court Disposals', *Policing*, 8 (4): 353–367.

Smith, A. (2011) *The Deliberative Impulse: Motivating Discourse in Divided Societies*. Plymouth: Lexington Books.

Smith, E. (2016) 'Modern Diversion or Colonial Hangover? The History and Development of Suspended Sentences in South Australia', *Australian & New Zealand Journal of Criminology*, 49 (2): 240–257.

Smith, L. (2006) 'Norms in Human Development: Introduction' in L. Smith and J. Voneche (eds) *Norms in Human Development*. Cambridge: Cambridge University Press.

Sparks, R. F. (1971) 'The Use of Suspended Sentences' *Criminal Law Review* (no vol.): 384–481.

Sparks, R. (2001) 'Bringin' It All Back Home: Populism, Media Coverage, and the Politics of Crime Control' in K. Stenson and R. Sullivan (eds) *Crime, Risk, and Justice*. Cullompton: Willan.

Sparks R. (2002) 'Out of the Digger: The Warrior's Honour of the Guilty Observer', *Ethnography*, 3 (4): 556–581.

Sparks, R., and Bottoms, A. E. (1995) 'Legitimacy and Order in Prisons', *British Journal of Sociology*, 46 (1): 45–62.

Sparks, R., and A. Bottoms (2008) 'Legitimacy and Imprisonment Revisited: Notes on the Problem of Order Ten Years After' in J. Byrne, F. Taxman, and D. Hummer (eds) *The Culture of Prison Violence*. London: Allyn and Bacon, pp. 91–104.

Sparks, R., Bottoms, A. E., and Hay, W. (1996) *Prisons and the Problem of Order*. Oxford: Clarendon Press.

Sparks, R., Hay, W., and Bottoms, A. E. (1990) *Control Problems and the Long-Term Prisoner (Report submitted to the Home Office Research and Planning Unit)*. London: Home Office Research and Planning Unit.

Sparrow, M. K. (2011) *Governing Science: New Perspectives in Policing*. Washington, DC: Department of Justice, National Institute of Justice.

Spring, I. (1990) *Phantom Village: The Myth of the New Glasgow*. Edinburgh: Polygon.

Staffordshire and West Midlands Probation Trust (2013) 'Justice Minister Visits Birmingham Women's Centre'. http://www,swmprobation.gov.uk/2013/06/19/justice-minister-visits-birmingham-womens centre/.

Stedman Jones, Gareth (1983) *Languages of Class: Studies in English Working Class History 1832–1982*. Cambridge: Cambridge University Press.

Sternberg, D. (1968) 'Legitimacy' in D. L Sills (ed.) *The International Encyclopaedia of the Social Sciences IX*. New York: Free Press, pp. 244–248.

Stephen, I. (1982) 'The Role of Education in the Special Unit' in C. Carrell and J. Laing (eds) *The Special Unit: Its Evolution through Art*. Glasgow: Third Eye Centre.

Stephen, I. (1987) 'The Barlinnie Special Unit: A Penal Experiment' in S. Backett, J. McNeill, and A. Yellowlees (eds) *Imprisonment Today: Current Issues in the Prison Debate.*

Steven, A. (2007) 'Obituary for Ken Murray', *The Scotsman* 15 October 2007.

Stewart, L., and Gobeil, R. (2015) 'Correctional Interventions for Women Offenders: A Rapid Evidence Assessment', *Journal of Criminological Research, Policy and Practice*, 1 (3): 116–130.

Storrs A. (1972) *The Dynamics of Creation*. London: Secker and Warburg.

Stouthamer-Loeber, M., Wei, E., Loeber, R., and Master, A. (2004) 'Desistance from Persistent Serious Delinquency in the Transition to Adulthood', *Development and Psychopathology*, 16: 897–918.

Strang, H. (2002) *Repair or Revenge: Victims and Restorative Justice*. Oxford: Clarendon Press.

Strang, H. (2012) 'Coalitions for a Common Purpose: Managing Relationships in Experiments', *Journal of Experimental Criminology*, *8*, 3: 211–227.

Strang, H., Sherman, L. W., Mayo-Wilson, E., Woods, D., and Ariel, B. (2013) 'Restorative Justice Conferencing (RJC) Using Face-to-Face Meetings of Offenders and Victims: Effects on Offender Recidivism and Victim Satisfaction. A Systematic Review'. *Campbell Collaboration in Crime and Justice*: http://www.campbellcollaboration.org/lib/project/63/

Strawson, P. F. (1997) 'Freedom and Resentment' in D. Pereboom (ed.) *Free Will*. Indianapolis: Hackett Publishing Company, pp. 119–142.

Streng, F. (1984) *Strafzumessung und relative Gerechtigkeit. Eine Untersuchung zu rechtlichen, psychologischen und soziologischen Aspekten ungleicher Strafzumessung*. Heidelberg: v.Decker.

Stroud, S., and Tappolet, C. (2003) *Weakness of Will and Practical Irrationality*. Oxford: Clarendon Press.

Stuntz, William (2011) *The Collapse of American Criminal Justice*. Cambridge, MA: Harvard University Press.

Sunshine, J., and Tyler, T. (2003) 'The Role of Procedural Justice and Legitimacy in Shaping Public Support for Policing', *Law & Society Review*, 37 (3): 313–348.

Sztompka, P. (1999) *Trust: A Sociological Theory*. Cambridge: Cambridge University Press.

Taggart, Paul (2000) *Populism*. Milton Keynes: Open University Press

Tait, D. (1995) 'The Invisible Sanction: Suspended Sentences in Victoria 1985–1991', *Australian & New Zealand Journal of Criminology*, 28 (1): 143–162.

Tankebe, J. (2007) *Policing and Legitimacy in a Post-Colonial Democracy: A Theoretical and Empirical Study of Ghana*. PhD dissertation, University of Cambridge.

Tankebe, J. (2009) 'Self-Help, Policing and Procedural Justice: Vigilantism and the Rule of Law in Ghana', *Law & Society Review*, 43 (2): 245–269.

Tankebe, J. (2010) 'Legitimation and Resistance: Police Reform in the (Un)Making' in L. K. Cheliotis (ed.) *Roots, Rites and Sites of Resistance: The Banality of Good*. London: Palgrave, pp. 197–219.

Tankebe, J. (2013) 'Viewing Things Differently: The Dimensions of Public Perceptions of Police Legitimacy', *Criminology*, 51: 103–135.

Tankebe, J. (2019) 'In Their Own Eyes: An Empirical Examination of Police Self-Legitimacy', *International Journal of Comparative and Applied Criminal Justice*, 43: 99–116.

Tankebe, J., and Liebling, A. (eds.) (2013) *Legitimacy and Criminal Justice: An International Exploration*. Oxford: Oxford University Press.

Tankebe, J., Boakye, K. E., and Amagnya, M. A. (2019) 'Traffic Violations and Cooperative Intentions among Drivers: The Role of Corruption and Fairness', *Policing and Society*. DOI: 10.1080/10439463.2019.1636795

Tavuchis, N. (1991) *Mea Culpa: A Sociology of Apology and Reconciliation*. Stanford: Stanford University Press.

Taylor, C. (1985) *Philosophy and the Human Sciences: Philosophical Papers 2*. Cambridge: Cambridge University Press.

Taylor, C. (1989) *Sources of the Self: The Making of the Modern Identity*. Cambridge: Cambridge University Press.

Taylor, C. (2004) *Modern Social Imaginaries*. Durham: Duke University Press.

Thomas, D. A. (1970) *Principles of Sentencing*. London: Heineman.

Thomas, J., Capps, J., Carr, J., Evans, T., Lewin-Gladney, W., Jacobson, D., Maier, C., Moran, S., and Thompson, S. (2003) 'Critiquing the Critics of Peacemaking Criminology: Some Rather Ambivalent Reflections on the Theory of "Being Nice"' in K. McEvoy and T. Newburn (eds) *Criminology, Conflict Resolution and Restorative Justice*. London: Palgrave.

Tisdall, C. (1974) *Joseph Beuys—Coyote*. London: Thames and Hudson

Tomasky, Michael (2014) 'A New Populism', *New York Review of Books* 6 March.

Tonry, M. (1994) 'Proportionality, Parsimony, and Interchangeability of Punishments' in R. A. Duff, S. Marshall, R. E. Dobash, and R. P. Dobash (eds), *Penal Theory and Practice: Tradition and Innovation in Criminal Justice*. Manchester: Manchester University Press, pp. 59–83.

Tonry, M. (ed) (2019a) *American Sentencing: What Happens and Why?* Chicago: Chicago University Press.

Tonry, M. (2019b) 'Fairness, Equality, Proportionality and Parsimony: Towards a Comprehensive Jurisprudence of Just Punishment' in A. du Bois-Pedain and A. E. Bottoms (eds), *Penal Censure: Engagements Within and Beyond Desert Theory*. Oxford: Bloomsbury, pp. 277–297.

Tonry, M., and M. Lynch. 1996. 'Intermediate Sanctions'. *Crime and Justice* 20 (1): 99–144.

Traverse Theatre (2011) *The Hard Man by Tom McGrath and Jimmy Boyle: Education Resource Pack*. Edinburgh: Traverse Theatre.

Trevelyan, S. (2017) *Freedom Found: A Memoir*. Edinburgh: Scotland Street Press.

Tyler, T. R. (1990/2006) *Why People Obey the Law*, 2nd edition. Princeton: Princeton University Press.

Tyler, T. R. (1998) 'Public Mistrust of the Law: A Political Perspective', *University of Cincinnati Law Review*, 66, 847–876.

Tyler, T., and Blader, S. (2000) *Cooperation in Groups: Procedural Justice, Social Identity, and Behavioral Engagement*. Philadelphia: Psychology Press.

Tyler, T., and Huo, Y. (2002) *Trust in the Law: Encouraging Public Cooperation with the Police and Courts*. New York: Russell Sage Foundation.

Tyler, Tom, and Weber, R. (1982) 'Support for the Death Penalty: Instrumental Response to Crime or Symbolic Attitude?' *Law & Society Review*, 17 (1): 21–46.

Tyler, T., Callahan, P., and Frost, J. (2007a) 'Armed, and Dangerous(?): Motivating Rule Adherence among Agents of Social Control', *Law & Society Review*, 41: 457–492.

Tyler, T., Jackson, J., Huq, A., and Bradford, B. (2012) 'Going Outside the Law: The Role of the State in Shaping Attitudes to Private Acts of Violence', *Public Law & Legal Theory Working Papers* No. 372.

Tyler, T., Sherman, L., Strang, H., Barnes, G., and Woods, D. (2007b) 'Reintegrative Shaming, Procedural Justice, and Recidivism: The Engagement of Offenders' Psychological Mechanisms in the Canberra RISE Drinking-and-Driving Experiment', *Law and Society Review*, 41 (3): 553–586.

Umbreit, M. S., Coates, R. B., Kalanj, B., Lipkin, R., and Petros, G. (1995) *Mediation of Criminal Conflict: An Assessment of Programs in Four Canadian Provinces*. St Paul, Minnesota: Centre for Restorative Justice and Mediation, University of Minnesota.

Unger, R. (1987) *Social Theory: Its Situation and Its Task*. Cambridge: Cambridge University Press.

Unger, R. (1998) *Democracy Realized: The Progressive Alternative*. London: Verso.

Unger, R. (2005) 'The Future of the Left' (interview with James Crabtree), *Renewal*, 31 (2/3): 173–184.

Unger, R. (2007) *The Self Awakened: Pragmatism Unbound*. Cambridge, MA: Harvard University Press.

Unger, R. (2014) 'What Is Wrong with the Social Sciences Today?' *Social Science Bites*. http://www.socialsciencespace.com/2014/01/roberto-mangabeira-unger-what-is-wrong-with-the-social-sciences-today/

United Nations (2002) ECOSOC Resolution 2002/12 '*Basic principles on the use of restorative justice programmes in criminal matters*'. New York: UN.

Useem, B., and Kimball, P. (1989) *States of Siege*. Oxford: Oxford University Press.

Uslaner, E. M. (2002) *The Moral Foundation of Trust*. Cambridge: Cambridge University Press.

Van Camp, T. (2014) *Victims of Violence and Restorative Practices: Finding a Voice*. London: Routledge.

van Ginneken, E. F. J. C., and Hayes, D. J. (2017) '"Just" Punishment? Offenders' Views on the Meaning and Severity of Punishment', *Criminology and Criminal Justice*, 17 (1): 62–78.

van Zyl Smit, D., and Snacken, S. (2011) *Principles of European Prison Law and Policy*. Oxford: Oxford University Press.

van Zyl Smit, D., Snacken, S., and Hayes, D. J. (2015) '"One cannot legislate kindness": Ambiguities in European Legal Instruments on Non-Custodial Sanctions', *Punishment and Society*, 17 (1): 3–26.

Vanstone, M. (2004) *Supervising Offenders in the Community: A History of Probation Theory and Practice*. Aldershot: Ashgate.

Vitale, A. (2017) *The End of Policing*. New York: Verso.

von Hirsch, A. (1990) 'The Ethics of Community Based Sanctions'. *Crime and Delinquency*, 36 (1): 162–173.

von Hirsch, A. (1993) *Censure and Sanctions*. Oxford: Oxford University Press.

von Hirsch, A. (1994) 'Sentencing Reform: Its Goals and Prospects' in R. A. Duff, S. Marshall, R. E. Dobash, and R. P. Dobash (eds), *Penal Theory and Practice: Tradition and Innovation in Criminal Justice*. Manchester: Manchester University Press, pp. 27–41.

von Hirsch, A., and Ashworth, A. (2005) *Proportionate Sentencing: Exploring the Principles*. Oxford: Oxford University Press.

von Hirsch, A., Wasik, M., and Greene, J. (1989) 'Punishments in the Community and the Principles of Desert', *Rutgers Law Journal*, 20 (3): 595–618.

von Hirsch, A., and Rex, S. (1998) 'Community Orders and the Assessment of Punishment Severity', *Federal Sentencing Reporter*, 10 (5): 278–282.

Von Hirsch, A., Bottoms, A. E., Burney, E., and Wikström, P.-O. H. (1999) *Criminal Deterrence and Sentence Severity: An Analysis of Recent Research*. Oxford: Hart Publishing.

Von Mayr, G. (1914) 'Strafrechtspflege, Kriminalstatistik, Kriminalpolitik', *Mitteilungen der Internationalen Kriminalistischen Vereinigung*, 21: 404–414.

Wacquant, L. (2009) *Prisons of Poverty*. Minneapolis: University of Minnesota Press.

Walgrave, L. (2008) *Restorative Justice, Self-Interest and Responsible Citizenship*. Cullompton: Willan Publishing.

Walker, N. (2003) *A Man Without Loyalties: A Penologists Afterthoughts*. London: Barry Rose.

Waller, I. (2014) *Smarter Crime Control: A Guide to a Safer Future for Citizens, Communities and Politicians*. Lanham, MA: Rowman and Littlefield.

Warr, M. (2002) *Companions in Crime: The Social Aspects of Criminal Conduct*. Cambridge: Cambridge University Press.

Wasik, M. (1994) 'Sentencing Guidelines: The Problem of Conditional Sentences', *Criminal Justice Ethics*, 13 (1): 50–57.

Weatheritt, M. (1986) *Innovations in Policing*. London: Police Foundation.

Weber, M. (1922/1978) *Economy and Society: An Outline of Interpretive Sociology* (edited by H. H. Gerth and C. W. Mills). Berkeley: University of California Press.

Weber, M. (1948) 'Politics as a Vocation' in H. Gerth and C. Wright Mills, *From Max Weber*. London: Routledge, Kegan and Paul.

Weber, M. (1948) 'Science as a Vocation' in H. Gerth and C. Wright Mills, *From Max Weber*. London: Routledge, Kegan and Paul.

Weber, M. (2009) *From Max Weber: Essays in Sociology* (edited by H. H. Gerth and C. W. Mills). London: Routledge.

Weisburd, D. W., and Hinkle, J. C. (2012) 'The Importance of Randomised Experiments in Evaluating Crime Prevention', in B. C. Welsh and D. P. Farrington (eds) *The Oxford Handbook of Crime Prevention*. Oxford: Oxford University Press.

Weisburd, D. W., and Neyroud, P. W. (2011) *Police Science: Towards a New Paradigm*. Washington DC: Department of Justice, National Institute of Justice.

Weisburd, D., Groff, E. R., and Yang, S-M. (2012) *The Criminology of Place and Our Understanding of the Crime Problem*. New York. Oxford University Press.

Weisburd, D., Eck, J. E., Braga, A., Telep, C. W. Cave, B. Bowers, K., Bruinsma, G., Gill, C., Groff, E. R., Hibdon, J., Hinkle, J. C., Lawton, B., Lum, C., Ratcliffe, J. H.,

Rengert, G., Taniguchi, T., and Yang, S-M (2016) *Place Matters. Criminology for the Twenty-First Century*. Cambridge: Cambridge University Press.

Welch, M. (2015) *Escape to Prison: Penal Tourism and the Pull of Punishment*. Oakland, CA: University of California Press

Wells, G, Steblay, N., and Dysart, J. (2011) *A Test of the Simultaneous vs. Sequential Lineup Methods: An Initial Report of the AJS National Eyewitness Identification Field Studies*. Des Moines, Iowa: American Judicature Society.

Welsh, B. C., and Farrington, D. P. (2012) 'Crime Prevention and Public Policy' in B. C. Welsh and D. P. Farrington (eds) *The Oxford Handbook of Crime Prevention*. Oxford: Oxford University Press.

Westman, H. (1961) *The Springs of Creativity*. London: Routledge and Kegan Paul.

Whatmore, P. (1987) 'The Barlinnie Special Unit: An Insider's View' in A. E. Bottoms and R. Light (eds) *Problems of Long Term Imprisonment*. Aldershot: Gower.

Whatmore, P. (1990) 'The Special Unit at Barlinnie Prison, Glasgow' in P. Bowden and R. Bluglass (eds) *Principles and Practice of Forensic Psychiatry*. Edinburgh: Churchhill Livingstone.

White, S. (1989) 'Mothers in Custody and the Punishment of Children', *Probation Journal*, 36 (3): 106–109.

Whitley, S., Briggs, D., and Turner, M. (1972) *Dealing with Deviants*. London: Hogarth Press.

Wiggins, D. (1995) 'Categorical Requirements: Kant and Hume on the Idea of Duty' in R. Hursthouse, G. Lawrence, and W. Quinn (eds) *Virtues and Reasons: Philippa Foot and Moral Theory*. Oxford: Clarendon Press, pp. 297–330.

Wikström, P.-O. H. (1985) *Everyday Violence in Contemporary Sweden: Ecological and Situational Aspects*. Stockholm: Liber förlag.

Wikström, P.-O. H. (1990) 'Age and Crime in a Stockholm Cohort', *Journal of Quantitative Criminology*, 6: 61–84.

Wikström, P.-O. H. (1991) *Urban Crime, Criminals and Victims*. New York: Springer verlag.

Wikström P.-O. H. (1998) 'Communities and Crime' in M. Tonry (ed) *The Oxford Handbook of Crime and Punishment*. New York: Oxford University Press.

Wikström, P.-O. H. (2006) 'Individuals, Settings and Acts of Crime. Situational Mechanisms and the Explanation of Crime' in P.-O. H. Wikström and Robert J. Sampson (eds) *The Explanation of Crime: Context, Mechanisms and Development*. Cambridge: Cambridge University Press.

Wikström, P.-O. H. (2007) 'The Social Ecology of Crime. The Role of the Environment in Crime Causation' in H. J. Schneider (ed.) *Internationales Handbuch der Kriminologie. Volume 1*. Berlin, New York: de Gruyter.

Wikström, P.-O. H. (2010) 'Explaining Crime as Moral Action' in S. Hitlin and S. Vaysey (eds) *Handbook of the Sociology of Morality*. New York: Springer verlag.

Wikström, P.-O. H. (2017) 'Character, Circumstances and the Causes of Crime: Towards an Analytical Criminology' in A. Liebling, S. Maruna, and L. McAra (eds) *The Oxford Handbook of Criminology*, 6th edition. Oxford: Oxford University Press, pp. 501–521.

Wikström, P.-O. H. (2019a) 'Explaining Crime and Criminal Careers. The DEA model of Situational Action Theory', *Journal of Developmental and Life-Course Criminology.* (https://doi.org/10.1007/s40865-019-00116-5)

Wikström, P.-O. H. (2019b) 'Situational Action Theory: A General, Dynamic and Mechanism-Based Theory of Crime and its Causes' in M. D. Krohn, N. Hendrix, G. P. Hall and A. J. Lizotte (eds) *Handbook on Crime and Deviance*, 2nd edition. Cham, Switzerland: Springer Nature.

Wikström, P.-O. H., Oberwittler, D., Treiber, K., and Hardie, B. (2012) *Breaking Rules: The Social and Situational Dynamics of Young People's Urban Crime.* Oxford: Oxford University Press.

Wikström, P.-O. H., and Sampson, R. J. (2003) 'Social Mechanisms of Community Influences on Crime and Pathways in Criminality' in B. B. Lahey, T. E. Moffitt, and A. Caspi (eds) *Causes of Conduct Disorder and Juvenile Delinquency.* New York: The Guilford Press.

Wikström, P.-O. H., and Treiber, K. (2015) 'Situational Theory: The Importance of Interactions and Action Mechanisms' in A Piquero (ed.) *The Handbook of Criminological Theory*. Chichester: Wiley Blackwell.

Wikström, P.-O. H., and Treiber, K. (2016) 'Social Disadvantage and Crime: A Criminological Puzzle', *American Behavioral Scientist*, 60: 1232–1259.

Wikström, P.-O. H., and Wikström S. (2019) Att förklara män och kvinnors brott. En situationell handlingsteori. In A. Heber and L. Roxell (eds) *Att odla kriminologi. Perspektiv på brott & utsatthet. Kriminologiska Instititionen. Stockholms universitet.*

Wikström, P.-O. H., Mann, R., and Hardie, B. (2018) 'Young People's Differential Vulnerability to Criminogenic Exposure: Bridging the Gap Between People- and Place-Oriented Approaches in the Study of Crime Causation', *European Journal of Criminology*, 15: 10–31.

Wikström, P.-O. H., Treiber, K., and Hardie, B. (2011) 'Examining the Role of the Environment in Crime Causation: Small Area Community Surveys and Space-Time Budgets' in S. Messner, D. Gadd, and S. Karsted (eds) *The SAGE Handbook of Criminological Research Methods.* Beverly Hills: SAGE Publications.

Wikström, P.-O. H., Treiber, K., and Roman, G. (2022) *Character, Circumstances and Criminal Careers: Towards a Dynamic Development and Life-Course Criminology.* Oxford. Oxford University Press.

Wikström, P.-O. H., Ceccato, V., Hardie, B., and Treiber, K. (2010) 'Activity Fields and the Dynamics of Crime. Advancing Knowledge about the Role of the Environment in Crime Causation', *Journal of Quantitative Criminology*, 26: 55–87.

Williams, B. (1973/1976) *Morality: An Introduction to Ethics*, 2nd edition. Cambridge: Cambridge University Press.

Williams, B. (1981) *Moral Luck*. Cambridge: Cambridge University Press.

Williams, B. (1985/2006) *Ethics and the Limits of Philosophy. First published in 1985 by Fontana Press; republished with a commentary by A.W. Moore.* London: Routledge.

Williams, B. (2005) *In the Beginning was the Deed: Realism and Moralism in Political Argument*. Princeton: Princeton University Press.

Williams, R. (1989) *Resources of Hope: Culture, Democracy, Socialism*. London: Verso.

Williams, R. (2018) *Being Human: Bodies, Minds, Persons*. London: SPCK.

Williams, R., and Liebling, A. (2018) 'Faith Provision, Institutional Power and Meaning among Muslim Prisoners in two English High Security Prisons' in Kerley K. R. Praeger (ed.) *Finding Freedom in Confinement: The Role of Religion in Prison Life*, pp. 269–291. https://doi.org/10.17863/CAM.18069

Wilson, B. (2007) 'Obituary for Ken Murray', *The Guardian* 11 October 2007.

Wilson, D. (2010) 'Review of I. Loader and R. Sparks, Public Criminology?' *Howard Journal of Criminal Justice*, 49 (5): 546–547.

Wilson, D. W., Brenna, I., and Olaghere, A. (2018) 'Police Initiated Diversion for Youth to Prevent Future Delinquent Behaviour: A Systematic Review', *Campbell Systematic Reviews*, 14 (1): 1–88.

Wilson, J. Q. (1983) *Thinking about Crime*. New York: Basic Books.

Wilson, J. Q. (1993) *The Moral Sense*. New York: Free Press Paperbacks.

Wincup, E. (1996) 'Mixed Hostels: Staff and Resident Perspectives', *Probation Journal*, 43 (3): 147–151.

Winters, L. (1979) *The Silent Scream*. Edinburgh: EUSPB.

Wood, P., and Grasmick, H. (1999) 'Toward the Development of Punishment Equivalencies: Male and Female Inmates Rank the Severity of Alternative Sanctions Compared to Prison', *Justice Quarterly*, 16 (1): 19–50.

Wood, P., and May, D. (2003) 'Racial Differences in Perceptions of the Severity of Sanctions: A Comparison of Prison with Alternatives', *Justice Quarterly*, 20 (3): 605–631.

Wootton, B. (1982) Foreword to Wright M., *Making Good: Prisons, Punishment and Beyond*. London: Burnett Books.

Worrall, A., and Gelsthorpe, L. (2009) '"What Works' with Women Offenders: The Past 30 Years', *Probation Journal*, 56 (4): 329–345.

Wright, L., and Kemshall, H. (1994) 'Feminist Probation Practice: Making Supervision Meaningful', *Probation Journal*, 41 (2): 73–80.

Wright, M. (1982) *Making Good: Prisons Punishment and Beyond*. London: Burnett Books.

Wrong, D. H. (1994) *The Problem of Order*. Cambridge, MA: Harvard.

Wrong, D. (1995) *Power: Its Forms, Bases and Uses*. London: Transaction Publishers.

Young, J. (1981) 'Thinking Seriously about Crime: Some Models of Criminology' in M. Fitzgerald, G. McLennan, and J. Pawson (eds) *Crime and Society: Readings in History and Theory*. London: Routledge/Open University, pp. 248–309.

Young, J. (1999) *The Exclusive Society*. London: Sage.

Zaplin, R. (ed.) (1998) *Female Offenders: Critical Perspectives and Effective Interventions*. Gaithersburg, MD: Aspen.

Zedner, L. (2002) 'Dangers of Dystopia in Penal Theory', *Oxford Journal of Legal Studies*, 22 (2): 341–366.

Zehr, H. (1990) *Changing Lenses: A New Focus for Crime and Justice*. Scottdale, PA: Herald Press.

Zhong, Y. (1996) 'Legitimacy Crisis and Legitimation in China', *Journal of Contemporary Asia*, 26: 201–220.

Zimring, Franklin, and Johnson, David (2006) 'Public Opinion and the Governance of Punishment in Democratic Political Systems', *Annals of the American Academy of Political and Social Science*, 605: 266–80.

Zimring, Franklin, Hawkins, Gordon, and Kamin, Sam (2003) *Democracy and Punishment: Three Strikes and You're Out in California*. New York: Oxford University Press.

Index

For the benefit of digital users, indexed terms that span two pages (e.g., 52–53) may, on occasion, appear on only one of those pages.

Tables and figures are indicated by *t* and *f* following the page number